Political Behavior of the American Electorate

Fifteenth Edition

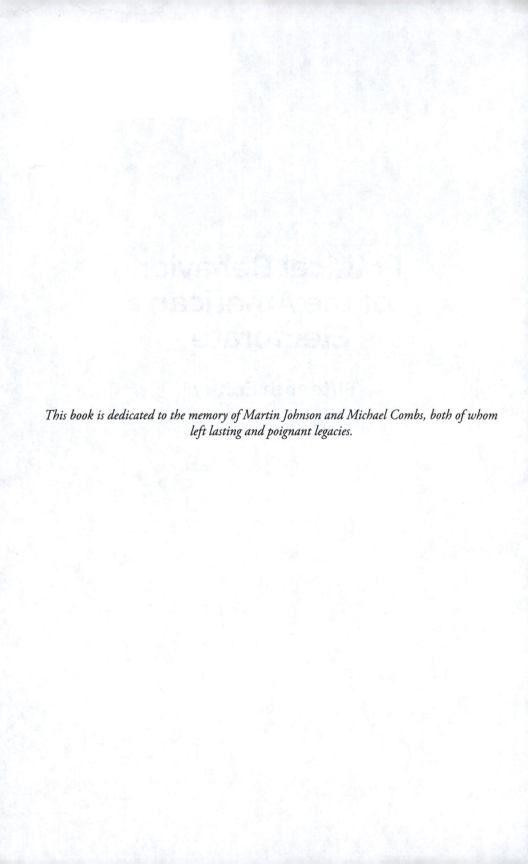

This book is dedicated to the memory of Martin Johnson and Michael Combs, both of whom left lasting and poignant legacies.

Political Behavior of the American Electorate

Fifteenth Edition

Elizabeth A. Theiss-Morse

University of Nebraska–Lincoln

Michael W. Wagner

University of Wisconsin–Madison

FOR INFORMATION:

CQ Press
2455 Teller Road
Thousand Oaks, California 91320
Email: order@sagepub.com

SAGE Publications Ltd.
1 Oliver's Yard
55 City Road
London EC1Y 1SP
United Kingdom

SAGE Publications India Pvt. Ltd.
B 1/I 1 Mohan Cooperative Industrial Area
Mathura Road, New Delhi 110 044
India

SAGE Publications Asia-Pacific Pte. Ltd.
18 Cross Street #10-10/11/12
China Square Central
Singapore 048423

Printed in the United States of America

ISBN: 9781071822173

This book is printed on acid-free paper.

Acquisitions Editor: Scott Greenan
Product Associate: Lauren Younker
Production Editor: Astha Jaiswal
Copy Editor: Melinda Masson
Typesetter: C&M Digitals (P) Ltd.
Cover Designer: Scott Van Atta
Marketing Manager: Jennifer Jones

SUSTAINABLE FORESTRY INITIATIVE

Certified Chain of Custody
At Least 10% Certified Forest Content
www.sfiprogram.org
SFI-01028

22 23 24 25 26 10 9 8 7 6 5 4 3 2 1

CONTENTS

TABLES AND FIGURES

Tables

Figures

ACKNOWLEDGMENTS

THIS IS our third go-round revising the franchise that Bill Flanigan and Nancy Zingale built. We remain honored and delighted to add to the wonderful work they have done over the decades. We are grateful for the opportunity to put our stamp on this book.

We are indebted to the National Science Foundation (NSF), which funds our primary data source, the American National Election Studies (ANES). The NSF's willingness to champion ANES investigations of what people think, what they want, what they do, and how well they think our democracy is working is crucial to the understanding and improvement of the American experiment.

Given the quick turnaround time between the point that the 2020 ANES data became available and our publication deadline, we relied on an enormous amount of thorough-but-quick research assistance from Rochelle Snyder and Joseph Maestas. We greatly appreciate and admire their professionalism, skill, and speed. We could not have finished the book without them.

As we began the process of making the book our own, we benefited from conversations with many wonderful friends and scholars who generously gave their time and perspectives regarding things for us to think about as we embarked on this journey. We thank Dona-Gene Barton, the late Jim Baughman, Barry Burden, Kathy Cramer, Bill Flanigan, Jordan Foley, Lew Friedland, Amanda Friesen, John Hibbing, Carly Jacobs, Nathan Kalmoe, Jianing Li, Randy Morse, Mallory Perryman, Katie Searles, Dhavan Shah, Kevin Smith, Sergio Wals, Rachelle Winkle-Wagner, and Nancy Zingale.

We also wish to thank Charisse Kiino at CQ Press for asking us to come along on this adventure and for supporting us through it. We thank Scott Greenan for his energy and his helpful editorial hand on this edition. We also thank Lauren Younker, Astha Jaiswal, and Melinda Masson for their quick, professional work that was instrumental in bringing the book to completion. It is a pleasure to work with such wonderful people who are committed to the study of American democracy and to the education of the citizenry.

E. T.-M.

M. W. W.

Sara Miller McCune founded SAGE Publishing in 1965 to support the dissemination of usable knowledge and educate a global community. SAGE publishes more than 1000 journals and over 600 new books each year, spanning a wide range of subject areas. Our growing selection of library products includes archives, data, case studies and video. SAGE remains majority owned by our founder and after her lifetime will become owned by a charitable trust that secures the company's continued independence.

Los Angeles | London | New Delhi | Singapore | Washington DC | Melbourne

INTRODUCTION

I N THE 2016 PRESIDENTIAL ELECTION, THE RESULT WAS A SURPRISE. Donald Trump, a reality-television star and real estate mogul who had never held elective office, won the presidency via the Electoral College despite losing the popular vote to former secretary of state, U.S. senator, and First Lady Hillary Rodham Clinton. In 2020, it was President Trump's churlish refusal to accept that he had lost that led some of his supporters to attempt a "dissident coup"[1] at the U.S. Capitol as the Electoral College votes were being certified by Congress, plunging the nation into a bitter acrimony that continues to threaten the foundations of our democratic republic.

After winning acquittals in the U.S. Senate for two separate impeachments in the House of Representatives, facing a historic global pandemic and its associated economic collapse, as well as a summer of Black Lives Matter protests from coast to coast, President Trump's reelection bid mustered 232 electoral votes to Joe Biden's 306—the worst performance by an incumbent since 1992. As fellow Democrat Hillary Clinton did before him in 2016, Biden won the popular vote, 51.3 percent to 46.8 percent.[2] While both Trump campaigns for the White House were unique in several important ways, much of what happened can be explained by carefully engaging with what political scientists have discovered about political behavior in the American electorate.

THE 2020 CAMPAIGN

While the 2016 election was a high-octane ratings bonanza filled with giant rallies and dramatic debates, much of the 2020 election was conducted virtually due to the COVID-19 pandemic. However, the campaign began long before the word *coronavirus* had entered the American lexicon. President Trump announced his reelection bid on February 17, 2017, barely one year into his first term and before both of his impeachments. Tech entrepreneur Andrew Yang was one of the first Democrats to announce his opposition to the president, doing so in November 2017.[3] Twenty-six Democrats would eventually spend some time in the 2020 race for the White House.[4]

In the United States, each election is in some way a product of the elections that came before it. The United States was a deeply divided country entering the 2020 election cycle. In the 2018 midterms, the Democrats gained forty-one seats, taking control of the House of Representatives. The Republicans expanded their U.S. Senate majority by two seats. President Trump's approval rating never enjoyed the highs of his most recent predecessors, Barack Obama and George W. Bush, leaving him more vulnerable than the typical incumbent. Even so, President Trump enjoyed sky-high approval ratings among Republicans, signaling the difficulty Democrats would face in taking the White House from the president.

At the beginning of 2019, the Democratic primary had the most diverse field of candidates in the nation's history. Frontrunner and former vice president Joe Biden; Massachusetts senator Elizabeth Warren; 2016 Democratic primary runner-up and Vermont senator Bernie Sanders; California senator Kamala Harris; South Bend, Indiana, mayor Pete Buttigieg; Minnesota senator Amy Klobuchar; former Texas congressman Beto O'Rourke; and New Jersey senator Cory Booker were among the most prominent candidates vying for the chance to compete against Trump in the general election. While Biden led the national polls for all of 2019 and all but two and a half weeks of 2020,[5] pundits and some party insiders considered him to be a weak candidate, too focused on middle-of-the-road voters.[6]

In a June 2019 debate, Senator Harris went on the offensive, attacking Biden for his position on school busing in the 1970s, claiming that Biden's position on race and busing would have kept a little girl from going to a good school:

> There was a little girl in California who was a part of the second class to integrate her public schools and she was bused to school every day. And that little girl was me.

Briefly, Harris vaulted into second place, but could not capitalize on the momentum in terms of public support or fundraising. Senator Warren's "I've got a plan for that" messaging earned positive media attention in the later summer and early fall with Warren tying Biden in the polls in October, but by November, Warren began to fade and, in a repeat of 2016, the Democratic Party frontrunner's main opponent was Senator Sanders.

When the Iowa caucuses and New Hampshire primary kicked off the voting, Buttigieg eked out a win in Iowa and essentially tied Sanders for delegates in New Hampshire, becoming the first openly gay candidate for the presidency to win a statewide primary or caucus. Biden began facing questions about his electability—the very factor he had been claiming made him the best person to be the nominee in the first place. After Sanders won Nevada on February 22, Biden's campaign was on fumes. As the important South Carolina primary approached, Biden received an endorsement from Congressman Jim Clyburn. Clyburn's endorsement carried weight in the Palmetto State's African American community, and Biden won a convincing victory—and ten of the next sixteen contests. In early March, most of the candidates had dropped out. After Biden won the Wisconsin primary on April 7, Sanders dropped out of the race the next day. Biden went to work on unifying the party, meeting with more liberal contenders and adopting some of their issue positions.[7]

Around the same time Biden began to wrap up the primary contest, the COVID-19 pandemic shut down the American economy. President Trump generally downplayed the seriousness of the potential pandemic, saying in February 2019 that the virus would, "like a miracle, disappear." At the end of March, the president claimed that the country would be on its way to recovery by June 1.[8]

He was wrong.

The growing pandemic was infecting tens of thousands of citizens, closing down schools and businesses, and spurring a spike in the unemployment rate. By April 2020, the unemployment rate was 14.8 percent, the highest it had been since the Bureau of Labor Statistics began measuring the unemployment rate in 1948.[9]

Then, in May, Minneapolis police officer Derek Chauvin was captured on video murdering a Black man named George Floyd.[10] Chauvin kept his knee on Floyd's neck for more than nine minutes. Despite the pandemic, people in Minneapolis, and all across the nation, began a series of sustained protests. Biden spoke with the Floyd family and condemned the murder[11] while President Trump called Floyd's death terrible and as bad as it can get,[12] but hastened to add that more white people than Black people are killed by police.[13] Biden's campaign adopted the pandemic response and racial justice as key themes.

The COVID-19 pandemic led the Democratic Party to delay their convention from mid-July—canceling the in-person event in Milwaukee, the largest city in the battleground state of Wisconsin (which Trump surprisingly won in 2016)— to mid-August, when they hosted a highly produced and carefully choreographed virtual event. The Republican Party held part of their convention as originally scheduled, in Charlotte, North Carolina, but the pandemic shifted most of the festivities to Washington, DC. The president even delivered his acceptance speech from the South Lawn of the White House, a highly unusual decision that was criticized for politicizing the "people's house."[14]

When the time came for the debates in late September, Biden had a six-point lead over the president. The first debate was plagued by dozens of interruptions and false statements—most of which came from President Trump. Critics called for the rules of future debates to change so that candidates' microphones would be off when it was not their turn to speak.[15] A few days after the debate, President Trump was diagnosed with COVID-19 and had to be hospitalized. The Commission on Presidential Debates announced the second debate would be held virtually, but President Trump declined to participate. Instead, the candidates participated in dueling town hall meetings, Biden's airing on ABC and Trump's airing on NBC, MSNBC, and CNBC. Both candidates squared off again for the third scheduled debate a few weeks later.

THE ELECTION

On the night of the election, it was clear that Biden would win the popular vote; he eventually earned a record 81,284,666 votes to Trump's 74,224,319.[16] Trump lost by more than 7 million votes, despite winning nearly 12 million more votes than he had won in 2016!

Of course, the popular vote does not determine the winner in the American political system. It was unclear on Election Day who won the Electoral College. On the Saturday after the election, the Associated Press and several other national media outlets declared that Biden would be the forty-sixth president of the United States after he crossed the threshold of 270 electoral votes by winning Pennsylvania. Biden continued to collect victories in most of the states wrapping up their initial counts—and engaging in recounts over the coming days.

How did he do it? This is a question we answer from multiple points of view in the pages that come. From a purely practical standpoint, however, Biden flipped Trump wins in Arizona, Wisconsin, Georgia, Michigan, Pennsylvania, and Nebraska's Second Congressional District (which Obama won in his 2008 election as well) to his column.

Despite clearly losing a free and fair election, President Trump continued to claim that the election had been stolen from him. On December 18, he demanded that congressional Republicans fight harder to overturn the election he falsely claimed he had won.[17] The next day, he tweeted out a promotion of a rally in Washington, DC, to "stop the steal" of the election he had lost. On the morning of January 6, 2021, two weeks before Joe Biden would take the oath of office, Trump spoke at this rally, saying,

> Our country has had enough. . . . We will not take it anymore and that's what this is all about. To use a favorite term that all of you people really came up with, we will stop the steal. . . . And after this, we're going to walk down, and I'll be there with you. We're going to walk down. We're going to walk down any one you want, but I think right here. We're going to walk down to the Capitol, and we're going to cheer on our brave senators, and congressmen and women. We're probably not going to be cheering so much for some of them, because you'll never take back our country with weakness. You have to show strength, and you have to be strong.

Shortly after Trump's speech, the joint session of Congress started the process of certifying the Electoral College vote certification. Prominent senators, like 2016 Republican presidential hopeful Ted Cruz of Texas, objected to certifying Arizona's electoral votes for Biden, even though Biden clearly won. About twenty minutes later, much of the crowd at the president's speech had made their way to the Capitol building, overtaking Capitol police and approaching entrances to the building.

Around that same time, suspicious packages containing pipe bombs were found at both the Democratic and Republican National Convention headquarters. Forty minutes later, around 2:15 p.m., the pro-Trump mob broke into the Capitol, breaking windows and climbing inside the building. Five minutes later, both houses of Congress voted to adjourn and take cover. At about 3:40 a.m., more than half a day after the Capitol was breached, Congress met in the secured Capitol to certify the election for Biden.[18] A total of five people died due to injuries sustained during the coup attempt.[19]

Why do we use the term *attempted dissident coup*, not *insurrection* as so many news organizations and politicians do? We are bound to present to you what the best scholarship reports about American political behavior. The Cline Center for Advanced Social Research Coup D'état Project concluded that the storming of the Capitol was "an organized, illegal attempt to intervene in the presidential transition by displacing the power of Congress to certify the election."[20] We do no one any favors by watering down the severity of what happened on January 6, 2021, at the U.S. Capitol.

The aftermath of the election leaves the United States as an asymmetrically polarized country.[21] How we got here, how individual attitudes and behaviors are organized today, and what we should look for in the future will be described in the pages that follow.

THE APPROACH OF THE BOOK

In this fifteenth edition, we follow a question-and-answer approach by asking critical questions about people's attitudes, behaviors, and perceptions of government and answering them with the best longitudinal data available. We focus attention on the major concepts and characteristics that shape Americans' responses to politics: Are Americans committed to upholding basic democratic values? Who votes, and why? How does partisanship affect political behavior? How and why does partisanship change? How are preferences about diversity, equity, and inclusion related to individuals' politics? How much does the flow of information—both accurate news stories and misinformation or "fake news"—in the news and on social media influence attitudes and political choices? How do party loyalties, candidates' personalities, issues, and events influence voters' choices among candidates? Throughout the book, we place the answers to these and other questions in the context of the changes that have occurred in American political behavior with respect to concerns regarding diversity, equity, and inclusion. We compare individual attitudes and behaviors by factors such as partisanship, ideology, race, gender, religion, region, education, and income.

To do this, we rely heavily on data from surveys conducted by the American National Election Studies (ANES). The ANES surveys, covering a broad range of political, social, and psychological topics and offering the best time-series data available, have been conducted during the fall of every presidential election year since 1952. Unless otherwise noted, the data come from this extraordinarily rich series of studies. We hope that the numerous tables and figures contained in this book will be used not only for documenting the points made in the book but also for learning to read and interpret data. Moreover, the ANES surveys allow students to learn how to interpret data over time. What factors in American politics have been stable over the past eight decades? What things have changed? How can we tell? That is, the tables and figures in this book serve as a gateway to data literacy and engaged citizenship. Students interested in asking their own questions of the data can also explore a much wider range of topics from the ANES at www.electionstudies.org. The data from the ANES and other studies are available for classroom use through the Inter-university Consortium for Political and Social Research (to see the full range of political studies available to the academic community, visit www.icpsr.umich.edu). An especially good introduction to the analysis of ANES data is a website at the University of California, Berkeley, that is open to all users: http://sda.berkeley.edu.

We have written this book to help students foster the building of professional skills and analytical abilities with respect to data literacy and an accurate understanding of American politics so that students can apply that knowledge to productively engage civically and politically, applying the lessons of this book to their own lives and their own desires for how our society should be organized and governed.

THE ORGANIZATION OF THE BOOK

We tell the story of political behavior in the American electorate. Since a deep understanding of American political history helps inform our understanding of American politics, we engage deeply with evidence from the last seventy years of public opinion research conducted by the ANES to put contemporary findings into historical context.

We begin by analyzing the 2020 election in the context of the foundational beliefs required to maintain a democracy. Chapter 1 explores the necessity of free and fair elections, trust in government, and support for democracy over undemocratic alternatives. The opening chapter sets the stakes for the book, and the country, as U.S. democracy is in peril as a nontrivial number of Americans do not believe in a democratic system and democratic electoral administration. Readers will be able to engage critically with the question of whether American democracy is in crisis, in danger, or moving along as normal.

Chapter 2 pulls back to a structural view of the American political system during presidential campaigns, highlighting the critical roles of features like the state of the economy, presidential approval, whether a state is a "swing state," how seemingly apolitical behaviors like getting a COVID-19 vaccine are related to state voting patterns, and why elections turn out the way that they do. Students will develop the ability to apply data literacy skills to interpreting how structural features shape individual behaviors in electoral contexts.

In Chapter 3, we describe voter turnout and other kinds of campaign participation in U.S. national elections. In particular, we pay attention to historical efforts to make voting harder for certain groups of people, in particular Black Americans, and to new innovations to make voting easier, such as the growth of early voting and voting by mail, that are currently being contested. Students will see how the rules of the game shape who is allowed to play and what the outcome of contests over these rules can be.

Chapter 4 is new to this edition of the book, focusing on the importance of unconventional participation in American politics, especially for groups who feel their voice is not being heard. While from an economic perspective not participating in unconventional activities is "rational," we focus on how involvement in major events, like the 2020 Black Lives Matter movement, hinges upon three factors: opportunities, recruitment, and politicized social identities. Students will begin to see how political behavior is the result of how contextual factors interact with individual-level factors.

Chapter 5 maintains our decades-long look at political party identification and change in the United States. We focus on over-time comparisons so that readers will understand both the stability of the party system and the dynamic ways in which party identification has changed over the past eight decades. In particular, we focus on how partisanship interacts with structural factors like the region one lives in and individual-level factors like one's religious beliefs. Readers will get a rich description of how changes in partisanship and partisan identity have ushered in our current era of asymmetric polarization.

Chapter 6 explores U.S. public opinion, showing how attitudes toward some issues, like government spending, have varied over time and how contemporary issues, like support for the Black Lives Matter movement or the Green New Deal, array across factors like one's partisanship and ideology. Students will also come to grips with the difficulties of measuring public opinion, helping them to increase their accuracy-motivated skepticism rather than their directionally motivated skepticism when it comes to understanding what a majority of citizens prefer on a major issue.

We live in a mediated democracy.[22] Chapter 7 explores how the information we get from the news media, social media, and conversation influences what we believe, want, and do. We pay particular attention to the role that news use can play in fostering partisan polarization, how the media repertoires used by different groups influence what people believe to be true, and how perceptions of media use affect what we think of other actors in the political world. Readers will be encouraged to think about how their own media diets contribute to their attitudes and behaviors in the political system.

Finally, we close the book with an analysis of the determinants of vote choice in 2020, looking at the impact of both long-term and short-term factors. Many people have called for reforming the Electoral College, but students need to think through what impact any given reform will have on the electoral system. Students will put together what they have learned with respect to data literacy, theories of political behavior, and applying theory and evidence to contemporary politics to thoughtfully explain electoral outcomes in the twenty-first-century American political system.

NEW TO THIS EDITION

American politics has always been contentious. However, the changing roles of social groups, growing—both asymmetric and affective—polarization, historic protests for racial justice, and, of course, a once-in-a-century global pandemic are contemporary features that deserve special attention from scholars and students alike. As such, we have updated the fifteenth edition in the following ways:

- A new chapter focusing on social groups and unconventional political participation

- Multiple analyses of support for and opposition to the Black Lives Matter movement

- Examination of beliefs in QAnon and other false rumors and elements of misinformation

- Reports of public assessments of President Trump's handling of the COVID-19 pandemic and analyses of pandemic-related behaviors' relationship with presidential voting

- Descriptions of postelection attitudes about the January 6 coup attempt, confidence in electoral administration, and shifting beliefs in democracy

- Updated longitudinal tables and figures with evidence from the 2020 presidential campaign

- Learning objectives at the beginning and study questions at the end of each chapter

Long before the Democratic Party primary season ended with Biden as the major party challenger to President Trump, the last two national public opinion polls of 2019 that asked about the 2020 presidential election showed the former vice president beating the incumbent by four and five points, respectively.[23] Nearly one year later, Biden defeated Trump by . . . four and a half points. This book tells the story of what happened in between—and how structural, event-related, and individual-level factors can help us make sense of American politics, understand political behavior in the American electorate, and more effectively engage as citizens of a democratic republic.

Notes

1. Cline Center for Advanced Social Research, "It Was an Attempted Coup: The Cline Center's Coup D'état Project Categorizes the January 6, 2021 Assault on the US Capitol," University of Illinois at Urbana-Champaign, January 27, 2021, https://clinecenter.illinois.edu/coup-detat-project-cdp/statement_jan.27.2021.

2. "Presidential Results," CNN Politics, accessed June 23, 2021, https://www.cnn.com/election/2020/results/president.

3. Hunter Schwarz, "Here's How 2020 Democrats Announced Their Campaigns," CNN Politics, February 13, 2019, https://www.cnn.com/2019/02/03/politics/2020-dem-announcements/index.html.

4. Renee Klahr, Alena Sadiq, Domenico Montanaro, and Alyson Hurt, "2020 Presidential Candidates: Tracking Which Democrats Ran," NPR, January 31, 2019, https://www.npr.org/2019/01/31/689980506/which-democrats-are-running-in-2020-and-which-still-might.

5. "Polls: Democratic National Convention," RealClear Politics, accessed June 23, 2021, https://www.realclearpolitics.com/epolls/2020/president/us/2020_democratic_presidential_nomination-6730.html.

6. E. J. Graff, "The New Rules of 'Electability' Mean Joe Biden Can't Win. Guess Who Can?," *Boston Globe*, October 9, 2019, https://www.bostonglobe.com/magazine/2019/10/09/the-new-rules-electability-mean-joe-biden-can-win-guess-who-can-biden-can-win-guess-who-can/HznRjHMCRuhy0AOyWO7ZEI/story.html.

7. Adrian Carrasquillo, "Biden Adopts Sanders' Agenda Items—Here's Where He Aligns With the Left," *Newsweek*, July 10, 2020, https://www.newsweek.com/biden-adopts-sanders-agenda-itemsheres-where-he-aligns-left-1517078.

8. Kathryn Watson, "A Timeline of What Trump Has Said on Coronavirus," CBS News, April 3, 2020, https://www.cbsnews.com/news/timeline-president-donald-trump-changing-statements-on-coronavirus/.

9. Bureau of Labor Statistics, "The Employment Situation—May 2021," U.S. Department of Labor, June 4, 2021, press release, https://www.bls.gov/news.release/pdf/empsit.pdf.

10. Chao Xiong and Paul Walsh, "Derek Chauvin, Convicted of Murdering George Floyd in Minneapolis, Is Led Away in Handcuffs," *Star Tribune*, April 21, 2021, https://www.startribune.com/derek-chauvin-convicted-of-murdering-george-floyd-in-minneapolis-is-led-away-in-handcuffs/600048324/.

11. Alana Wise, "Biden Calls George Floyd Killing 'an Act of Brutality,'" NPR, May 29, 2020, https://www.npr.org/2020/05/29/865511082/biden-calls-george-floyd-killing-an-act-of-brutality.

12. Allyson Chiu, "'Who Could Watch That?': Trump Says He Hasn't Seen Full Video of George Floyd's Death," *Washington Post*, June 18, 2020, https://www.washingtonpost.com/nation/2020/06/18/trump-floyd-video-fox/.

13. Mark DeCambre, "President Trump Says George Floyd's Death Was 'Terrible' but Says 'More White People' Die at Hands of Police Than Blacks in U.S.," MarketWatch, July 15, 2020, https://www.marketwatch.com/story/president-trump-says-george-floyds-death-was-terrible-but-says-more-white-people-die-at-hands-of-police-than-blacks-in-us-2020-07-14.

14. Zach Montague, "What Is the Hatch Act? Is Trump Violating It at the R.N.C.?," *New York Times*, August 26, 2020, https://www.nytimes.com/2020/08/26/us/politics/hatch-act-trump-rnc.html.

15. Michael W. Wagner, "Take Back Our Presidential Debates," Isthmus, September 30, 2020, https://isthmus.com/opinion/opinion/taking-back-our-presidential-debates/.

16. "Presidential Election Results: Biden Wins," *New York Times*, November 3, 2020, https://www.nytimes.com/interactive/2020/11/03/us/elections/results-president.html?action=click&pgtype=Article&state=default&module=styln-elections-2020&region=TOP_BANNER&context=election_recirc.

17. Amy Sherman, "A Timeline of What Donald Trump Said Before the Capitol Riot," Poynter, February 11, 2021, https://www.poynter.org/fact-checking/2021/a-timeline-of-what-donald-trump-said-before-the-capitol-riot/.

18. Shelly Tan, Youjin Shin, and Danielle Rindler, "How One of America's Ugliest Days Unraveled Inside and Outside the Capitol," *Washington Post*, January 9, 2021, https://www.washingtonpost.com/nation/interactive/2021/capitol-insurrection-visual-timeline/.

19. Kelly McLaughlin, "5 People Died in the Capitol Insurrection. Experts Say It Could Have Been So Much Worse," Business Insider, January 23, 2021, https://www.businessinsider.com/capitol-insurrection-could-have-been-deadlier-experts-say-2021-1.

20. Cline Center for Advanced Social Research, "It Was an Attempted Coup."

21. Mathew Grossmann and Daniel A. Hopkins, *Asymmetric Politics: Ideological Republicans and Group Interest Democrats* (New York: Oxford University Press, 2016).

22. Michael W. Wagner and Mallory R. Perryman, *Mediated Democracy: Politics, the News and Citizenship in the 21st Century* (Washington, DC: CQ Press, 2020).

23. "General Election: Trump vs. Biden," RealClear Politics, accessed June 24, 2021, https://www.realclearpolitics.com/epolls/2020/president/us/general_election_trump_vs_biden-6247.html#polls.

DEMOCRATIC BELIEFS AND AMERICAN DEMOCRACY

ELECTIONS ARE AT THE HEART of representative democracies. It is through elections that citizens have a voice in choosing who will represent them and the opportunity to hold elected representatives accountable for what they have done, or not done, while in office. Americans know when the next election is coming as elections for national office are always held on the Tuesday after the first Monday in November of even-numbered years. People who want to run for office can start their efforts far in advance of Election Day. On the day Donald Trump was inaugurated as president—January 20, 2017—he filed a letter with the Federal Election Commission indicating he qualified to run for reelection in 2020.[1] On the day he became president, he was already running for reelection.

What he couldn't have foreseen was that 2020 would be unlike any other election year. A *New York Times* timeline lays out the staggering spread and effects of the pandemic.[2] The first coronavirus (COVID-19) case was reported in Wuhan, China, in December 2019. By January 20, 2020, the United States had its first known case, a man in the state of Washington. The disease spread quickly, with the United States leading the world in confirmed cases by the end of March. Stay-at-home orders and mask mandates became the norm in the hardest-hit areas. Schools went remote, businesses closed their doors, restrictions on travel were put in place, and sports were sidelined. Millions of Americans were out of work, and countries worldwide tumbled into a recession. By Election Day, the United States had more than ten million infections and was nearing a quarter of a million deaths.

Adding to the tumult of 2020 was the murder of George Floyd and the subsequent Black Lives Matter (BLM) protests across the United States. On May 25, a store clerk in Minneapolis called 911 saying that a Black man had bought cigarettes with a counterfeit $20 bill. Within seventeen minutes of police arriving at the scene, Floyd was dead, his neck pinned under the knee of a police officer.[3] Protests erupted in Minneapolis and quickly spread across the country. On June 6 alone there were over five hundred protests. Some experts estimate that the number of BLM protesters was the largest in U.S. history.[4] Unlike past seasons that saw protests against police brutality, the summer of 2020 witnessed what appeared to be a major shift in support for the movement. Protests were occurring in predominantly white counties, and diverse organizations, including the NFL and NASCAR, publicly supported efforts to stop racism.[5]

Even Election Day—November 3, 2020—was not normal. According to Charles Stewart III, in-person voting on Election Day has been dropping since the early 1990s, but it took a nosedive in 2020. Whereas 60 percent of voting was done in person on Election Day in 2016, that number dropped to 28 percent in 2020. Mail and absentee voting shot from 21 percent in 2016 to 46 percent in 2020. (The remaining 26 percent of 2020 voters voted early in person.)[6] The partisan gap in Election Day versus mail-in and early voting was huge, with many Democrats voting absentee or early and many Republicans voting on Election Day.[7] Part of this difference was due to Democrats' greater fears about the coronavirus and not wanting to take the risk of catching it by going to the polls. A large part of the explanation, though, was Trump's frequent questioning before the election of the security of voting by mail. From arguing that mail ballots could be stolen to claiming that foreign countries would mail in millions of fraudulent ballots, Trump caused many Republicans to be uneasy about voting by mail and to choose instead to vote in person.[8]

Trump's claims about voting by mail fed into his argument that the only way he could lose the election was "if the election is rigged."[9] Many experts pointed out that the differences in voting method between Democrats and Republicans would lead to election returns coming in unevenly. On Election Night, the numbers favored Trump, but as the ballots that were mailed in started to be counted, the numbers started to favor the Democratic candidate, former vice president Joe Biden. This is what happened, but Trump's framing of mail-in ballots as illegitimate and his Election Night speech claiming he had won because he was ahead in the vote count, along with his tweet claiming "We are up BIG, but they are trying to STEAL the Election," led many Republicans to believe the election had been stolen and that Trump had really won.

Not surprisingly, claims of fraud were rampant. Trump and his followers claimed that more votes were cast in nineteen Michigan counties than there were people who lived there (although the counties listed were actually in Minnesota and the turnout in these areas was all under 100 percent); that surges in the count of Democratic votes implied malfeasance (claims deemed not credible by a judge); that the voting machines made by Dominion Voting Systems flipped millions of votes (a claim denied by Dominion and for which no evidence has been found by Edison Research) because it was owned by Bill and Hillary Clinton and other Democrats (Dominion claims to be a nonpartisan company, is not owned by top

Democrats, and has made campaign donations to both Democrats and Republicans); and that thousands of dead people had voted (proved untrue when people on the list of dead voters came forward to prove they were alive).[10] Approximately sixty cases brought by lawyers trying to overturn the election either were dismissed by the courts or made claims that judges ruled against, arguing that the courts needed facts, not innuendo.[11] These lawsuits were only brought in swing states in which Biden won even though other states used the Dominion voting system and had made similar minor alterations in how the elections were run due to the impact of COVID-19.

The insurrection that occurred on January 6, 2021, was the culmination of the constant claim from Trump and his fellow Republican supporters that the election had been stolen. His supporters stormed the Capitol building in Washington, DC, after Trump gave a speech reiterating false claims that the election had been stolen, extolling his followers to "fight like hell. And if you don't fight like hell, you're not going to have a country anymore," and encouraging them to walk down Pennsylvania Avenue to the Capitol to give congressional Republicans "the kind of pride and boldness that they need to take back our country."[12] These supporters held signs saying "Stop the Steal" and shouted such things as "We will not take it anymore!" and "Arrest Congress!"[13]

The attempted dissident coup[14] combined with the rhetoric surrounding the 2020 election and the efforts by the outgoing president to undermine the peaceful transfer of power to Biden raise serious concerns about Americans' support for elections, democratic government, and the processes that distinguish democracies from authoritarian regimes. Do Americans have confidence that elections are free and fair? Do they trust their government and each other, or has this trust disappeared? Do they continue to want to live in a democracy, or would they prefer a less messy, more efficient authoritarian system? Throughout this book, we examine in depth the political behavior and attitudes of the American electorate while taking into account the context within which those behaviors and attitudes occur. In this chapter, we address whether Americans have lost their affection for democracy and their belief in democratic principles, beginning with their attitudes toward elections. Gauging Americans' beliefs and values about democratic processes sets the groundwork for what happens in specific elections.

Learning objectives for Chapter 1 include:

- Exploring the perceptions and reality of what makes elections free and fair with a focus on the 2020 presidential election

- Understanding why trust in government has plummeted and what impact this has on politics in the United States

- Learning to appreciate the messiness of democratic practices and processes

- Addressing concerns about maintaining democracy in the United States given current public opinion

ARE ELECTIONS FREE AND FAIR?

One aspect of democracy that political theorist Robert Dahl highlights is "free, fair, and frequent elections."[15] Elections are a basic component of a democratic political system. At regular intervals, competitive elections give ordinary citizens the power to choose their leaders and, just as important, to throw them out of office. Competitive elections require that all citizens must be free to participate fully in campaign activities before the election itself. Such campaign activities include the freedom to express one's views and the freedom to organize with others during the nominating phase and the campaign to make preferences known and to persuade others. Implicit in this is the freedom to receive information about the choices before the voters. Citizens must also be free to vote, and the right to vote should not be undermined by substantial economic or administrative barriers. No physical or social intimidation should take place. Citizens legally eligible to vote should have full and convenient access to polling places. The right to vote and the right to express one's choices freely require a secret ballot. In fair elections, the ballots cast should reflect the intention of the voters, and the votes should be counted accurately. Votes should be weighted equally, or as equally as possible, in translating votes into representation.

Americans take great pride in their democracy, but recent presidential elections provide an opportunity to reassess the extent to which the requirements for being fair and free have been met in the American political system. Elections in the twenty-first century have been close and intensely contested, and it is during extremely close elections that irregularities matter the most. Many observers questioned how free and fair the 2000 presidential election was, but questions have been raised in other recent elections as well, especially in the 2020 election. From concerns about the role of money in politics to people being kept from voting to votes not being counted, there is good reason to keep an eye on what happens during elections. Acknowledging the importance of keeping an eye on elections is very different, however, from questioning the integrity of elections. Trump's claim in October 2016 that "the election is absolutely being rigged" and his postelection claims in 2020 that "the only way we're going to lose this election is if the election is rigged"[16] can be adjudicated by looking at the evidence.

The evidence shows clearly that there is no need for concern about who really won in 2020. Biden won 81,268,924 votes to Trump's 74,216,154 in the 2020 presidential election, a difference of over 7 million votes. In the Electoral College, Biden had 306 votes to Trump's 232.[17] For Trump to have won the election, enough voter fraud would have had to occur in close states to give Trump 38 more Electoral College votes. The three closest states were Arizona (Biden won by 10,457 votes), Georgia (Biden won by 11,779 votes), and Wisconsin (Biden won by 20,682 votes). Their combined Electoral College votes, 37, were not enough to give Trump the election, even if there had been enough fraudulent votes to flip the winner in those states.[18] The next state on the list is Nevada, which Biden won by 33,596 votes. Nevada has 6 Electoral College votes and, combined with the other three states, would have put Trump over the threshold needed to win. Another state that received a lot of attention after the election was Pennsylvania, a state with 20 Electoral College votes. Biden won Pennsylvania by 80,555 votes.

To win the election, the Trump campaign would have had to prove that there were large numbers of fraudulent votes, all of which had been cast for Biden, not Trump, or that there was serious election malfeasance that would allow large numbers of votes to be tossed out. To back up their claims of widespread fraud and malfeasance, Trump and his Republican supporters filed many lawsuits. *New York Times* reporters Jim Rutenberg, Nick Corasaniti, and Alan Feuer summarized the outcomes:

> After bringing some 60 lawsuits, and even offering financial incentive
> for information about fraud, Mr. Trump and his allies have failed to
> prove definitively any case of illegal voting on behalf of their opponent in
> court—not a single case of an undocumented immigrant casting a ballot,
> a citizen double voting, nor any credible evidence that legions of the
> voting dead gave Mr. Biden a victory that wasn't his.[19]

The Associated Press fact-checked Trump's claims that vote rigging had occurred and found them "all wrong."[20] The *New York Times* called election officials in every state, all of whom reported "that there was no evidence that fraud or other irregularities played a role in the outcome of the presidential race."[21] U.S. Attorney General William Barr told the Associated Press after the FBI investigated complaints about voting irregularities that "to date, we have not seen fraud on a scale that could have effected a different outcome in the election."[22] The Heritage Foundation's "Election Fraud Cases" website lists cases that have been serious enough to get to court. While many of these cases have to do with ballot initiatives and voter registration, there are occasional cases of people voting twice or fraudulently using an absentee ballot that belonged to someone else. For example, a man in Michigan forged his daughter's signature on an absentee ballot in the 2020 general election; a woman in Colorado switched her party identification and was sent two absentee ballots, both of which she mailed in.[23] Election fraud does occasionally occur, but there is no evidence, even in all of the lawsuits filed in the 2020 election, that there was enough fraud to give Trump anywhere near the number of votes he needed to overturn the presidential election.

Some of the conspiracy theories, though, suggested that there might be something nefarious happening behind the scenes. Questions about foreign interference and Dominion voting machines raise the possibility that finding individual fraud cases isn't going to uncover the alleged deep fraud. These concerns can be allayed, though, via statistical analyses that can determine if the election results were statistically out of whack compared to what would be considered normal and feasible. In a thorough analysis, Andrew Eggers, Haritz Garro, and Justin Grimmer did just this when they analyzed claims that the 2020 election results were statistically inconsistent with results that would occur in a free and fair election. After extensive analyses, they state, "In all cases we find that the supposed anomaly is not an anomaly once we compare the properly computed test statistic to a reasonable null distribution. In other words, facts that are purportedly so surprising as to throw the 2020 election result into question are either not facts or not surprising."[24] The combined evidence from the lawsuits, state officials, the attorney general of the United States, and statistical analyses of the vote shows that Biden won the presidency in a free and fair election and that Trump lost.

The lack of evidence for election fraud in the United States is not surprising. Researchers have carefully analyzed evidence on voter fraud and have concluded that if voter fraud has occurred, it "is an isolated and rare occurrence in modern U.S. elections."[25] Just because there is a lack of evidence for voter fraud occurring at the level needed to affect election outcomes, however, doesn't mean that people do not believe the allegations. A Monmouth University poll fielded after the 2020 election found that among all respondents, 60 percent thought Biden won fair and square, and 32 percent thought his win was due to fraud. Looking just at Trump voters, however, fully 77 percent thought Biden's win was based on fraud.[26] The questioning of the election results by Trump and his followers in 2020 occurred within a challenging context for the integrity of the election process. When the political parties are highly polarized, when the winner of the popular vote does not win the Electoral College (as happened in 2000 and 2016), and when a major party candidate questions the legitimacy of the election outcome (as happened with Trump in 2016 and 2020), it is important for people to believe that the electoral system is fair and effective. Belief in the integrity of U.S. elections acts as a bulwark against the various events and claims made by opposing partisans.

Unfortunately, belief in election integrity has become highly polarized in the United States. In both 2016 and 2020, people were asked in the American National Election Studies (ANES) survey how often votes are counted fairly in American elections. The response options were "all of the time," "most of the time," "about half of the time," "some of the time," and "never." Figure 1-1 shows the percentage of people who answered "all of the time" or "most of the time" in the two years surveyed. While more people gave the stronger answer of "all of the time" in 2020 compared to 2016, the total percentage of people giving a positive response was quite similar across these two years: 74 percent in 2016 and 69 percent in 2020. These results would suggest little change between the two election years. Figure 1-2, however, shows that this would be a mistaken interpretation. While there was essentially no difference between Democrats and Republicans in assessments of election fairness in 2016 (a difference of only 3 percentage points), the difference in 2020 was huge (38 percentage points). It is likely that people in both parties were reacting to Trump's statements about election fraud: Republicans believed what he said, and Democrats became more positive as a counter to Trump's position. Many people on the left and the right worried that the then president's accusations would make people question the integrity of elections in the United States. These data suggest that the concern should be focused on Republicans.

The ANES asked additional questions dealing with election integrity in 2020: Are votes counted accurately, do elections make the government pay attention, and do people trust election officials? Americans overwhelmingly think elections make the government pay attention (82 percent gave a positive response), but they are much more skeptical about election officials (only 44 percent gave positive responses) and that votes are counted accurately (only 38 percent gave positive responses). It is not clear what distinction people are making between fairness and accuracy when it comes to counting votes, but they are much more likely to think that votes are counted fairly than to think that they are counted accurately.

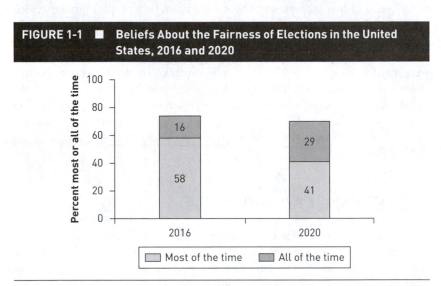

FIGURE 1-1 ■ Beliefs About the Fairness of Elections in the United States, 2016 and 2020

Source: 2016, 2020 American National Election Studies, available at www.electionstudies.org.

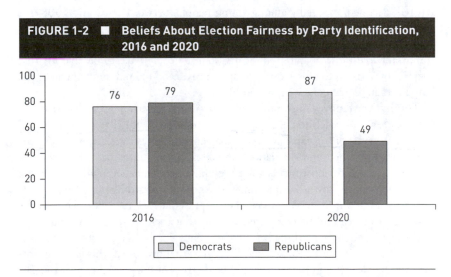

FIGURE 1-2 ■ Beliefs About Election Fairness by Party Identification, 2016 and 2020

Source: 2016, 2020 American National Election Studies, available at www.electionstudies.org.

Americans have a long history of accepting election outcomes, even when the elections were close or when the Electoral College vote did not uphold the popular vote. It is also the case that American elections have become more fair and accurate over the country's history. In recent elections, the number of cases of voter fraud has been miniscule compared to the number of votes cast, and certainly not large enough to overturn the results in virtually all elections from local school boards to president. The narrative propagated by Trump that the election was rigged and that the counting of votes did not reflect people's preferences led many Americans, especially Republicans, to reject the 2020 election outcome. In their minds, Trump had legitimately, and Biden had illegally, won the presidency. The storming of the U.S. Capitol on January 6, 2021, when the House and Senate were meeting to certify the Electoral College votes was meant to keep the normal process of declaring the winner of the presidency from happening, based on the belief that the election results were fraudulent. Never before had this happened in all of American history. Allowing the peaceful transfer of power in a democratic political system is essential, even when people, including the losing candidate, do not like the outcome.

TRUST IN GOVERNMENT

It is not just trust in the electoral system that matters in a democracy. Trust is a major part of all human interactions. People trust other people to behave according to accepted rules of behavior across all aspects of life, from having a vendor send the item purchased through an online site to having a friend not betray a secret. Interpersonal trust, or the generalized sense that people as a whole can be trusted, declined, especially among young people, between 2002 and 2008 (see Figure 1-3). There was an uptick in interpersonal trust in the 2010s, which is important since this type of trust, according to social capital scholars, plays an important role in democratic political systems. People have to be able to trust their fellow citizens to follow through on promises and to hold up their end of the bargain to have democracy run smoothly.

Political trust moves trust into the domain of the government. Jack Citrin and Christopher Muste define political trust as the "confidence that authorities will observe the rules of the game and serve the general interest."[27] Citizens elect people to represent their and the nation's interests in the government. Elected officials report back to constituents what they have accomplished, and local media outlets often cover town-hall meetings or votes on major bills, but people have relatively limited information about their representatives' behavior. This means that the people cannot be completely certain that their representatives have not misbehaved or done something behind the scenes that went against the constituents' or nation's interests. Russell Hardin argues that because of this lack of information, people's default position should be distrust of the government.[28] Indeed, some political distrust in a democracy is good. People need to stay informed and

FIGURE 1-3 ■ Social Trust and Age, 1964–2020

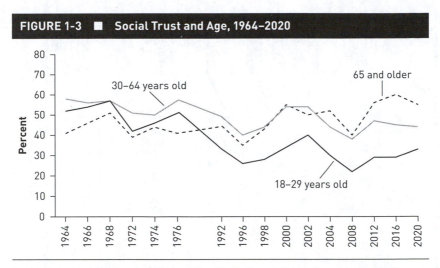

Source: Trust data from American National Election Studies, available at www.electionstudies.org.

Note: From 1964 through 2008, the question wording was "Generally speaking, would you say that most people can be trusted, or that you can't be too careful in dealing with people?" From 2012 through 2020, the question wording was "Generally speaking, how often can you trust other people?" with response options "always," "most of the time," "about half of the time," "some of the time," and "never." Responses of "always" and "most of the time" are included in the figure.

engaged enough to hold elected officials accountable for their actions, and some distrust can be the motivator for people to remain vigilant.

Political trust in 2016, however, dropped to alarmingly low levels, and 2020 didn't show any improvement. For years, the ANES has asked respondents how often they thought "the government in Washington could be trusted to do the right thing." The solid black line in Figure 1-4 shows the percentage of people who responded "all of the time" or "most of the time" to this question. The high point of political trust in the late 1950s and early 1960s, when over three-quarters of Americans gave trusting responses, was followed by a steep decline. Trust has been on something of a roller-coaster ride ever since. Certain contextual factors lead to upticks in trust: Ronald Reagan's presidency and his message of American greatness, the booming economy in the Bill Clinton years, and the rally-around-the-flag effect after the terrorist attacks in 2001. Figure 1-4 includes two gray lines, the darker one showing positive responses to a question about whether or not people are satisfied with the way things are going in the United States and the lighter one showing positive responses to a question about whether the country is on the wrong track or heading in the right direction. Clearly, political trust increases when people are happy with what is happening in the country and decreases when people are dissatisfied.

Political trust in the 2016 election—the lowest level ever recorded by the ANES surveys at only 14 percent—was quite a bit lower than satisfaction with how things were going. This pattern persisted in 2020. While only a quarter to

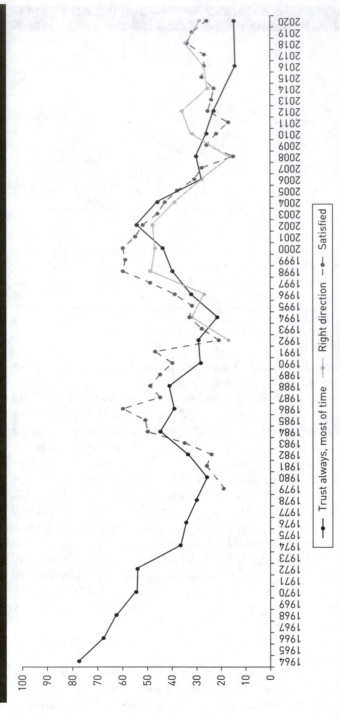

FIGURE 1-4 ■ Trust and Attitudes About How Things Are Going in the United States, 1958–2020

--- Trust always, most of time   --- Right direction   --- Satisfied

Sources: Trust data from American National Election Studies, available at www.electionstudies.org. Right direction data from NBC News/*Wall Street Journal* Poll, available at www.pollingreport.com (1996 to 2020), and from ANES (1992 to 1994), available at www.electionstudies.org. Satisfaction data from Gallup, available at https://news.gallup.com/poll/1669/general-mood-country.aspx.

[a] "How much of the time do you think you can trust the government in Washington to do what is right—just about always, most of the time, or only some of the time?"

[b] "All in all, do you think things in the nation are generally headed in the right direction, or do you feel that things are off on the wrong track?"

[c] "In general, are you satisfied or dissatisfied with the way things are going in the United States at this time?"

a third of Americans thought the United States was doing well, this is far more than the 14 percent who said they could trust the government to do what is right. Trump tapped into that feeling of distrust and was an important part of the context surrounding the 2016 and 2020 presidential elections. Many Americans were fed up with government and wanted change. Trump's promise to "drain the swamp," referring to the federal government in Washington, DC, was a favorite rallying cry at Trump rallies, even after he had served as president for four years.

Another measure used by Gallup over the years is the extent to which people have confidence in various institutions in the United States. The percentage of people expressing "a great deal" or "quite a lot" of confidence in the military has increased significantly since the 1970s, from 58 percent in 1975 to 72 percent in 2020. Confidence in the three branches of government have not fared so well. While confidence in the Supreme Court only dropped from 49 to 40 percent, confidence in the presidency dropped from 52 to 39 percent, and confidence in Congress dropped from 40 to 13 percent.[29]

Why Is Trust Lower?

Why do so few Americans trust the U.S. government in recent years? Political scientists have expended considerable effort answering this question and have pointed to such things as the state of the economy (people have a much more positive view of the world, including the government, when times are good) and whether politicians have been involved in scandals or other bad behaviors (people do not look kindly on scandals, and their opinion of the government goes down).[30] We briefly explore three possible explanations that have received varying levels of attention: direct experience, media coverage, and negative attacks on the government.

People's direct experiences with the government or with government officials could affect their levels of political trust. If people have bad experiences when they interact with government officials or if they do not receive the government benefits they expect, they can easily become jaded, and their trust can subsequently decline. The direct experience explanation, however, appears not to be viable. People who have had contact with federal employees, such as an employee of the U.S. Postal Service (USPS), the National Park Service (NPS), or the Supplemental Nutrition Assistance Program (SNAP), are positive about the experience. A *Washington Post* poll in 2010 found that three-quarters of respondents who had had direct experience with federal employees thought the employees had done their job fairly or very well.[31] Similarly, the Pew Research Center asked respondents in 2019 about their views of a variety of federal agencies. They found that a vast majority of Americans had a favorable view of the USPS (90 percent), the NPS (86 percent), the National Aeronautics and Space Administration (NASA, 81 percent), and the Centers for Disease Control and Prevention (CDC, 80 percent). In fact, a majority of Americans had a favorable view of fourteen out of the sixteen governmental agencies about which they were asked, including the Internal Revenue Service (IRS, 55 percent), which is the agency that collects taxes. Only the Department of Education (48 percent) and Immigration and Customs Enforcement (ICE, 42 percent) did not get favorable ratings from a majority of Americans.[32]

People are also much more positive about their own member of Congress than Congress as a whole. Gallup found a 20-percentage-point difference in comparisons of one's own member and all of the other members of Congress on whether they are corrupt, focused on special interests, and out of touch with average Americans.[33] People tend to think of their own member of Congress as "one of us," which Richard Fenno labels *identification*. Members of Congress speak and act in ways that send the message, "You can trust me because we are like one another."[34] When people see their representative at a town-hall meeting or giving a talk to the local Rotary Club, their sense of identification improves their level of trust in their own representative. This feeling of trust remains focused on the individual representative and is not generalized to Congress as a whole.

The second explanation for declining trust focuses on the media and people's negative reactions to media coverage, in terms of both what the media cover and how they cover it. Media coverage tends to focus on conflict, disagreement, and incivility to keep people tuned in. With so many entertainment options available, having two politicians sedately discuss a policy quickly loses an audience, and this leads to a loss in advertising revenue. To keep people engaged, and therefore tuning in, the media prefer covering conflict and, if possible, dramatic conflict. Politicians who engage in uncivil behavior tend to get more media coverage, and the up-close, in-your-face camera work brings the conflict right into people's living rooms. Diana Mutz and her colleagues have shown that the close-up coverage of incivility leads to greater distrust of government, although some researchers have argued that when politicians are highly civil, people have greater distrust as well.[35]

The media's constant negativity has also been associated with broader societal distrust. People are less trusting not only of government but also of each other and of a variety of institutions that used to be highly trusted, such as education, medicine, and religion. When people read and hear about only the negative things that happen in society, they begin to distrust everything around them. This "media malaise" encompasses government and therefore can explain the decline in trust.[36] Politicians recognize this behavior and use it to their advantage when campaigning. Trump regularly castigated the media as spreading "fake news" and of covering stories in "unfair" and "nasty" ways in both 2016 and 2020. At some of his large and occasionally raucous rallies, Trump would point out particular reporters whose coverage he did not appreciate. NBC's Katy Tur even needed Secret Service protection after being called out by name at a rally in August 2016. Some researchers, however, have argued that the relationship between the media and lower political trust is more nuanced, with the effect being more pronounced among the highly educated and informed. Others have found no relationship.[37]

The third explanation we address is the idea that the constant verbal attacks, especially from elected representatives themselves, have undermined people's faith in the government. Fenno, in his book *Home Style*, noted that members of Congress often run for Congress by running against the institution.[38] In this way, the public's disdain for Congress is constantly reinforced, and members of Congress get reelected at astounding numbers because the problems with Congress are the fault of everyone else. If incumbents running for reelection are actively bashing Congress and this bashing has an impact on people's disapproval, we should see an increase in disapproval as an election nears. David Brady and Sean Theriault tested this argument by examining whether disapproval of Congress increases closer to an election. They found that approval of Congress increases almost one-third of a point each month away from an election and increases seven points after an election.[39]

The Impact of Lower Trust

Trust has decreased significantly, but what impact does lower trust have on a political system? One impact can be seen directly in the 2016 presidential election. Presidential candidates who were "Washington insiders," including Republicans Ted Cruz (a U.S. senator), Marco Rubio (another U.S. senator), and Jeb Bush (former governor of Florida but brother of former president George W. Bush and son of another former president, George H. W. Bush), had difficulties gaining traction as they tried to convince voters that they were not part of the problem. Trump ran gleefully as an outsider, and voters responded. On the Democratic side, political insider Hillary Clinton was expected to easily win her party's nomination but faced stiff competition in the primary from Bernie Sanders, a U.S. senator from Vermont who could point to his independence from the two political parties (he is the longest-serving independent in Congress) as a measure of his outsider status in Washington. In 2020, Trump continued to run as an outsider, even though as president he was an insider, whereas Biden embraced his long service in government, beginning as a U.S. senator in 1972 and serving as vice president during the Barack Obama administration.

Not only does lower political trust increase the appeal of outsider candidates; it has policy consequences as well. Marc Hetherington has examined extensively the relationship between political trust and redistributive versus distributive policy outcomes. Redistributive policies are policies that end up redistributing wealth, such as welfare policies. People pay taxes, with the wealthier paying in more money than the poor, and this money is then used to fund programs such as SNAP and Temporary Assistance for Needy Families (TANF). Distributive policies, such as Social Security, involve the beneficiaries bearing the costs of the program. Decreased trust in government leads to less support for redistributive policies but not distributive policies. Hetherington argues that when people are being asked to sacrifice some of their wealth for the benefit of others, they need to trust those asking them to make the sacrifice: "When people know for certain that they will not readily or materially gain from a program but that they will have to help pay the costs, it is essential that they trust the agent asking such sacrifice."[40] During times when Americans have higher levels of political trust, politicians are more likely to pass liberal policies, such as welfare policies. Politicians pass more conservative policies when Americans are more distrusting of the government.[41]

Another possible consequence of lower trust concerns support for democratic processes. We discuss in the next section Americans' attitudes toward democracy, but it is important to consider whether the heightened distrust in the United States actually acts to undermine democracy. In a preliminary test of this idea, survey respondents were asked about their support for two basic democratic processes, debating with the other side to fully air considerations surrounding the policy and compromising with the other side to get policy passed.[42] Higher political trust was strongly related to support for both debate and compromise. Debating and compromising on contentious issues involves trusting that both the process and the outcome will be fair. The more people distrust the government, the more likely they are to think the system is rigged and that efforts to debate issues fully and to find a compromise that takes into account the views of the other side are a waste of time.

Political trust has declined sharply over the past fifty years, and it reached its lowest point during the 2016 and 2020 presidential elections. Trump's appeal to many Americans was in part due to his outsider status. Many Americans saw him as a businessman, not a political hack in Washington, even after serving four years as president. His support for conservative policies, such as putting severe restrictions on immigration and cutting government spending on social, but not military, programs, was seen as a way to move the country in the right direction by many of his voters. By 2020, however, many Americans were eager to embrace Biden, a Washington insider who promised to work with both Democrats and Republicans to achieve his more liberal policy goals. We examine policy support in greater depth in Chapter 6.

ATTITUDES TOWARD DEMOCRACY

The main ideas underlying American democracy are (a) that power must be broadly dispersed and not concentrated in the hands of a small number of people and (b) that democratic citizens must have the ability to influence political outcomes. For the latter to occur, citizens must have access to information, preferably accurate information, and the opportunity to voice their opinions and participate in the political sphere. Not everyone will get what they want in a democracy, but people must have the opportunity to try to get what they want.

The United States has democratic structures well in place to allow for these outcomes, but these structures can be used to pursue democratic or undemocratic goals. In democratic theory, much depends on the set of values and beliefs held by citizens that support democratic processes and institutions. Citizens need to accept the idea of rule by the majority and, equally, to believe that the rights of the minority should be respected. They should have some sense of their rights and obligations to participate in the political process, at a minimum through exercising the right to vote. The political elite—those who hold elected or appointed office and those who are informed about and engaged in politics—need to be willing to play by the democratic rules of the game and respect the will of the majority, even when it means the loss of their positions. Finally, elites and the public in general need to understand that democratic solutions do not come quickly and easily. Democratic solutions require allowing diverse interests to have a voice in debates over policy options, and they require accepting that many of these solutions will be based on compromises made with the opposing side. We examine the content of Americans' beliefs and values concerning democracy and assess them as a foundation for the maintenance of democracy.

Freedom of Expression and the Press

A distinction is often made between democratic *goals*, such as equality and individual freedom, and democratic *procedures*, such as majority rule, due process of law, and protection of the political rights of freedom of speech, press, and assembly. The distinction is an important one when the extent to which these ideals are supported within a political system is under consideration because democratic goals can be pursued through undemocratic means or democratic procedures can be used for antidemocratic ends. Likewise, mass support may exist for democratic goals but not for democratic procedures, or vice versa.

A widely held and perfectly plausible expectation is that the American people support the values underlying democratic goals and procedures. At an abstract level, this is true enough. American citizens overwhelmingly subscribe to the basic rules and goals of democracy when the commitment is kept vague. The near-unanimous support for democratic goals and procedures disappears when specific applications of these concepts are considered. Majorities historically have been happy to infringe on the right to speak, to organize, and to run for office of unpopular groups such as atheists, Communists, and the Ku Klux Klan (KKK).

The willingness to give disliked groups their basic constitutional rights is referred to as political tolerance.[43] Americans overwhelmingly support freedom of speech and assembly, for example, but they are much more reluctant to allow a group they abhor, such as the KKK, to speak or assemble in a public place. So long as there is not a widespread consensus on which groups Americans believe are so noxious that they should not be given their rights, and so long as there are people who believe that rights should be given to all groups (known as civil libertarians), there will be enough people available to defend the rights of the noxious group to speak and assemble. The real problem occurs when a majority of Americans turn against a group and want group members' rights taken away. Examples in U.S. history include the internment of people of Japanese descent during World War II and the treatment of suspected communists during the McCarthy Era in the early 1950s.

More recently, protection of the rights of Muslims and Arab Americans in the United States has been a major concern for civil libertarians. The September 11, 2001, attacks on the United States led many Americans to feel highly threatened, and this perceived threat significantly increased their willingness to support policies that would infringe on the rights of Arab Americans. For example, almost a third of Americans (29 percent) supported the idea that Arabs and Arab Americans should be put under special surveillance by the U.S. government, and the more threatened people felt, the more they supported this policy. Threat also increased support for government surveillance of all Americans and of viewing security as more important than civil liberties.[44] Americans' willingness to sacrifice rights and freedoms in waging the war on terrorism can be seen in their support of the 2001 USA PATRIOT Act, which expanded the government's authority to monitor and regulate citizens. Over time, Americans have shifted their opinion to be more pro–civil liberties. Gallup has asked respondents which of two options comes closer to their views: The government should take all steps necessary to prevent additional acts of terrorism in the United States even if it means your basic civil liberties would be violated, or the government should take steps to prevent additional acts of terrorism but not if those steps would violate your basic civil liberties. The percentage of Americans choosing the first option (accepting the violation of civil liberties) dropped from 47 percent in January 2002 to 30 percent in June 2015, whereas the percentage saying civil liberties should not be violated increased from 49 percent to 65 percent across the same time span.[45]

A major topic of the 2016 and 2020 presidential elections was the role of a free press in American politics. Trump frequently targeted the media as evil or as the enemy both during his two campaigns and while serving as president.[46] Upon taking office in January 2017, his administration indicated a desire to change libel laws to make it easier to try and punish reporters for writing negative stories.[47] The First Amendment of the Constitution offers protection for a free press. Politicians would often prefer not to have the press investigating what they are doing, but the framers viewed the role of the press as so important that it needed to be constitutionally protected. Americans, however, are somewhat divided on whether the media should be free to criticize political leaders. The Pew Research Center, in a survey administered in February 2017, asked respondents whether having news organizations free to criticize political leaders was important to maintaining a strong democracy in the United States. Two-thirds (64 percent) agreed that this was very important, although there was a pronounced partisan divide: 49 percent of Republicans said a press free to criticize was very important compared to 76 percent of Democrats.[48] Since the survey was done when Republican Donald Trump was in office, perhaps the partisan division is due to Republicans not wanting the press to criticize their president and Democrats wanting the media to criticize him. This argument, however, does not appear to be the case. A Pew survey fielded in October 2016, when Democrat Barack Obama was still president, reveals the same partisan divide, with 49 percent of Republicans and 72 percent of Democrats viewing a free press critical of political leaders as very important.[49]

Democratic Processes

In addition to believing in the integrity of elections, trusting the government and each other, and upholding basic rights, the healthy functioning of democracy rests on people's understanding of and support for basic democratic processes. The U.S. political system is set up as a representative system in which people elect representatives to positions in government and these representatives both follow the rule of law and represent the interests of their constituents when debating and compromising on policy outcomes. The people do not have a direct vote, at the national level, on these outcomes. The framers intentionally, through federalism and the separation of powers, made it difficult for a majority to have its way without taking into consideration the interests of the minority. What this means is that the American political system is intentionally slow and inefficient and not easily swayed by the passions of the time. The framers hoped that this system would allow cooler heads to prevail, thereby leading to wiser decisions.

Putting aside the question of whether decisions are indeed wiser, what this system has done is to increase Americans' frustration with what they see as politicians' unwillingness or inability to solve the major problems facing the nation. This frustration could make Americans question basic democratic processes and prefer instead more efficient undemocratic processes, such as having experts or a strong leader make decisions rather than elected representatives. The left side of Figure 1-5 provides evidence that many Americans are not averse to having undemocratic processes in place. A vast majority are positive about having a democratic political system (85 percent), but a surprisingly large proportion think experts, not the government, should be making political decisions (53 percent) or that a strong leader who does not have to bother with the legislature or elections should be making the decisions (38 percent).[50] A third of respondents agree or strongly agree that having a strong leader is good, even if the leader bends the rules to get things done (this 2020 result is down from almost half, 46 percent, who agreed or strongly agreed in 2016). A 2020 postelection survey of Wisconsin voters showed that 33 percent felt that the American way of life is changing so much that force may be required to save it.

When looking at specific democratic processes, many Americans are similarly skeptical. Three major features of the American political system are that it is a representative democracy, which means that elected officials, not the people, make the decisions; that political decisions are the outcome of debate and compromise; and that even though the majority has more say in outcomes, the minority's interests and rights must be protected. The right side of Figure 1-5 shows that

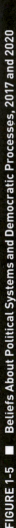

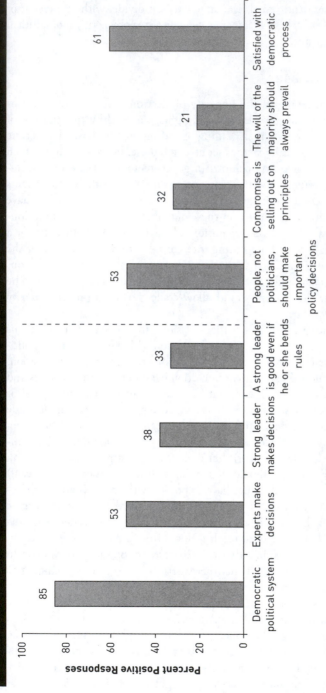

FIGURE 1-5 ■ Beliefs About Political Systems and Democratic Processes, 2017 and 2020

Percent Positive Responses

- Democratic political system — 85
- Experts make decisions — 53
- Strong leader makes decisions — 38
- A strong leader is good even if he or she bends rules — 33
- People, not politicians, should make important policy decisions — 53
- Compromise is selling out on principles — 32
- The will of the majority should always prevail — 21
- Satisfied with democratic process — 61

Source: 2020 American National Election Studies, available at www.electionstudies.org; 2017 World Values Survey, available at https://www.worldvaluessurvey.org/wvs.jsp.

World Values Survey: "I'm going to describe various types of political systems and ask what you think about each as a way of governing this country. For each one, would you say it is a very good, fairly good, fairly bad or very bad way of governing this country? Having a strong leader who does not have to bother with parliament or elections; Having experts, not government, make decisions according to what they think is best for the country; Having a democratic political system."

2020 ANES: "Having a strong leader in government is good for the United States even if the leader bends the rules to get things done"; "The people, and not politicians, should make our most important policy decisions"; "The will of the majority should always prevail, even over the rights of minorities"; "On the whole, are you very satisfied, fairly satisfied, not very satisfied, or not at all satisfied with the way democracy works in the United States?"

while only 21 percent think the United States should be a purely majoritarian democracy, a third look askance at compromise, and over half think the United States should be a direct democracy instead of a representative one. When asked if they were satisfied with democratic processes in 2020, only 61 percent said yes.

Some of Americans' preferred processes raise practical concerns. How is the will of the majority determined? If people had to make all of the important decisions, how would they find the time to become knowledgeable about the issues, how would their voices and votes be tallied, and what decision rule (plurality, simple majority, or supermajority) would be used to determine the outcome? These preferences also raise questions about Americans' commitment to principles that are foundational to American democracy, such as minority rights and separation of powers. Questions must also be raised about the compatibility of some of these opinions. For example, a preference for having the people decide appears to be inconsistent with the preference for having a strong leader who presumably makes the decisions. There would be no inconsistency, however, if people who agreed with one option disagreed with the other. Table 1-1 provides evidence that about a third of Americans hold consistent attitudes: 25 percent liked the idea of the people deciding policy and opposed having a strong leader, and 6 percent liked the strong leader idea and did not think the people should decide. The 21 percent who agreed with both options hold inconsistent attitudes. They both want to have people make the important decisions and want to have a strong leader who would presumably be making the decisions. Perhaps the people who agree with both options just want anything but the current system. Interestingly, only 11.5 percent of the respondents are consistent supporters of the current American political system (not wanting a strong leader and not wanting the people to directly decide important policies).

TABLE 1-1 ■ Support for Alternative Political Processes

		People, not politicians, should make important policy decisions		
		Agree	Neither agree nor disagree	Disagree
Strong leaders are good even if they bend the rules	Agree	21	7	6
	Neither agree nor disagree	7	10.5	3
	Disagree	25	10	11.5

Source: 2020 American National Election Studies, available at www.electionstudies.org.

Note: Cell entries are total percentages.

The sustainability of the political system rests in part on Americans choosing democracy over the alternatives. Two things could cause worry in this regard. First, if the most pro-democracy citizens are older and those less supportive of democracy are younger, then the trajectory might lead to a less democratic America over time. Using the World Values Survey data from 2017, Figure 1-6 breaks down support for democratic and undemocratic systems by age. While a vast majority of Americans say that a democratic system is very or fairly good, those under thirty years of age are significantly less positive about democracy than people fifty and older. Younger people have spent their whole lives in a time of extreme polarization, diminishing government efforts, and debilitating crises (including the terrorist attacks of September 11, 2001). Older people, in contrast, lived through major accomplishments, including World War II, the tremendous expansion of the U.S. economy, the civil rights movement, and so on. They also were more directly aware of what can result from having strong leaders who do not have to play by the rules of the game, including Adolf Hitler and Benito Mussolini. Having decisions made by undemocratic experts or strong leaders might look appealing when the gridlock in Washington appears so intractable, but history provides numerous examples of the horrific outcomes that can come from these types of leaders.

Second, having a segment of the population support undemocratic alternatives is not likely to undermine the democratic system if these preferences are located in small fringe parties or are spread across the two major parties. Third parties have a difficult time gaining traction in the two-party system, and most often have an impact on policies when a major party picks up their cause. The real problem arises if one of the major parties chooses not to support democratic processes. In 2020, Trump refused to say he would support the peaceful transfer of power if he lost the

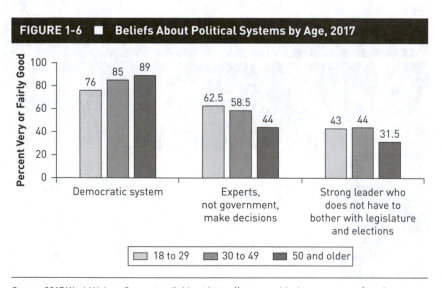

FIGURE 1-6 ■ Beliefs About Political Systems by Age, 2017

Legend: 18 to 29; 30 to 49; 50 and older

Source: 2017 World Values Survey, available at https://www.worldvaluessurvey.org/wvs.jsp.

election. After the election, Senator Lindsey Graham (R-SC) said on Fox News, "If Republicans don't challenge and change the U.S. election system, there will never be another Republican president elected again."[51] If these individuals reflect the preferences of Republicans as a group not to accept basic democratic processes, then the undermining of American democracy is more likely. Democracy itself becomes a polarized issue, and no longer is part of the foundational beliefs upon which the American political system rests. Figure 1-7 shows the breakdown of support for democratic and undemocratic processes by party identification. Partisans on both sides of the aisle overwhelmingly support having a democratic political system (94 percent of Democrats and 81 percent of Republicans). There is also not a big difference between Democrats and Republicans in their support for having experts make the decisions, although over half of Democrats support this approach. The biggest difference is in support of a strong leader making decisions without the democratic controls of a popularly elected legislature or elections themselves. Almost half of Republicans (46 percent) like this approach, compared to under a third of Democrats (29 percent). If support for democracy becomes more polarized, American democracy may well be in trouble.

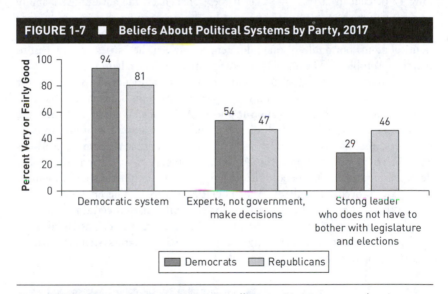

FIGURE 1-7 ■ Beliefs About Political Systems by Party, 2017

Source: 2017 World Values Survey, available at https://www.worldvaluessurvey.org/wvs.jsp.

MAINTAINING A DEMOCRACY

Belief in democratic ideals is essential to the preservation of a democratic system, both because such beliefs inhibit citizens from undemocratic actions and because the public will demand proper behavior on the part of political leaders. Belief that the system and its leaders meet democratic expectations in adhering to democratic procedures and responding to the wishes of the public is also important.

A third factor is perhaps less obvious. A democratic system must meet some standard for effectiveness in solving societal problems. If not, the public may conclude that democracy does not work, and that some other form of government—such as a dictatorship—is needed to maintain order, fend off an enemy, or provide economic well-being.

The United States is facing some big challenges at this point in its history. The threat of a terrorist attack looms constantly. America's education system is less competitive internationally than was historically the case. The economy, while strengthening, remains weaker than most Americans would like. Income inequality is increasing at dramatic rates. The Gini coefficient, which measures gross income inequality, has been increasing dramatically and is higher in the United States than in other G7 nations (0.434 in 2018). The gap in wealth between upper-income and lower-income families has similarly increased. In 1983, lower-income families held 7 percent and upper-income families held 60 percent of U.S. aggregate wealth. By 2016, lower-income wealth dropped to 4 percent while upper-income wealth increased to 79 percent. The hardest-hit group, though, is middle-income Americans, who dropped from holding 32 percent of aggregate wealth in 1983 to holding only 17 percent in 2016.[52] With all of these challenges, the government's ability to deal with such problems is hampered by the polarization that currently grips Washington. This polarization is based not simply on the parties trying to win political points but on deep-seated differences between the parties on how best to handle the problems. The unwillingness of political leaders to hammer out compromise solutions with the opposition, and the increased tendency of voters to throw out incumbents willing to compromise in primary elections, leads to stalemate.

Given the lack of sophistication in the public's understanding of democratic values and procedures, the declining levels of trust in government and in elections, and the increased support for undemocratic alternatives, some uneasiness emerges about public support for American democracy—and perhaps for any democratic regime. Democratic theory implies that the public should demand values and procedures embodying democratic principles. The hope or expectation is that the public in a democratic society will insist on certain values and processes. Leaders' positive support for a political system is also essential to its existence. If some leaders are willing to oppose the democratic system, it is crucial that few people are open to their appeal.

Study Questions

1. What makes for free and fair elections? Was the 2020 election free and fair given the evidence?

2. What is it about government that people don't trust? Why should we care about the decline in trust?

3. Does the American public support democracy as a form of government?

Suggested Readings

Achen, Christopher H., and Larry M. Bartels. *Democracy for Realists: Why Elections Do Not Produce Responsive Government*. Princeton, NJ: Princeton University Press, 2016. An important book on the influence of identities and party loyalties and the potential of democratic governance.

Almond, Gabriel, and Sidney Verba. *The Civic Culture*. Princeton, NJ: Princeton University Press, 1963. A classic study of political culture in five nations, including the United States.

Herrnson, Paul S., Richard G. Niemi, Michael J. Hanmer, Benjamin B. Bederson, Frederick G. Conrad, and Michael Traugott. *Voting Technology: The Not-So-Simple Act of Casting a Ballot*. Washington, DC: Brookings Institution, 2008. An in-depth look at voting systems and their impact on voters' ability to vote as they intended and their confidence in voting.

Hetherington, Marc J. *Why Trust Matters: Declining Political Trust and the Demise of American Liberalism*. Princeton, NJ: Princeton University Press, 2005. An important study of the policy implications of declining trust.

Hibbing, John R., and Elizabeth Theiss-Morse. *Stealth Democracy: Americans' Beliefs About How Government Should Work*. Cambridge, England: Cambridge University Press, 2002. A provocative analysis of the public's attitudes toward American political processes.

Marcus, George E., John L. Sullivan, Elizabeth Theiss-Morse, and Sandra L. Wood. *With Malice Toward Some*. Cambridge, England: Cambridge University Press, 1995. An in-depth study of the public's tolerance of unpopular groups.

McClosky, Herbert, and John Zaller. *The American Ethos*. Cambridge, MA: Harvard University Press, 1984. An analysis of the public's attitudes toward democracy and capitalism.

Putnam, Robert D. *Bowling Alone: The Collapse and Revival of American Community*. New York: Simon & Schuster, 2000. An analysis of the decline of participation in civic affairs.

Skocpol, Theda, and Morris P. Fiorina, eds. *Civic Engagement in American Democracy*. Washington, DC: Brookings Institution, 1999. A collection of readings on civic engagement in historical perspective.

Stimson, James A. *The Tides of Consent: How Public Opinion Shapes American Politics*. Cambridge, England: Cambridge University Press, 2004. Mainly about policy views and their impact, but also an interesting discussion of trust in government.

Verba, Sidney, Kay L. Schlozman, and Henry E. Brady. *Voice and Equality: Civic Voluntarism in American Politics*. Cambridge, England: Cambridge University Press, 1995. A survey of various forms of political participation, their determinants, and their impact on representative democracy.

Internet Resources

The website of the American National Election Studies, www.electionstudies.org, offers extensive data on topics covered in this and other chapters. Click on the Resources menu and then choose "Guide to Public Opinion and Electoral Behavior." Scroll down to "Support for the Political System." Some of the attitudinal data cover 1952 to the present. For every political item, there is a breakdown for each social characteristic in every election year.

If you have access through your school, go to https://ropercenter.cornell.edu/ and click on Search iPOLL menu. Follow the sign-in instructions to search the hundreds—perhaps thousands—of items related to political culture from surveys taken from the 1930s to the present.

Notes

1. Matea Gold, "President Trump Tells the FEC He Qualifies as a Candidate for 2020," *Washington Post*, January 21, 2017, https://www.washingtonpost.com/local/2017/live-updates/politics/live-coverage-of-trumps-inauguration/president-trump-tells-the-fec-he-qualifies-as-a-candidate-for-2020/.

2. Derrick Bryson Taylor, "A Timeline of the Coronavirus Pandemic," *New York Times*, January 10, 2021, https://www.nytimes.com/article/coronavirus-timeline.html?.

3. Evan Hill, Ainara Tiefenthäler, Christiaan Triebert, Drew Jordan, Haley Willis, and Robin Stein, "How George Floyd Was Killed in Police Custody," *New York Times*, May 31, 2020, updated February 23, 2021, https://www.nytimes.com/2020/05/31/us/george-floyd-investigation.html.

4. Larry Buchanan, Quoctrung Bui, and Jugal K. Patel, "Black Lives Matter May Be the Largest Movement in U.S. History," *New York Times*, July 3, 2020, https://www.nytimes.com/interactive/2020/07/03/us/george-floyd-protests-crowd-size.html.

5. Ibid.

6. "A Summary of the 2020 Election: Survey on the Performance of American Elections," MIT Election Lab, January 22, 2021, https://medium.com/mit-election-lab/a-summary-of-the-2020-election-survey-on-the-performance-of-american-elections-7a8d3f7bb83.

7. Nathaniel Rakich and Jasmine Mithani, "What Absentee Voting Looked Like in All 50 States," *FiveThirtyEight* (blog), February 9, 2021, https://fivethirtyeight.com/features/what-absentee-voting-looked-like-in-all-50-states/.

8. Miles Parks, "Fact Check: Trump Spreads Unfounded Claims About Voting by Mail," NPR, June 22, 2020, https://www.npr.org/2020/06/22/881598655/fact-check-trump-spreads-unfounded-claims-about-voting-by-mail.

9. Terrance Smith, "Trump Has Longstanding History of Calling Elections 'Rigged' If He Doesn't Like the Results," ABC News, November 11, 2020, https://abcnews.go.com/Politics/trump-longstanding-history-calling-elections-rigged-doesnt-results/story?id=74126926.

10. "U.S. Election 2020: Fact-Checking Trump Team's Main Fraud Claims," BBC News, November 23, 2020, https://www.bbc.com/news/election-us-2020-55016029.

11. Jim Rutenberg, Nick Corasaniti, and Alan Feuer, "Trump's Fraud Claims Died in Court, but the Myth of Stolen Elections Lives On," *New York Times*, December 26, 2020, updated January 7, 2021, https://www.nytimes.com/2020/12/26/us/politics/republicans-voter-fraud.html.

12. Brian Naylor, "Read Trump's Jan. 6 Speech, a Key Part of Impeachment Trial," NPR, February 10, 2021, https://www.npr.org/2021/02/10/966396848/read-trumps-jan-6-speech-a-key-part-of-impeachment-trial.

13. Nicholas Bogel-Burroughs, "Police Brush Back Protesters During Clash," *New York Times*, January 6, 2021, https://www.nytimes.com/live/2021/01/06/us/washington-dc-protests#lock-the-door-the-scene-inside-and-outside-the-capitol.

14. Cline Center for Advanced Social Research, "It Was an Attempted Coup: The Cline Center's Coup D'état Project Categorizes the January 6, 2021 Assault on the US Capitol," University of Illinois at Urbana-Champaign, https://clinecenter.illinois.edu/coup-detat-project-cdp/statement_jan.27.2021. Researchers at the Cline Center at the University of Illinois at Urbana-Champaign have classified the January 6, 2021, storming of the U.S. Capitol as an attempted coup because of the attempt by the perpetrators to disrupt the constitutional transition process and to keep the legally elected president, Joe Biden, from taking power. We use their recommended term, *attempted dissident coup*, when talking about the January 6 events.

15. Robert A. Dahl, *On Democracy* (New Haven, CT: Yale University Press, 1998), 85.

16. Smith, "Trump Has Longstanding History of Calling Elections 'Rigged.'"

17. "Official 2020 Presidential General Election Results," Federal Election Commission, January 28, 2021, https://www.fec.gov/resources/cms-content/documents/2020presgeresults.pdf.

18. The Electoral College votes for each of these states were 11 (Arizona), 16 (Georgia), and 10 (Wisconsin).

19. Rutenberg et al., "Trump's Fraud Claims Died in Court."

20. Hope Yen, Ali Swenson, and Amanda Seitz, "AP Fact Check: Trump's Claims of Vote Rigging Are All Wrong," AP News, December 3, 2020, https://apnews .com/article/election-2020-ap-fact-check-joe-biden-donald-trump-technology-49a24edd6d10888dbad61689c24b05a5.

21. Nick Corasaniti, Reid J. Epstein, and Jim Rutenberg, "The Times Called Officials in Every State: No Evidence of Voter Fraud," *New York Times*, November 10, 2020, updated November 19, 2020, https://www.nytimes.com/2020/11/10/us/politics/voting-fraud.html.

22. Michael Balsamo, "Disputing Trump, Barr Says No Widespread Election Fraud," AP News, December 1, 2020, https://apnews.com/article/barr-no-widespread-election-fraud-b1f1488796c9a98c4b1a9061a6c7f49d.

23. "Election Fraud Cases," The Heritage Foundation, accessed March 16, 2021, https://www.heritage.org/voterfraud/search.

24. Andrew C. Eggers, Haritz Garro, and Justin Grimmer, "Comment on 'A Simple Test for the Extent of Voter Fraud With Absentee Ballots in the 2020 Election,'" Hoover Institution, January 4, 2021, https://www.hoover.org/research/comment-simple-test-extent-voterfraud-absentee-ballots-2020-presidentialelection.

25. Ray Christensen and Thomas J. Schultz, "Identifying Election Fraud Using Orphan and Low Propensity Voters," *American Politics Research* 42, no. 2 (2014): 311–337, p. 313; see also David Cotrell, Michael C. Herron, and Sean Westwood, "An Exploration of Donald Trump's Allegations of Massive Voter Fraud in the 2016 General Election," *Electoral Studies* 51 (2018): 123–142.

26. "More Americans Happy About Trump Loss Than Biden Win," Monmouth University Polling Institute, November 18, 2020, https://www.monmouth.edu/polling-institute/reports/monmouthpoll_us_111820/.

27. Jack Citrin and Christopher Muste, "Trust in Government," in *Measures of Political Attitudes*, vol. 2, eds. J. P. Robinson, P. R. Shaver, and L. S. Wrightman (San Diego, CA: Academic Press, 1999), 465–532.

28. Russell Hardin, "Do We Want Trust in Government?," in *Democracy and Trust*, ed. M. E. Warren (Cambridge, England: Cambridge University Press, 1999), 22–41.

29. "Confidence in Institutions," Gallup, accessed June 25, 2021, http://www .gallup.com/poll/1597/confidence-institutions.aspx. The data for the earlier years were from 1975. The most recent data are from 2020.

30. See, for example, Russell J. Dalton, "Political Trust in North America," in *Handbook on Political Trust*, eds. Sonia Zmerli and Tom W. G. van der Meer (Cheltenham, England: Edward Elgar, 2017), 375–394.

31. Lisa Rein and Ed O'Keefe, "New Post Poll Finds Negativity Toward Federal Workers," *Washington Post*, October 18, 2010, http://www.washingtonpost .com/wp-dyn/content/article/2010/10/17/AR2010101703866.html?sid=ST2010101703889.

32. "Public Expresses Favorable Views of a Number of Federal Agencies," Pew Research Center, October 1, 2019, https://www.pewresearch.org/politics/2019/10/01/public-expresses-favorable-views-of-a-number-of-federal-agencies/.

33. "Congress and the Public," Gallup, accessed June 25, 2021, http://www.gallup.com/poll/1600/congress-public.aspx. Data are taken from a September 9–13, 2015, poll.

34. Richard Fenno, *Home Style* (New York: Addison-Wesley, 2003 [1977]), 59.

35. Diana C. Mutz and Byron Reeves, "The New Videomalaise: Effects of Televised Incivility on Political Trust," *American Political Science Review* (February 2005): 1–15; Diana C. Mutz, *In-Your-Face Politics: The Consequences of Uncivil Media* (Princeton, NJ: Princeton University Press, 2015); Eran N. Ben-Porath, "Interview Effects: Theory and Evidence for the Impact of Televised Political Interviews on Viewer Attitudes," *Communication Theory* (August 2010): 323–347.

36. See, for example, Ken Newton, "Political Trust and the Mass Media," in *Handbook on Political Trust*, eds. Sonja Zmerli and Tom W. G. van der Meer (Cheltenham, England: Edward Elgar, 2017), 353–372, for a good overview of these arguments.

37. See, for example, Pippa Norris, *A Virtuous Circle: Political Communications in Postindustrial Societies* (Cambridge, England: Cambridge University Press, 2000); Doris A. Graber, *Processing Politics: Learning From Television in the Internet Age* (Chicago: University of Chicago Press, 2001); Dhavan V. Shah, "Civic Engagement, Interpersonal Trust and Television Use: An Individual-Level Assessment of Social Capital," *Political Psychology* (September 1998): 469–496.

38. Fenno, *Home Style*, 914.

39. David W. Brady and Sean M. Theriault, "A Reassessment of Who's to Blame: A Positive Case for the Public Evaluation of Congress," in *What Is It About Government That Americans Dislike?*, eds. John R. Hibbing and Elizabeth Theiss-Morse (Cambridge, England: Cambridge University Press, 2001), 175–192.

40. Marc J. Hetherington, *Why Trust Matters* (Princeton, NJ: Princeton University Press, 2005), 48.

41. Ibid., 53.

42. Elizabeth Theiss-Morse, Dona-Gene Barton, and Michael W. Wagner, "Political Trust in Polarized Times," in *Motivating Cooperation and Compliance With Authority: The Role of Institutional Trust, Nebraska Symposium on Motivation*, vol. 62, eds. B. H. Bornstein and A. Tomkins (New York: Springer, 2015).

43. For the major study of the 1950s, see Samuel Stouffer, *Communism, Conformity, and Civil Liberties* (Garden City, NY: Doubleday, 1955). See also James W. Prothro and Charles M. Grigg, "Fundamental Principles of Democracy: Bases

of Agreement and Disagreement," *Journal of Politics* 22 (May 1960): 276–294; John L. Sullivan, James Piereson, and George E. Marcus, *Political Tolerance and American Democracy* (Chicago: University of Chicago Press, 1982).

44. Leonie Huddy, Stanley Feldman, Charles Taber, and Gallya Lahav, "Threat, Anxiety, and Support of Antiterrorism Policies," *American Journal of Political Science* 49 (July 2005): 593–608.

45. "Civil Liberties," Gallup, accessed June 25, 2021, http://www.gallup.com/poll/5263/civil-liberties.aspx.

46. Alexander Burns and Nick Corasaniti, "Donald Trump's Other Campaign Foe: The 'Lowest Form of Life' News Media," *New York Times*, August 12, 2016, https://www.nytimes.com/2016/08/13/us/politics/donald-trump-obama-isis.html; Manuel Roig-Franzia and Sarah Ellison, "A History of the Trump War on Media—The Obsession Not Even Coronavirus Could Stop," *Washington Post*, March 29, 2020, https://www.washingtonpost.com/lifestyle/media/a-history-of-the-trump-war-on-media--the-obsession-not-even-coronavirus-could-stop/2020/03/28/71bb21d0-f433-11e9-8cf0-4cc99f74d127_story.html.

47. Adam Liptak, "Can Trump Change Libel Laws?" *New York Times*, March 30, 2017, https://www.nytimes.com/2017/03/30/us/politics/can-trump-change-libel-laws.html?_r=0.

48. "Large Majorities See Checks and Balances, Right to Protest as Essential for Democracy," Pew Research Center, March 2, 2017, http://www.people-press.org/2017/03/02/large-majorities-see-checks-and-balances-right-to-protest-as-essential-for-democracy/.

49. "As Election Nears, Voters Divided Over Democracy and 'Respect,'" Pew Research Center, October 27, 2016, http://www.people-press.org/2016/10/27/as-election-nears-voters-divided-over-democracy-and-respect/.

50. In the 1994–1998 World Values Survey, 90 percent of Americans were positive about democracy, 37 percent were positive about experts making decisions, and 25 percent were positive about a strong leader making decisions.

51. Stephanie Saul, "Lindsey Graham's Long-Shot Mission to Unravel the Election Results," *New York Times*, November 17, 2020, https://www.nytimes.com/2020/11/17/us/politics/lindsey-graham-georgia-trump-biden.html?searchResultPosition=10.

52. Juliana Menasce Horowitz, Ruth Igielnik, and Rakesh Kochhar, "Trends in Income and Wealth Inequality," Pew Research Center, January 9, 2020, https://www.pewresearch.org/social-trends/2020/01/09/trends-in-income-and-wealth-inequality/.

2

ELECTORAL CONTEXT
AND STRATEGY

IT IS NOT EXCITING, but after nearly $7 billion in campaign spending, dramatic debates, a global pandemic, a summer of protests for racial justice, and a growing phalanx of conspiratorial misinformation clogging social media, the factors that political scientists call "the fundamentals" did a good job predicting the outcome of the 2020 presidential election. A predictive model from Peter Enns and Julius Lagodny, made more than one hundred days before the election, correctly predicted the results in forty-nine of fifty states, missing only Georgia, a state that surprisingly flipped to Joe Biden's column on the heels of the voter registration and organizing work of voting rights activist and Georgia politician Stacey Abrams.[1] While news coverage and pundits focus on things like candidate personality, strategy, and swing voters, much of what predicts the end result of a presidential campaign is beyond candidates' control.

There are a variety of ways to predict election results with "structural" variables such as presidential approval, economic growth, aggregated polls, and other fundamental aspects of politics and social life. Table 2-1 summarizes many of the major political science forecasts made months before Election Day. Forecasters use data from these fundamental measures of politics and the economy to predict the election, often before each party has even selected its nominee. The average number of electoral votes predicted for President Donald Trump by the political scientists doing the forecasting was 237, only 5 more than he actually received. The average prediction of his two-party vote total was 47.8 percent; he received 47.7 percent.

This chapter examines how the economic and political conditions scholars use give us a baseline from which to understand elections in American politics, how the rules that govern elections can influence the outcome, and the basic strategic choices candidates and other interested groups make in an election season. Thus, this chapter serves as a lens through which we can think about the structural

TABLE 2-1 ■ Political Scientists' 2020 Election Forecasts

Author(s)	Trump Electoral Vote	Trump Two-Party Popular Vote Share
Abramowitz	219	N/A
DeSart	188	45.2
Enns and Lagodny	248	45.5
Jerome et al.	230	48.3
Lewis-Beck and Tien	68	43.3
Murr and Lewis-Beck	346	50.4
Norpoth	362	N/A
Erikson and Wlezien	N/A	45.0
Graefe	N/A	47.2
Lockerbie	N/A	55.2
Gruca and Rietz	N/A	49.9
Average	**237**	**47.8**

Source: Alan I. Abramowitz, "How Did the Political Science Forecasters Do?," in *Sabato's Crystal Ball*, ed. Larry J. Sabato, Kyle Kondik, and J. Miles Coleman (University of Virginia Center for Politics, December 3, 2020), https://centerforpolitics.org/crystalball/articles/how-did-the-political-science-forecasters-do/.

conditions that help us understand how the political behavior of the American electorate works. Everything else that we analyze in this book—political partisanship, public opinion, group characteristics and social identity, the media, and the elements of individual vote choice—does not occur in a vacuum, but takes place in a specific context that, when properly understood, can help us to make fairly accurate predictions about election results months before any ballots are cast. As is the case throughout the book, in this chapter we will use examples from the 2020 election and data showing trends over time to illustrate our points.

Learning objectives for Chapter 2 include:

- Understanding how fundamentals like the state of the economy and presidential approval are related to the presidential vote

- Learning how the administrative "rules of the game" influence how elections are conducted

- Exploring how electoral structures influence campaign strategy

- Engaging with how campaigns deal with unexpected factors that have the potential to interact with or even upend "the fundamentals"

- Lay the groundwork to assess how fundamentals interact with other factors to affect election results

THE FUNDAMENTALS

For decades, the state of the American economy has been the most celebrated fundamental factor related to presidential vote choice, and 2020 provided a particularly complicated test of the relationship between the economy and vote choice. The COVID-19 pandemic led the nation's gross domestic product (GDP) to an astronomical 31.4 percent drop in the second fiscal quarter of 2020 and an equally huge 33.4 percent spike in the third fiscal quarter of 2020.[2] Typically, change in the nation's GDP ranges between –3 percent and +7 percent. How voters would apply their experience of the yo-yoing economy to their evaluations of President Trump was a great unknown heading into the 2020 election.

In nonpandemic times, presidents are keenly aware of how the performance of the economy is tied to their electoral fortunes. About one month into his first term as commander in chief, Barack Obama said on the *Today* show, "If I don't have this [improving the economy] done in three years, then there's gonna be a one-term proposition."[3] As far back as 2014, political scientists argued that the slowly growing economy and President Obama's relatively low approval rating at the time gave Democrats an "uphill battle" to 270 electoral votes.[4] By the beginning of 2016, the economy had picked up slightly and President Obama's approval was north of 50 percent, but neither measure had improved enough to make most political scientists think the 2016 election was much more than a coin flip. Political scientist Larry Bartels wrote that the 2012 race was a coin flip election that the Democrats won, while the 2016 race was a coin flip race the Republicans won.[5]

In a world of campaign war rooms, instantaneous media coverage, billions of dollars of television advertising, dramatic debates, raucous campaign rallies, gaffes, special interest spending, and messaging, can a few elements of data correctly predict the winner of almost every election of the past sixty years, months before any ballots are counted?

Historically, the American people have responded to a growing economy by awarding the incumbent or the incumbent's political party another term in the White House. A clear relationship exists between growth in the nation's GDP (and/or real disposable income per capita, or RDI) and the percentage of the two-party vote earned by the incumbent's party in presidential elections. People generally reward the occupant of 1600 Pennsylvania Avenue at the ballot box when the economy is on the rise. Figure 2-1 shows a linear relationship with a growing GDP from January to June of the election year and an increase in the incumbent party's share of the two-party presidential vote. If we look at just 1956, 1964, 1972, 1980, 1984, 1992, 1996, 2004, and 2012 (the years the incumbent president himself was seeking reelection), the relationship is even stronger than it is for years when a presidential hopeful from the same party is running for president.

There are exceptions to this rule. Figure 2-1 shows that the economy was growing in 1976 when Republican president Gerald Ford lost to Democrat Jimmy Carter. In 1992, the economy was actually rebounding out of the recession that doomed President George H. W. Bush's reelection bid when third-party candidate Ross Perot achieved a strong showing and Bill Clinton rode his "it's the economy, stupid" campaign strategy into the Oval Office. But in general, a growing economy is good for the president seeking reelection. Indeed, of the sixteen presidential elections examined in Figure 2-1, only five saw the incumbent or incumbent's party earn less than 50 percent of the popular vote if the economy was growing at all.

Using second-quarter GDP change in 2020 (–31.4 percent), President Trump, even though he lost, dramatically overperformed what we would expect of him. But using third-quarter GDP growth (+33.4 percent), the president dramatically underperformed what we would expect, given the previous seventy years of presidential elections. Given the incredibly large GDP shifts in 2020, we do not include 2020 data in Figure 2-1 as it would skew how we interpret the previous seven decades of data.

Not all economic indicators are created equal, however. GDP and RDI are generally good estimators that help predict election results. Some popular data providing evidence about the economy are less well suited to the task of helping students of American politics understand elections. For example, hundreds of stories were written about how the nation's high unemployment in 2011 and 2012 spelled disaster for Obama. However, unemployment has what former *New York Times* election blogger Nate Silver called a "maddening" relationship with election results. For example, unemployment was relatively high (over 7 percent) for Ronald Reagan's popular and electoral vote thumping of Walter Mondale during Reagan's reelection victory in 1984. Unemployment *rose* from the beginning of the terms to Election Day for Dwight Eisenhower's 1956 reelection victory, Richard Nixon's reelection in 1972, and George W. Bush's reelection in 2004.[6] Unemployment actually dropped during Jimmy Carter's term, but he was not able to defend the White House from Reagan's advances.

Unemployment rates are certainly an important indicator about the health of the economy, but they are not highly correlated with presidential election results. Trump actually performed better in 2020 in locales with high unemployment.[7] In 2012, media coverage regularly pointed out that one "reason" that Obama was in trouble was that no president in the post–World War II era had ever won reelection with an unemployment rate above 7.4 percent. Of course, and much to our dismay, no one in the history of humankind has ever won any election after the Minnesota Vikings won the Super Bowl.[8] In other words, some claims are factually accurate without being substantively meaningful.

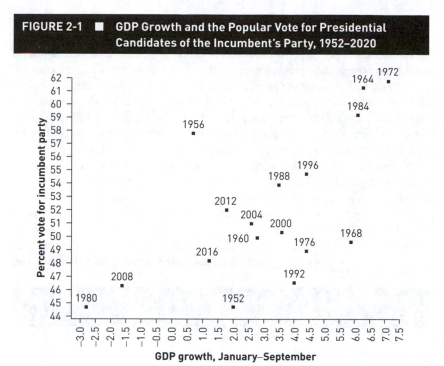

FIGURE 2-1   ■   GDP Growth and the Popular Vote for Presidential Candidates of the Incumbent's Party, 1952–2020

Sources: GDP data from the U.S. Department of Commerce Bureau of Economic Analysis, National Economic Accounts, Gross Domestic Product, at http://www.bea.gov/national/; presidential voting data from John Woolley and Gerhard Peters, The American Presidency Project, at https://www .presidency.ucsb.edu/statistics/elections.

Gas prices are also a popular indicator of the state of the economy. Republican presidential primary candidate Newt Gingrich went as far as to promise that gas prices would drop to $2.50 per gallon if he were elected president, something that even HBO's *The Newsroom* mocked in its dramatic, fictional treatment of the 2012 campaign in which the anchorman character Will McAvoy pointed out the president does not control gas prices. On a more serious note, political scientist John Sides has argued that while rising gas prices can affect presidential approval, they are not a major player in predicting presidential elections.[9]

The volatile changes in the economy, caused by the national response to the COVID-19 pandemic, meant that any Republican presidential candidate would have a difficult path to victory in 2020. But the state of the economy is not the only fundamental factor that helps us predict election results. In July 2020, political scientists Olivia Quinn, Amanda Brush, and Eric R. A. N. Smith noted, "Without a significant change in Trump's approval rating and a swift recovery of the pandemic-depressed economy, Republicans seem unlikely to prevail in November."[10] In other words, presidential elections are not just a function of economic performance; they are also structured by the nation's approval of the job the president is doing.

Presidential approval plays a key role in forecasting elections. It should not be terribly surprising that public approval of the job the president is doing has something to do with whether the president gets a chance at a second term. Figure 2-2 shows the relationship between presidential approval in an election year and the incumbent party's share of the two-party vote. If you recall from Figure 2-1 that there were five elections in which a growing economy was not enough for the incumbent party to earn 50 percent of the popular vote, a quick look at Figure 2-2 highlights the fundamental importance of presidential approval as an independent indicator of presidential elections. In 1952, Democratic president Harry Truman left office with a 32 percent approval rating, which helped drag down the effect of a growing economy and allowed Republican Dwight Eisenhower to win the election. It is true that in 1992, President George H. W. Bush lost some support to the surprisingly strong third-party candidacy of Ross Perot, but he was also hurt by a dismal approval rating. Gerald Ford, who was appointed (not elected) to be

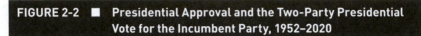

FIGURE 2-2 ■ Presidential Approval and the Two-Party Presidential Vote for the Incumbent Party, 1952–2020

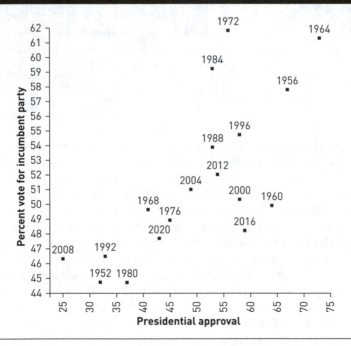

Source: Presidential approval and vote share data are from John Woolley and Gerhard Peters, The American Presidency Project, Presidential Job Approval, http://www.presidency.ucsb.edu/data/popularity.php.

Percentage of two-party vote for incumbent presidential party data from John Woolley and Gerhard Peters, The American Presidency Project, https://www.presidency.ucsb.edu/statistics/elections.

vice president and ascended into the Oval Office after Richard Nixon resigned in disgrace, presided over a booming growth in GDP, but his pardoning of Nixon and problems with high inflation sank his approval rating and his bid for a presidential victory in his own right. Hubert Humphrey has been blamed for underperforming as a candidate, but his commander in chief, Lyndon Johnson, had the approval of only 41 percent of the country in 1968.

With respect to presidential approval in 2020, President Trump peaked at 49 percent—with only 43 percent approving of his job performance on Election Day. While presidents typically see their approval rating rise on the way to their reelection bid, President Trump's dropped from a high point in May to rest between 39 and 43 percent from June to Election Day.[11] In 2016, President Obama's approval rating rose steadily during his last year in office. While an unpopular George W. Bush was largely kept off the campaign trail in 2008, the popular Obama was a key surrogate for Hillary Clinton, visiting several swing states in the waning days of the election season. Clinton regularly referenced her time in the Obama administration as secretary of state, trying to tie her candidacy to Obama's service and legacy. Political scientist Drew Linzer suggested that the 2016 election forecasting showed the election was a normal one as Clinton netted almost exactly the percentage of the two-party vote as would be expected given President Obama's approval rating.[12] Figure 2-2 shows the vote share of all voters that presidential candidates of the president's party earned as compared to the approval rating of the president. Looking at the two-party vote as a function of presidential approval suggests Trump slightly underperformed in 2020.

In addition to economic fundamentals and those related to approval of the president, political fundamentals can influence election results. This is especially the case in congressional elections. Putting election results into the proper context requires understanding the political structure heading into the election and the complexion of the electorate within electoral boundaries, such as a congressional district or a state.

For an example of the political structure's influence on elections, we can turn to the 2010 congressional contests. The Democratic Party went into the 2010 midterms with a solid majority, holding 255 seats in the 435-member House of Representatives. Democrats had taken back both houses of Congress in 2006 and brought their party back into the White House in 2008. However, one political fundamental of congressional elections is that both success in previous elections and the size of a party's majority in a house of Congress tend to beget more vulnerable seats in the *next* election. For example, forty-eight Democratically represented House districts voted for John McCain in the 2008 presidential election. Districts in which the congressional representative is of a different party from the district's preferred presidential candidate are generally the hardest to hold in midterm contests.

These "swing districts" are an example of how the partisan complexion of a district can affect election results. Since they often have an incumbent who represents a district in which the majority of voters identify with the opposite political party, more qualified challengers are often inspired to enter the race. In competitive districts in 2010, the Republican Party fielded more quality challengers (those who have previously held elective office) than ever before. Over 39 percent of Democratic representatives holding competitive seats faced a quality Republican challenger in 2010, compared to 28 percent in 2008. Regardless of whether an incumbent faces a quality challenger, the fundamental truth is that a district's general ideology holds great predictive power in congressional elections. As we noted in our supplement to this volume, *Political Behavior in Midterm Elections*, 2015 edition,[13] simply knowing whether a congressional district voted for Obama or McCain, and nothing else, correctly predicted the results of 85 percent of the races for the House of Representatives in 2010.

In 2020, changes in real gross national product in the first and second quarters, the president's approval rating in July, and the fact that it was a presidential year predicted modest gains in the House and Senate for the Democrats, albeit with quite a bit of variance.[14] In the end, Democrats captured the Senate majority, gaining 3 seats, and held onto the House majority despite losing 12 seats.

THE RULES OF THE GAME

One of us authors likes to play pickup basketball with fellow faculty members, graduate students, and understanding undergraduates who don't mind a slower game consisting of older players with rapidly diminishing skills. He is most valuable to his team when the game rewards three-point baskets (rather than counting all baskets by ones, which is a conventional way of scorekeeping in pickup games). This is because he is slow-footed, middle-aged, short, and a loafer on defense. When the rules of the game reward long-distance shooting, the one element of the game in which he has some skill, his teams are more likely to win. The rules of the game are important in the confines of pickup basketball at public universities, but they are even more important (and more consequential!) in the world of elections.

Election rules affect access to the ballot, the ability to participate in debates, the schedule of primary elections, the date of the general election, who can run for office, and what type of vote is most important (the popular vote or that of the Electoral College). Rules are especially important in primary elections. The Democratic and Republican Parties award their delegates differently, which leads to different campaign strategies in primary elections for candidates of both parties. The Democrats award their delegates proportionately (so long as the candidate wins above 15 percent of the popular vote in the primary) so that a candidate who wins 35 percent of the vote will win 35 percent of the delegates. Thus, it is in Democratic candidates' interest to campaign hard in every state in which they might win enough of the vote to earn some delegates. The Texas primary/caucus is so unique that even though Hillary Clinton won more votes than Barack Obama in the 2008 Texas primary, his strong performance in the caucus there resulted in Obama winning more delegates. Some analysts attributed Obama's defeat of Clinton to his campaign's more strategic understanding of the party's rules regarding the awarding of delegates, especially in states that held caucuses rather than primaries. Democrats also can win "superdelegates"—typically, lawmakers and high-ranking officials in the party. These superdelegates are not bound to the popular vote in their state's primary when deciding which candidate they will vote for at the Democratic National Convention. Clinton dominated her chief competitor, Bernie Sanders, in superdelegates by a margin of 570½ to 44½.

Some Republican primaries are winner take all. That is, whoever wins the most votes gets all the delegates. Other Republican primaries elect to award delegates on a proportional basis. The different rules for these primaries can affect the number of visits a candidate makes to a state, the size of an advertising buy in that state, and the media momentum a candidate might enjoy (or suffer) after all the votes are counted.

Regardless of how delegates are awarded, Marty Cohen, David Karol, Hans Noel, and John Zaller have persuasively argued that party leaders typically unite behind a candidate, and when they do, that candidate becomes the nominee.[15] To be sure, there are times when party leaders stay on the sidelines, perhaps wary of the risk involved in supporting a candidate who falters, but in general, even in the era of primary elections and caucuses, "the party decides" who their nominee will be for president. Even though the rules of party nominations have changed a great deal, the somewhat hidden "fundamental" of endorsements from party insiders plays a crucial role in selecting nominees for president.

Of course, authors Cohen et al. of *The Party Decides* took a bit of a beating in 2016 because the Republican Party establishment did not want Donald Trump to be their party's nominee. This simple fact led many to declare the "party decides" thesis to be dead. The question we should ask as political scientists is whether 2016's Republican primary results suggest that the "party decides" theory is incorrect or whether there were other factors at play that uniquely contributed to the results. Presidential scholar Julia Azari argued that the Republican Party simply decided not to decide.[16] The Grand Old Party (GOP) fielded a large number of qualified candidates for president, and no single candidate ran away with the endorsement primary. The party never coalesced around Jeb Bush, Scott Walker, John Kasich, or Ted Cruz. Political parties scholar Seth Masket reminded election watchers that the "party decides" thesis was alive and well on one side of the aisle.[17] Democratic Party elites clearly settled on Hillary Clinton—and she won her closely contested race with Bernie Sanders. They did the same thing in 2020, preferring Joe Biden in the crowded field.

Perhaps no other rule shapes presidential campaigns as much as the awarding of Electoral College votes. Forty-eight states award electoral votes on a winner-take-all basis. Nebraska and Maine give a candidate two electoral votes for winning the state's popular vote and one electoral vote for each congressional district the candidate wins. In 2008, Barack Obama won the Second Congressional District in Nebraska, but lost the Cornhusker State's popular vote and the contests in the First and Third Congressional Districts, giving him one electoral vote from Nebraska to John McCain's four. Obama's 2008 campaign manager David Plouffe called the history-making result in Nebraska's Second Congressional District his favorite electoral vote. In 2016, Maine awarded one electoral vote to Donald Trump, who won the Second Congressional District, and Hillary Clinton won the statewide contest and the First Congressional District, netting three electoral votes. In 2020, once again Trump won an electoral vote in Maine while Biden collected Nebraska's second district for the Democrats.

Given the Electoral College's structure, candidates spend the most amount of time in swing states that possess a large number of electoral votes. Even the most casual observer of American politics can name a few of the states that regularly enjoy a high volume of candidate visits and an even higher volume of campaign advertising—states such as Ohio, Florida, Wisconsin, Pennsylvania, Michigan, and Virginia. A candidate must win 270 electoral votes to become the president. However unlikely it may be, given that there are 538 total electoral votes up for grabs, a 269 to 269 stalemate is possible.

Table 2-2 shows that while there is a correlation between electoral votes and popular votes, these two measures of campaign success are not the same. For example, John F. Kennedy earned more electoral votes in 1960 than Jimmy Carter did in 1976 and George W. Bush did in 2004 even though Kennedy won less of the popular vote. Bill Clinton won more electoral votes in 1992 than presidents in seven other elections—all seven of whom got a higher percentage of the popular vote than he did. Of course, you will recall that Clinton's share of the popular vote was diminished as he beat President George H. W. Bush *and* strong third-party candidate Ross Perot in that election. One reason political scientists are far more skeptical about declaring that a winning presidential candidate has a "mandate" is that Electoral College blowouts, like the ones in 2012, 1996, 1992, and 1980, mask much narrower victories in the popular vote. In 2016, Donald Trump's big Electoral College win came while losing the popular vote, just as George W. Bush's victory in 2000 did.

Campaign finance rules are also important to understand. Individuals are limited in the amount of money they can give to a campaign, but candidates face no such limit, in terms of how much they spend or how much they can give themselves. Some, notably John Kerry in 2004 and Mitt Romney in 2008, have spent substantial amounts of their own money in (unsuccessful) bids for the White House. Donald Trump spent $66.1 million of his own money in his successful White House bid in 2016. Self-financed candidates have been more successful in congressional races; Jon Corzine of New Jersey spent nearly the same amount, about $62 million, of his own money to get to the Senate in 2000. Despite Corzine's victory, self-funded candidates are by no means guaranteed victory. Wrestling mogul Linda McMahon has spent nearly $100 million in unsuccessful bids for U.S. Senate seats in Connecticut.

In fact, enormous campaign spending by incumbent members of Congress, whether they are self-financed or financed conventionally by individuals and political action committees (PACs), is negatively correlated with vote totals.

TABLE 2-2 ■ Popular Vote Percentage and Electoral Vote Count for the Winning Presidential Candidate, 1952–2020		
Year	Popular Vote (%)	Electoral College Votes
1952	54.9	442
1956	57.4	457
1960	49.7	303
1964	61.1	486
1968	43.4	301
1972	60.7	520
1976	50.1	297
1980	50.7	489
1984	58.8	525
1988	53.4	426
1992	43.0	370
1996	49.2	379
2000	47.9	271
2004	50.7	286
2008	52.9	365
2012	51.1	332
2016	45.9	306
2020	51.3	306

Source: John Woolley and Gerhard Peters, The American Presidency Project, available at https://www.presidency.ucsb.edu/statistics/elections.

This is because the more members of Congress have to spend to get reelected, the more likely it is that they represent a swing district, are facing a stiff challenge, or both. In other words, the more money one has to spend to hold onto a congressional seat, the more danger that seat tends to be in during an election. On the other hand, plenty of incumbents who spend a ton of money do win reelection, and spending too much money is far more preferable than not having enough to compete.

Though the rules of the game are difficult to change, the times that they are altered introduce greater uncertainty into our ability to understand how elections will work. One example of a recent major change comes from a controversy commonly referred to as "Citizens United." The Federal Election Commission (FEC) had objected to the airing of *Hillary: The Movie*, a movie critical of Hillary Clinton, within thirty days of the 2008 presidential primaries. The FEC claimed that the movie, produced by a nonprofit organization called Citizens United, was electioneering and thus prohibited by law to air the movie that close to an election. The Supreme Court's decision in *Citizens United v. Federal Election Commission* determined that while corporations and unions are not literal humans, they do have the constitutional right to free speech afforded to "associations of persons." Thus, banning corporations and unions from spending money to engage in electioneering at any point in a campaign was unconstitutional.

Citizens United, and other subsequent decisions from the court, opened the door to major spending from PACs and "super PACs," such as Restore Our Future (which supported Mitt Romney) and Priorities USA Action (which supported Barack Obama), to the tune of $142 million and $65 million, respectively, in 2012.[18] PACs are outside groups not officially connected with a campaign. Spending was up in congressional races too, though it should be noted that independent expenditures began their rapid rise after the Bipartisan Campaign Reform Act (BCRA) in 2002 and not after *Citizens United*. Regardless, it is worth asking whether all the spending was consequential. The early returns on that question suggest that spending did not do much to affect the result of the 2020 presidential election.

Figure 2-3 shows the total presidential and congressional expenditures in millions of dollars from 1976 to 2020. Before the BCRA was passed, the average increase in spending from one congressional election to the next was $34 million. The average increase after the BCRA was $83.75 million. As Figure 2-3 shows, the difference on the presidential side is even greater.

STRATEGY

Even if candidates can accurately assess whether the economic, partisan, and structural fundamentals favor them or their opponents, candidates and their advisers need to develop and execute strategies designed to help them win elections. Increasingly, these strategies—at least at the presidential level—appear to be rooted in empirical evidence regarding what drives voter turnout (see Chapter 3), who is most likely to be persuaded to change their vote, and where the most efficient use of television advertising might be located.

Given the crucial role that economic conditions play in affecting presidential and congressional elections, successful candidates are more likely to rely on economic messages when the economic fundamentals favor them and focus on meeting other criteria when the prevailing economic headwinds are bad news for

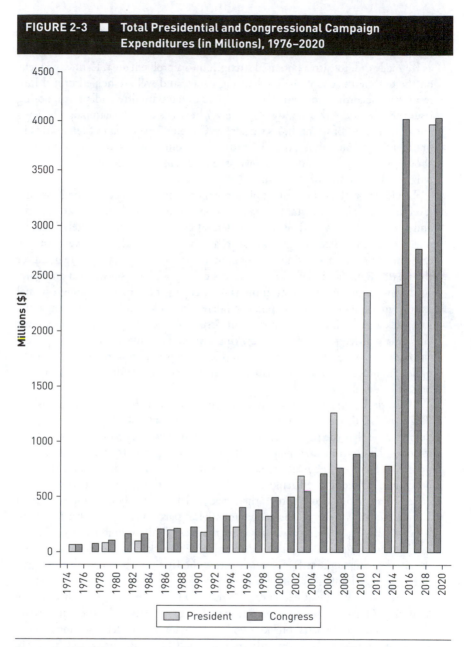

FIGURE 2-3 ■ Total Presidential and Congressional Campaign Expenditures (in Millions), 1976–2020

Sources: Presidential campaign expenditures data from OpenSecrets, at http://www.opensecrets.org/ pres16/totals.php, and for 2016 "2016 Presidential Race," OpenSecrets, at http://www.opensecrets.org/ pres16/index.php; congressional campaign expenditures data from "House Campaign Expenditures, 1974–2016," Campaign Finance Institute, available at http://www.cfinst.org/data.aspx, "Elections Overview" at https://www.opensecrets.org/elections-overview?cycle=2018, and "2020 Presidential Race" at https://www.opensecrets.org/2020-presidential-race/.

their campaigns. When candidates ignore a growing economy (recall Figure 2-1), as Vice President Richard Nixon did by focusing on foreign policy in his 1960 campaign against John F. Kennedy, opponents can use their media megaphone, as Kennedy did, to turn a potential strength into a problem area. Kennedy's focus on the decline in school quality, housing issues, and welfare helped propel him to victory, according to Lynn Vavreck.[19] Candidates are often adept at ignoring issues they would rather not discuss in favor of issues that the campaign believes are a greater area of strength. As we note in Chapter 7, candidates even do this in presidential debates, doing their best to reverse course on the topic of a question about a strategically disadvantageous issue to discuss an issue that fits the campaign's theme or area of strength.

Deciding on the issue content of campaigns is important at the congressional level as well. While constant press attention, millions of dollars in attack ads, and the like make it difficult for presidential candidates to completely ignore a major issue on the campaign trail or in a debate, candidates in lower-visibility races have a much easier time focusing on a small set of issues that are good for their campaign. Jamie Druckman and his colleagues have shown, via an analysis of campaign websites, a stunning lack of engagement between congressional campaigns on issues.[20] Simply put, candidates do not spend much time engaging in a back-and-forth debate over the same issues. Rather, they focus on an almost completely different set of issues, making it more difficult for the public to sort through which candidate is the best fit. Candidates tend to avoid engaging their opponent unless the issue is so salient to the voters that avoiding the issue would be campaign suicide.

How do candidates know upon which issues to base their campaigns? In Chapter 7, we discuss the issue ownership and trait ownership hypotheses, which demonstrate that the public believes that one party handles particular issues better or exudes particular traits more than the other party. If candidates can get people to focus on the issues their party owns, they can improve their electoral outcomes. While it is difficult to steal issues from the opposing party, it is far easier to steal traits to improve their electoral fortunes. For example, though Democrats are viewed as the more empathetic party, George W. Bush ran for office in 2000 as a "compassionate conservative." While Republicans get higher marks from the public on the trait of strength, Barack Obama was fond of saying on the campaign trail, "We never throw the first punch, but we'll throw the last."[21] In addition to searching for an issue focus, candidates work hard to get out the vote (GOTV). The Obama campaign's GOTV efforts in 2012 relied on the analysis of "big data," massive voter files that were merged with other bits of data exploring potential voters' previous voting behavior, party identification, spending habits, and, if known, favored candidate in 2012. As discussed in Chapter 3, after the campaign made predictions about which supporters were least likely to vote, volunteers were sent to knock on those people's doors, call them to remind them to vote, and send them mail that was tailored to their particular profile. The campaign even ran experiments to see whether volunteers were more successful at persuading undecided voters if the volunteer callers read a script about Obama's economic performance or asked the undecided voters which issues they wanted to discuss (the economic script performed better). It has been harder to discern the role of data analytics in the 2016 elections. Donald Trump employed a company previously used by failed GOP presidential candidate Ted Cruz to help the campaign identify potential voters via their personality characteristics and discourage potential opponents from turning out to vote. Hillary Clinton's campaign relied on an algorithm called "Ada" that ran hundreds of thousands of simulations of the battle between Clinton and Trump, helping to guide the campaign's behavior. The performance of the algorithm was spotty, as it correctly identified Pennsylvania as an important state to visit (Clinton lost the state Democrats had won from 1992 to 2012), but it did not send Clinton to Wisconsin—a state Trump captured for Republicans for the first time since 1984.

Candidates also must consider where to buy television advertisements and what to say in them. Contrary to advertisers who want to get their brand in front of as many eyes as possible, presidential campaigns are more interested in where their audience lives than in reaching the highest number of people. As you might have guessed, this means that candidates almost exclusively focus their advertising spending in a small number of states. In the last month of the 2012 presidential campaign, Barack Obama aired television ads in just over one-quarter of the country's media markets, ignoring the largest ones in New York City and Los Angeles. Mitt Romney aired ads in about one-third of the nation's markets over the course of the campaign, but his choices in the last month of the 2012 contest suggested that he spent money in places he should not have. In the summer and fall of 2012, Romney put ads up in seventy-three media markets, but was down to fifty in the final weeks of the campaign. Obama aired ads in sixty-two markets and was still airing them in fifty-seven during the last month of the campaign. In 2016, Hillary Clinton dominated the airwaves, but her advertising strategies may not have served her well in the end. In 2020, Joe Biden aired nearly double the television ads Donald Trump did during the critical period from the end of September to mid-October.[22]

Most congressional candidates who can afford television advertisements do not have to worry as much about where to air their ads. Many districts overlap into more than one media market, but typically, most of a district lies within a single market. Of course, the ranking of the market determines, in part, how expensive the advertisements will be. For example, the First Congressional District in Nebraska does not have its own NBC station. One NBC station is located in Hastings, a small city of twenty-five thousand people in the Third Congressional District. The other NBC station is in the Omaha media market, which is in the Second Congressional District. Omaha is the 76th-ranked media market in the country, while Lincoln, located in the First District, is part of the 106th market, allowing Omaha stations to charge more for their ads. Thus, ads aired in First District races during the local and national news on the NBC affiliate reach far more voters who live outside the district than voters who live within the First District boundary, while having the added problem of costing more precious campaign dollars.

The tone of the ads the candidates air is largely determined by the closeness of the race. A great deal of evidence shows that incumbents who are running against opponents who are not well funded, have not held elective office, and so forth tend to air positive advertisements. Congressional incumbents typically air negative ads only in close races or after they have been attacked. However, well-financed candidates fearing future attacks may try to gain the upper hand by going negative first. In Wisconsin's 2012 Senate race, Democrat Tammy Baldwin was on the air first with a series of ads blasting her opponent, Republican and former governor Tommy Thompson, as someone who is "not for you anymore." By the time Thompson got on the air to attack Baldwin, she had climbed ahead in the polls, eventually upsetting the popular Thompson in November. Showing how much things can change from one election to the next, Baldwin's reelection bid against state lawmaker Leah Vukmir was not competitive, leaving Baldwin to air mostly positive ads in 2018.

In presidential races, the question is not whether to go negative, but how much. Kathleen Hall Jamieson makes a distinction between advertisements that purely attack the opponent and those that contrast the opponent's record or position on an issue with the candidate's own record or views.[23] As shown in Table 2-3, contrast ads made up about a quarter of all presidential campaign ads in 2016. The biggest change in ad tone from 2012—the most negative election of the last five—was the 11-percentage-point increase in positive ads and concomitant 12-percentage-point drop in negative ads. What we cannot see in Table 2-3 are the incredible differences in advertising strategy deployed by Hillary Clinton and Donald Trump in 2016 and Joe Biden and Trump in 2020. While Mitt Romney aired more ads on cable television than Barack Obama (260,210 to 216,363) in 2012, Trump essentially did not air ads on cable television in 2016. Meanwhile, Clinton aired 332,817 cable ads. In 2020, Trump and Biden spent similar amounts on both national and local cable ads.

The other major difference in the 2016 presidential campaign ads as compared to years past went beyond issues of volume—where Clinton enjoyed a 3:1

TABLE 2-3 ■ Tone of Presidential Campaign Advertisements, 2012–2020 (April 9–Election Day)			
	Percent Negative	Percent Contrast	Percent Positive
2012	63.8	24	12.2
2016	51.5	25	23.5
2020	34	39	27

Source: Based on initial Wesleyan Media Project coding of Kantar/CMAG data. See "Political Ads in 2020: Fast and Furious," Wesleyan Media Project, March 23, 2021, https://mediaproject.wesleyan .edu/2020-summary-032321/.

Note: Totals include all sponsors, including outside groups.

advantage—to placement. The Wesleyan Media Project reported that Clinton did not air many ads in three key states that she lost—Michigan, Wisconsin, and Pennsylvania—until the last week of the election. Moreover, the content of Clinton's ads was far different from her opponent's and that of presidential candidates in previous years. Typically, about 60 percent of candidates' ads focus on some kind of policy discussion while other ads focus on personal features of the candidates or both the policy and the personal. Erika Franklin Fowler and her colleagues reported that only about 25 percent of Clinton's ads had policy content. Most of her ads focused on her campaign's belief that Trump was personally unfit for office.[24]

In 2020, analysis from the Wesleyan Media Project, the premier U.S. political advertising tracking project in political science, showed that Trump spent more resources on digital advertising on outlets like Facebook and Google than Biden did while Biden continued the Democratic Party's dominance of the television airwaves.[25] Most of Biden's ads were about taxes, COVID-19, and social security. Most of Trump's ads were about jobs, COVID-19, and China.[26]

Beyond the tone, advertising can prime voters to consider specific factors when preparing to cast their ballots. For example, an analysis by Mirya Holman, Monica Schneider, and Kristin Pondel showed that women candidates could prime women voters' gender identity whereas men running for office could not.[27]

Candidates also want to find new ways to reach voters, especially potential voters. The Obama campaign tried to reach out to young voters in a variety of ways in 2008 and 2012. For example, the campaign broke the news of Obama's choice of Joe Biden as his running mate in 2008 to supporters via text message. In 2016, Donald Trump used Twitter to communicate to voters. One analysis of the 2016 primaries revealed that when Trump's news attention started to dip, he could generate increased media coverage by going on "tweet storms" where his provocative use of social media, and the thousands of retweets he generated from his followers, inevitably resulted in more media attention—attention his opponents in the primary were not getting.

Campaigns spend an enormous amount of resources on advertising, but they also pay for pollsters, consultants, advance staff, administrative staff, yard signs, stickers, buttons, travel, and more. Red "Make America Great Again" hats were a best seller for Trump in 2016. When one of us authors asked a top Obama campaign staffer about why the campaign was trying so many different strategies to reach voters, he replied, "We know that some of these things are working, but we aren't 100% sure about which ones they are. So we'll keep doing them all."

THE UNEXPECTED

Campaigns cannot plan for everything. Much of the day-to-day life of the campaign falls outside considerations of how closely the strategic messaging hews to the latest relevant economic data. Rather, campaign staff spend a great deal of time responding to press inquiries, reacting to moves made by their opponent, and dealing with problems and opportunities they had not anticipated. While 2020 had fewer dramatic moments than 2016 did, the surprises in 2020 were longer lasting. In 2020, the COVID-19 pandemic cast a shadow over the entire general election campaign. President Trump gave wildly inconsistent messages about the seriousness of the pandemic and what the government's response would be, and he even made dozens of false statements about COVID-19, how it spreads, how it can be treated and prevented, and how dangerous it is. While at times the president took the coronavirus seriously, he spent just as much time downplaying the severity of the crisis, leading Republicans to follow their party's leader—compared to Democrats, Republicans were less likely to wear masks, less likely to socially distance, and less likely to want to get a COVID-19 vaccine.

Figure 2-4 shows the strong, positive relationship between the percentage of people in each state fully vaccinated as of June 1, 2021, and the percentage of people who voted for Biden in the 2020 election. A higher Biden vote is clearly associated with a higher vaccination rate. Biden's emphasis on vaccination during the campaign and in the early days of his presidency integrated the structural challenges of the COVID-19 pandemic and individual voters' assessments of who would handle the pandemic better.

Another unexpected sustained moment in 2020 involved the racial justice protests in support of the Black Lives Matter movement that began after a Minneapolis police officer named Derek Chauvin murdered a Black man named George Floyd. Protests broke out over the whole country, with 55 percent of American adults supporting the movement in September—after a summer of high-profile protests (discussed in greater depth in Chapter 4).[28]

Sometimes, the unexpected events fit well with the theme a campaign is trying to portray. Regarding COVID-19, Biden portrayed himself as a president who would follow the science, saying in his convention speech that, "as president, the first step I will take will be to get control of the virus that's ruined so many lives."[29] On racial justice issues, Biden promised to root out systemic racism.

As noted, though, 2016 had more than its share of unexpected moments. Trump's use of Twitter was so unconventional that the *New York Times* actively kept a list of the "people, places, and things" that Trump had insulted on Twitter.[30] The leak of the *Access Hollywood* video in which Trump told TV host Billy Bush how he could sexually assault women because he is a celebrity was one of many moments that caused pundits to declare that what had just occurred was something from which the Trump campaign could not recover. But recover the campaign did. Whether led by spirited defenses from his chief spokesperson Kellyanne Conway or Trump himself, the campaign was always able to explain away the latest controversy, blame the media for it, blame his opponents for it, blame the electoral system for it, or change the subject. Hillary Clinton's campaign was not immune from unexpected moments that were damaging as well. Clinton's husband, former president Bill Clinton, generated controversy on multiple occasions, most notably when he met privately with Attorney General Loretta Lynch—which was seen as an attempt by the former commander in chief

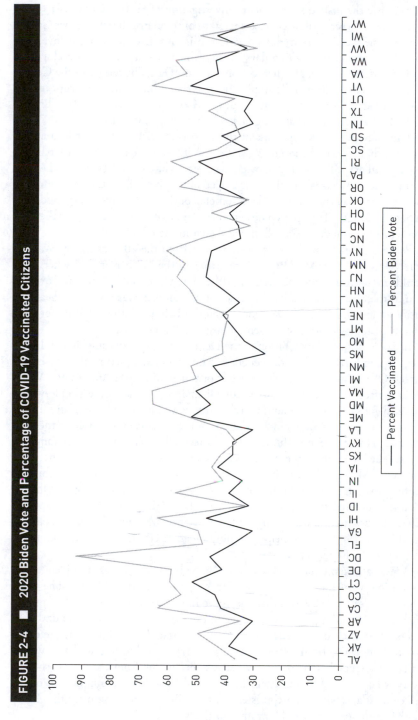

FIGURE 2-4 ■ 2020 Biden Vote and Percentage of COVID-19 Vaccinated Citizens

—— Percent Vaccinated   —— Percent Biden Vote

Sources: David Wasserman, Sophie Andrews, Leo Saenger, Lev Cohen, Ally Flinn, and Griff Tatarsky, "2020 National Popular Vote Tracker," Cook Political Report, accessed June 28, 2021, https://cookpolitical.com/2020-national-popular-vote-tracker.

to influence the Justice Department's investigation of Hillary Clinton's use of a private email server while serving as secretary of state. FBI director James Comey said that the meeting spurred his decision to inform the public of his investigation of Clinton in the waning days of the campaign—a dramatic development Clinton partially blamed for her loss on Election Day. The release of the Comey letter in the fall of 2016 fit Trump's narrative that Clinton was a corrupt insider who was part of a rigged system. Trump's *Access Hollywood* video fit Clinton's narrative that Trump was a misogynist who was unfit for office.

The unexpected developments of the 2016 race even led to a renaissance for the comedy program *Saturday Night Live*. With cast member Kate McKinnon playing Hillary Clinton and movie star Alec Baldwin impersonating Donald Trump, the presidential election was played out each week on the news, and the satirical version of the stunning developments of the week found a large audience on Saturday night. Trump even hosted *Saturday Night Live* a year before the election while Clinton guest starred in one sketch in the fall of 2015.

Perhaps the most well-known media event from the 2012 campaign was the secret video taken of Mitt Romney referring to the "47 percent" of voters who would not be voting for the GOP in 2012. The video and subsequent coverage fit into the Obama campaign's argument that Romney was a wealthy, heartless businessman who would leave middle America behind. Although Romney later offered an apology for the comment, it largely fell on deaf ears.

In 2008, both Hillary Clinton in the Democratic primary campaign and John McCain and Sarah Palin in the general election painted a picture of then senator Barack Obama as an elitist who was out of touch with "real Americans." When audio surfaced late in the primaries of Obama saying that some people would "cling to guns or religion or antipathy to people who aren't like them" in difficult times, his opponents were quick to jump on the gaffe as an example of the "real Obama." However, the kerfuffle did not affect Obama's campaign for long. Of course, the cratering of the nation's economy was the major event of the 2008 campaign. McCain filled in his own narrative that he was a "maverick" by suspending his campaign and calling for a postponement of a debate with Obama. Obama countered that there are no time-outs for the president and that chief executives have to deal with many problems at once. McCain relented and participated in the debate, which helped amplify Obama's efforts to steal the "strength" trait owned by Republicans.

A few days before the 2004 election, Osama bin Laden released a video taking responsibility for the September 11 attacks against the United States. The video might have reminded voters that they gave high marks to President George W. Bush on his handling of the war on terror even though an increasing number of voters were critical of his leadership of the war in Iraq. Meanwhile, trying to drum up votes in Ohio, Bush's opponent John Kerry went hunting and was widely ridiculed for pandering to rural voters as the photos from that event showed Kerry, who had an F rating from the National Rifle Association, decked out in full camouflage, which was consistent with the Bush team's argument that Kerry was a flip-flopper who would say anything to get elected.

UNDERSTANDING FUNDAMENTALS AND WINNING ELECTIONS

After billions of dollars of spending and nearly two years of campaigning, Joe Biden won back typically Democratic Party strongholds Pennsylvania, Michigan, and Wisconsin from Donald Trump. He also won the swing states of Georgia, Arizona, and Nevada. Republicans lost the Senate, after both Senate elections in Georgia went to Democratic Party candidates, giving Vice President Kamala Harris the tiebreaking vote in a 50-50 Senate. Republicans gained seats in the House of Representatives, but not enough to get the 218 they needed to take back a majority. Overall, the fundamentals predicted a close presidential election in which the Democrat would narrowly win the popular vote. That is just what happened. The fundamentals also predicted that the vast majority of congressional incumbents would win, which they did. This is not to say that the campaigns did not matter. Each of the campaigns turned out an enormous number of voters, had evidence that they had persuaded fence-sitters to their side, and thought that they were going to win on Election Day. In the end, whether by design or by luck, the Biden team was successful. In the remainder of the book, we take detailed looks at the context of these conclusions. We also engage in examinations, over time, of American political behavior and public attitudes. While the rest of the book shows analyses of American partisanship, public opinion, group identities and social characteristics, media use, and determinants of vote choice, keep in mind that each of those factors occurs in the context of the framework described in this chapter.

Study Questions

1. What are the major structural, or fundamental, factors that influence presidential election results?

2. In what ways was the 2020 election a typical election? In what ways did it differ from the norm?

3. How do the ways in which candidates react to the unexpected affect how U.S. presidential elections turn out?

Suggested Readings

Cohen, Marty, David Karol, Hans Noel, and John Zaller. *The Party Decides.* Chicago: University of Chicago Press, 2008. A new classic in election research.

Issenberg, Sasha. *The Victory Lab: The Secret Science of Winning Campaigns.* New York: Crown, 2012. An accessible account of the "analytical revolution" in campaign management.

Shaw, Daron R. *The Race to 270: The Electoral College and the Campaign Strategies of 2000 and 2004*. Chicago: University of Chicago Press, 2006. A careful treatment of how and why Republicans and Democrats targeted specific media markets in presidential campaigns.

Sides, John, Michael Tesler, and Lynn Vavreck. *Identity Crisis: The 2016 Presidential Campaign and the Battle for the Meaning of America*. Princeton, NJ: Princeton University Press, 2019. A book that shows how the stories claiming the 2016 election violated fundamentals of American politics were wrong.

Theiss-Morse, Elizabeth, and Michael W. Wagner. *2018 Congressional Elections*. Washington, DC: CQ Press, 2018. A short, and readable, take on the 2018 midterms.

Notes

1. Peter K. Enns and Julius Lagodny, "We Predicted the States Biden Would Win 100 Days Before the Election," *Monkey Cage* (newsletter), *Washington Post*, November 12, 2020, https://www.washingtonpost.com/politics/2020/11/12/we-predicted-states-biden-would-win-100-days-before-election/.

2. "Gross Domestic Product, First Quarter 2021 (Advance Estimate)," Bureau of Economic Analysis, April 29, 2021, press release, https://www.bea.gov/sites/default/files/2021-04/gdp1q21_adv.pdf.

3. Barack Obama, interview with Matt Lauer, *Today*, NBC, February 2, 2009.

4. John Sides, "The Democratic Party's Uphill Battle to 270 Electoral Votes," *Monkey Cage* (newsletter), *Washington Post*, January 18, 2014, https://www.washingtonpost.com/news/monkey-cage/wp/2014/01/18/the-democratic-partys-uphill-battle-to-270-electoral-votes-in-2016/?tid=a_inl&utm_term=.fa6fe3c8bc7a.

5. Larry Bartels, "2016 Was an Ordinary Election, Not a Realignment," *Monkey Cage* (newsletter), *Washington Post*, November 10, 2016, https://www.washingtonpost.com/news/monkey-cage/wp/2016/11/10/2016-was-an-ordinary-election-not-a-realignment/?utm_term=.51e27306ed05.

6. Nate Silver, "On the Maddeningly Inexact Relationship Between Unemployment and Re-election," *FiveThirtyEight* (blog), *New York Times*, June 2, 2011, http://fivethirtyeight.blogs.nytimes.com/2011/06/02/on-the-maddeningly-inexact-relationship-between-unemployment-and-re-election/?_r=0.

7. Elliott Ramos, "Where Did Trump Make Election Gains? Unemployment Data Tell a Surprising Story," NBC News, November 16, 2020, https://www

.nbcnews.com/news/us-news/where-did-trump-make-election-gains-unemployment-data-tells-surprising-n1247935.

8. Something the Vikings have never done.

9. John Sides, "The Political Consequences of Gas Prices," *Monkey Cage* (blog), March 12, 2012, http://themonkeycage.org/2012/03/12/the-political-consequences-of-gas-prices/.

10. Olivia Quinn, Amanda Brush, and Eric R. A. N. Smith, "A Simple Forecast Suggests a Democratic Sweep in 2020," *Monkey Cage* (newsletter), *Washington Post*, July 7, 2020, https://www.washingtonpost.com/politics/2020/07/07/simple-forecast-suggests-democratic-sweep-2020/.

11. "Presidential Job Approval Center," Gallup, accessed June 28, 2021, https://news.gallup.com/interactives/185273/presidential-job-approval-center.aspx.

12. Drew Linzer, "The Forecasts Were Wrong. Trump Won. What Happened?," Votamatic, November 16, 2016, https://votamatic.org/2016/11/.

13. Elizabeth Theiss-Morse, Michael W. Wagner, William H. Flanigan, and Nancy H. Zingale, *Political Behavior in Midterm Elections*, 2015 ed. (Washington, DC: CQ Press, 2015).

14. Quinn et al., "Simple Forecast Suggests a Democratic Sweep in 2020."

15. Marty Cohen, David Karol, Hans Noel, and John Zaller, *The Party Decides* (Chicago: University of Chicago Press, 2008).

16. Julia Azari, "What If the Party Decided Not to Decide?," Vox, January 26, 2016, https://www.vox.com/mischiefs-of-faction/2016/1/26/10834512/party-decides-establishment.

17. Seth Masket, "The 2020 Invisible Primary in Light of 2016," Vox, January 7, 2019, https://www.vox.com/mischiefs-of-faction/2019/1/7/18170894/2020-invisible-primary-2016-democrats.

18. "Super PACs," OpenSecrets, accessed June 28, 2021, http://www.opensecrets.org/pacs/superpacs.php.

19. Lynn Vavreck, *The Message Matters: The Economy and Presidential Campaigns* (Princeton, NJ: Princeton University Press, 2009).

20. James N. Druckman, Cari Lynn Hennessy, Martin J. Kifer, and Michael Parkin, "Issue Engagement on Congressional Candidate Web Sites," *Social Science Computer Review* 28, no. 1 (2010): 3–23.

21. ABC News, "Obama: 'We Don't Throw the First Punch, but We'll Throw the Last,'" *HuffPost*, accessed June 29, 2021, https://www.huffpost.com/entry/post_169_n_132323.

22. "Biden Continues to Dominate Advertising" (Table 1: Top Spenders in Presidential Race), Wesleyan Media Project, October 15, 2020, https://mediaproject.wesleyan.edu/releases-101520/#table1.

23. Kathleen Hall Jamieson, conversation with Bill Moyers, *Bill Moyers Journal*, PBS, February 29, 2008, http://www.pbs.org/moyers/journal/02292008/profile.html.

24. Erika Franklin Fowler, Travis N. Ridout, and Michael M. Franz, "Political Advertising in 2016: The Presidential Election as Outlier?," De Gruyter, February 22, 2017, https://www.degruyter.com/document/doi/10.1515/for-2016-0040/html, as cited in "2016 Election Study Published," Wesleyan Media Project, March 6, 2017, http://mediaproject.wesleyan.edu/blog/2016-election-study-published/.

25. "Biden Continues to Dominate Advertising" (Table 2: Digital Ad Spending by Presidential Candidates and Single-Candidate Super PACs), Wesleyan Media Project, October 15, 2020, https://mediaproject.wesleyan.edu/releases-101520/#table2.

26. "Biden Continues to Dominate Advertising" (Figure 1: Advertising Advantage in the Presidential Race on Television), Wesleyan Media Project, October 15, 2020, https://mediaproject.wesleyan.edu/releases-101520/#fig1.

27. Mirya R. Holman, Monica C. Schneider, and Kristin Pondel, "Gender Targeting in Political Advertisements," *Political Research Quarterly* 68, no. 4 (2015): 816–829.

28. Deja Thomas and Juliana Menasce Horowitz, "Support for Black Lives Matter Has Decreased Since June but Remains Strong Among Black Americans," Pew Research Center, September 16, 2020, https://www.pewresearch.org/fact-tank/2020/09/16/support-for-black-lives-matter-has-decreased-since-june-but-remains-strong-among-black-americans/.

29. Jacob Pramuk, "Read Joe Biden's Full 2020 Democratic National Convention Speech," CNBC, August 21, 2020, https://www.cnbc.com/2020/08/21/joe-biden-dnc-speech-transcript.html.

30. Jasmine C. Lee and Kevin Quealy, "The 359 People, Places and Things Donald Trump Has Insulted on Twitter," *Upshot* (newsletter), *New York Times*, January 28, 2016, updated August 15, 2017, https://www.nytimes.com/interactive/2016/01/28/upshot/donald-trump-twitter-insults.html?_r=0.

TURNOUT AND PARTICIPATION IN ELECTIONS

I N EVERY election cycle, stories in the media question who and how many will vote. Are Trump voters more fired up than Biden voters, or is it the other way around? Will Hispanic voter turnout be higher than normal in reaction to Trump's immigration policies? Will Black people vote at a higher rate because of Trump's crackdown on Black Lives Matter protests? What about youth? What about the Republican or Democratic base? Voter turnout is a major strategic concern for candidates running for office. This concern was especially pronounced in 2020 given mask mandates and stay-at-home orders due to COVID-19. Elections can normally be won or lost by getting one's supporters to the polls and keeping the opponent's supporters at home. In 2020, the Biden campaign encouraged Americans to take advantage of the opportunity to use mail-in or early voting, whereas the Trump campaign raised questions about the security of votes that were not cast in person.

The activity surrounding get-out-the-vote (GOTV) efforts in any given election occurs against the backdrop of historically anemic turnout rates in the United States over the past fifty years. Turnout rates declined dramatically after 1960, leading many commentators to worry about the future of American democracy and many scholars to examine what was going on. Two major explanations were the focus of this research: institutional impediments to voting and individual-level attitudes that might increase or decrease turnout. We look at historical trends in voter turnout and at the institutional and attitudinal factors that affect whether people vote. We also address mobilization efforts by political parties and candidates and their impact on turnout.

While turnout is obviously important in a democracy, the American electorate can participate in many other ways that have an impact on elections.

Americans can donate money to a campaign, put a sign in their yard or a bumper sticker on their car, make telephone calls on behalf of a candidate, go door-to-door canvassing for a candidate, write letters to the editor supporting a candidate, and so on. Donald Trump's strategy of holding rallies across the country, even during the pandemic, and Joe Biden's socially distanced approach point to the importance of campaign activists and enthusiasts. We therefore examine in this chapter not only who votes but who gets involved more actively in campaigns as well.

Learning objectives for Chapter 3 include:

- Understanding turnout trends and who the voters and nonvoters are

- Exploring the institutional impediments that those in power have used to keep especially Black people from voting

- Examining the psychological motivations that set voters apart from nonvoters

- Learning what campaigns do to increase turnout and who the activists are who get more involved in elections

TURNOUT IN AMERICAN ELECTIONS

One of the most persistent complaints about the recent American electoral system is its failure to achieve the high rates of voter turnout found in other countries and common in the United States in the nineteenth century. U.S. voter turnout was close to 80 percent before 1900; modern democracies around the world frequently record similarly high levels. Turnout in the United States over the past one hundred years, in contrast, has exceeded 60 percent only in presidential elections, and throughout most of the twentieth century it rarely did even that.

These unfavorable comparisons are somewhat misleading. The *voting turnout rate* is the percentage of the eligible population that votes in a particular election (the number of voters divided by the number of eligible voters). This seems straightforward, but it isn't. As Michael McDonald and Samuel Popkin point out, most reports on voter turnout use the voting age population (VAP) as the denominator rather than the voting eligible population (VEP).[1] Not all people who are of voting age are eligible to vote because of state laws restricting voting to, for example, U.S. citizens and people who fulfill residency requirements. The voting turnout rate is ideally calculated taking into account all state-level restrictions. When the denominator includes the VAP rather than the VEP, the turnout rate appears lower than it actually is because the denominator is inflated. On the flip side, in some states, Blacks, women, and eighteen-year-olds were given the right to vote before suffrage was extended to them nationwide by the Fifteenth, Nineteenth, and Twenty-Sixth Amendments to the U.S. Constitution. Since the Constitution originally left it up to the states to determine voter eligibility, states varied in whom they let vote. Not including these groups in the denominator when they were actually eligible to vote within their states makes the turnout rate in earlier years appear higher than it actually was because of a deflated denominator.

Determining the numerator in the turnout rate is also surprisingly difficult. The total number of ballots cast throughout the country is unknown; some states report the total vote only for particular races. For example, not included are those who went to the polls but skipped the presidential race or who inadvertently invalidated their ballots. This "undercount" of votes cast also reduces the estimate of turnout. Most often, the number of votes cast for the highest office on the ballot is used as the numerator, but this method could miss some votes.

McDonald, who runs the United States Elections Project, has attempted to calculate turnout more accurately by correcting both the numerator and the denominator of the official figures on a state-by-state basis starting in 1980. The turnout rate is slightly higher when total ballots cast, rather than total votes for the highest office, is used, but the difference is usually less than 1 percentage point. The most pronounced difference comes from using the VEP instead of the VAP, especially when looking at recent elections. The VEP-based turnout rate in the 1980s was about 2 percentage points higher than the VAP-based turnout rate. This difference increased to just under 5 percentage points beginning in 2004, largely due to both an increase in the number of noncitizens in the United States and an increase in the number of ineligible felons. In 1980, 3.5 percent of the U.S. population was made up of noncitizens, and just over 800,000 were ineligible felons. By 2020, 7.8 percent of the population was composed of noncitizens, and 3.29 million were ineligible felons.[2] Rather than the official VAP highest office turnout rate of 62 percent in 2020, the VEP highest office turnout rate was 66.7 percent. Thus, turnout tends to be low in the United States compared to other established democracies, but it is not as low as official statistics suggest.

Despite the difficulties in estimating turnout, the data in Figure 3-1 show that dramatic shifts in the rate of voter turnout have occurred over time. During the nineteenth century, national turnout appears to have been extremely high— always more than 70 percent. The biggest drop in turnout occurred after 1896, especially in the South. The steep drop in the South from 1900 to 1916 is in part attributable to the restrictions placed on African American voting and to the increasing one-party domination of the region. In many Southern states, whoever won the Democratic primary won the general election, making turnout in the primary much more important than turnout in the general election.

Political maneuverings in the South, however, cannot explain the decline in turnout in the rest of the country that occurred at about the same time. While the Republican Party became dominant in the non-South, leading to less competition and therefore less interest in general elections, the Progressive Era reforms of the late 1800s and early 1900s likely affected turnout rates across the United States.[3] Party organizations in the latter part of the 1800s, referred to as party machines, "delivered" or "voted" substantial numbers of votes via party loyalists casting multiple votes, "voting tombstones" (dead people), or vote buying. The decline in voter turnout in the early twentieth century coincides with the introduction of electoral reforms, including the introduction of the secret, or Australian, ballot and the imposition of a system of voter registration.[4] Prior to the electoral reforms, voters were given distinctively colored ballots from their political party and openly placed them in the ballot box. The Australian ballot provided for secret voting and an official ballot with all candidates' names appearing on it, thereby decreasing party control of voting. Without the color-coded ballots, the parties couldn't know for whom people voted, which meant they couldn't reward or punish people according to their vote. Voter registration requirements were another useful tool for combating corruption, by limiting the opportunity for fraudulent voting, but they also created an additional barrier to voting that had the effect of decreasing the turnout of less motivated potential voters. Turnout in national elections reached a low in the early 1920s and then fluctuated up and down before experiencing the recent uptick in the early years of the twenty-first century. The year 2020 saw an especially high turnout, reaching almost 67 percent. Turnout hadn't been this high since 1904.

Great differences in turnout among the states are concealed within these national data. Rates of voting in the South, as shown in Figure 3-1, were consistently low until recently, when they nearly converged with northern turnout, but state variation is still considerable. For example, states with the lowest turnout in 2020 were Oklahoma at 55 percent and Arkansas at 56 percent. States with the highest turnout were Colorado at 76 percent and Minnesota at 80 percent.[5] Variation in turnout is considerable not only from state to state but also from one type of election to another. Elections vary in the amount of interest and attention they generate in the electorate. As Figure 3-2 demonstrates, high-salience presidential elections draw higher turnout, whereas low-salience elections, such as off-year congressional elections, are characterized by turnout levels that are 10 to 20 percent lower. Even in a presidential election year, fewer people vote for a candidate in U.S. House races than for president, although in 2020 the percentages of votes for each of these two races based on VEP were close. Primaries and local elections elicit still lower turnout. Most of these differences in turnout can be accounted for by the lower visibility of nonpresidential elections; when less information about an election is available to voters, their interest is diminished.

Voters and Nonvoters

While turnout rates vary across time and across states, political scientists are pretty clear on the demographic characteristics of those who vote and of those who choose not to vote. Campaign staffs care a great deal about who the voters and nonvoters are as well because what matters is whether their party's base is getting to the polls and the other party's base is staying home. We look at the voter turnout rates of various demographic groups in 2020 and compare these results to previous elections.

Socioeconomic status is a key predictor of turnout. People who are better educated, wealthier, and in more professional occupations consistently turn out

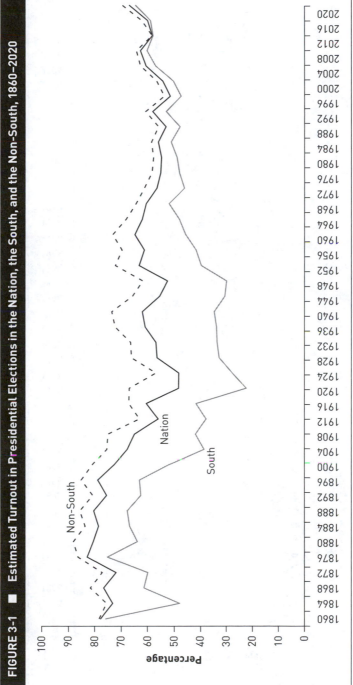

FIGURE 3-1 ■ Estimated Turnout in Presidential Elections in the Nation, the South, and the Non-South, 1860–2020

Sources: Curtis Gans, *Voter Turnout in the United States, 1788–2009* (Washington, DC: CQ Press, 2010) for the data from 1860 to 2010; Michael McDonald, "Voter Turnout," United States Elections Project, accessed June 30, 2021, http://www.electproject.org/home/voter-turnout/voter-turnout-data.

Note: The states included in the South were Alabama, Arkansas, Delaware, Florida, Georgia, Kentucky, Louisiana, Maryland, Mississippi, North Carolina, Oklahoma, South Carolina, Tennessee, Texas, Virginia, and West Virginia. All other states were counted as non-South. The data on Southern states from 1864 were limited to only four states.

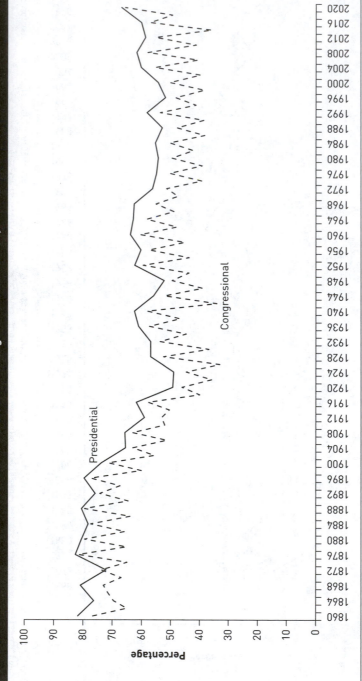

FIGURE 3-2 ■ Estimated Turnout in Presidential and Congressional Elections, 1860–2020

Presidential

Congressional

Percentage

1860 1864 1868 1872 1876 1880 1884 1888 1892 1896 1900 1904 1908 1912 1916 1920 1924 1928 1932 1936 1940 1944 1948 1952 1956 1960 1964 1968 1972 1976 1980 1984 1988 1992 1996 2000 2004 2008 2012 2016 2020

Sources: Curtis Gans, *Voter Turnout in the United States, 1788–2009* (Washington, DC: CQ Press, 2010) for the data from 1860 to 2010; Michael McDonald, "Voter Turnout," United States Elections Project, accessed June 30, 2021, http://www.electproject.org/home/voter-turnout/voter-turnout-data.

to vote at a higher rate than those from a lower socioeconomic status. When respondents were asked in the American National Election Studies (ANES) surveys from 1972 to 2016 if they voted in the presidential election, slightly over 91 percent of those with a college education or postgraduate degree said they voted compared to only about 69 percent of those with a high school education or less. In 2020, both groups had slightly higher reported turnout rates: 94 percent of those with a college degree and 76 percent of those without a college degree cast a ballot. Even in this year of heightened participation among the less educated, the college educated voted at a higher rate. Granted, self-reported turnout is always higher than actual turnout numbers, in part due to the social desirability problem of people not wanting to admit they did not vote when they know they should have.[6] Research suggests that the better educated seem to be more affected by the social desirability bias than the less educated when it comes to voting and therefore are more likely to claim to have voted when they did not. For example, the well educated are much more likely to view voting as very much a duty (62 percent) compared to the less well educated (45 percent), who are more likely to believe voting is a choice. It is harder to admit to not doing one's duty than it is to admit that one simply chose not to vote. Even taking into account exaggerated turnout numbers, education is highly related to voting for a variety of reasons, including having a better understanding of the voter registration process, having greater interest in and knowledge about politics, and being part of a more politically active social network.[7] Not surprisingly, family income plays out in much the same way. In the past forty years, ANES data show that 86 percent of those in the top third of family income say they voted in the previous presidential election compared to just over 61 percent of those in the bottom third. The most recent presidential election had increases in both, the bottom third reaching 69 percent and the top third reaching 93 percent, but the pattern remains. Clearly, socioeconomic status matters in American elections.

The elections of 2020 fit the pattern of demographic shifts that have been taking place over the past seventy years. It used to be the case that men turned out to vote at a higher rate than women, sometimes by as much as 12 percentage points (as happened in 1956). As Figure 3-3 shows, this tendency reversed itself in 2004 when women began to vote at a higher rate than men, especially in 2008 when there was a 6-percentage-point difference in reported turnout between women and men. There has been little change in the difference in voting rates between men and women since 2012, about 3 percentage points, including in 2020.

Race has long been a key factor when discussing turnout. Whites discriminated against Blacks primarily but not exclusively in the South when it came to registering and voting. National turnout figures for Blacks consistently showed them voting at a much lower rate than whites because of these discriminatory practices that decreased their voting eligibility. When registration and voting laws that discriminated against Blacks were removed, the turnout rate among Black voters increased. Figure 3-4 shows that while Blacks closed the distance with whites after the Voting Rights Act passed in 1965, they did not surpass whites in

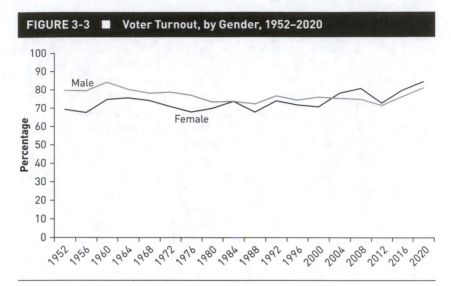

FIGURE 3-3 ■ Voter Turnout, by Gender, 1952–2020

Source: American National Election Studies, available at www.electionstudies.org.

turnout until 2008, when Barack Obama first ran as the Democratic nominee for president. Black Americans voted at a higher rate than whites in both 2012 and 2016, but their turnout rate dropped to below that of white people in 2020.

The ethnic group that has voted at a level lower than whites and Blacks is Latinos and Latinas. They voted at a higher rate than Blacks in 1988 and at parity in 1996, but since then they have had a significantly lower turnout rate than both Blacks and whites. Part of the reason behind these lower turnout rates is voter eligibility. In the past, some states gave noncitizens the right to vote, but today only citizens are allowed to vote in federal and state elections. Immigrants who are not U.S. citizens might be asked in a survey if they voted, but they are not eligible to vote. Even taking eligibility into account, however, Latin@s vote at a lower rate than whites and Blacks, as can be seen in Figure 3-4. One potential explanation is the possible language barrier some Latin@s might experience. A more likely explanation is that campaigns have been slow or inconsistent in targeting Latino and Latina voters. As this population has grown in the United States and as their vote has become more critical to election outcomes, future campaigns will be smart to target Latin@s in a meaningful way.

One demographic group that consistently gets a lot of attention for not voting is young people. People in the eighteen to thirty-four age cohort consistently vote at a lower rate than older people, sometimes by 20 percentage points (see Figure 3-5). Even in a good year, such as 2004, youth turned out to vote significantly less than older people. The increase in reported turnout in 2004 and 2008 was most impressive among the youngest group of eighteen- to twenty-five-year-olds, whose turnout increased from 48 percent in 2000 to 64 percent in 2008

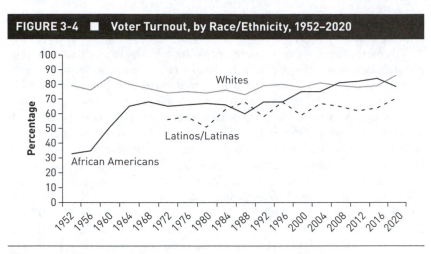

FIGURE 3-4   ■   Voter Turnout, by Race/Ethnicity, 1952–2020

Source: American National Election Studies, available at www.electionstudies.org.

(data not shown). Many analysts wondered what would happen to youth turnout in 2016. Bernie Sanders garnered enthusiastic support from young people during the primaries, and his failure to get the Democratic Party's nomination was frustrating to many of his supporters. Some Sanders supporters insisted they could not vote for Hillary Clinton, which raised the specter of a decline in voter turnout especially among young people. Figure 3-5 shows this was not the case. The turnout of young people increased slightly between 2012 and 2016, suggesting there was not a pronounced Sanders effect on young adult turnout. Those under thirty-five had their highest turnout since 1960 in the 2020 election, when 73 percent reported voting, an 11-percentage-point increase over 2016.

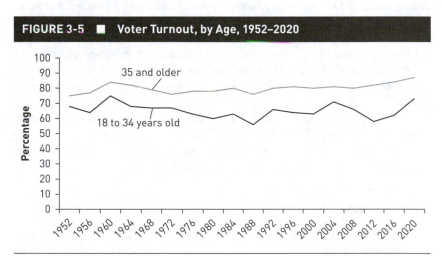

FIGURE 3-5   ■   Voter Turnout, by Age, 1952–2020

Source: American National Election Studies, available at www.electionstudies.org.

Older people also increased their turnout in 2020 but not anywhere near as much as younger people.

There are many reasons why young people are less likely to vote than older people, including motivational and institutional factors. Young people often incorrectly think that politics doesn't have much to do with their lives when in reality it does. Aside from the direct connection with certain issues, such as student loan rates, many laws debated by Congress have a big impact on young people, such as health care reform, the spending of money on defense versus social programs, and so on. A contextual factor that likely affects youth turnout is the attention, or lack of attention, they receive from the candidates running for office. Candidates know that young people vote at a much lower rate than older people and therefore often tailor their messages to older people to capture their votes. When candidates take the time to talk specifically to younger people, as Obama did in 2008 and 2012, they are able to both increase youth turnout and gain a big share of their vote. Finally, much of the nonvoting among young people may be attributed to the unsettled circumstances of this age group rather than to simple disinterest in politics. Military service, being away at college, geographic mobility with the possible failure to meet residence requirements, and the additional hurdle of initial registration, along with receiving less attention from candidates, all create barriers to voting for young citizens that are less likely to affect older ones.

RACE AND INSTITUTIONAL IMPEDIMENTS TO TURNOUT

Political behavior, including whether people vote or not, takes place within a certain context. That context includes the institutional arrangements that make up the electoral system in the United States. Would turnout be higher if elections were held on a weekend instead of a Tuesday? Would it be higher if the government automatically registered its citizens instead of having citizens take the initiative to get registered? Would it be higher if the United States had more competitive electoral districts? People have jobs, take care of families, and attend school, all of which make it difficult at times to fit politics into their already busy lives. The institutional arrangements surrounding elections can make it easier or more difficult for people to get to the polls. In essence, the easier it is to vote, the more people will turn out to vote. Unfortunately, institutional impediments have frequently been used by whites to keep Blacks from voting.

Restrictions of Suffrage

Decisions about the institutional arrangements used in elections are inherently political and often partisan because they affect who can vote and how easily they can vote. After the Civil War, Republicans were eager to enfranchise Blacks, figuring that this new group of voters would vote Republican. In the early 1970s, Democrats were eager to enfranchise eighteen- to twenty-year-olds, figuring that they would vote Democratic. Reformers of all sorts encouraged the enfranchisement of women as a means of promoting their own goals. Many optimistically saw women voters as the cure for corruption in government, as unwavering opponents of alcohol consumption, and as champions of virtue in the electorate. Expansions of suffrage are quite rare, however, compared to attempts to restrict suffrage. The most notorious of these efforts was the effective disenfranchisement of Blacks in the South during the late nineteenth through the mid-twentieth centuries.

Several techniques for disenfranchising Blacks were used after Reconstruction in the South, and from time to time some of these techniques were applied in the North on a more limited basis to restrict the electoral participation of immigrants. The most common methods included white primaries, the poll tax, literacy tests, discriminatory administrative procedures, and intimidation. In some Southern states, only whites were allowed to vote in the party primary (the crucial election in one-party states), under the rationale that primaries to nominate candidates were internal functions of a private organization. In 1944, the U.S. Supreme Court ruled such white primaries unconstitutional on the ground that the selection of candidates for election is a public function in which discrimination on the basis of race is prohibited. The now-unconstitutional poll tax, whereby each individual was charged a flat fee as a prerequisite for registration to vote, was used for years and no doubt disenfranchised both poor Blacks and poor whites. The literacy test gave local officials a device that could be administered in a selective way to permit registration of whites while prohibiting that of Blacks. Registrars could ask Blacks to read and interpret the state constitution, for example, and insist they had not done a satisfactory job, whereas they might ask whites only to sign their names. To remain effective over long periods of time, these and other similar administrative devices probably depended on intimidation or the use of violence against Blacks.[8] The outlawing of the poll tax through constitutional amendment and the suspension of literacy tests by the Voting Rights Act of 1965 and its extensions eliminated two important restrictions on the right to vote.

Felon disenfranchisement remains a major state restriction on suffrage, although there is great variation from state to state. In all but two states (Maine and Vermont) and the District of Columbia, prison inmates cannot vote. In many states, convicted felons cannot vote until they have served their entire sentence—in other words, served their time in prison and completed probation or parole. In some states, a felony conviction entails a permanent forfeiture of voting rights. With the prison population growing, this amounts to a sizable restriction of the franchise. A study by the Sentencing Project estimates that in 2016, over 6 million citizens were ineligible felons, compared to 3.34 million in 1996 and 1.17 million in 1976. This means that in 2016 approximately 2.5 percent of the VAP was disenfranchised because of a felony conviction. Over 10 percent of the VAP was disenfranchised in Florida, which had particularly strict laws until Florida voters passed an amendment in 2018 allowing most people who have served their sentences to vote. A legal battle ensued over whether all legal financial obligations have to be paid before people regain their right to vote.[9]

The number of felons who were disenfranchised dropped between 2016 and 2020 to 5.17 million, or 2.27 percent of the U.S. VEP. Blacks remain the group hardest hit by felon disenfranchisement laws because of their higher rates of incarceration and because they tend to live in states that disenfranchise felons for life, even after they have served all of their sentence. The Sentencing Project study estimates that 6.2 percent of Black adults are disenfranchised because of felony convictions (down from 7.4 percent in 2016), although certain states have much higher percentages. Over 20 percent of Blacks in Tennessee and Wyoming are disenfranchised. The disenfranchisement rate of non-Blacks is 1.7 percent, although this figure includes Latin@s who have a higher disenfranchisement rate than whites (over 2 percent). Women make up approximately one-fifth of the total disenfranchised population.[10]

Felon disenfranchisement clearly decreases the VEP, but does it decrease voter turnout? This question is more difficult to answer. On the one hand, if the people who are disenfranchised because of a felony conviction would not have voted anyway, then voter turnout is not affected by these state laws. Felons often come from certain demographic groups—primarily young people, the less educated, and the poor—that are less likely to vote. Based on these arguments, various researchers have found that felon disenfranchisement laws do not have a significant impact on turnout rates after taking into account several demographic factors.[11] Other scholars, however, have estimated a much larger impact. By matching felons and nonfelons on such characteristics as gender, race, age, and education, Christopher Uggen and Jeff Manza estimate that just over a third (35 percent) of disenfranchised felons would have voted in presidential elections in recent years. They also estimate that a large proportion of these disenfranchised felons would vote for Democratic candidates.[12] In states with higher percentages of disenfranchised felons and in close elections, these disenfranchised nonvoters could affect election outcomes. Putting felon disenfranchisement aside, some research shows that even being arrested (and not convicted) increases distrust in government and decreases attachment to the political system, leading to significantly lower turnout rates among those who have experienced the criminal justice system.[13] Even if states do not have severe felon disenfranchisement laws, they likely have citizens who do not vote in part because of their experiences with the criminal justice system. Evidence suggests, however, that simple outreach campaigns providing information to felons who have served their sentences can increase the participation rate of this population.[14]

Reforms and Institutional Impediments to Voting

Historically, the United States has stood out as being less voter friendly than many Western democracies. In many of these countries, governments maintain registration lists instead of placing the burden of registration on the individual.

In the United States, citizens in all states but one—North Dakota—must register to be able to vote. States vary dramatically in how many days prior to the election people must register, ranging from Election Day registration in such states as Minnesota and Colorado, where people can register immediately prior to casting their vote, to registering thirty days in advance of the election in such states as Texas and Ohio. West Virginia has a twenty-one-day deadline, Virginia a nineteen-day deadline, California a fifteen-day deadline, and Massachusetts a ten-day deadline. Not only must people register when they first vote; they must reregister each time they move. According to the U.S. Census Bureau, 9 to 11 percent of Americans move in any given year.[15] College students are especially mobile. Regulations also typically cancel the registration of people who fail to vote in a few consecutive elections. With the various registration deadlines along with different rules concerning residency requirements set by each state, simply getting registered can appear daunting, and registration requirements raise the costs of political involvement, costs that a significant number of citizens choose not to assume.

Registering is much easier today than it was in the past, when people had to travel to the county seat to register, but this added step increases the costs of voting. Classic studies estimated that turnout in the United States would increase by 9 to 14 percent if people could register to vote on Election Day.[16] Because of concern over low voter turnout and the role registration requirements likely play in that low turnout, reformers have worked hard to make registering easier. In 1993, Congress passed the "motor voter" bill, which provides that registration forms will be available at various governmental agencies that citizens visit for other purposes. These include agencies where motor vehicles are registered and driver's licenses are obtained; however, because of a Republican-sponsored amendment, states are not required to provide them at unemployment and welfare offices. Because the unregistered tend to be poorer and less well educated, Democrats, who traditionally represent such groups, hoped (and Republicans feared) that reducing registration obstacles would increase the number of Democratic voters.

Many of the same political considerations were at play in the passage of the Help America Vote Act (HAVA) of 2002, which mandated that states provide provisional ballots for those citizens who believe they are registered to vote but whose names are not on the registration rolls. Congress passed HAVA in reaction to the voting debacle in Florida in the 2000 presidential election between Al Gore and George W. Bush. Aside from poorly designed butterfly ballots, hanging chads, and miscounted overseas absentee ballots,[17] some voters were turned away from polling places because they did not appear on the voter lists even though they insisted they were registered. At a primarily Black precinct in Fort Lauderdale, election workers turned away about one hundred people who came to vote because the voter list indicated they had not registered.[18] Similar scenes were played out across Florida. As noted, a provision in HAVA was designed to ensure that registered voters could vote by allowing people to cast a provisional ballot.

If people show up to vote on Election Day and their name does not appear on the voter list, election workers must now offer them a provisional ballot. If they are registered, their vote will be counted. Much of the debate in Congress over this provision in HAVA involved the form of identification that voters seeking to cast provisional ballots would need to produce at the polls or within a certain time period after the election. Republican legislators sought more rigid standards to prevent voter fraud; Democratic legislators generally argued for keeping the barriers to a minimum.[19] Despite Republican fears that easing registration requirements would bring more Democrats to the polls, the main impact of making it easier to register seems to have been a decline in the percentage of people not registered to vote and a slight increase in the proportion of the officially registered who do not vote (see Figure 3-6). Overall, the effect has been relatively small. Failure to register prohibits voting, but registering does not ensure turnout.

Registration requirements are not the only institutional impediment to voting. Traditionally, voting in national elections has been done on just one day, the Tuesday after the first Monday in November, at polling sites located in the precincts near where people live. These polling sites are open at a set time, in many states from 7 a.m. to 7 p.m., although the opening and closing times vary by state. Reformers have argued that having elections on a weekday, when many people work, decreases turnout. The more inconvenient voting is for people, the less likely they are to vote.

To lessen the impact of these obstacles, reforms have opened up when and where people can vote by making it easier to vote through mail ballots, early voting, absentee ballots, and the use of voting centers. Some states mail ballots to registered voters and allow them to vote by mail. Oregon has pursued these

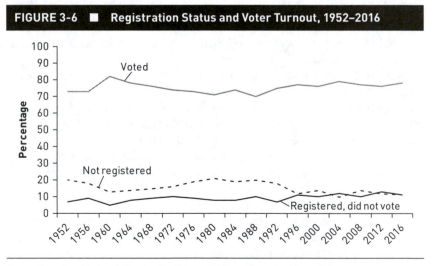

FIGURE 3-6 ■ Registration Status and Voter Turnout, 1952–2016

Source: American National Election Studies, available at www.electionstudies.org.

possibilities most aggressively since 2004, sending the entire electorate mail-in ballots rather than having in-person voting. Four states (Colorado, Hawaii, Utah, and Washington) have moved to all-mail elections, following Oregon's lead, although other voting options are available. Other states have loosened the conditions under which voters can request absentee ballots or have set up systems for in-person early voting in the weeks prior to the election, referred to as nontraditional voting. Only 11 percent of votes cast in 1996 were nontraditional votes. The percentage of nontraditional votes rose to 31 percent in 2008 and by 2016 was at 40 percent. Fears about how people would get to the polls during the pandemic led many states to open up early voting and mail ballot opportunities, and many people took advantage of these opportunities. In 2020, the percentage of nontraditional votes jumped to 69 percent.[20] The largest increase came in the use of mail or absentee ballots, which jumped from just over 20 percent in 2016 to almost 50 percent of all votes cast in 2020.[21]

If making voting more convenient is the answer to higher turnout, then the series of reforms put in place in recent years should lead to a significant increase in votes cast. The act of voting is much more convenient than it used to be, thereby lowering the costs associated with voting. Research on the impact of these reforms, however, has not shown the effects many reformers had hoped would occur. The people taking advantage of these reforms tend to be those who would vote anyway; it is just easier for them now. And these reforms have not increased substantially the turnout of underrepresented groups, such as people of color or young people.[22] It can't be denied, though, that turnout has been increasing since the mid-1990s over the time that voting has become more convenient.

In response to the increased access to voting, some states and localities have taken steps to make voting potentially less convenient. Many of these efforts occurred long before the 2020 elections, including the closing of polling places and the requirement instituted by some states that voters provide an official form of identification to be able to vote. In 2013, the Supreme Court struck down, in *Shelby County v. Holder*, the restrictions in Section 5 of the 1965 Voting Rights Act that required states with a history of voting discrimination to get federal court permission to make changes in how their elections are carried out. Since that decision, many counties, especially in the South, have closed voting stations. Between 2012 and 2018, over 1,600 polling places were closed, including 1 in 10 in Texas and 1 in 5 in Arizona. Almost 1,200 of these occurred after the 2014 elections.[23] The argument for closing these voting stations was that they were underutilized and it was therefore cost efficient to close them. Opponents of the closures argued that having fewer polling sites would make voting less convenient and would increase the time needed to vote.[24] The availability of voting stations and ease of access to them vary for people of different racial backgrounds. One study of Wisconsin voters in 2018 showed that Latin@ voters systematically faced longer waits in line than other voters and Black voters had longer commutes to their polling places.[25]

Instituting voter identification (ID) laws has also increased. After the 2000 presidential election, states began passing voter ID laws in droves. According to the National Conference of State Legislatures, thirty-six states have voter ID laws in place (although North Carolina's law had not gone into effect by the end of 2020 due to court cases in the works).[26] These state laws vary, with some states requiring an official photo ID, others requiring a nonphoto ID, and still others requesting but not requiring an ID. What happens if people do not have an appropriate form of identification also varies by state. In some states, people who do not have an appropriate ID can vote using a provisional ballot but must bring their ID to election officials within a few days of the election to have their vote counted. Other states allow those without an acceptable ID to vote if they sign a voucher attesting to their identity or if a poll worker vouches for them.

A University of Massachusetts Amherst/WCVB poll released in April 2021[27] found a large majority of Americans, 67 percent, favor the requirement that voters show a photo ID to be able to vote. Partisanship played a role in this support, with 94 percent of Republicans, 71 percent of independents, and 45 percent of Democrats supporting a voter ID requirement. Supporters of voter ID laws are more likely to worry about voter fraud, arguing that people who are ineligible to vote are casting ballots and potentially swaying election outcomes, whereas opponents are more likely to worry about voter suppression, arguing that people who are eligible to vote but cannot afford a photo ID are being turned away from the polls. Not surprisingly, Republicans are more likely than Democrats to believe that preventing election fraud is a priority even if it makes voting harder (88 percent of Republicans vs. 22 percent of Democrats). Democrats, in contrast, are much more likely than Republicans to support automatic voter registration (84 percent to 24 percent), vote by mail (90 percent to 23 percent), and automatic absentee ballots (76 percent to 13 percent).

Little evidence exists that there is actual widespread voter fraud, especially of the type that a voter ID law would presumably stop. When Indiana passed its photo ID law among claims of widespread voter fraud, no cases of in-person fraud had been prosecuted, and a special investigation over almost two years of voter fraud in Texas led to only thirteen indictments, six of which involved people helping friends with a mail-in ballot.[28] Fears of widespread voter fraud appear to be misplaced. One study found that Americans were more likely to claim that they had been abducted by an alien than to have impersonated another voter.[29] It could be the case, however, that regardless of the reality of voter fraud, having voter ID laws could increase confidence in the election process. This argument was made by the Supreme Court in its *Crawford v. Marion County Election Board* (2008) decision. Whether fraud exists or not, increasing confidence in elections might be an important outcome and a reason to pass voter ID laws. Research shows, however, that people who live in states with strict voter ID laws are no more confident in election outcomes, or no less likely to believe that fraud exists, than people who live in states with no voter ID laws.[30]

Evidence on the effects of voter ID laws on turnout has been mixed, although any effects appear to be small. Some researchers have found a moderate impact on turnout among people who are the least likely to have the type of identification required in the state, especially people of color. Others, however, present evidence for minuscule effects.[31] Stephen Ansolabehere found that less than two-tenths of 1 percent (seven people out of four thousand) did not vote in 2008 because of voter ID problems. It is certainly possible that the most strict voter ID laws, which have only more recently been passed, could have a detrimental impact on turnout, a potential that will need to be watched. For example, research shows that Hispanics and Blacks are much more likely to be asked by poll workers to show some type of identification, especially photo IDs, even when there is no state law in place requiring identification to vote.[32] The unequal treatment of voters at the polls based on race raises serious concerns about voter ID laws.

After the 2020 election, states have ramped up their efforts to put more restrictions on voting. According to the Brennan Center for Justice, legislators in forty-seven states have introduced bills to restrict voting in one way or another. By May 2021, five states had passed restrictive legislation. For many states, the bills were still moving through the legislative process. In response, legislators have proposed codifying in law the more expansive practices of 2020, and the U.S. House of Representatives passed H.R. 1 in March 2021 to expand voter registration and increase voter access.[33] The bill at the time of this writing sits in the U.S. Senate. The current fights over institutional impediments to voting matter because they affect voter turnout, and who votes matters in a democracy.

PSYCHOLOGICAL MOTIVATION, GENETICS, AND TURNOUT

Election processes and rules clearly play a role in encouraging or dampening voter turnout. Any obstacles increase the cost of voting, and even the smallest cost can cause people to find other things to do on Election Day. But many people vote even when obstacles and costs exist, just as many people do not vote even when voting is relatively easy. Making the effort to register, to become informed about an upcoming election, and to cast a ballot demands a certain level of interest and engagement in politics that cannot be created simply by reducing institutional obstacles.

The people most likely to vote, especially in midterm or local elections, are highly interested in politics, are more likely to be knowledgeable about politics, and feel strongly attached to a political party, largely because strong identifiers care more about who wins.[34] Even though interest in politics is strongly correlated with voting, about half of those who say they have hardly any interest (not very and not at all interested) do vote in presidential elections (and in 2020, a whopping 72 percent of the uninterested said they voted), suggesting that other factors are also at work. One of these is a sense of civic duty—the attitude that a good citizen has an obligation to vote. Many Americans see voting as an obligation of citizenship (51 percent see it more as a duty than a choice), and when they vote, they feel a sense of gratification that overrides any cost of voting they might incur.[35] When voting is viewed as a civic norm, people with a strong sense of civic duty vote because of the intrinsic satisfaction they get from doing what they know is right, or they vote because of extrinsic pressure to conform to a social norm. In a clever experiment, Alan Gerber, Donald Green, and Christopher Larimer found that when people were reminded of the obligation to vote, turnout increased by 1.8 percentage points compared to people who received no message. The biggest impact on turnout, however, came from people who were told that their neighbors would know whether they voted or not. In this case, turnout increased by over 8 percentage points.[36] A similar effect was found in a study of Facebook users that manipulated whether people saw posts in their Facebook feed that showed their friends voting.[37] Civic duty increases turnout not just because people feel good when they have done what they know they ought to do; it also increases turnout because people experience social pressure to vote. It should come as no surprise that polling places often hand out "I voted" stickers, allowing voters to publicly display the fact that they fulfilled their civic obligation to vote.

Political scientists have begun to wonder more recently if there are even deeper explanations for people's voting behavior, deeper in the sense that there might be a genetic component that leads people to vote or not to vote. Testing genetic influences is not easy, given that there is obviously not a gene for voting, but scholars have been able to use studies of twins to compare monozygotic twins (popularly known as identical twins, who share 100 percent of their genes) and dizygotic twins (popularly known as fraternal twins, who share only 50 percent of their genes, which is true for all biological siblings). We know that parents who vote are much more likely to have children who grow up to vote, and this is likely affected somewhat more by genetic influences than socialization influences. James Fowler and his colleagues found that over 50 percent of people's turnout behavior can be explained by genetic heritability, whereas about 35 percent can be explained by shared environment. Environment matters, but genes play a big role. The influence of genetics on voting might well occur through the large role they play in explaining attitudes related to turnout, such as interest, partisanship, civic duty, and political efficacy.[38]

CAMPAIGN ACTIVITY AND MOBILIZATION IN AMERICAN ELECTIONS

Our discussion of voter turnout thus far has implied that there are people who vote (sharing certain demographic characteristics, such as higher education level and income; certain attitudes, such as interest and civic duty; and certain genetics) and people who do not vote (those who do not share these characteristics). This is clearly not the case. Some people never vote, estimated to make up about 10 percent of eligible voters, and they are unlikely to go to the polls regardless of what institutional rules are in place or what is done to get them to vote. Constant voters, about 25 percent of eligible voters, do not need to be prompted to go to the polls, and they will overcome whatever obstacles might get in their way. They always vote. It is the remaining 65 percent who are the intermittent voters. They are more likely to vote in high-salience elections (e.g., presidential elections) and when voting is convenient. Since reforms have, in general, made voting easier, the trick now is to get these intermittent voters to vote regularly. Getting these voters to the polls is a target of mobilization efforts.[39]

Millions of dollars are spent by campaigns, partisan groups, and nonpartisan organizations to get people to the polls on Election Day. These GOTV efforts include door-to-door canvassing, leaflets, door hangers, direct mail, email, and phone calls. In a series of field experiments, political scientists have tested the varying effects of these GOTV strategies to determine which lead to higher turn-out.[40] Door-to-door canvassing, where campaign volunteers ring doorbells and ask the targeted individuals to be sure to vote, tends to be more effective than using the phone or mail. Personal, face-to-face requests elicit greater compliance than impersonal requests, but people also tend to follow through when they have made a commitment publicly.[41] People like to think of themselves as consistent, and the only way to be consistent after telling a canvasser that they will vote in the upcoming election is to vote. Given this logic, it makes sense that phone calls can be effective as well if there is a more personal touch involved—for example, when the call is made by volunteers or when professional phone banks use a more inter-active and conversational approach rather than robotic calls.[42] Major advances in GOTV efforts came into play in the 2012 presidential election with the use of "big data" and microtargeting. Both the Barack Obama and Mitt Romney campaigns bought demographic data from companies that gather personal data on everything from shopping habits to financial problems. They gathered online data themselves on such things as social networks. As *New York Times* reporter Charles Duhigg wrote before the election,

> They have access to information about the personal lives of voters at a scale never before imagined. And they are using that data to try to influence voting habits—in effect, to train voters to go to the polls through subtle cues, rewards, and threats in a manner akin to the marketing efforts of credit card companies and big-box retailers.[43]

The campaigns used the information to contact potential voters and apply tar-geted pressure to get them to vote, although appearing to know too much personal information can backfire by seeming creepy.

The Obama campaign was especially advanced in microtargeting. Jim Messina, Obama's campaign manager in 2012, set up campaign headquarters in

Illinois and hired sixty data analysts to analyze all the data needed to microtarget. Being able to microtarget gave the Obama campaign a definite edge over the Romney campaign. In a story told by Messina, Obama volunteers were canvassing a neighborhood at the same time as Romney volunteers. The Romney volunteers knocked on every door on one side of the street, finding that half of the people were not home and the other half were Obama supporters. The Obama volunteers were told to knock on only two doors and to speak with certain people at those houses, people who fit the profile of being potential Obama supporters and who could be nudged to get to the polls on Election Day. Because of the analysis of big data, Messina said, the Obama campaign was able to target the houses of undecided voters who had a good probability of voting, and they were able to tell their volunteer canvassers what to say. The Obama volunteers knocked on the relevant doors, talked to the relevant people, and were able to move on to the next neighborhood, while the Romney volunteers were still knocking on doors that would not elicit Romney voters.[44] The Obama campaign even ran experiments on volunteer phone calls to potential supporters to test whether it was more effective to control the message in the calls or let the voters talk about issues of their own choosing; the campaign persuaded more people to support Obama when sticking to the campaign script than when letting the voters lead the discussion.

GOTV efforts were decidedly skewed in 2016. While Hillary Clinton's campaign had a less robust ground game than Obama's did in 2012, she had more than twice as many field offices as Trump. Field offices are places where people can go to volunteer their services for the campaign. They therefore are the hub from which volunteers go out into neighborhoods to knock on doors and from which phone calls are made to energize voters. Trump's strategy was to piggyback on the efforts of the Republican National Committee, which was a more efficient approach but less under the control of the candidate.[45] The Trump campaign's emphasis was on utilizing untraditional methods to increase enthusiasm and the desire to vote, including his signature rallies that generated significant media coverage.

The campaign strategies of the top two contenders in 2020 could not have been more different. In the midst of the pandemic, with mask mandates and stay-at-home orders in effect in many parts of the country, Democrat Joe Biden chose to hold occasional small events with strict social distancing, but he focused more on holding virtual gatherings and airing television ads. Rather than going door-to-door to mobilize voters, the Biden campaign staff used mobile offices to try to generate enthusiasm and engagement. Republican Donald Trump, in contrast, held large rallies at which his supporters wearing "Make America Great Again" caps gathered to cheer their candidate on. Trump traveled far and wide across the country and often chastised his opponent for hiding in his basement while he was out meeting with voters.[46] Turnout was historically high in 2020, likely not because of the differing GOTV efforts of the two candidates but because people cared so much about which candidate won. Most Democrats (91 percent) and almost as many Republicans (84.5 percent) said they cared a lot or a great deal about who won the election.

Even if voter mobilization efforts were highly successful, turnout rates would not be consistently high across all elections. Context still matters. Good candidates, competitive races, and high-salience elections are more likely to bring out voters than are other, less invigorating races.[47] In low-salience races, such as a local race for mayor or even a midterm congressional election, mobilization efforts are aimed at intermittent voters who vote frequently but not always and just need a nudge. GOTV campaigns can also be successful by targeting probable voters who are undecided. The problem is that there have been relatively few undecided voters in most recent elections. Defining undecided voters as those who stated in a survey that they were undecided and did not say they were leaning toward one candidate or the other when pushed, Larry Bartels and Lynn Vavreck found that only 5 percent of survey respondents in 2012 were actually undecided in the months before the election. These undecided voters not surprisingly tended to identify as independents and moderates, were not terribly knowledgeable about politics, and tended not to follow political news much.[48] While people might not be able to make a conscious decision, however, they often have implicit leanings toward one candidate or the other, and this unconscious preference is a good predictor of who they will actually vote for on Election Day.[49] In 2016, the number of people who claimed to be undecided was higher than normal (10 percent of the ANES respondents). They also turned out to vote in unusually high numbers, and they tended to vote for Trump.[50] By 2020, the undecideds had dropped to the more normal 5 percent.

Who Participates in Campaigns?

Getting out the vote is what candidates need to do to win, but campaigns would be hard-pressed to get out the vote without a large amount of unpaid help. Candidates and political parties rely heavily on volunteers during the election season to do the canvassing, the stuffing of envelopes, and the calling of potential voters. They hope their supporters get out the word on their candidate by putting up yard signs or placing bumper stickers on their cars or talking to friends, relatives, and coworkers to drum up support for the candidate. And with the tremendous cost of campaigns, especially in recent years, campaign organizations eagerly solicit supporters' donations. Voting is a relatively easy way to participate in politics compared to the initiative and costs (in time and, for donations, money) associated with other types of campaign activity. Campaign activists have to be highly motivated both to figure out what they need to do to be involved and to participate in the activity. Most Americans are not motivated to be activists. A focus group participant summed it up nicely when she said, "When I leave here [the focus group discussion], when I walk out this door, I'm not going to volunteer for anything. I'm not going to get involved in anything. I mean I know this. I'm not going to pretend I'm some political activist. I'm lazy. I'm not going to do it. I'm too busy obsessing on other things going on in my life."[51] It comes as no surprise that fewer people are involved in campaign activities than vote.

Figure 3-7 shows Americans' involvement in various campaign activities over time. The first thing that stands out is that Americans are much more likely to try to influence other people in how they should vote than to be involved in other campaign activities. ANES respondents were asked, "During the campaign, did you talk to any people and try to show them why they should vote for or against one of the parties or candidates?" On average, about a third of the respondents said yes, they did try to influence people's votes. This percentage skyrocketed to just under 50 percent in the 2004 election and dropped to 43 percent in 2008. The percentage of those trying to influence other people's votes has remained at this level over the recent election cycles, between 40 and 44 percent, but this level was still higher than the average over the time period covered by ANES. Making the effort to try to persuade people how to vote indicates a strong interest in the outcome of the election and enough knowledge about the campaign to be able to make an argument on behalf of a party or candidate. It is interesting to note that while voters are the most likely to try to influence others, people who end up not voting do so as well. Over the past several elections, approximately 50 percent of voters and just over 20 percent of nonvoters tried to influence others' vote choice. These percentages were 42 percent of voters and 26 percent of nonvoters in 2020. We can't know what the nonvoters had to say while trying to persuade other people, but we do know that in the past election, half (51 percent) of nonvoters claimed to "care a great deal" or "a lot" about which party won the election. Granted, voters were more likely to care (87 percent), but it is clear that a lot of nonvoters care enough about the outcome of the election to want to persuade others for whom to vote. The other campaign activities are not as popular, with only 3 to 5 percent of Americans working on campaigns and just under 10 percent attending political meetings. With the pandemic limiting social gatherings in 2020, attendance at meetings, rallies, speeches, and dinners dropped to just over 5 percent. Many more people, 12 percent, said they had attended *online* meetings, rallies, speeches, and dinners, a reflection of the limits on social gatherings during the pandemic.

The second aspect of Figure 3-7 that stands out is that campaign activities overall increased significantly in 2004 but by 2012 had dropped to more normal levels (except for trying to influence people). People's willingness to display buttons or stickers and to donate money increased in 2020, but 2004 still stands out as a particularly engaged election. So what is special about 2004? Much of the commentary leading up to the 2004 election focused on energized youth and upset Democrats who were still smarting after the 2000 election and the debacle in Florida. The closeness of the 2000 election led Democrats to emphasize the need for their followers to vote. The stepped-up efforts of Rock the Vote and Sean P. Diddy Combs's "Vote or Die," both aimed at increasing youth turnout, and the large number of Democrats thinking that year's presidential election was "the most important of their lifetimes" led to speculation that youth and Democrats would be much more engaged in 2004 than was usual.[52] The uptick in campaign activities in 2020 is likely due to a similar dynamic: Democrats were upset about

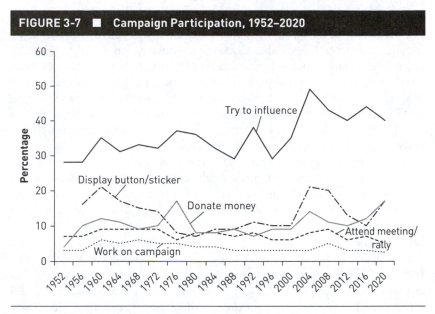

FIGURE 3-7 ■ Campaign Participation, 1952–2020

Source: American National Election Studies, available at www.electionstudies.org.

winning the popular vote but losing the Electoral College vote in 2016, especially given their dislike of Trump (more on this in Chapter 5). Youth were highly energized by the Black Lives Matter protests over the summer of 2020, a topic we address in the next chapter.

We have raised a number of different aspects of campaigns and voting that could influence whether people get engaged in campaigns. We are now going to put much of it together to analyze who is most likely to be engaged in campaigns, from voting to donating. Looking at certain factors, such as age or income, tells us a lot, but sometimes these variables overlap. For example, older people are more likely to have higher incomes than younger people. When looking at the relationship between age and participation in politics, is it age that explains what is going on? Or is it income level that is driving participation, and it just happens that older people have more income? To figure out the unique effects of each of the factors we have discussed, we need to run a regression analysis. The results tell us how much of an effect each variable has on campaign participation, controlling the effects of all of the other variables. Using this method, we can see whether, for example, age matters (controlling all else) and whether income matters (controlling all else).

We created a Campaign Activities Scale using ANES data that includes whether people voted, tried to influence others' vote, worked on a campaign, attended a meeting in person, attended a meeting online, displayed a button or sticker, or donated money. A score of 0 means they did none of these (12 percent of the sample), and a score of 7 means they did all of these (only 0.4 percent had a score of 7). The mean score was 1.7, which means that the average person did just under two of these activities. To explain campaign activities behavior, we included as independent variables demographic information (sex, race, age, education, and income), interest in the election (whether the respondent cares about who wins the presidency and partisan strength, because strong partisans tend to care more about winning elections than those with a weaker or no partisanship), GOTV contact (whether anyone talked to the respondent about registering or voting), and believing voting is a duty (vs. thinking it is just a choice people can make). Table 3-1 shows the results of the regression analysis.

The results are easy to interpret. All of the independent variables were scaled to range from 0 to 1. For example, an eighteen-year-old is coded 0, and someone who is 80 or older is coded 1. Everyone else falls somewhere between these two extremes. For race, we coded whites as 1 and people of color as 0. If the regression coefficient (B) is positive and the p value is smaller than .05, then the variable significantly increases campaign activity. If B is negative and the p value is smaller than .05, then the variable significantly decreases campaign activity. How big B is tells us how much a unit increase in the independent variable has an impact on campaign activities. For example, sex is coded 1 for males and 0 for females. The B is positive but extremely small (.011), and the p value is way above .05, which means that men and women are basically the same when it

TABLE 3-1 ■ Explaining Who Is Involved in Campaign Activities

Independent Variables	B (unstandardized coefficient)	Standard Error	Significance (p value)
Sex (Male)	.011	.036	.766
Race (White)	.229	.039	.000
Age	.292	.068	.000
Education	.478	.070	.000
Income	.211	.063	.001
Partisan strength	.428	.055	.000
Cares who wins	1.135	.078	.000
GOTV contact	.428	.036	.000
Voting as a duty	.469	.047	.000
Constant	−.628	.073	.000
F	144.2		.000
Adj. R^2	.231		
N	4296		

Source: 2020 American National Election Studies, available at www.electionstudies.org.

comes to campaign activity. In contrast, whites are more likely to participate in campaign activities than people of color, although whites only do .23 more campaign activities than people of color. (Keep in mind that the campaign activities scale ranges from 0 to 7, so an increase of .23 is very small.) Among the other demographic variables, older people are more likely to participate than younger people, the better educated are more likely to participate than the less educated, and wealthier people are more likely to participate than poorer people, all else equal.

The political motivation variables also explain involvement in campaign activities. The stronger people's partisanship, the more likely they are to participate (by almost half of an activity). Being encouraged to vote by someone and believing voting is a duty have similar significant impacts on campaign activity. The best predictor of campaign participation, though, is caring who wins. The more people cared if Trump or Biden won, the more they participated in the campaign. Moving from not caring at all to caring a great deal moved people up the campaign activities scale by more than one activity. This result is hardly surprising, but it does suggest that holding everything else constant, if we can increase how much people care about who wins, participation in campaigns will increase quite dramatically. The downside, of course, is that if people care a great deal about who wins, then losing the election becomes much more difficult to accept.

Electoral context matters. What happens in the political world—being upset about previous election outcomes, having GOTV efforts target certain groups of people, caring passionately about who wins—can influence people's behavior, making them more or less active in any given election. A common theme among democratic theorists is a desire for people to get more involved in politics. People need to vote, be informed about politics, participate in campaigns, and join organizations. The data throughout this chapter show that while many Americans achieve this standard of good citizenship, a great many do not. Political scientists have made significant advances in ascertaining what causes low participation rates and what can be done to increase citizens' engagement in the political system. Having people care a great deal about politics because of what they see happening in Washington and around the country matters.

Study Questions

1. Voter turnout has gone up and down over time. Who are the voters, and who are the nonvoters?

2. How have institutional restrictions on voting been used to affect political outcomes, especially when it comes to restricting Blacks' right to vote?

3. What are the psychological motivations that increase turnout?

4. What do campaign activists do, and who are they?

Suggested Readings

Green, Donald P., and Alan S. Gerber. *Get Out the Vote! How to Increase Voter Turnout*. Washington, DC: Brookings Institution Press, 2015. Recommendations on how to mobilize voters and increase turnout based on rigorous research.

Holbein, John B., and Sunshine Hillygus. *Making Young Voters: Converting Civic Attitudes Into Civic Action*. New York: Cambridge University Press, 2020. Combining psychological, economic, and child development theories, this book shows how education and civic reforms can increase younger voters' turnout.

Leighley, Jan E., and Jonathan Nagler. *Who Votes Now? Demographics, Issues, Inequality, and Turnout in the United States*. Princeton, NJ: Princeton University Press, 2013. In-depth, thorough analysis of the characteristics of voters versus nonvoters.

Manza, Jeff, and Christopher Uggen. *Locked Out: Disenfranchisement and American Democracy*. New York: Oxford University Press, 2008. An indispensable examination of felon disenfranchisement laws and their impact on American elections.

McDonald, Michael P., and Samuel L. Popkin. "The Myth of the Vanishing Voter." *American Political Science Review* 95, no. 4 (December 2001): 963–974.

Patterson, Thomas E. *The Vanishing Voter: Public Involvement in an Age of Uncertainty*. New York: Alfred A. Knopf, 2002. An analysis of political participation based on a huge, yearlong survey in 2000.

Rusk, Jerrold D., and John J. Stucker. "The Effect of the Southern System of Election Laws on Voting Participation." In *The History of American Electoral Behavior*, edited by Joel Silbey, Allan Bogue, and William Flanigan. Princeton, NJ: Princeton University Press, 1978. A sophisticated analysis of the disenfranchisement of voters in the South in the nineteenth century.

Teixeira, Ruy A. *The Disappearing American Voter*. Washington, DC: Brookings Institution Press, 1992. A sophisticated and thorough analysis of the factors that have contributed to the decline in turnout in the United States and a discussion of the impact of proposed reforms.

Internet Resources

An important website for the analysis of aggregate turnout data is the United States Elections Project, www.electproject.org. Michael McDonald, the host of this website, uses strategies for reducing the error in turnout estimates and offers commentary on turnout.

The website of the American National Election Studies, www.electionstudies.org, offers data on turnout in both presidential and off-year elections since 1952. In the Resources menu, click on the link for tables and graphs under "The ANES Guide to Public Opinion and Electoral Behavior" and then scroll down to "Political Involvement and Participation in Politics." You also can examine turnout of numerous social groups from 1952 to the present.

Turnout and registration data for the nation and the states are available at the U.S. Census Bureau website, www.census.gov. Click on "Browse by Topic" in the menu bar, then click on "Public Sector," and then click on "Voting and Registration."

Notes

1. Michael P. McDonald and Samuel L. Popkin, "The Myth of the Vanishing Voter," *American Political Science Review* 95, no. 4 (2001): 963–974.

2. See United States Elections Project, accessed June 29, 2021, www.electproject.org; and McDonald and Popkin, "Myth of the Vanishing Voter."

3. On the one-party dominance argument, see E. E. Schattschneider, *The Semisovereign People* (New York: Holt, Rinehart, and Winston, 1960), especially Chapter 5; and Walter Dean Burnham, "The Changing Shape of the American Political Universe," *American Political Science Review* 59 (March 1965): 7–28. On electoral manipulations and the subsequent electoral reforms, see Philip E. Converse, "Change in the American Electorate," in *The Human Meaning of Social Change*, eds. Angus Campbell and Philip E. Converse (New York: Russell Sage Foundation, 1972), 263–337. For an analysis that alters the estimates of turnout, see Ray M. Shortridge, "Estimating Voter Participation," in *Analyzing Electoral History*, eds. Jerome M. Clubb, William H. Flanigan, and Nancy H. Zingale (Beverly Hills, CA: SAGE, 1981), 137–152.

4. Jerrold D. Rusk, "The Effect of the Australian Ballot Reform on Split-Ticket Voting: 1876–1908," *American Political Science Review* 64 (December 1970): 1220–1238.

5. See "Voter Turnout," United States Elections Project, accessed June 29, 2021, http://www.electproject.org/home/voter-turnout/voter-turnout-data.

6. Allyson L. Holbrook and Jon A. Krosnick, "Social Desirability Bias in Voter Turnout Reports," *Public Opinion Quarterly* 74 (Spring 2010): 37–67.

7. Brian D. Silver, Barbara A. Anderson, and Paul R. Abramson, "Who Overreports Voting?," *American Political Science Review* 80 (June 1986): 613–624; Rachel Milstein Sondheimer and Donald P. Green, "Using Experiments to

Estimate the Effects of Education on Voter Turnout," *American Journal of Political Science* 54 (January 2010): 174–189.

8. For a treatment of these and many additional topics, see J. Morgan Kousser, *The Shaping of Southern Politics* (New Haven, CT: Yale University Press, 1974). See also Jerrold D. Rusk and John J. Stucker, "The Effect of the Southern System of Election Laws on Voting Participation," in *The History of American Electoral Behavior*, eds. Joel Silbey, Allan Bogue, and William Flanigan (Princeton, NJ: Princeton University Press, 1978).

9. Christopher Uggen, Ryan Larson, Sarah Shannon, and Arleth Pulido-Nava, "Locked Out 2020: Estimates of People Denied Voting Rights Due to a Felony Conviction," Sentencing Project, October 30, 2020, https://www .sentencingproject.org/publications/locked-out-2020-estimates-of-people-denied-voting-rights-due-to-a-felony-conviction/.

10. Ibid.

11. Randi Hjalmarsson and Mark Lopez, "The Voting Behavior of Young Disenfranchised Felons: Would They Vote If They Could?," *American Law and Economics Review* 12 (2010): 356–393; Thomas J. Miles, "Felon Disenfranchisement and Voter Turnout," *Journal of Legal Studies* 33 (January 2004): 85–129.

12. Christopher Uggen and Jeff Manza, "Democratic Contraction? Political Consequences of Felon Disenfranchisement in the United States," *American Sociological Review* 67 (December 2002): 777–803, p. 786.

13. Vesla M. Weaver and Amy E. Lerman, "Political Consequences of the Carceral State," *American Political Science Review* 104 (November 2010): 817–833, p. 818.

14. Alan S. Gerber, Gregory A. Huber, Marc Meredith, Daniel R. Biggers, and David J. Hendry, "Can Incarcerated Felons Be (Re)integrated Into the Political System? Results From a Field Experiment," *American Journal of Political Science* 59 (October 2015): 912–926.

15. "CPS Historical Migration/Geographic Mobility Tables" (Table A-1 Annual Geographic Mobility Rates, by Type of Movement: 1948–2020), U.S. Census Bureau, U.S. Department of Commerce, December 2020, https://www.census .gov/data/tables/time-series/demo/geographic-mobility/historic.html.

16. Raymond E. Wolfinger and Steven J. Rosenstone, *Who Votes?* (New Haven, CT: Yale University Press, 1980); G. Bingham Powell, "American Voter Turnout in Comparative Perspective," *American Political Science Review* 80 (March 1986): 17–43.

17. Henry E. Brady, Michael C. Herron, Walter R. Mebane Jr., and Jasjeet Singh Sekhon, "'Law and Data': The Butterfly Ballot Episode," *PS: Political Science*

and Politics 34 (March 2001): 59–69; David Barstow and Don Van Natta Jr., "Examining the Vote; How Bush Took Florida: Mining the Overseas Absentee Vote," *New York Times*, July 15, 2001.

18. Mireya Navarro and Somini Sengupta, "Contesting the Vote: Black Voters; Arriving at Florida Voting Places, Some Blacks Found Frustration," *New York Times*, November 30, 2000.

19. *CQ Almanac Plus 2002* (Washington, DC: Congressional Quarterly, 2003), 143.

20. Zachary Scherer, "Majority of Voters Used Nontraditional Methods to Cast Ballots in 2020," U.S. Census Bureau, April 29, 2021, https://www.census .gov/library/stories/2021/04/what-methods-did-people-use-to-vote-in-2020-election.html.

21. "Voting by Mail and Absentee Voting," MIT Election Data + Science Lab, accessed May 7, 2021, https://electionlab.mit.edu/research/voting-mail-and-absentee-voting.

22. See, for example, Adam Berinsky, "The Perverse Consequences of Electoral Reform in the United States," *American Politics Research* 33 (July 2005): 471–491; Jeffrey A. Karp and Susan A. Banducci, "Going Postal: How All-Mail Elections Influence Turnout," *Political Behavior* 22, no. 3 (2000): 223–239; Robert M. Stein and Greg Vonnahme, "Voting at Non-precinct Polling Places: A Review and Research Agenda," *Election Law Journal* 10 (October 2011): 307–311.

23. Andy Sullivan, "Southern U.S. States Have Closed 1,200 Polling Places in Recent Years: Rights Group," Reuters, September 9, 2019, https://www .reuters.com/article/us-usa-election-locations/southern-u-s-states-have-closed-1200-polling-places-in-recent-years-rights-group-idUSKCN1VV09J.

24. Elena Mejia Lutz, "Report: Texas Has Closed Most Polling Places Since Court Ruling," *Texas Tribune* (Austin), November 4, 2016, https://www.texastribune .org/2016/11/04/report-texas-holds-highest-number-polling-place-cl/; John Whitesides, "Polling Places Become Battleground in U.S. Voting Rights Fight," Reuters, September 16, 2016, http://www.reuters.com/article/us-usa-election-vote-precincts-insight-idUSKCN11M0WY.

25. Jordan Foley, Michael W. Wagner, Ceri Hughes, Jiyoun Suk, Katherine J. Cramer, Lewis A. Friedland, and Dhavan V. Shah, "Free and Fair? The Differential Experiences of Voting Barriers and Voting Policies in American Midterm Elections," *International Journal of Public Opinion Research* (Forthcoming).

26. These numbers are accurate as of March 2021. "Voter Identification Requirements/ Voter ID Laws," National Conference of State Legislatures, May 25, 2021, https://www.ncsl.org/research/elections-and-campaigns/voter-id.aspx.

27. UMassAmherst UMass Poll, Toplines and Crosstabs April 2021 Election Reform, April 28, 2021, accessed May 7, 2021, https://polsci.umass.edu/toplines-and-crosstabs-april-2021-election-reform?_gl=1*1yrvk7t*_ga*MjczNjg5NjIzLjE2 MjA0MTQ0NzE.*_ga_21RLS0L7EB*MTYyMDQxNDQ3MC4xLjAuMTYyMDQxN DQ3MC4w&_ga=2.2687155.222364461.1620414471-273689623.1620414471.

28. Chandler Davidson, "The Historical Context of Voter Photo-ID Laws," *PS: Political Science & Politics* 42 (January 2009): 93–96.

29. John S. Ahlquist, Kenneth R. Mayer, and Simon Jackman, "Alien Abduction and Voter Impersonation in the 2012 U.S. General Election: Evidence From a Survey List Experiment," *Election Law Journal: Rules, Politics and Policy* 13, no. 4 (2014): 460–475.

30. Stephen Ansolabehere and Nathaniel Persily, "Vote Fraud in the Eye of the Beholder: The Role of Public Opinion in the Challenge to Voter Identification Requirements," *Harvard Law Review* 121 (2008): 1737–1774; "Voter Identification," MIT Election Data + Science Lab, accessed June 29, 2021, https://electionlab.mit.edu/research/voter-identification.

31. Benjamin Highton, "Voter Identification Laws and Turnout in the United States," *Annual Review of Political Science* (2017): 149–167; R. Michael Alvarez, Delia Bailey, and Jonathan N. Katz, "The Effect of Voter Identification Laws on Turnout" (California Institute of Technology Social Science Working Paper No. 1267R), January 17, 2008. Available at SSRN: https://ssrn.com/abstract=1084598; Zoltan Hajnal, Nazita Lajevardi, and Lindsay Nielson, "Voter Identification Laws and the Suppression of Minority Votes," *Journal of Politics* 79 (April 2017): 363–379.

32. Stephen Ansolabehere, "Effects of Identification Requirements on Voting: Evidence From the Experiences of Voters on Election Day," *PS: Political Science and Politics* 42, no. 1 (January 2009): 127–130; Lonna Rae Atkeson, Lisa Ann Bryant, Thad E. Hall, Kyle L. Saunders, and R. Michael Alvarez, "A New Barrier to Participation: Heterogeneous Application of Voter Identification Policies," *Electoral Studies* 29 (March 2010): 66–73.

33. "State Voting Laws," Brennan Center for Justice, accessed May 26, 2021, https://www.brennancenter.org/issues/ensure-every-american-can-vote/voting-reform/state-voting-laws.

34. Markus Prior, "You've Either Got It or You Don't? The Stability of Political Interest Over the Life Cycle," *Journal of Politics* 72 (July 2010): 747–766; Markus Prior, *Post-broadcast Democracy: How Media Choice Increases Inequality in Political Involvement and Polarizes Elections* (New York: Cambridge University Press, 2007); Michael X. Delli Carpini and Scott Keeter, *What Americans Know About Politics and Why It Matters* (New Haven, CT: Yale University Press, 1996); Larry M. Bartels, "Partisanship and Voting Behavior, 1952–1996," *American Journal of Political Science* 44 (January 2000): 35–50.

35. Angus Campbell, Philip E. Converse, Warren E. Miller, and Donald E. Stokes, *The American Voter* (New York: John Wiley, 1960); Sidney Verba, Kay Lehman Schlozman, and Henry E. Brady, *Voice and Equality* (Cambridge, MA: Harvard University Press, 1995); Elizabeth Theiss-Morse, "Conceptualizations of Good Citizenship and Political Participation," *Political Behavior* 15 (December 1993): 355–380.

36. Alan S. Gerber, Donald P. Green, and Christopher W. Larimer, "Social Pressure and Voter Turnout: Evidence From a Large-Scale Field Experiment," *American Political Science Review* 102 (February 2008): 33–48.

37. Robert M. Bond, Christopher J. Fariss, Jason J. Jones, Adam D. I. Kramer, Cameron Marlow, Jaime E. Settle, and James H. Fowler, "A 61-Million-Person Experiment in Social Influence and Political Mobilization," *Nature* 489: 295–298.

38. James H. Fowler, Laura A. Baker, and Christopher T. Dawes, "Genetic Variation in Political Participation," *American Political Science Review* 102 (May 2008): 233–248; Christopher T. Dawes and James H. Fowler, "Partisanship, Voting, and the Dopamine D2 Receptor Gene," *Journal of Politics* 71 (July 2009): 1157–1171; Robert Klemmensen, Peter K. Hatemi, Sara Binzer Hobolt, Inge Petersen, Axel Skytthe, and Asbjørn S. Nørgaard, "The Genetics of Political Participation, Civic Duty, and Political Efficacy Across Cultures: Denmark and the United States," *Journal of Theoretical Politics* 24 (June 2012): 409–427; Robert Klemmensen, Peter K. Hatemi, Sara Binzer Hobolt, Inge Petersen, Axel Skytthe, and Asbjørn S. Nørgaard, "Heritability in Political Interest and Efficacy Across Cultures: Denmark and the United States," *Twin Research and Human Genetics* 15, no. 1 (2012): 15–20.

39. The estimates of the percentages of those who never vote, the constant voters, and the transient voters come from Adam Berinsky, Nancy Burns, and Michael W. Traugott, "Who Votes by Mail? A Dynamic Model of the Individual-Level Consequences of Vote-by-Mail Systems," *Public Opinion Quarterly* 65 (June 2001): 178–197. See also Berinsky, "Perverse Consequences of Electoral Reform in the United States."

40. See, for example, Alan S. Gerber and Donald P. Green, "The Effects of Canvassing, Telephone Calls, and Direct Mail on Voter Turnout: A Field Experiment," *American Political Science Review* 94 (September 2000): 353–363; Donald P. Green, Alan S. Gerber, and David W. Nickerson, "Getting Out the Vote in Local Elections: Results From Six Door-to-Door Canvassing Experiments," *Journal of Politics* 65 (November 2003): 1083–1096; Alan S. Gerber, Donald P. Green, and Christopher W. Larimer, "An Experiment Testing the Relative Effectiveness of Encouraging Voter Participation by Inducing Feelings of Pride or Shame," *Political Behavior* 32 (September 2010): 409–422; Kevin Arceneaux and David W. Nickerson, "Who Is

Mobilized to Vote? A Re-analysis of 11 Field Experiments," *American Journal of Political Science* 53 (January 2009): 1–16; David W. Nickerson, "Quality Is Job One: Professional and Volunteer Voter Mobilization Calls," *American Journal of Political Science* 51 (April 2007): 269–282.

41. Robert B. Cialdini and M. R. Trost, "Social Influence: Social Norms, Conformity, and Compliance," in *The Handbook of Social Psychology*, 4th ed., vol. 2, eds. D. T. Gilbert, Susan T. Fiske, and G. Lindzey (Boston: McGraw-Hill, 1998), 151–192; Robert B. Cialdini and Noah J. Goldstein, "Social Influence: Compliance and Conformity," *Annual Review of Psychology* 55 (2004): 591–621.

42. Shang E. Ha and Dean S. Karlan, "Get-Out-the-Vote Phone Calls: Does Quality Matter?," *American Politics Research* 37 (March 2009): 353–369; Nickerson, "Quality Is Job One."

43. Charles Duhigg, "Campaigns Mine Personal Lives to Get Out Vote," *New York Times*, October 14, 2012, A1.

44. "Messina and Zeleny Discuss 2021 Presidential Campaign," Peter J. Hoagland Integrity in Public Service Lecture at the University of Nebraska–Lincoln, April 5, 2013, YouTube video posted April 10, 2013, accessed June 29, 2021, http://www.youtube.com/watch?v=N122vHLO03E; see also Sasha Issenberg, "When It Comes to Targeting and Persuading Voters, the Obama Campaign Has a Massive, Insurmountable Advantage," Slate, October 29, 2012, http://www.slate.com/articles/news_and_politics/victory_lab/2012/10/obama_s_secret_weapon_democrats_have_a_massive_advantage_in_targeting_and.html.

45. Joshua Darr, "Where Clinton Is Setting Up Field Offices—and Where Trump Isn't," *FiveThirtyEight* (blog), October 7, 2016, https://fivethirtyeight.com/features/trump-clinton-field-offices/; Susan Milligan, "The Fight on the Ground," *U.S. News and World Report*, October 14, 2016, https://www.usnews.com/news/the-report/articles/2016-10-14/donald-trump-abandons-the-ground-game.

46. Sean Sullivan, Michelle Ye Hee Lee, Anu Narayanswamy, and Josh Dawsey, "Trump Aims for Adulation. Biden Goes Virtual. The Two Presidential Candidates Are Running Vastly Different Campaigns as Election Day Nears," *Washington Post*, October 21, 2020, https://www.washingtonpost.com/politics/trump-biden-rallies-spending/2020/10/21/474d7738-13d9-11eb-bc10-40b25382f1be_story.html.

47. Arceneaux and Nickerson, "Who Is Mobilized to Vote?"

48. Larry M. Bartels and Lynn Vavreck, "Meet the Undecideds," *Campaign Stops* (blog), *New York Times*, July 30, 2012, http://campaignstops.blogs.nytimes.com/2012/07/30/meet-the-undecided/.

49. Luciano Arcuri, Luigi Castelli, Silvia Galdi, Cristina Zogmaister, and Alessandro Amadori, "Predicting the Vote: Implicit Attitudes as Predictors

of the Future Behavior of Decided and Undecided Voters," *Political Psychology* 29 (June 2008): 369–387; but see Malte Friese, Colin Tucker Smith, Thomas Plischke, Matthias Bluemke, and Brian A. Nosek, "Do Implicit Attitudes Predict Actual Voting Behavior Particularly for Undecided Voters?," *PLoS ONE* 7 (August 2012): e44130. doi:10.1371/journal.pone.0044130.

50. Nate Silver, "The Invisible Undecided Voter," *FiveThirtyEight* (blog), January 23, 2017, http://fivethirtyeight.com/features/the-invisible-undecided-voter/.

51. John R. Hibbing and Elizabeth Theiss-Morse, *Stealth Democracy* (New York: Cambridge University Press, 2002), 127.

52. E. J. Dionne Jr., "The Intensity Gap," *Washington Post*, October 26, 2004, A25.

4

UNCONVENTIONAL PARTICIPATION AND SOCIAL IDENTITY

VOTING AND PARTICIPATING MORE ACTIVELY IN CAMPAIGNS are attempts to influence political outcomes through institutional channels. Whom voters elect to office matters because these elected representatives not only directly make laws that affect everyone, including people who didn't vote; they also have a large say both in who sits on the courts and in who works in the bureaucratic agencies that make the rules and decisions that affect people's everyday lives. Working through institutional channels, however, rests on the assumption that there is a cycling through of winners and losers, and that if one loses an election this time around, there is a good chance of winning in the next election or the election after that.[1] A person might lose at $Time_1$ but hold the expectation of winning at $Time_2$ or $Time_3$. If people believe their voice will be heard at some not-too-distant point, then voting, participating in campaigns, and writing letters to elected officials make a great deal of sense. What happens, though, when people keep losing or the gains made year after year are so small that it begins to feel as if nothing is going to change?

This question is especially pertinent for groups in the United States that are always in the political minority, especially people of color. The reciprocity of winning and losing can appear to be a pipe dream if the majority whites always get their way and people of color rarely do. When voting and other types of conventional participation don't seem to have any effect, groups often turn to unconventional participation. The civil rights movement used protests, marches, and civil disobedience to force the majority to take notice of the injustices experienced by Black people in America. Protests against the killing of Black people by police officers, which had been getting some press coverage in recent years, erupted in the summer of 2020 after the murder of George Floyd by a Minneapolis police officer.

Many Americans felt that this egregious murder was the last straw and that police departments and cities across the country had to change.

The use of protests by people who feel they do not have a voice and who want to push openly for change is a common occurrence in American politics. In 2006, after the U.S. House of Representatives passed legislation to restrict immigration, numerous protests were held across the country to express outrage over the legislation, culminating on May 1 when over two million people marched in over 150 U.S. towns and cities. Some demonstrations were held during the workweek to show the impact on businesses of a "Day Without Immigrants."[2] On January 21, 2017, approximately five million people participated in Women's Marches held in over 650 localities across the United States, including an estimated half a million people who marched in the Women's March on Washington, DC. These protesters were showing their support for women's rights and their opposition to Donald Trump's election to office given the disparaging comments he made toward women during his campaign and earlier in his public life.[3] And in a "National Day of Action and Healing" on March 27, 2021, thousands of protesters took to the streets across the country to protest the increase in violence against Asian Americans after six women of Asian descent were killed in a mass shooting in Atlanta. Violent attacks against Asian Americans had been increasing over the previous year, prompting many Asian Americans to decry the stereotyping of and violence toward people of Asian descent in the United States.[4]

We address in this chapter political participation that takes place outside of institutional channels, what is known as unconventional participation. While only a small portion of the U.S. population gets involved in protests, demonstrations, marches, and riots, these events get a lot of media attention, and people can feel that they have a voice that has been denied to them through institutional channels. To get a handle on unconventional participation, we look more closely at social groups and group identities. Voting or putting a candidate's sign in one's yard is relatively easy and does not demand much time or effort. Attending a rally, protesting, or joining a social movement demands more from participants. Connecting one's behavior to a broader social goal and having people in one's social network who support and even join the effort can significantly increase the likelihood of joining a rally, boycotting a business, and traveling to Washington, DC, to participate in a march. Understanding the role social context plays in how people think and act when it comes to politics is essential for understanding political behavior. We end the chapter by looking at Americans' support for the use of violence to pursue political goals.

Learning objectives for Chapter 4 include:

- Understanding what unconventional participation is and who participates in this way

- Being able to explain what increases the likelihood of participating in protests even if free riding is the easier route

- Exploring the increase in support for using political violence
- Examining how unconventional participation and political violence fit within a democratic political system

UNCONVENTIONAL PARTICIPATION

In Chapter 3, we focused on participation in elections (such as voting or working on campaigns). These conventional, or institutional, forms of participation are widely accepted as legitimate and encouraged as fundamental to good citizenship. Focusing on conventional participation, however, misses all of the political actions that take place outside the normal, institutional channels of politics. Key social movements have transformed American politics and culture, and unconventional activities, such as petitions, protests, civil disobedience, occupying buildings, and even violence, have been used by activists to bring attention to issues and to sway public opinion.[5] It is hard to imagine the leaders of the civil rights movement, for example, simply asking their followers to vote or to donate money to a campaign. The problems faced by Black people in mid-twentieth-century America included widespread and successful efforts to keep them from voting. Encouraging voting wouldn't solve the problem. Other groups that make up a political minority face problems being heard when the reciprocity of winning and losing never happens. Taking strong action and trying to project strength in numbers can help groups move their agendas forward.

Unfortunately, there is much less data on unconventional participation than conventional participation. Everyone knows when the next election for national office will take place in the United States, and surveys can easily be put in the field to measure voting behavior. We can't be certain when the next protest or occupation of a building will happen. Issues also arise when surveys include questions on people's involvement in unconventional activities. It's easy to ask people if they voted in the last election. It is trickier figuring out how to ask about unconventional activities, especially since some of them happen out of public view.[6] Should the time frame of the activity be short, such as protesting in the past year, or should it be open ended, implying protesting at any time in one's life? Social desirability can also affect results. When asked about voting, people know they should vote, so they are inclined to say they have voted even if they haven't. When asked about unconventional activities, though, the opposite problem can occur. Americans tend to be less approving of unconventional activities, especially those that are illegal or involve violence, so respondents might be inclined to say they haven't participated in certain ways even if they have. On top of all of this, there tend to be few people who have taken more extreme actions, meaning that asking a random sample of people if they have engaged in certain activities will lead to very few yes responses. It is difficult to analyze a very small number of cases in a survey.

In the 1970s, researchers fielded a set of surveys, called the Political Action surveys, in eight countries that asked a large battery of questions on unconventional participation.[7] The U.S. portion of the survey was administered in 1974. We will examine more recent data from the American National Election Studies (ANES) and the World Values Survey (WVS), but these older data include a much broader array of activities and reveal not only how often they are used but also how acceptable they are to the public. Respondents were asked, for each activity, if they had actually done it in the past ten years, if they would do it if it were important to them, if they might do it in a particular situation, or if they would never do it under any circumstances. Figure 4-1 shows the results. In 1974, the survey respondents readily admitted to having signed a petition. Many fewer said they had attended a lawful demonstration or joined in a boycott (12 percent and 16 percent, respectively), but a large proportion said they either would do it or might do it if given the opportunity. Only about a third said they would never do any of these activities. Each of the remaining activities has had fewer participants (only between 1 and 2 percent), and the number of people who adamantly say they would never do it under any circumstances increases dramatically, from two-thirds (for refusing to pay rent or taxes and joining in a wildcat strike) to over 90 percent (for painting slogans on walls, using personal violence, and damaging property). The more damage done by the activity (to person or property), and therefore the more illegal the activity, the less likely people are to admit having done it, and the less willing they are to entertain the possibility of taking part in it. Not surprisingly, when asked the extent to which they approved or disapproved of each of these activities, respondents overwhelmingly said they strongly disapproved of the more aggressive activities (data not shown).

The year 1974 came a long time ago, at the end of the civil rights and Vietnam War eras. While more recent surveys do not ask about the same range of activities as the Political Action survey, we can get a sense of Americans' more recent involvement in some of these activities. The ANES asked respondents in 2020 if, during the past twelve months, they had signed a petition on the internet or on paper about a political or social issue and if they had joined a march, rally, or demonstration. The response options were *yes* and *no*. Respondents were also asked how often, in the past twelve months, they had "either bought or declined to buy a certain product or service because of the social or political values of the company that provides it." Response options ranged from *never* to *all the time*, but we focus on those who answered *most of the time* or *all the time*. The WVS asked about these same activities in 2017, but there are two big differences with this survey. First, the response options are more similar to those of the Political Action survey: *have actually done*, *might do*, and *would never do it under any circumstance*. Second, unlike the ANES survey that puts a time limit on the activity (in the past twelve months), the WVS includes no time frame. Respondents could therefore answer the question thinking about their whole lifetime.

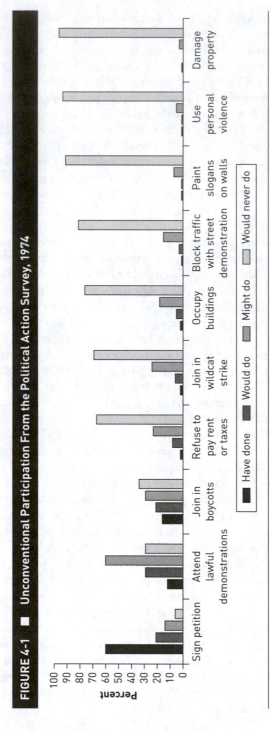

FIGURE 4-1 ■ Unconventional Participation From the Political Action Survey, 1974

Legend: Have done | Would do | Might do | Would never do

Categories: Sign petition | Attend lawful demonstrations | Join in boycotts | Refuse to pay rent or taxes | Join in wildcat strike | Occupy buildings | Block traffic with street demonstration | Paint slogans on walls | Use personal violence | Damage property

Percent (y-axis): 0, 10, 20, 30, 40, 50, 60, 70, 80, 90, 100

Source: Samuel H. Barnes and Max Kaase, et al., "Political Action: An Eight Nation Study, 1973–1976" [ICPSR 7777], Inter-university Consortium for Political and Social Research, available at http://web.stanford.edu/group/ssds/dewidocs/icpsr7777/cb7777.all.pdf.

The data in Table 4-1 that can most easily be compared to the 1974 data are from the WVS. There has been a slight increase (of 4 to 5 percentage points) in the number of people who say they have boycotted a product or business or participated in a protest or demonstration, and the number of petition signers has remained steady. The ANES asks specifically about the previous twelve months, so not surprisingly, the number of participants tends to be lower than for the WVS. Interestingly, the activity over which people have the most personal control—each individual can decide whether to boycott a company or product regardless of what anyone else does—is the least affected by the time frame. The activities that depend on others, protesting and signing petitions, have much lower numbers in the ANES than in the WVS.

In a 2020 survey of adults in the swing states of Wisconsin, Pennsylvania, Michigan, and North Carolina, 32 percent of people had boycotted products or businesses for expressly political reasons while 27 percent had purchased particular products for political reasons. A 2018 survey of adults in the same states, taken prior to the decrease in in-person participation caused by the COVID-19 pandemic, 20 percent indicated having participated in a political protest in the past year.[8]

We take a closer look at people who say they have joined in a protest, march, or demonstration, again drawing on the ANES and WVS data, to determine who has protested and who is likely to protest in the future. Table 4-2 shows the results broken down by demographic categories. Some of the demographic results stand out. First, protesters overall are not more likely to be overrepresented by

TABLE 4-1 ■ Recent Unconventional Participation, WVS (2017) and ANES (2020)			
	Sign a petition	Boycott product or business	Protest, march, or demonstrate
WVS			
Have done	60%	21%	17%
Might do	31	48	55
Would never do	9	31	28
ANES			
Yes	27%	22%	10%
No	73	78	90

Source: 2020 American National Election Studies, available at www.electionstudies.org; 2017 World Values Survey, available at https://www.worldvaluessurvey.org/wvs.jsp.

TABLE 4-2 ■ Who Protests? WVS (2017) and ANES (2020)				
	WVS			ANES
	Have protested	Might protest	Would never protest	Protested in past 12 months
Sex				
Male	20%	55%	25%	9%
Female	14	56	30	10
Race				
White, non-Hispanic	17	56	27	10
Black	14	62	25	8
Hispanic	17	49	35	10
Asian/Pacific Islander				12
Native American				11
Mixed races	21	49	30	15
Age				
18–29	14	61	25	16
30–64	17	55	28	8
65 and older	19	51	30	6
Education				
Less than college degree	11	55	34	7
College degree or higher	29	56	15	14
Income				
Low	15	54	31	9
Medium	14	58	28	9
High	24	55	21	12
Location of residence				
Rural area	12	61	27	6
Small town				8

	WVS			ANES
	Have protested	**Might protest**	**Would never protest**	**Protested in past 12 months**
Suburb				9
City	18	55	28	14
Party identification				
Democrats and leaners	25	56	20	14
Independents	14	54	32	6
Republicans and leaners	9	57	33	6
Ideology				
Liberals	30	55	16	20
Moderates	11	55	33	6
Conservatives	10	58	32	6

Source: 2020 American National Election Studies, available at www.electionstudies.org; 2017 World Values Survey, available at https://www.worldvaluessurvey.org/wvs.jsp.

any given sex or race. In contrast, people who have protested in the past year are much more likely to be young (16 percent of those younger than thirty compared to only 6 percent of those sixty-five and older), although older people are more likely to have protested in their lifetime. This result isn't surprising since older people would have had more opportunities to protest over their lifetimes compared to younger people, and younger people are more likely to say they might protest than older people if given the opportunity. Education is also a significant predictor of protest. Those with a college education are much more likely to have protested. The opportunity to protest is likely higher among those attending college, especially given the social support networks college students have and the likely increased awareness that a protest will take place among this cohort. In terms of opportunity, living in a city and having a higher household income increase the likelihood of protesting, whereas living in a rural area or being poor makes it less likely that protest opportunities will arise. Whereas few rural people have protested, compared to urban dwellers, they are much more likely to say they might. The swing state survey found similar results, with the lion's share of people attending Black Lives Matter (BLM) protests coming from urban centers. Being poor, on the other hand, has a depressive effect on actual behavior and does not appear to be related to the willingness to protest.

Protesters differ from nonprotesters most strikingly in their political views. Democrats and especially liberals are much more likely to have protested in the last year and in their lifetime compared to Republicans and conservatives. This is partly due to the issue goals of protests over the years. Liberals have been more likely to turn to protests surrounding such issues as civil rights and opposing wars. Conservatives, however, have held many antiabortion marches, and Donald Trump was able to garner large turnout at his rallies. Interestingly, the higher protest rates of Democrats and liberals hold in rural areas as well. Over twice as many rural liberals (12 percent) as rural conservatives (5 percent) joined in a rally or demonstration over the past year. But it is urban liberals who participate at the highest rate (27 percent of urban liberals compared to only 8 percent of urban conservatives). Size of place matters for the opportunity to protest, but political beliefs also have a significant impact on this type of political behavior.

EXPLAINING UNCONVENTIONAL PARTICIPATION

Voting is a comparatively easy form of political participation. The costs associated with voting are relatively low, involving the time it takes to become informed and to get to the polling place (or to drop off one's absentee or mail ballot) along with the cost of gas or public transportation and perhaps child care. If there are long lines at the polls or if one's job makes it difficult to get away from work, the costs increase, but in general, voting is a relatively low-cost form of participation. Other types of participation, such as volunteering for a campaign or writing a letter to the editor in support of a candidate, take more time, and the participant has to be highly motivated to participate. It's no surprise that many more people vote than get more actively involved in campaigns. When it comes to unconventional participation, though, there is an even higher cost than extensive time and effort: both social disapproval and risks are likely to be higher for unconventional than for conventional participation. We discussed earlier the Political Action survey in which respondents indicated much higher disapproval of more extreme forms of unconventional participation. In addition, people involved in protests and civil disobedience know, based on historical events, that even peaceful protests can turn violent or prompt law enforcement to arrest participants.

Protests, rallies, and acts of civil disobedience are therefore potentially highly costly, and the likelihood of any one event succeeding in obtaining a group's goals is uncertain at best. Even if the group obtains its goal, say a more just policy, it is a collective outcome shared by everyone in the society, not just those who worked to get the policy passed. Mancur Olson argued that it is perfectly rational for people to be free riders, even when they very much want the shared outcome. If individuals participate, they incur high costs, whereas if they do not participate, they incur no costs. Since the positive outcome is shared by everyone, the inactive individual gains the benefits (the more just policy) and hasn't had to bear any costs. It is rational, then, not to participate. However, if everyone behaves rationally, then everyone free rides, and the preferred outcome will not be achieved.[9] The resulting outcome, in this instance the continuation of an injustice, is what the potential participants do not want, yet it is what they get.

But people do get involved in unconventional activities, sometimes a lot of people. For unconventional participation to happen, especially given the high costs associated with participating, certain factors need to fit into place. We focus on protest behavior (which includes protests, marches, demonstrations, and riots) and look at three major factors that explain this type of unconventional behavior: opportunities, recruitment, and motivation.

Opportunities

If people care deeply about an issue, they are likely to get involved in a political activity if there are opportunities to do so. The opportunity to protest, however, tends to be low. This type of participation is called "unconventional" because it is just that, unconventional. It is not the normal, conventional way that people participate in politics. Unlike voting or participating through institutional channels, such as working on a campaign or donating money to a candidate, protests and demonstrations occur erratically, and there is not a set place or time to participate. People might not be aware of an event in their area until it is too late, or a protest on an issue salient to a person might not take place nearby. Another defining feature of protest events is that they involve more than one person. That is, it is a social group event. While one individual might care a great deal about an issue and want to protest, it doesn't really work if no one else is protesting. For most people most of the time, the opportunity to engage in unconventional participation does not arise, either because the necessary mass of people isn't gathering or because the protest takes place far away or without people being aware. It is important, therefore, to take into account the opportunities associated with unconventional participation to understand the context within which this type of participation occurs.

In general, the more heavily populated the state, the more opportunities there are to participate in protests or riots. The Armed Conflict Location & Event Data Project (ACLED) defines protests as being peaceful and riots as involving disruption and violence. Using ACLED data, Figure 4-2 shows the number of protests and riots in the United States from January 1, 2020, to the end of March 2021.[10] In January 2020, there were 1,144 protests and riots across the United States. People living in California during that month could have participated in any one of 170 protests or riots. On January 4, for example, Californians could have attended 1 of 10 protests in support of or condemning the killing of Iranian general Qassem Soleimani, or they could have joined with a couple dozen people gathered in American Canyon to protest the eviction notices of low-income mobile-home owners. In contrast, people living in North Dakota in that same month had no protests or riots occur in their state. North Dakotans would have had to wait until February 14, 2020, for a protest held in Fargo by the Missing and Murdered Indigenous Women Task Force to raise awareness of missing and murdered Native American women and girls.

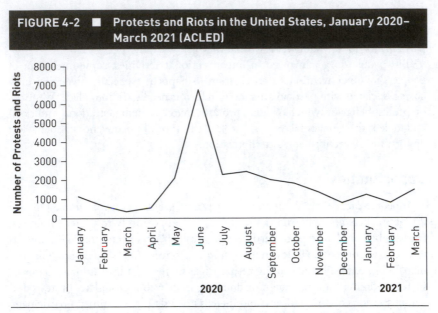

Source: Armed Conflict Location & Event Data Project (ACLED), available at https://www.acleddata.com.

The outcry over the murder of George Floyd by Minneapolis police officer Derek Chauvin changed the protest landscape dramatically. Floyd was killed on May 25, 2020, and in the few days remaining in that month, over 1,000 protests were held across the United States. In June 2020, there were a whopping 6,753 protests and riots. Every state experienced a large increase: North Dakota went from having 0 in January to 15 in June, Oklahoma increased from 7 to 73, and California jumped from 170 to 737. Whereas the opportunity to protest was spotty in January 2020, by June protests were happening across the United States.

Just as living in a more populous state increases the opportunity to participate in a protest or rally, so does living in a city. We showed in Table 4-2 the impact of location of residence on whether people said they had joined a protest, march, rally, or demonstration in the past twelve months.[11] Under 6 percent of respondents living in rural areas had participated in a protest or rally compared to just under 14 percent for city dwellers. Living in a city simply gives one more opportunity to participate unconventionally. The protests that took place in June 2020, however, were widespread. Looking just at the two states in which the authors of this book reside, Nebraska had 44 protests or riots in that month. The two largest cities in the state, Omaha and Lincoln, had 12 and 17 protests, respectively, but protests occurred across the state from Auburn to Sidney. Wisconsin saw an even greater dispersal of protests, with the two largest cities, Milwaukee and Madison, accounting for only 26 and 19 of the total 164 protests, respectively.

June stands out in Figure 4-2 as a high protest month, but Americans remained unsettled throughout the summer of 2020. Almost all of the protests or riots from the end of May through late summer included BLM as one of the main groups of participants.[12] ANES respondents were asked how warm or cold they felt toward various groups, including BLM. Those who had attended a protest or similar event in the past twelve months felt warmer toward BLM (a mean of 71 degrees on a 101-point scale) compared to those who had not attended a protest (a mean of 53 degrees). Looked at in a different way, 16 percent of those who felt warm toward BLM said they had participated in a protest whereas only 6 percent of those who felt cold toward BLM had protested.

In the lead-up to and after the 2020 elections, there was a significant shift in the focus of the protests and riots. BLM protests continued, although in much smaller numbers, but there were more protests focused on frustration with COVID-19 measures and concerns about the election (from both sides). The most significant event was Trump's "Save America" rally followed by the storming of the U.S. Capitol on January 6, 2021, when Congress was in session to certify the Electoral College results. The size of the crowd was somewhat large—estimated in the thousands to tens of thousands—but the acts of breaking into the Capitol building, destroying property, and threatening the lives of the elected representatives in the building at the time, along with the delay of the certification process and the deaths of a participant and police officers, made it an event that few Americans will forget. In terms of obstacles and costs, people from around the country had to travel to Washington, DC, pay for someplace to stay and for meals, and take the time off of work to make the trip. Some participants lost their jobs after being seen on social media. Still others are facing court cases and time in jail.

If we look at only the opportunities, costs, and benefits of unconventional participation, it seems unlikely that anyone would participate in this way. The opportunities are scattered and uneven, the costs (especially if violence occurs) are high, and the benefits for any single individual are small. Whether a given individual participates or not is unlikely to affect the outcome and bring the protesters closer to their goal. Focusing solely on the individual and on the costs and benefits of unconventional participation cannot explain this behavior. To get a better sense of what is going on, we turn to the influence of groups.

Recruitment and Social Networks

Social groups have a pronounced impact on individual attitudes and behavior. Some of this impact occurs directly through face-to-face interactions with primary groups, such as family, friends, and coworkers. Social networks are the people with whom one interacts either face-to-face or via social media, and these social networks affect our political attitudes and behaviors in important ways. Social groups can have an impact in less direct ways as well, especially when secondary groups are involved. Secondary groups are those organizations or collections of individuals with which one identifies, or is identified, that have some common interest or goal instead of personal contact as their major basis. We focus in this section on social networks and look more closely at large social groups in the next section.

People tend to have social networks that are politically homogeneous and that reinforce their political views. Democrats rarely have Republican discussion partners (only 16 percent of all discussion partners), and Republicans are reluctant to have Democratic discussion partners (only 22 percent of all discussion partners).[13] Where one lives affects the likelihood of having talk partners who identify with the other party. In the swing state of Wisconsin, people living in the liberal city of Madison were more likely to have Democratic Party talk partners while those living in rural Wisconsin were less likely to have Democratic Party political discussants. Interestingly, the rate at which having a talk partner in the other party declines at different rates depending on geography. Republicans living in liberal areas that were also urban centers had a more rapid decline in the likelihood of having Democratic discussion partners while Republicans living in rural areas and small towns had a slower decline in the same outcome.

Whether looking at friends or spouses, people are attracted to those who hold similar values and attitudes, including about politics. The tendency of people not to like conflict or disagreement increases the likelihood that friends will hold the same views, or that they will not talk politics when they disagree. Groups of coworkers appear to be somewhat more mixed politically. Workplace groups are formed with a task-oriented goal as the key, leading coworkers to be more diverse in their political leanings but also less likely to talk politics.[14]

Social networks are particularly important in explaining political behavior because of the role they play in recruitment. Sidney Verba, Kay Lehman Schlozman, and Henry Brady raise the important point that if people are asked to participate in a political activity, they are likely to say yes. They found that about half of their respondents had been asked to participate in a political activity, and about half of those asked said yes.[15] Recruitment works for several reasons. People like to feel wanted. They also might not be aware that an opportunity to participate is available, so being asked to participate lets them know of the opportunity. Finally, participating in the activity with friends, family members, or coworkers could make participating more fun. Of course, people who have larger social networks are more likely to be asked. The more people a person interacts with on a daily basis, the more likely it is that the person will learn about a political event and be recruited by one of the discussion partners. These recruitment efforts can be as simple as having a friend say, "Hey, are you going to the protest today? You should. It'll be fun." Even seeing a friend or relative involved in a political activity can increase participation. For example, people who see in their Facebook newsfeed that their friends have voted are more likely to vote themselves.[16]

Social networks play an especially important role when it comes to participating in social movements and unconventional activities. Getting a large group of people to attend a rally or demonstration is much easier with the rise of social media. An Instagram feed urging people to meet at a certain place at a certain time to oppose a recent governmental action or to support a candidate for office can generate enough enthusiasm and participation to make it onto the local or national news, thereby giving the movement an even stronger following. The BLM protests attracted a great deal of media attention, as did the various rallies Trump held in key spots around the United States. Organizers and participants used Twitter, Facebook, Instagram, and other social media to spread the word about all of these rallies and protests, increasing the number of people who participated.

In 2014, the International Social Survey Programme (ISSP) asked a sample of Americans how many people they had contact with on a typical weekday. The respondents were also asked if they had been involved in a variety of political activities in the past year, including unconventional activities. Figure 4-3 shows the relationship between social network size and participation rates. We include voting as a highly institutionalized activity that is done regularly and publicized heavily in the media. When everyone knows when the election will be held and get-out-the-vote (GOTV) campaigns work to ensure that people get to the polls, it is perhaps not surprising that voting is not strongly related to social network size. People who have very few discussion partners are no more or less likely to vote than people who have over fifty discussion partners. All of the unconventional activities, on the other hand, are significantly affected by social network size. The larger the social network, the more likely people are to sign a petition, boycott a product or business, or join a demonstration. The bottom line is that people who are socially engaged are more likely to hear about and be asked to participate in activities that are not standard activities like voting. This is true even when discussions with others are not focused on politics.

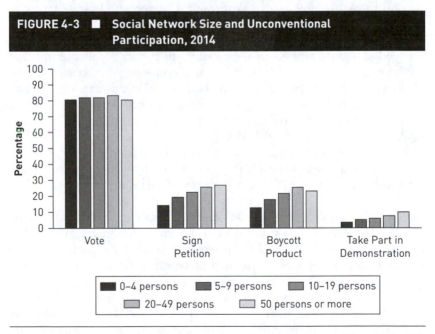

FIGURE 4-3 ■   Social Network Size and Unconventional Participation, 2014

Source: ISSP Research Group (2016): International Social Survey Programme: Citizenship II—ISSP 2014. GESIS Data Archive, Cologne. ZA6670 Data file Version 2.0.0, doi:10.4232/1.12590, U.S. sample.

Motivation and Social Group Identity

Not all groups that influence behavior involve direct communication. Large social groups matter as well. Research on social identity has found that when people feel like part of a group—feeling attached to the group, thinking of themselves as members of the group, and evaluating the group as a positive part of who they are—they shift their behavior and attitudes in ways that help out the group.[17] Henri Tajfel and many other researchers have shown that simply being a member of a group leads participants to discriminate in favor of their in-group and to do what they can to benefit the group, even at personal expense.[18] People who identify strongly with their race or ethnicity, gender, profession, sports team, religion, political party, or nation, just to take a few examples, are deeply influenced by that group attachment.

Everyone is born into certain ascriptive groups, such as race and sex, and categorized based on their visually distinguishable traits. Individuals are also categorized into groups based on their preferences and beliefs. While people often assume that those who share the group's characteristics identify strongly with the group, the fact is that the strength of people's group identities varies.[19] In addition, context matters. For example, some women might strongly identify with women, and this social identity will always be a major influence on their perceptions and behaviors. For others, whether the identity is salient might depend on context. A woman might not identify very strongly as a woman in general, but when she is the only female in a meeting, that identity might take on added significance. One study showed that women in rural Texas who favored Hillary Clinton engaged in secret meetings to discuss politics. Living with what Emily Van Duyn called "networked silence," people were silent about their politics in public settings and met secretly to express their views.[20] At times, people might reject an ascriptive identity depending on the context. People born in the United States are American citizens and part of that national group, but if the United States does something that people find objectionable, they might reject their American identity and hold, instead, their state or a global identity.

In contrast to ascriptive groups, voluntary groups tend to yield strong identities. People can choose to be a Minnesota Vikings football fan or not. Those who stick with the team, through years of heartache, are strong identifiers, whereas those who shift their support to the Green Bay Packers or the New England Patriots, depending on the chances of winning the Super Bowl, are much weaker identifiers. Within the realm of politics, children might learn their parents' party identification, if the parents are politically engaged, but most people do not form a stable, crystalized party identification until they are in their early thirties.[21] They choose which party to identify with depending on a host of factors, including what they learned from their parents but also which policy beliefs they hold, what they think of recent presidents, and what they hear from friends and coworkers. We will have much more to say about party identification in Chapter 5, but the same social group dynamics are at play with this voluntary group membership.

Most important for our purposes is that group identity is related to group attitudes and behaviors. Loving one's in-group does not necessarily mean hating the out-group, but it does mean that people will prioritize their in-group's well-being and view the in-group members more positively.[22] The more strongly people identify with a group, the more they cooperate with fellow members, and the more active and participatory they are on behalf of helping the group attain its goals. The successes of the in-group and the accomplishment of its goals take on personal importance for the strong identifier, and doing what is necessary to ensure those successes is an important part of feeling like one of the group.[23] On the flip side, when the in-group experiences a loss or is treated unjustly, strong identifiers' reactions are personal and often not only psychological but also physiological. The in-group's wins and losses and hurts and joys are experienced as personal.[24] What this means is that people don't have to experience an injustice personally to be motivated to do something about it. For strong identifiers, seeing injustices occur against any group member becomes a catalyst for action.

This collective impact of in-group experiences is important for understanding political behavior and what motivates people to overcome the collective action dilemma described by Mancur Olson. Why are some people willing to shoulder steep costs when their own individual gain is likely to be small? Why don't they just free ride and hope for the best? There must be something motivating them to bear the high costs of unconventional participation, and that something, according to Bert Klandermans and his colleagues, is social identity.[25] Goals like social justice or racial equality or making America great again are collective goods shared by everyone, including those who contribute nothing to obtain the goal. Driven by the desire to have one's group succeed, people are willing to bear a lot of cost for the good of the group. Feeling like part of a group can also increase one's sense of efficacy, the feeling that one's actions can have a positive impact on policy. One individual might not be able to change the world, but a whole bunch of people working together can make a difference. Finally, a sense of injustice, that the group has been mistreated or harmed, can be a strong motivator for those who identify strongly with the group. When people see someone in their group hurt or treated unfairly because of membership in the group, then the injustice is experienced by everyone who shares that group identity.

Group identities are important to people. They drive, consciously or unconsciously, people's attitudes and behavior. Not all identities, however, are politically meaningful. A person can identify strongly as an artist or a Minnesota Vikings fan, for example, but identifying with these groups will not affect one's political attitudes or behavior unless the identity becomes politicized. The more politics becomes contentious and polarized, the more likely political opinions begin playing a role in activities and behaviors that have not been previously thought of as political.[26] Feeling a strong sense of grievance and injustice on behalf of the group can be the politicizing agent.[27] Watching the video of Minneapolis police officer Derek Chauvin kneeling on George Floyd's neck for over nine minutes, especially after seeing many recent news stories about police use of force targeting people of color, was more than just an individual incident for many Black people.

It symbolized the mistreatment of Black people across American history, and this injustice motivated many to take to the streets in the summer of 2020. The pain felt in the Black community was palpable.

As happened during the civil rights movement in the 1950s and 1960s, though, it was not only racial group identity that came into play in the 2020 BLM protests. Many Americans who are not Black took to the streets in part to show their solidarity with Black people but also because another group identity was important. Many protesters argued that the murder of George Floyd, and all of the other Black people who have recently been killed by police, showcased an America that did not reflect their values or beliefs. Some of the people marching in solidarity with Black people did so because they wanted their nation, of which they are members, to head down a different path when it comes to racial equality. These people wanted to reclaim an American identity that they could respect, and they wanted to contribute to making that change.

Many Americans, especially Democrats, view race as a major issue facing the nation, and one that undermines the American value of equality. In a poll fielded in June 2020, Democrats were over 50 percentage points more likely than Republicans to agree that the criminal justice system treats whites better than Blacks, that police killings of African Americans are signs of a broader problem, that Blacks and whites are not treated equally by the police, that there is a problem with systemic racism in America, and that systemic racism in policing is a bigger problem than violence and vandalism in protests.[28] To people on the left, American history is replete with racism, and this must stop. In a different survey fielded in 2020, respondents were asked to choose between two statements: "The United States has not made nearly enough progress on racial equality since the 1960s, and our society should prioritize racial justice" or "The United States has made considerable progress on racial equality since the 1960s, and people should be patient as progress continues." Just under 70 percent of Democrats chose the first statement whereas 90 percent of Republicans chose the second.[29]

To get a better sense of the relationship between social identity, grievance, and protest behavior, we turn to the 2020 ANES data. ANES asked respondents questions about police actions, the unfair treatment of Black people, personal experiences with police and discrimination, and attitudes about a more diverse America. Unfortunately, the racial and American identity questions were not available in time for us to analyze them, but Table 4-3 shows how strongly perceptions of injustice are related to protest behavior in 2020. People who attended a protest in 2020 were much more likely than those who did not to believe that Black people were treated particularly unfairly by police and by the government and society at large. About three-quarters of protesters thought the police treated white people better than Black people and that the latter faced significant discrimination. Only about half of those who did not protest held these views.

Table 4-3 also provides evidence for the argument that, in general, it is not personal, individual experiences or self-interest that matters. Whether people had been arrested or not is unrelated to protest behavior. Police stopping and

TABLE 4-3   ■   Protest Behavior and Racial Grievance, 2020

	Have attended a protest, march, or demonstration	Have not attended a protest, march, or demonstration
Police use force more than necessary (most/all of the time)	44%	24%
Police treat whites better (moderately/much better)	77	54
Has respondent ever been arrested (have been)	20	19
Has respondent or any family member been stopped or questioned by police	22	15
Federal government treats whites better (moderately/much better)	69	39
Discrimination against Blacks (a lot/a great deal)	74	53
Respondent personally faced race discrimination (a lot/a great deal)	11	10
Respondent personally faced race discrimination (a lot/a great deal)	Whites 3 Blacks 53 Hispanics 13	Whites 3 Blacks 36 Hispanics 13
Increasing diversity makes U.S. a better place to live (a little/a lot better)	76	51

Source: 2020 American National Election Studies, available at www.electionstudies.org.

questioning the respondent or a family member of the respondent had a small impact (a 7-percentage-point difference), but the effect isn't large. Personally facing racial discrimination also did not increase the likelihood of protesting, although it is unlikely that white people who feel they have been discriminated against for their race would feel much affinity with the BLM movement. Breaking down responses to this question by race, it is clear that whether whites and Hispanics had experienced discrimination was not related at all to protest behavior. For Black people, on the other hand, it was. Over half of Black protesters said they had experienced racial discrimination compared to only a third of those who did not protest. Overall, though, it is people's beliefs that Black people as a group are treated unfairly by the police, the government, and society that set protesters apart from those who do not take to the streets.

People who participated in the BLM protests in 2020 were likely motivated by a desire to see real change in the United States, especially on race issues. One question in the ANES survey, asking if diversity makes the United States a better place to live in, gets at the idea that some protesters want their country to reflect the values they think are important. Three-quarters of protesters said diversity would make the United States a little or a lot better (the two most positive responses) compared to just half of people who did not protest. People on the left tend to identify less strongly as Americans than people on the right, and this is in part connected to their belief in constructive patriotism and the idea that the country has a lot of work left to do to achieve its laudatory goal of equality.[30]

The clash over American identity was front and center in the 2020 presidential election, as was the idea of suffering an injustice and a grievance. Donald Trump ran in 2016 under the slogan "Make America Great Again" (MAGA). In a fascinating study by Rachel Blum and Christopher Parker,[31] MAGA supporters, Trump's loyal base, expressed a high level of grievance, with over 80 percent believing that "real Americans are losing freedoms," "the American way of life is disappearing," and "forces are changing our country for the worse." They thought Trump had spent his four years as president turning things around or at least being the first president in a long time to try to slow down the terrible things they thought were happening. Trump's reelection in 2020 was therefore essential if the America they wanted was to be saved, yet almost all MAGA supporters thought the 2020 election results were fraudulent and couldn't be trusted.[32] In the 2020 swing state study referenced earlier, 30 percent of people thought that the traditional American way of life was changing so fast, force might be required to save it. Another 21 percent agreed with the idea that patriotic Americans might need to take the law into their own hands, and 30 percent believed that strong leaders might have to bend rules to get things done.

If the outcome of the election was deeply important and people believed the lie that the election was stolen, they had a strong motivation to protest. From their perspective, a democratic country must follow the will of the people, and going against the people's will by accepting fraudulent election results must not be allowed to happen in America. The injustice of losing the election when Trump so clearly won, MAGA supporters believed, must not be tolerated. With Trump and his backers rallying people to "Stop the Steal," many MAGA supporters participated in local rallies or traveled to Washington, DC, to stop Joe Biden from becoming president. They were also willing to bear substantial costs to participate in the attempted coup at the U.S. Capitol on January 6, 2021, to try to correct what they perceived to be an injustice. The fact that the injustice was based on a lie does not make the impact of group identity any less strong. Trump supporters thought they were being harmed, and they could join together as a group to insist that Trump be reinstated as president for a second term.

The ANES survey was fielded in late 2020, so the survey does not ask about the January 6 event. Fortunately, a poll fielded on January 6, 2021, can give us some insight about the storming of the U.S. Capitol. Respondents were asked, "Supporters of President Trump have stormed the U.S. Capitol to protest lawmakers certifying Joe Biden's election victory. Based on what you have read or heard about this, do you support or oppose these actions?" Ninety-six percent of Democrats and 67 percent of independents said they strongly or somewhat opposed the storming of the Capitol. Among Republicans, 43 percent opposed the actions, and among voters who thought the election was fraudulent, only 34 opposed the actions. When asked how to characterize those who stormed the Capitol, Democrats overwhelmingly said they were "extremists" (74 percent) and "domestic terrorists" (78 percent). Republicans were less likely to label them anything, but the two highest characterizations were "protestors" (50 percent) and "patriots" (30 percent).[33] Among Americans who thought the 2020 election results were fraudulent, 18 percent supported or strongly supported the storming of the Capitol, compared to only 2 percent who thought the election results were accurate.[34] Unfortunately, we do not have data on the people who actually participated in the insurrection on January 6. It is not too far a stretch, though, to guess that they strongly identified as MAGA supporters and felt highly aggrieved given the election results. Opinions about the veracity of the election were also related to other major political issues. The swing state study conducted a follow-up panel survey in the spring of 2021, finding that a belief that the election was stolen from President Trump was positively correlated with a refusal to get a COVID-19 vaccine.

THE USE OF VIOLENCE TO ACHIEVE POLITICAL ENDS

The vast majority of protests, marches, and demonstrations that occur in the United States are peaceful. For example, and contrary to the widespread narrative surrounding the BLM protests in the summer of 2020, almost all of the protests were peaceful. According to Erica Chenoweth and Jeremy Pressman, of the over seven thousand BLM protest events in the summer of 2020, only 3.7 percent involved property damage, 1.6 percent involved injury to protesters or bystanders, and 1 percent involved injury to police officers.[35] Yet Americans have persisted in believing that the protests were violent. ANES respondents were asked if the protests "during the past few months," which refers primarily to the BLM protests, had been mostly violent or mostly peaceful. About a third (31 percent) said they had been mostly violent, a third said they had been equally violent and peaceful, and another 13 percent said they had been a little more peaceful. Under a quarter (23 percent) said they were a lot more peaceful. The media overwhelmingly covered any violence to person or property that occurred, which explains public misperceptions, but the data clearly show the protests were mostly peaceful.

But incidents of political violence have increased significantly in recent years. Hate crimes increased 3 percent in 2019, with over seven thousand incidents for the third year in a row, and the attacks were more violent than usual. According to FBI data, anti-Jewish hate crimes rose 14 percent, and anti-Hispanic hate crimes rose 9 percent.[36] There was also an increase in anti-Asian hate crimes beginning with the rise of the pandemic in March 2020.[37] Perceptions of political violence reflect the actual increase in violence. Respondents to the ANES survey thought the use of violence to pursue political goals had increased over the previous four years, with almost half, 45 percent, thinking it had increased a great deal and another 31 percent thinking it had increased a little or a moderate amount. Only 3 percent thought it had decreased.

Political analysts have become increasingly concerned about Americans' acceptance of the use of violence to gain political goals. Bright Line Watch has fielded surveys several times a year since 2017 to gauge expert and public opinion about the state of democracy and democratic practices.[38] Starting in October 2020, based on questions from Nathan Kalmoe and Lilliana Mason, the Bright Line Watch respondents were asked about political violence used by their own or the opposing party. The results in Table 4-4 show that Americans in general do not think political violence is justified. When asked how often it is justified for one's

TABLE 4-4 ■ How Often Is Political Violence Justified? (2020, 2021)			
	How often do you feel it is justified for [your own party] to use violence in advancing their political goals these days?	What if the [opposing party] win[s] an election? How often is it justified to respond with violence?	If the [opposing party] engage[s] in violence during an election, how often is it justified to respond with violence?
October 2020			
Never	85	79	61
Occasionally	8	11	20
Frequently or Always	7	11	19
November 2020			
Never	88	86	66
Occasionally	7	7	18
Frequently or Always	6	7	16
January/February 2021			
Never	88	88	69
Occasionally	7	7	18
Frequently or Always	5	6	13

Source: Bright Line Watch, 2020 and 2021, "Bright Line Watch Waves 12, 13, and 14 Public Surveys," available at https://brightlinewatch.org/survey-data-and-replication-material/.

own party to use violence, almost all respondents said never, and this remained stable across the three surveys. Most people were also unwilling to entertain the use of violence if the opposing party won the election. Interestingly, fewer people thought using violence in this circumstance was never justified before the election (79 percent) than thought it was never justified after the election (86 percent in November and 88 percent in early 2021). Political violence becomes much more palatable to people when they view it as reciprocity. Only about two-thirds of respondents said violence was never justified as a response to the opposing party engaging in violence.

To get a sense of who opposes the use of political violence, we return to the ANES data. In the 2020 survey, respondents were asked, "How much do you feel it is justified for people to use violence to pursue their political goals in this country?" We focus on those who said *not at all*. Other possible responses were *a little*, *a moderate amount*, *a lot*, and *a great deal*, so anyone who did not say *not at all* was condoning some use of political violence. Figure 4-4 breaks down responses by demographic and political variables. Those who most oppose the use of political violence are whites, older people, the college educated, and conservatives. Younger people, people of color, and those who said they had attended a protest in the past twelve months were the least likely to oppose the use of violence to pursue political goals.

Most Americans do not condone the use of political violence, and as we noted earlier, most protests are peaceful in the United States. We have seen an uptick, though, in the number of people who think using violence for political gains

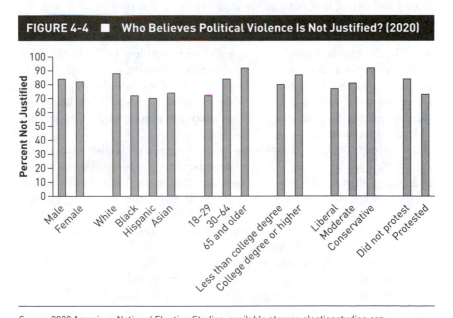

FIGURE 4-4 ■ Who Believes Political Violence Is Not Justified? (2020)

Source: 2020 American National Election Studies, available at www.electionstudies.org.

is justified. What explains the increase in political violence and its acceptance? Recent research suggests that people are more likely to endorse the use of political violence when they moralize the issue and when they think other people share their moral values on the matter.[39] Both the increased moralization of partisan differences and the widespread use of social media feeding people's politically homogeneous social networks raise the possibility that there will be more political violence in the future. The more people believe political violence is justified, the more likely they are to use it and to condone it even if they haven't been involved.

UNCONVENTIONAL PARTICIPATION AND DEMOCRACY

In Chapter 1, we discussed Americans' support for democracy and for undemocratic alternatives that might seem appealing at a time when major problems loom over the country and the world. Using violence to obtain political goals is not only illegal; it is also undemocratic. We might therefore expect to find a relationship between support for democracy and the belief that political violence is not justified. According to the ANES data, this is the case. Eighty-seven percent of people who are very satisfied with democracy think political violence is not justified, compared to 79 percent of those who say they are not at all satisfied with democracy. A better way to look at the situation, though, might be to determine if those who hold undemocratic beliefs are more likely to support the use of political violence. It does not take many people to turn a peaceful protest into violent mayhem. While the numbers are small, they are disconcerting. Among people who like the idea of having a strong leader who is willing to "bend the rules" to get things done, 7 percent believe that political violence is *always* justified. Similarly, 9 percent of people who think the will of the majority should always prevail also think political violence is *always* justified. Almost no one who opposes these approaches to government decision making is supportive of using political violence to get one's way.

In contrast, the U.S. Constitution protects Americans' right to free speech and assembly. People can sign petitions, boycott products and businesses, and engage in peaceful protests, marches, and demonstrations as much as they want. People who have been marginalized in the American political system—political minorities for whom the reciprocity of winning and losing hasn't been real—and their political allies have been the most likely to get involved in peaceful unconventional activities. Their efforts have led to meaningful change in the American political system. Conventional participation, including voting, has a major impact on political outcomes, but unconventional participation can give voice to those who have historically been kept silent.

Study Questions

1. Why are some people more likely to engage in unconventional participation than others?

2. How would you weigh the factors that influence unconventional participation? Do opportunities, recruitment, or group identities and grievances have the biggest impact on whether people protest?

3. The vast majority of Americans do not think political violence is ever justified, but there has been an increase in support for political violence in recent years. Why?

4. Is unconventional participation good or bad for democracy?

Suggested Readings

Barnes, Samuel H., Max Kaase, et al. *Political Action: Mass Participation in Five Western Democracies*. Beverly Hills, CA: SAGE, 1979. A classic in the study of participation, and especially unconventional participation, from a comparative perspective.

Gillion, Daniel. *The Loud Minority: Why Protests Matter in American Democracy*. Princeton, NJ: Princeton University Press, 2020. Innovative look at the impact of protests on electoral politics.

Hibbing, John R. *The Securitarian Personality: What Really Motivates Trump's Base and Why It Matters for the Post-Trump Era*. Oxford: Oxford University Press, 2020. An in-depth look at Donald Trump's most loyal base.

Ransby, Barbara. *Making All Black Lives Matter: Reimagining Freedom in the 21st Century*. Berkeley: University of California Press, 2018. A powerful look at the Black Lives Matter movement and the tactics it has used to push for systemic change in America.

Theiss-Morse, Elizabeth. *Who Counts as an American? The Boundaries of National Identity*. New York: Cambridge University Press, 2009. An examination of the dynamics of American identity and how it can marginalize and silence those who don't "fit."

Walsh, Katherine Cramer. *Talking About Politics: Informal Groups and Social Identity in American Life*. Chicago: University of Chicago Press, 2004. A fascinating study of how ordinary Americans use their group identities to make sense of politics in their everyday lives.

Internet Resources

Data on protests and riots are not as readily available as data on voting. Fortunately, the Armed Conflict Location & Event Data Project (ACLED) provides event data on protests, riots, and other political violence events around the world. The data set includes a vast amount of information on events, including dates, major actors, if political violence occurred, and a short synopsis of what took place. See https://acleddata.com/#/dashboard.

Bright Line Watch is a website that brings together political science data and research to monitor the state of democracy and the threats against democracy in the United States. For current data and reports, the web address is https://brightlinewatch.org/.

The World Values Survey website (www.worldvaluessurvey.org/wvs.jsp) provides access to public opinion data starting in the early 1980s through the present. Surveys are done worldwide, and numerous questions are asked about involvement in protests, beliefs about democracy, and other pertinent topics.

Notes

1. Lani Guinier, *Tyranny of the Majority: Fundamental Fairness in Representative Democracy*, reprint ed. (New York: Free Press, 1995).

2. Xóchitl Bada, Jonathan Fox, and Jane Guskin, "Immigrant Rights Protests—Spring 2006," Mapping American Social Movements Project, University of Washington, accessed May 3, 2021, http://depts.washington.edu/moves/2006_immigrant_rights.html.

3. Erica Chenoweth and Jeremy Pressman, "This Is What We Learned by Counting the Women's Marches," *Monkey Cage* (newsletter), *Washington Post*, February 7, 2017, https://www.washingtonpost.com/news/monkey-cage/wp/2017/02/07/this-is-what-we-learned-by-counting-the-womens-marches/.

4. Li Cohen, "Thousands Protest Violence Against Asian Americans During National Day of Action Protest," CBS News, March 27, 2021, https://www.cbsnews.com/news/asian-american-protests-national-day-of-action-condemn-violence-against-asian-americans/.

5. Edwin Amenta, Neal Caren, Elizabeth Chiarello, and Yang Su, "The Political Consequences of Social Movements," *Annual Review of Sociology* 36 (2010): 287–307; Edwin Amenta and Francesca Polletta, "The Cultural Impacts of Social Movements," *Annual Review of Sociology* 45 (2019): 279–299.

6. Emily Van Duyn, "Hidden Democracy: Political Dissent in Rural America," *Journal of Communication* 68 (2018): 965–987.

7. Samuel H. Barnes and Max Kaase, et al., "Political Action: An Eight Nation Study, 1973–1976" (ICPSR 7777), Inter-university Consortium for Political and Social Research, accessed June 3, 2021, https://www.icpsr.umich.edu/web/ICPSR/studies/7777.

8. 2020 Swing State Survey, conducted by the Center for Communication and Civic Renewal, University of Wisconsin–Madison.

9. Mancur Olson, *The Logic of Collective Action: Public Goods and the Theory of Groups* (Cambridge, MA: Harvard University Press, 1965).

10. Armed Conflict Location & Event Data Project (ACLED), accessed July 3, 2021, www.acleddata.com. The region was limited to the United States. The event type was filtered to include only riots and protests. ACLED defines *protests* as "public demonstration[s] against a political entity, government institution, policy or group in which the participants are not violent" and *riots* as "violent events where demonstrators or mobs engage in disruptive acts or disorganised acts of violence against property or people" (see "User Quick Guide," April 2019, https://acleddata.com/acleddatanew/wp-content/uploads/dlm_uploads/2019/04/General-User-Guide_FINAL-1.pdf).

11. These questions were asked by ANES in late 2020, after the election, so the reference to "the past twelve months" encompasses all of 2020.

12. ACLED, www.acleddata.com.

13. Betsy Sinclair, *The Social Citizen: Peer Networks and Political Behavior* (Chicago: University of Chicago Press, 2012), 124. We combined strong, weak, and leaning partisans.

14. Diana C. Mutz and Jeffery J. Mondak, "The Workplace as a Context for Cross-Cutting Political Discourse," *Journal of Politics* 68 (February 2006): 140–155.

15. Sidney Verba, Kay Lehman Schlozman, and Henry E. Brady, *Voice and Equality: Civic Voluntarism in American Politics* (Cambridge, MA: Harvard University Press, 1995).

16. Robert M. Bond, Christopher J. Fariss, Jason J. Jones, Adam D. I. Kramer, Cameron Marlow, Jaime E. Settle, and James H. Fowler, "A 61-Million-Person Experiment in Social Influence and Political Mobilization," *Nature* 489 (September 13, 2012): 295–298.

17. Henri Tajfel, *Differentiation Between Social Groups: Studies in the Social Psychology of Intergroup Relations* (London: Academic Press, 1978).

18. Henri Tajfel, *Social Identity and Intergroup Relations* (Cambridge, England: Cambridge University Press, 1982); Naomi Ellemers, Russell Spears, and Bertjan Doosje, eds., *Social Identity: Context, Commitment, Content* (Oxford: Blackwell, 1999); Michael A. Hogg and Dominic Abrams, *Social Identifications:*

A Social Psychology of Intergroup Relations and Group Processes (London: Routledge, 1988); Roderick M. Kramer and Marilynn B. Brewer, "Effects of Group Identity on Resource Utilization in a Simulated Commons Dilemma," *Journal of Personality and Social Psychology* 46 (1984): 1044–1057.

19. Elizabeth Theiss-Morse, *Who Counts as an American? The Boundaries of National Identity* (New York: Cambridge University Press, 2009).

20. Emily Van Duyn, "Hidden Democracy: Political Dissent in Rural America," *Journal of Communication* 68 (2018): 965–987.

21. M. Kent Jennings and Gregory B. Markus, "Partisan Orientations Over the Long Haul: Results From the Three-Wave Political Socialization Panel Study," *American Political Science Review* 78 (December 1984): 1000–1018; M. Kent Jennings, "The Crystallization of Orientations," *Continuities in Political Action* (Berlin, Boston: De Gruyter, 2014), 313–348.

22. Marilynn B. Brewer, "The Psychology of Prejudice: Ingroup Love or Outgroup Hate?," *Journal of Social Issues* 55, no. 3 (1999): 429–444; C. W. Perdue, John F. Dovidio, M. B. Gurtman, and R. B. Tyler, "'Us' and 'Them': Social Categorization and the Process of Intergroup Bias," *Journal of Personality and Social Psychology* 59 (1990): 475–486; Hogg and Abrams, *Social Identification*.

23. Marilynn B. Brewer, *Intergroup Relations*, 2nd ed. (Buckingham, England: Open University Press, 2003); Naomi Ellemers, Russell Spears, and Bertjan Doosje, eds., *Social Identity: Context, Commitment, Content* (Oxford: Blackwell, 1999); Daniel L. Wann and Nyla R. Branscombe, "Die-Hard and Fair-Weather Fans: Effects of Identification on BIRGing and CORFing Tendencies," *Journal of Sport and Social Issues* 14, no. 2 (1990): 103–117.

24. Daniel L. Wann, *Sport Fans: The Psychology and Social Impact of Spectators* (New York: Routledge, 2001).

25. Bert Klandermans, "How Group Identification Helps to Overcome the Dilemma of Collective Action," *American Behavioral Scientist* 45, no. 5 (January 2002): 887–900; Jacquelien van Stekelenburg, Bert Klandermans, and Wilco W. van Dijk, "Combining Motivations and Emotion: The Motivational Dynamics of Protest Participation," *Revista de Psicologia Social* 26, no. 1 (2011): 91–104; Jacquelien van Stekelenburg, "The Political Psychology of Protest," *European Psychologist* 18, no. 4 (2013): 224–234.

26. Chris Wells, Katherine J. Cramer, Michael W. Wagner, German Alvarez, Lewis A. Friedland, Dhavan V. Shah, Leticia Bode, Stephanie Edgerly, Itay Gabay, and Charles Franklin, "When We Stop Talking Politics: The Maintenance and Closing of Conversation in Contentious Times," *Journal of Communication* 67 (2017): 131–157; Michael W. Wagner, Chris Wells,

Lewis A. Friedland, Katherine J. Cramer, and Dhavan V. Shah, "Cultural Worldviews and Contentious Politics: Evaluative Asymmetry in High-Information Environments," *The Good Society* 23, no. 2 (2014): 126–144.

27. P. G. Klandermans, "Identity Politics and Politicized Identities: Identity Processes and the Dynamics of Protest," *Political Psychology* 35, no. 1 (2014): 1–22; Arthur H. Miller, Patricia Gurin, Gerald Gurin, and Oksana Malanchuk, "Group Consciousness and Political Participation," *American Journal of Political Science* 25 (August 1981): 494–511.

28. Michael Tesler, "Republicans and Democrats Agree on the Protests but Not Why People Are Protesting," *FiveThirtyEight* (blog), June 17, 2020, https://fivethirtyeight.com/features/republicans-and-democrats-increasingly-agree-on-the-protests-but-not-why-people-are-protesting/.

29. Jeff Spinner-Halev and Elizabeth Theiss-Morse, "Social Justice and Solidarity Survey," July/August 2020.

30. Leonie Huddy and Nadia Khatib, "American Patriotism, National Identity, and Political Involvement," *American Journal of Political Science* 51 (January 2007): 63–77.

31. Rachel M. Blum and Christopher Sebastian Parker, "Panel Study of the MAGA Movement," accessed May 22, 2021, https://sites.uw.edu/magastudy/.

32. Ibid.

33. Matthew Smith, Jamie Ballard, and Linley Sanders, "Most Voters Say the Events at the US Capitol Are a Threat to Democracy," YouGovAmerica, January 6, 2021, accessed May 22, 2021, https://today.yougov.com/topics/politics/articles-reports/2021/01/06/US-capitol-trump-poll.

34. Domenico Montanaro, "Poll: Majority of Americans Blame Trump for Violence at Capitol," NPR, January 15, 2021, https://www.npr.org/2021/01/15/956850131/poll-majority-of-americans-blame-trump-for-violence-at-capitol; PBS NewsHour/Marist Poll, conducted January 7, 2021, http://maristpoll.marist.edu/npr-pbs-newshour-marist-poll-results-trump-the-insurrection/#sthash.upYvWaDn.dpbs.

35. Erica Chenoweth and Jeremy Pressman, "This Summer's Black Lives Matter Protesters Were Overwhelmingly Peaceful, Our Research Finds," *Monkey Cage* (newsletter), *Washington Post*, October 16, 2020, https://www.washingtonpost.com/politics/2020/10/16/this-summers-black-lives-matter-protesters-were-overwhelming-peaceful-our-research-finds/.

36. Hannah Allam, "FBI Report: Bias-Motivated Killings at Record High Amid Nationwide Rise in Hate Crimes," NPR, November 16, 2020, https://www.npr.org/2020/11/16/935439777/fbi-report-bias-motivated-killings-at-record-high-amid-nationwide-rise-in-hate-c.

37. Kimmy Yam, "There Were 3,800 Anti-Asian Racist Incidents, Mostly Against Women, in Past Year," NBC News, March 16, 2021, https://www.nbcnews.com/news/asian-america/there-were-3-800-anti-asian-racist-incidents-mostly-against-n1261257.

38. Bright Line Watch, "Bright Line Watch Waves 12, 13, and 14 Public Surveys," October and November 2020 and January/February 2021, https://brightline watch.org/survey-data-and-replication-material/.

39. Marlon Mooijman, Joe Hoover, Ying Lin, Heng Ji, and Morteza Dehghani, "Moralization in Social Networks and the Emergence of Violence During Protests," *Nature Human Behaviour* 2 (2018): 389–396.

5

PARTISANSHIP AND PARTY CHANGE

"PARTISANSHIP IS A HELLUVA DRUG," political scientist Brendan Nyhan told CNN's Don Lemon on May 13, 2021, when describing why so many Republican politicians were saying things that were not true about the January 6 riot and insurrection at the U.S. Capitol. For good and for ill, people tend to see the world through partisan-colored glasses. Over the past few decades, as the two major parties have become more polarized, individuals' partisan identity has come to shape how people think about themselves and their political opponents to the extent that even when people agree across party lines, they view the other side with distaste and distrust.[1] One analysis showed that, after a contentious, partisan policy curtailing organizing rights in Wisconsin was passed in 2011, more than a third of Badger State residents stopped talking to people they disagreed with about the policy—a sign that partisan identity is deeply ensconcing itself into the daily lives of people.[2]

Partisanship is the centerpiece of American politics. Indeed, if you want to predict how someone is going to vote for president on Election Day and you can only learn one fact about that person before making your forecast, asking for that person's political partisanship will give you enough information to make a correct prediction nine times out of ten. As E. E. Schattschneider put it in his 1942 book *Party Government*, "Modern democracy is unthinkable save in terms of parties."[3] Political parties are organized coalitions working to win elections and govern. They structure public debate, dominate news columns and airtime, and continue to play a central role in American politics.

This chapter addresses *partisanship*—the sense of attachment or belonging that an individual feels for a political party—and offers a brief history of American parties, an examination of the implications partisanship has for political behavior, and an assessment of the factors that influence partisan change. In Chapter 6, we explore how partisanship helps to shape and constrain public opinion, while

Chapter 7 considers, in part, how partisan identification influences media choice and individual susceptibility to media effects.

Learning objectives for Chapter 5 include:

- Developing a historical understanding of party identity and party loyalty in the United States

- Understanding affective partisanship

- Exploring how partisanship influences voting behavior

- Analyzing the conditions for realignment

- Learning the factors that are correlated with partisan change

- Building a framework to think about the future of parties and partisanship

PARTY LOYALTY AND IDENTIFICATION

For a century and a half, the U.S. electorate has supported a two-party system of Republicans and Democrats in national politics. Such remarkable stability is largely unknown in other democracies. Within this stable party system, however, voter support for Republicans and Democrats has fluctuated widely, and significant numbers of voters occasionally abandon the traditional parties to support third-party or independent candidates, as occurred in 1992. The aggregate division of partisans in the electorate, shown in Figure 5-1, reveals a wide range of the structure of political conflict from 1952 to 2020, even in elections close together in time. While Democrats have outnumbered Republicans in the electorate for more than half a century, students of American politics know that holding the majority of partisans nationwide is not enough to promise victory at the ballot box. Moreover, the number of partisans in the electorate regularly vacillates. Years in which the total percentage of Democrats and Republicans drops a bit include elections with the third-party candidacies of George C. Wallace in 1968 and Ross Perot in 1992 and, to a lesser degree, 1996. Perot's 1992 showing of 19 percent was the largest percentage won by a third-party candidate since 1912. Although Ralph Nader's votes denied the presidency to Al Gore in 2000, his 2.7 percent of the popular vote was an unimpressive figure for a third-party candidate in recent years. Third-party candidates supporting the Green, Libertarian, and other parties garnered about 2 percent of the popular vote in 2012 and over 5 percent in 2016. A difference in vote choice of 0.006 voters across Wisconsin, Pennsylvania, and Michigan would have added an Electoral College vote victory to Hillary Clinton's popular vote win in 2016. In 2020, just as many people answered the American National Election Studies (ANES) partisanship question by saying they were independents as did so by identifying as Republicans, 31 percent each.

FIGURE 5-1   ■   Partisan Division of Americans, 1952–2020

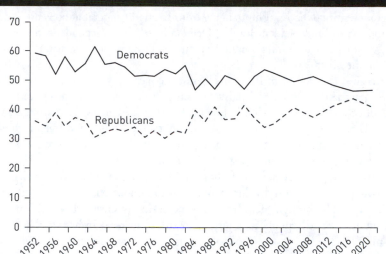

Source: American National Election Studies, available at www.electionstudies.org.

Despite variations in election outcomes and American voters' differentiated support for the candidates offered to them by the political parties, most voters have a basic and stable loyalty to one party or the other. This tendency of most individuals to be loyal to one political party makes the idea of partisanship, or *party identification* as it is often called, one of the most useful concepts for understanding the political behavior of individuals. After good survey data became available in the late 1940s, party identification assumed a central role in all voting behavior analysis.[4]

Party Identification

Party identification is a relatively uncomplicated measure determined by responses to the following questions:

- Generally speaking, do you usually think of yourself as a Republican, a Democrat, an independent, or what?

- [If Republican or Democrat] Would you call yourself a strong [Republican/Democrat] or a not very strong [Republican/Democrat]?

- [If independent] Do you think of yourself as closer to the Republican Party or to the Democratic Party?

Leaving aside for the moment the people who do not or cannot respond to such questions, this yields seven categories of participants in the electorate according to intensity of partisanship ranging from strong Democrat at one end to weak Democrat and independent-leaning Democrat to pure independent in the middle, to independent-leaning Republican and weak Republican to strong Republican on the other end.

Because this self-identification measure of party loyalty is the best indicator of partisanship, political analysts commonly refer to partisanship and party identification interchangeably. While many other influences are at work on voters in U.S. society, and partisanship varies in its importance in different types of elections and in different time periods, partisanship is the single most important influence on political opinions and voting behavior.

Partisanship represents the feeling of identification with and loyalty to a political party that an individual acquires—sometimes during childhood—and generally holds through life, often with increasing intensity. This self-image as a Democrat or a Republican is useful to the individual in a special way. For example, individuals who think of themselves as Republicans or Democrats respond to political information partially by using party identification to orient themselves, reacting to new information in a way that fits in with the ideals and feelings they already have. A Republican who hears a Republican Party leader advocate a policy has a basis in party loyalty for supporting that policy, apart from other considerations. A Democrat may feel favorably inclined toward a candidate for office because that candidate bears the Democratic label. Partisanship orients individuals in their political environment, although it may also distort their picture of reality. Attaching a partisan label to an issue preference helps citizens determine what they find to be important and how they tend to think about their own preferences.[5]

Table 5-1 shows the stability of partisan conflict in the United States during the modern polling era. Democrats have held the party identification advantage, even in years such as 1956, 1972, 1980, and 1984, when Republicans ran away with the White House. One element of the data that jumps out is the fact that the percentage of self-identified independents has nearly doubled since the time series began. Even so, independent partisan leaners are among the most loyal party voters. Indeed, after asking independents which party they lean toward, under 10 percent of the public reveals itself to be truly independent from the two major parties.

The dramatic role that the Southern United States has played in American political history—from seceding from the Union to kick off the Civil War to the days of "solid South" Democratic presidential voting to a region where Republicans have the advantage today—merits a careful examination of partisanship in the South and non-South. Southerners' partisan loyalties shifted from a South that was almost twice as likely to identify as strongly Democratic compared to the non-South in 1952 to a region that displayed a significant loss of Democratic loyalty (but lack of gain for Republicans) by 1972 to one that was indistinguishable

TABLE 5-1 ■ Party Identification of the Electorate, 1952–2020

Party Identification	1952	1956	1960	1964	1968	1972	1976	1980	1984	1988	1992	1996	2000	2004	2008	2012	2016	2020
Democrats	47%	44%	46%	51%	45%	40%	39%	41%	36%	35%	35%	38%	36%	32%	34%	34%	31%	34%
Independents	22	24	23	22	29	35	36	35	34	36	38	32	42	38	40	37	37	31
Republicans	27	29	27	24	24	23	23	22	28	28	25	29	20	29	25	25	27	31
(N)	1,377	1,442	1,540	1,247	1,186	965	1,930	1,109	1,622	1,418	1,848	1,286	1,301	948	1,820	1,946	1,161	5,408

Source: American National Election Studies, available at www.electionstudies.org.

from the rest of the country across the party spectrum by 2012. We consider the changes in the South later, in the sections of the chapter dealing with party systems and realignment.

Partisanship is also interesting to political analysts because it provides a base against which to measure deviations in particular elections. In other words, individual voters' long-standing loyalty to one party means that, "other things being equal," or in the absence of disrupting forces, they can be expected to vote for candidates of that party. Of course, campaigns are not conducted in a vacuum; Republican presidential candidates do not simply say to themselves, "Well, there are more Democrats than Republicans, and I'll never be able to convince any Democrats to vote for me, so I guess I'll bow out of the race now!" Nor do Democratic presidential candidates say to themselves, "Well, looking at those party ID numbers, I see that there's no need to campaign—we have this in the bag!" Indeed, voters are responsive to a great variety of other influences that can either strengthen or weaken their tendency to support their usual party. Variations occur from election to election in such factors as the attractiveness of the candidates, the impact of foreign and domestic policy issues, and purely local circumstances. These current factors, often called *short-term forces*, may move voters away from their usual party choices. If the political predispositions of all the individuals in the electorate were added up, the result would be an "expected vote" or "normal vote."[6] This is the electoral outcome that would be expected if all voters voted according to their party identification. Departures from this expected vote in elections represent the impact of short-term forces, such as issues or candidates.

In assessing the partisanship of the American electorate historically, we have no data to add up individual party identifications to find an expected vote. Survey data of this type have been available only for the past seventy-five years or so. For the period from 1824 to 1968, we base our estimates on the only available data—election returns for aggregate units.[7] These data cannot tell us about the voting patterns of individuals, but they do allow us to make assessments of party loyalty and temporary deviations from party by collections of voters. Even though the same set of individuals does not turn out to vote in each election, we use the election returns over the years to indicate the collective partisanship of the electorate. From these data, an estimate is made of the expected vote for the Democratic and Republican Parties. It is then possible to say, for example, that the electorate deviated from its normal voting pattern in favor of the Republican Party in 1904 or that the voters departed from their normal Democratic loyalty in 1952.

Political scientist Philip E. Converse developed a method that can be used as an expectation about vote choice in the absence of short-term forces. This technique uses party identification, expected defection rates, and turnout to generate an estimate of the normal vote. Our analysis finds that the deviation of the actual Democratic vote meanders under the predicted Democratic normal vote, meaning that Democratic presidential candidates since 1968 have rarely done as well as would be expected, given the distribution of party identification. The elections of 2004, 2008, and 2012 were exceptions, as the Democratic candidates' performances matched Democratic partisan strength in the electorate. In elections in which a third-party candidate won a significant number of votes—1968, 1992, and 1996—both the Democratic and Republican candidates performed below what the normal votes would predict. Strong party support and turnout for Joe Biden in 2020 in Wisconsin, Michigan, and Pennsylvania overcame a problem of lower enthusiasm for Hillary Clinton in those same states in 2016.

Party identifiers are members of various demographic and social groups. There are a wide range of relationships in the U.S. electorate between social characteristics and political behavior. American journalists and party strategists often attribute political trends to such categories as "white populists," "soccer moms," or "born-again Christians"; frequently, these explanations rely on so-called bloc voting, such as "the Black vote," "the senior citizen vote," or "the Latin@ vote," implying that some social factors cause large numbers of people to vote in certain ways.

Social groups have a major impact on individual attitudes and behavior, including partisanship. As we discussed in Chapter 4, some of this impact occurs directly through face-to-face interactions with primary groups and social networks, but the secondary groups with which one identifies can also have an impact. The two major political parties in the United States have courted certain social groups and passed policies that benefit some groups over others. These connections have led to the political parties having an image or "brand" that people have in mind when they think of the parties. For example, the Democratic Party is widely associated with the poor and with people of color, whereas the Republican Party is widely associated with the wealthy and white people.

Table 5-2 shows the percentage of party identification in the United States by social characteristics. Men are almost evenly split between the two major parties and are nearly mirror images of each other in terms of partisan strength. However, more women identify as Democrats, particularly as strong Democrats, continuing the reversal of how things were in the 1950s and early 1960s when men were more likely to be Democrats. White people are more likely to be Republicans, especially strong Republicans, while both Black people and Latin@s are more likely to be Democrats. That said, it is worth noting that 19 percent of Latin@s identified as pure independents, the largest percentage of independents in Table 5-2.

Age is another factor that is related to party identification. Adults under forty-four are more likely to be Democratic identifiers. Those in the prime of their professional working years, forty-five to fifty-four, are equally distributed across the two parties while those between fifty-five and sixty-four and those seventy-five and older are more likely to identify as Republicans. Those sixty-five to seventy-four are stronger Democrats.

Education, union membership, and religious beliefs are also related to partisanship. Those who have a high school education or less as well as those with some time in college are equally distributed across the two parties while college graduates are more likely to be Democrats. Union members are more likely to be Democrats, especially strong Democrats. With respect to religious identification,

TABLE 5-2 ■ **Party Identification, by Social Characteristics, 2020**

Category (percentage of sample)	Democrats		Independents			Republicans	
	Strong	Weak	Lean Democrat	Pure Independent	Lean Republican	Weak	Strong
Men (48)	19	11	13	13	11	12	21
Women (52)	27	12	12	11	10	10	19
Whites (65)	18	9	12	10	12	13	26
Blacks (12)	51	13	17	10	4	2	3
Hispanics (13)	26	17	13	19	8	8	10
18–24 (14)	21	16	13	17	7	10	16
25–34 (17)	20	14	17	14	12	12	12
35–44 (17)	18	12	17	14	11	11	17
45–54 (16)	22	13	10	11	11	12	21
55–64 (16)	26	9	9	8	13	10	25
65–74 (13)	32	7	11	8	9	8	26
75 and over (7)	27	8	7	10	9	10	30

Category (percentage of sample)	Democrats		Independents			Republicans	
	Strong	Weak	Lean Democrat	Pure Independent	Lean Republican	Weak	Strong
High school education or less (36)	22	11	11	15	10	10	22
Some college (29)	21	11	11	12	12	11	23
College graduates (35)	26	13	16	9	10	11	15
Union households (15)	24	16	12	11	11	11	15
Mainline Protestants (12)	26	9	10	6	14	14	21
Fundamentalists, evangelicals (16)	16	7	5	8	10	13	41
Catholics (21)	20	13	11	10	12	13	21
Atheists or Agnostics (12)	33	18	23	12	8	4	3

Source: American National Election Studies, available at www.electionstudies.org.

there are more Republican mainline Protestants but more strong Democrats than strong Republicans who are mainline Protestants. Evangelical Christians are overwhelmingly Republican, and atheists or agnostics, the fastest-growing religious group in the country, are overwhelmingly Democrats. Catholics are evenly distributed across the parties.

Identification with these groups is related to vote choice as spouses tend to vote alike, as do neighbors, fellow churchgoers, and even coworkers. Even in workplaces, where crosscutting political conversations are more likely to occur, people are more likely to find like-minded people to talk to, if they talk about politics at all.

Affective Partisanship

As we have noted throughout the book, partisan polarization is on the rise in the United States. One way in which the divide between the parties is particularly acute, and that is different from issue divides among partisans, is with respect to the intense feelings partisans have for their own party as compared to the feelings they express toward the other major party. Alan Abramowitz attributes the rise of this emotional, or "affective," polarization to the growing intensity of ideological differences between liberals and conservatives.[8] The average intensity of one's partisan preferences, measured by a feeling thermometer asking how warmly or coolly (100 is warmest, 0 is coldest) one feels about one's party, has increased over 15 percent in the past few decades. Meanwhile, the average difference in temperature one feels toward one's party and the other party has gone from about 20 degrees to more than 40!

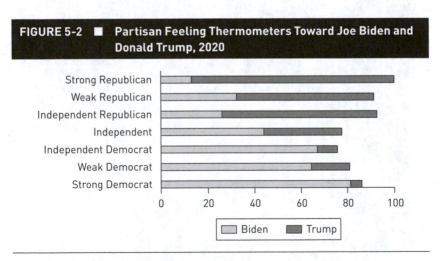

FIGURE 5-2 ■ Partisan Feeling Thermometers Toward Joe Biden and Donald Trump, 2020

Source: American National Election Studies, available at www.electionstudies.org.

Figure 5-2 shows the differential levels of animus that partisans felt toward Donald Trump and Joe Biden before the 2020 election. In general, Republicans loved Trump and were cool to Biden while Democrats liked Biden but were downright frozen in their feelings about Trump. Specifically, strong Republicans felt incredibly warmly toward Trump (87 degrees) and just as coolly toward Biden (13 degrees). Strong Democrats were not quite as warm to their party's candidate (81 degrees) as Republicans were to Trump, but they were almost wholly negative toward President Trump (5 degrees). Independents were warmer to Biden (44 degrees) than Trump (34 degrees), and the gap between feelings of independent-leaning Republicans for Trump as compared to Biden was smaller (41 degrees) than the gap between what independent-leaning Democrats felt for Biden and what they felt for Trump (58 degrees).

Some scholars argue that the roots of affective polarization are in the media messages partisans consume—many of which are quick to denounce the other side not just as wrong but as evil, dangerous, and a threat to the American way of life. Thinking of partisanship as a social identity enables analyses of partisans as members of an in-group and people in the other party as members of an out-group (see Chapter 4). Shanto Iyengar and colleagues found evidence, using this social identity perspective, that some partisans simply loathe the other side, and consuming messages that treat the other party as an out-group exacerbates the negative views partisans ascribe to their opponents across the aisle.[9]

One reason this happens is that many partisans get their news from different sources than folks in the other major party. Figure 5-3 shares data from the Pew Research Center that show how different Republican and Democratic Party identifiers are when it comes to the news sources they trust the most. Democrats trust more traditional, mainstream sources the most. The only source that garnered a majority of trust for Republicans was Fox News. Notably, three of the top five

FIGURE 5-3 ■ Partisan Trust in Major National News Sources, 2020

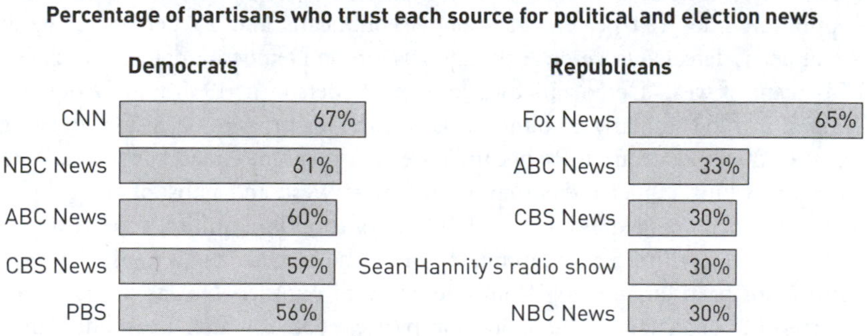

Percentage of partisans who trust each source for political and election news

Democrats		Republicans	
CNN	67%	Fox News	65%
NBC News	61%	ABC News	33%
ABC News	60%	CBS News	30%
CBS News	59%	Sean Hannity's radio show	30%
PBS	56%	NBC News	30%

Source: Mark Jurkowitz, Amy Mitchell, Elisa Shearer, and Mason Walker, "U.S. Media Polarization and the 2020 Election: A Nation Divided," Pew Research Center, January 24, 2020, https://www.journalism.org/2020/01/24/u-s-media-polarization-and-the-2020-election-a-nation-divided/.

most trusted sources are the same for each group of partisans (ABC, CBS, and NBC), though Democrats are twice as likely to trust them as Republicans are. The same Pew study also showed that of the thirty prominent news sources Pew asked people about, Republicans distrusted twenty-two of them, whereas Democrats only distrusted eight. We take up other relationships between the media and polarization in Chapter 7.

VOTING BEHAVIOR

As we noted earlier, the standard party identification question, used in almost all political surveys, asks respondents whether they are Republicans, Democrats, or independents and whether they are "strong" or "not very strong" Republicans or Democrats. The likelihood of voting loyally in support of one party varies with the strength of individuals' partisanship. The defection rates of strong and weak partisans in each presidential election since 1952 are shown in Figure 5-4. Declining party loyalty is apparent as the intensity of partisanship decreases. Strong partisans consistently support the candidate of their party at higher rates than do weak partisans. In most years, Republicans have been a bit more loyal to their party than Democrats, although this is partly accounted for by Southern Democrats who regularly deserted their party in presidential elections in the late twentieth century. By the end of the twentieth century, Southern Democrats were no longer distinctive in this regard; previously defecting Democrats had become independents or Republicans.

Differences in candidate appeal affect the propensity to defect. Few Republicans deserted Dwight D. Eisenhower in the 1950s, Richard M. Nixon in 1972, or Ronald Reagan in 1984; many more left Barry Goldwater in 1964. Similarly, most Democrats were loyal to Lyndon B. Johnson in 1964 but abandoned George McGovern in large numbers in 1972.

Another potential cause of defection is attractive third-party candidates. In 1992, Ross Perot drew defectors from both parties, although more from the Republican side. Ten percent of strong Republicans and 25 percent of weak Republicans defected to Perot. Although few strong Democrats defected to Perot, 17 percent of weak Democrats did. John B. Anderson in 1980 and George C. Wallace in 1968 similarly account for part of the upsurges in defections in those years. In 2020, Libertarian Party candidate Jo Jorgensen, Green Party candidate Howie Hawkins, rapper and entrepreneur Kanye West, and a host of other third-party candidates earned fewer than 3 million of the 158.3 million votes cast.[10]

Historically, third-party candidates often have been viewed as "halfway houses" for partisans moving from one party to another. Not as dramatic for a partisan as defection to the opposition party, a vote for such a candidate may be a first step away from party loyalty or a temporary blip related to a party's nominee for president, prevailing economic conditions, or an unusually effective third-party candidate. In any event, support for third parties and an increase in

FIGURE 5-4 ■ Defection Rates by Party Identifiers in Presidential Voting, 1952–2020

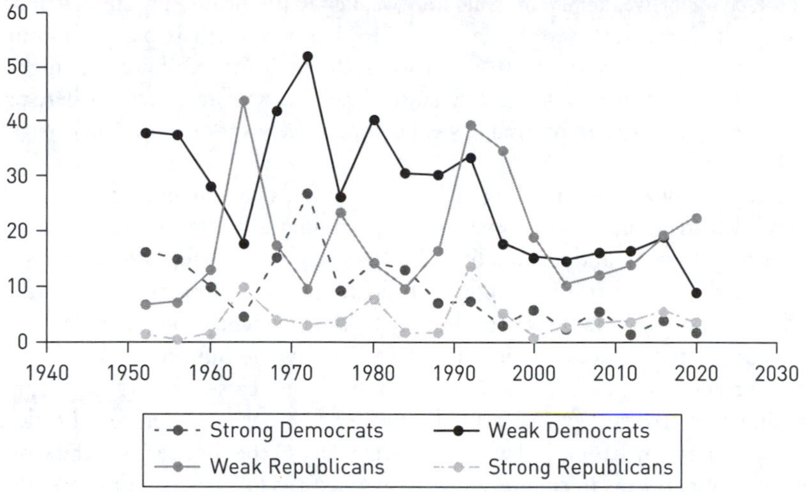

Source: American National Election Studies, available at www.electionstudies.org.

defection rates have generally been symptomatic of the loosening of party ties in eras of dealignment. (See discussion in the Partisans, Realignment, and Party Systems section.)

A different pattern—one of high party loyalty on both sides—was exhibited in the presidential elections of 1976, 1988, 1996, 2000, 2004, 2008, 2012, 2016, and 2020. In these elections, partisans of both parties remained loyal to candidates who were relatively balanced in their appeal.

In the twenty-first century, the high degree of loyalty is also a reflection of partisan polarization.[11] Although strong partisans vary in their loyalty from year to year, depending on the candidates offered by their party, this tendency is much more pronounced among weak partisans. For example, the defection rate of strong Republicans falls in a narrow range from around 2 percent in a good Republican year to 10 percent in a bad year. In contrast, weak Republicans are almost as loyal as strong Republicans when an attractive Republican candidate is on the ticket, but nearly 50 percent defected in the disastrous 1964 election. The behavior of Democrats is similar, although both strong and weak Democrats are more likely to desert their party than are Republicans. Clearly, marked departures from the expected vote of a party are accomplished by wooing away the weaker partisans of the opposite party. Figure 5-4 shows that 2016 brought higher defection rates from both strong Republicans and strong Democrats as compared to 2012. However, fewer strong Democrats defected in 2016, a year Democrat Hillary Clinton lost, as compared to 2008, the year Democrat Barack Obama won. While weak partisans on both sides tended to hold the party line, their defection rates were higher than those of weak Republicans and Democrats in 2012.

One way that the 2020 election was different from 2016 can be found in the behavior of weaker Democrats and weaker Republicans. Figure 5-4 shows that weak Democrats were far less likely to defect from their party's nominee in 2020 than they were in 2016 and weak Republicans exhibited the highest level of defection in two decades. Even so, 2020 was still an election where partisans, especially strong partisans, were comparatively very loyal to their party's candidates.

The tendency of both strong and weak partisans to vote according to their party identification becomes even more pronounced as one moves down the ticket to less-visible and less-publicized offices. Figure 5-5's focus on congressional races shows that this is a product of the dominant two-party system nationwide. Even highly successful third-party or independent candidates down the ticket are merely local disruptions that have virtually no impact on national patterns. (Data limitations for some midterm election years—the ANES stopped fielding midterm surveys early in the twenty-first century—prevent breaking down partisans by strong and weak for the entirety of the time series.) The voting behavior of partisans in congressional races since 1952 differs from the presidential data in two significant ways. First, differences between the party loyalty of strong and weak partisans are usually smaller. Second, the defection rate does not fluctuate from year to year nearly as much as in the presidential elections. Both differences are attributable to the lower visibility of congressional races. In a presidential election, the flood of available information means that a particularly attractive candidate or a stirring issue may touch the consciousness of the weak partisans, causing them to defect from traditional party ties; the firmly attached, strong partisans are more likely to resist. In the less-publicized congressional races, the information that might cause weak partisans to defect is less likely to even reach them. In the absence of information about the candidates and issues, weak partisans vote according to their party identification. Recent midterm races, in particular, have had historically low levels of partisan defection on both sides of the aisle. In 2020, Democrats defected in their congressional voting less than they did four years earlier while Republicans defected slightly more in 2020 than in 2016.

The intensity of partisanship affects political behavior beyond its influence on the likelihood of voting for or defecting from a party's candidate. Strong partisans are also more likely to vote in all kinds of elections than are either weak partisans or independents. Though it seems quaint today, one explanation sometimes offered for the low turnout in the late twentieth century was the declining partisanship of the American public.[12] The turnout rates of the various categories of partisans and independents for three types of elections—presidential, off-year congressional, and primary—are illustrated in Figure 5-6. Presidential primaries, despite all their accompanying publicity and frenetic campaigning, typically have a lower average turnout than off-year congressional elections. This is especially true in uncontested

FIGURE 5-5 ■ Defection Rates by Party Identifiers in Congressional Voting, 1952–2020

Sources: American National Election Studies, available at www.electionstudies.org. Data for 2006 and 2010 from Pew Research Center, November 2006 Postelection Survey and November 2010 Postelection Survey, available at https://www.pewresearch.org/topic/politics-policy/.

139

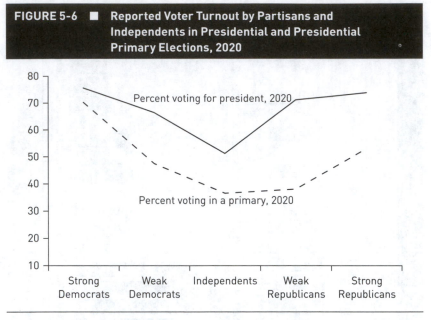

FIGURE 5-6 ■ Reported Voter Turnout by Partisans and Independents in Presidential and Presidential Primary Elections, 2020

Percent voting for president, 2020

Percent voting in a primary, 2020

Source: 2020 American National Election Studies, available at www.electionstudies.org.

primaries, which often occur when an incumbent president is seeking reelection. No serious opponents squared off against Donald Trump in 2020 (so much so that the Grand Old Party [GOP] in eight states canceled their primaries). Even so, Figure 5-6 shows the power of strong partisanship, as strong Republicans voted at comparable rates to weak Democrats in the primaries even though Democrats had a highly populated field of would-be nominees for their party.

In congressional voting, unlike presidential voting, Democrats were regularly more party loyal than were Republicans until 1994. This was both cause and effect of the recent disjuncture of national politics, whereby Republicans were stronger in presidential politics and Democrats dominated in congressional politics. Throughout the 1970s and 1980s, the Republicans were able to field more attractive presidential candidates than the Democrats, leading more Democratic partisans to defect in presidential races. In contrast, congressional races saw Republican partisans often defecting to vote for a long-term Democratic incumbent running against token Republican opposition. The situation changed dramatically in 1994, when the Republicans gained control of the House of Representatives in part by fanning the flames of anti-incumbent, anti-Democratic sentiment. Thereafter, with more Republican incumbents for whom to vote, Republican partisans were noticeably more party loyal than they had been in previous congressional elections. Even when the Democrats took back the House of Representatives in 2006, the percentage of GOP defectors in the electorate was low.

What can candidates do to try and orient persuadable voters to the things the candidates' parties do well? It turns out that the public has some strong opinions about which issues each major party "owns"—that is, handles better than the other party. The issue ownership hypothesis is that when parties can focus voter attention on the issues they are perceived to own, they are more likely to be successful at the ballot box. Figure 5-7 shows the issues the public thought Democrats and Republicans owned, respectively, in 2020. Perhaps most importantly, the public gave Democrats higher marks on handling the COVID-19 pandemic as compared to Republicans. Breaking down the results by the party of the survey respondent (not shown in the figure), 86 percent of Democrats and 44 percent of independents thought the Democrats would handle the pandemic better. Forty percent of independents and 30 percent of Republicans felt it would not make a difference. Less than 1 percent of Democrats thought Republicans would do a better job, and only (comparatively) 63 percent of Republicans thought their party was the better choice on COVID-19.

As is commonly the case, Democrats were perceived to own environmental and health care issues while Republicans were perceived to own the economy and taxes. With the economy and the pandemic serving as the issues that topped voters' minds in 2020, we might have expected for Trump to focus on advertising about the economy and taxes and Biden to focus on advertising about COVID-19 and health care. As noted in Chapter 2, Biden focused on COVID-19 in his ads, but actually aired more ads about taxes than anything else—a strategy political science research suggests might have worked on some Republicans. This is because partisans prefer it when candidates in the other party discuss the issues owned by the partisans' own party as compared to out-party candidates who only focus on what their party does well.[13]

Are Independents Apolitical?

Independents, who now account for more than one-third of the national electorate if leaners are included, are the most obvious source of additional votes for either party. Although partisans, especially weak partisans, sometimes abandon their party, year after year independents are the largest bloc of uncommitted voters available to both parties. Theoretically, in the current closely divided electorate, the vote of the independents can easily determine the outcome of an election.

The independents' capacity for shifting back and forth between the major parties is shown in Table 5-3. Each party has, on occasion, successfully appealed to the independents, winning over a large majority to its side. In 1984, the independents voted almost two to one for Reagan over Walter F. Mondale, and Johnson held a similar advantage over Goldwater in 1964. During the years in which the Democrats had a clear advantage in partisan identifiers, Republicans had to win a healthy majority of the independent vote even to stay in close contention. This was the case in the elections of 2012 (Romney vs. Obama), 1976 (Carter vs. Ford), and 1960 (Kennedy vs. Nixon). The election of George W. Bush in 2000

FIGURE 5-7 ■ Issue Ownership in the 2020 Presidential Election

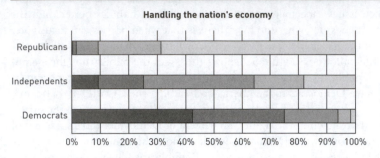

Handling the nation's economy

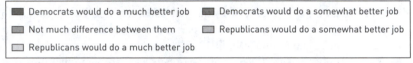

Democrats would do a much better job
Democrats would do a somewhat better job
Not much difference between them
Republicans would do a somewhat better job
Republicans would do a much better job

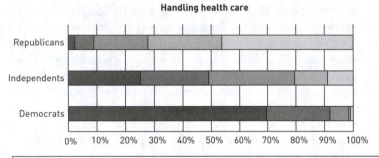

Handling health care

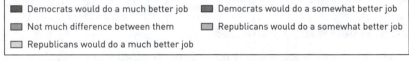

Democrats would do a much better job
Democrats would do a somewhat better job
Not much difference between them
Republicans would do a somewhat better job
Republicans would do a much better job

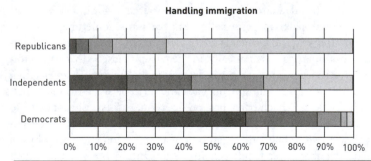

Handling immigration

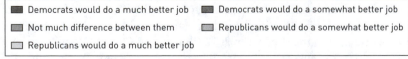

Democrats would do a much better job
Democrats would do a somewhat better job
Not much difference between them
Republicans would do a somewhat better job
Republicans would do a much better job

Source: 2020 American National Election Studies, available at www.electionstudies.org.

TABLE 5-3 ■ The Distribution of Votes for President by Independents, 1952–2020

	1952	1956	1960	1964	1968	1972	1976	1980	1984	1988	1992	1996	2000	2004	2008	2012	2016	2020
Democratic	34%	26%	46%	66%	26%	33%	46%	28%	34%	47%	43%	48%	46%	57%	58%	47%	38%	58%
Republican	66	74	54	34	57	67	54	58	66	53	30	36	54	42	42	50	42	36%
Other candidate					17			14			27	15		1		3	20	6%
Total	100%	100%	100%	100%	100%	100%	100%	100%	100%	100%	100%	99%	100%	100%	100%	100%	100%	100%
(N)	261	303	298	219	281	481	537	299	424	357	574	283	344	245	499	428	42	1269

Source: American National Election Studies, available at www.electionstudies.org.

depended on, among other things, the substantial advantage he enjoyed over Al Gore among independents. Bush's reelection in 2004 was a different story as Democratic candidate John Kerry handily carried the independent vote.[14] Obama matched Kerry's appeal to independent voters in 2008, though Mitt Romney scored more independent support than Obama did in 2012. In 2020, independent voters supported Joe Biden 58 to 36 percent, the largest gap since 1984.

Third-party or independent candidates find unaffiliated voters a major source of votes. In 1992, 27 percent of the independents voted for Perot. His failure to hold those votes in 1996 turned his earlier, impressive showing into a minor story. In 1968, more than 20 percent of the independents gave their votes to Wallace, and in 1980, 14 percent voted for Anderson. Looking at the composition of third-party candidates' votes, one sees more than half typically come from independents. Furthermore, independents may shift dramatically in voting for president and remain stable in voting for Congress.

On what basis do independents make their vote choices? Two views of independents have competed for popularity. The pundit's view is of an intelligent, informed, dispassionate evaluator of candidates and issues who, after careful consideration, votes for "the person, not the party." An alternate view—generally attributed to scholars—is of an uninformed and uninterested voter on whom issue-oriented appeals are less effective. Further analysis will help determine who is right.

The first thing we need to do is make two distinctions among independents. We note these distinctions and then drop them because they complicate the analysis and are usually ignored. First, important differences exist between nonpartisans who identify themselves as independents and those who lack any political identification. A sizable segment of the electorate answers the party identification question by saying that they identify as nothing or that they do not know what they are. According to the coding conventions used by the ANES, most nonidentifiers are included with the independents, but important conceptual distinctions may exist between them and self-identified independents.[15] The two types of nonpartisans are included in Table 5-4. Those in one set identify themselves as *independents*; the others do not think of themselves in terms of political labels. Since 1972, between about one-sixth and one-third of the nonpartisans failed to identify themselves as independents. Even though the electorate generally has become more nonpartisan, it is not necessarily more independent. These situations present different implications for the political parties. Self-identified independents think of themselves as having a political identity and are somewhat antiparty in orientation. The nonidentifying nonpartisans have a less clear self-image of themselves as political actors, but they are not particularly hostile to the political parties. They are less self-consciously political in many ways.

Second, within the large group of people who do not identify with either the Democratic or the Republican Party are many who say they "lean toward" one or the other. These leaners make up two-thirds of all nonpartisans, and they complicate analysis in a significant way. On crucial attitudes and in important forms

TABLE 5-4 ■ Party Identifiers, Self-Identified Independents, and People Claiming No Preference, 1968–2020

	1968	1972	1976	1980	1984	1988	1992	1996	2000	2004	2008	2012	2016	2020
Identify with a party	69%	64%	63%	64%	64%	63%	61%	64%	59%	61%	60%	59%	58%	68%
Identify as independents	26	28	29	24	25	31	32	28	28	33	33	35	37	31
Have no preference	3	8	8	12	10	6	7	8	12	5	6	3	3	0
Don't know										1	1	2	2	0
Not ascertained					1							1		1
Total	98%	100%	100%	100%	100%	100%	100%	100%	99%	100%	100%	100%	100%	100%
(N)	1,557	2,705	2,870	1,614	2,257	2,040	2,488	1,714	1,807	1,212	2,322	2,056	1,179	5,441

Source: American National Election Studies, available at www.electionstudies.org.

of political behavior, the leaning independents look like partisans. Independents who lean toward the Democratic Party behave somewhat like weak Democratic partisans, and independents who lean toward the Republican Party behave like weak Republicans.[16] As can be seen in Figure 5-8, independent leaners are more similar to weak partisans than strong and weak partisans are to each other.

Samara Klar and Yanna Krupnikov have found, in their research on independents, that people who have preferences that should land them in either the Republican or the Democratic Party are increasingly identifying as independents because they are so disgusted with partisan politics and the parties' favored candidates for office.[17] Increasingly, then, independents have preferences that make them appear like partisans, but they identify as independents because of their distaste for the parties and their candidates. These independents hide their partisanship from pollsters—and even their friends! The same forces that drive undercover partisans to identify as independents—media coverage of partisan sniping and polarization—also drive independents to candidates like Bernie Sanders and Donald Trump, who run under a party label but criticize the party system and party elites. Indeed, Figure 5-8 shows that pure independents favored Joe Biden. Higher percentages of independent-leaning Republicans and independent-leaning Democrats favored Biden in 2020 than favored Hillary Clinton in 2016.

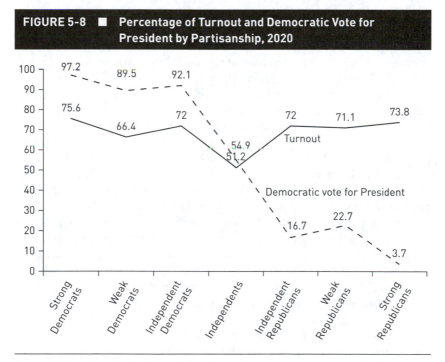

FIGURE 5-8   ■   Percentage of Turnout and Democratic Vote for President by Partisanship, 2020

Source: 2020 American National Election Studies, available at www.electionstudies.org.

How appropriate, then, is it to include all independents in one category? On some characteristics, such as ideological self-identification and interest in public affairs, much more variation is evident within the three independent categories than between the several partisan categories. The differences between leaners and pure independents are often greater than those among Republicans or Democrats. Because the concept of *independent* embraces these three dissimilar groups, there is little wonder that some disagreement exists over what the true independent is like. As we briefly consider in Chapter 6, some of these independents have ideological views on social and economic issues that directly contradict the views of other independents on the same issues. In any case, the point here is that independents are a very diverse group, and efforts to paint them with a broad brush and use that painting to make precise electoral predictions is a fool's errand.

In other words, as a consequence of including various types of people under the label "independent," making generalizations about the degree of political interest and information of independents is difficult. Some independents have considerable interest in politics, and others are apathetic. There are more informed, concerned voters among the leaning independents than among other nonpartisans, and the leaning independents are more likely to register and to vote. So are independents attentive or apathetic toward politics? The answer is they are both.

To the student of contemporary American politics, these characteristics of the independent remain important because they determine the independent's susceptibility to political appeals. We and others have argued that the American electoral system is presently at a time when a fairly large group of potential voters has weak ties to the political parties. The argument is that, when a large portion of the electorate either is independent or exhibits more independent behavior, these people form a pool of potential recruits for one of the parties or a new party. Given the diverse nature of beliefs among the ranks of independents, the likelihood of the emergence of a third party that appeals to a majority of independents is unlikely. Indeed, between 2006 and 2008, anti-Bush and pro-Obama sentiment combined to move some previous independents to begin calling themselves Democrats, at the same time moving some Republicans into the independent category. Several efforts were made to generate interest in a Libertarian Party and a Green Party in the 2016 elections, but each party's candidate for president struggled to get media attention, struggled to raise money, and, consequently, struggled at the ballot box. In 2020, many independent campaigns also struggled at getting on the ballot. Kanye West's campaign sued to get on the ballot in Wisconsin, but lost the case since the campaign turned in the required signatures supporting his nomination between 5:00 p.m. (the deadline) and 5:01 p.m. (what West's team argued the deadline should be). The court decided that time has meaning—and the meaning is that the deadline was at 5:00 p.m.[18] Since West turned in his signatures late, he was left off the ballot.

PARTISANS, REALIGNMENT, AND PARTY SYSTEMS

One type of departure from the expected level of partisan voting in an election is usually referred to as *deviating change:* the temporary deviations from normal party loyalty attributable to the short-term forces of candidate images or issues.[19] The amount of deviating change in an election tells how well a candidate or party did relative to the party's normal performance. In these terms, the Eisenhower victories in 1952 and 1956 and the Nixon landslide in 1972 appear even more dramatic because they represent big Republican margins during a time when the Democratic Party held an advantage in party loyalists. These deviating elections involved substantial departures from the underlying strength of the two parties in the electorate.

Temporary deviating changes may be dramatic and reflect important electoral forces, but another type of change is of even greater interest. On rare occasions in American national politics, a permanent, or *realigning*, change in voting patterns occurs. In such instances, the electorate departs from its expected voting pattern but does not return to the old pattern afterward. The changes sometimes are large and durable enough to alter the competitive balance between the parties, with significant consequences for the policy directions of the government. Such a period of change is usually referred to as a *partisan realignment*.[20] Electoral analysts usually discuss three major realignments in American history. One occurred during the time of the Civil War and the emergence of the Republican Party; another followed the depression of 1893 and benefited the Republicans; and the most recent followed the depression of 1929 and led to Democratic Party dominance. These abrupt changes in the expected votes of the parties can be seen in Figures 5-9 and 5-10. Each realignment of partisan loyalties coincided with a major national crisis, leading to the supposition that a social or economic crisis is necessary to shake loose customary loyalties. But major crises and national traumas have not always led to disruptions of partisanship, suggesting that other political conditions must also be present for a crisis to produce a realignment. The nature of the realignment crisis has political significance, however, because it generally determines the lines along which the rearrangement in partisan loyalties will take place, as different segments of the electorate respond differently to the crisis and to attempts to solve it.

In general, realignments appear to happen in the following way. At a time of national crisis, the electorate rejects the party in power, giving a decisive victory to the other party—a victory that includes not only the presidency but also large majorities in both houses of Congress. The new party in office acts to meet the crisis, often with innovative policies that are sharp departures from the past. *If* the administration's policy initiatives are successful in solving the nation's problems (or at least if they are widely perceived as successful), then significant numbers of voters will become partisans of the new administration's party and continue voting for this party in subsequent elections, thus causing a lasting change in the division of partisan strength in the electorate. If the administration in power is *not* perceived as successful in handling the crisis, then in all likelihood the voters will reject that party in the next election, and its landslide victory in the previous election will be regarded, in retrospect, as a deviating election.

In a realignment, the people who become partisans of the new majority party likely are independents and previously uninvolved members of the electorate, not partisans of the other party. In other words, in a realignment, few Democrats or Republicans switch parties. It appears more likely that independents drop their independent stance and become partisan. Thus, for a realignment to occur, a precondition may be a pool of people without partisan attachments who are available for realignment. This, in turn, suggests a longer sequence of events that forms a realignment cycle.

First there is the crisis that, if successfully handled, leads to a realignment. This initiates a period of electoral stability during which the parties take distinct stands on the issues that were at the heart of the crisis. Party loyalty is high during this period, both within the electorate and among the elected political leaders in government. However, as time passes, new problems arise, and new issues gradually disrupt the old alignment and lead to greater electoral instability. During this period, often referred to as a *dealignment*, voters are much more susceptible to the personal appeals of candidates, to local issues, and to other elements that might lead to departures from underlying party loyalty. As the time since the last realignment lengthens, more and more new voters come into the electorate without attachments to the symbols and issues of the past that made their elders party loyalists. This group of voters, who have no strong attachments to either party, may provide the basis for a new realignment should a crisis arise and one or the other of the parties be perceived as solving it. One conceptual problem for the realignment perspective is its "either-or" nature. Declaring whether an election is or isn't a realigning one can mask slow but important shifts in the electorate. As campaigns become more sophisticated and ideologues sort themselves into the party that is best for them, dramatic realigning elections have become less common.

Political historians often divide American electoral history into five *party systems*—eras that are distinguished from each other by the different political parties that existed or by the different competitive relationships among the parties.[21] The transition from one party system to another has usually been marked by a realignment.

The first party system, which extended from the 1790s until about 1824, saw the relatively rapid formation of two parties, the Federalists and the Jeffersonian Republicans. The issue that divided the parties most clearly was their attitude toward the power of the central government. The commercial and financial interests supported the Federalist position of increasing the authority of the central government, whereas Jeffersonian Republicans distrusted the centralizing and, in their view, aristocratic tendencies of their rivals. The parties began as factions within Congress, but before long they had gained organizations at the state and local level and had substantially broadened the base of political participation among the voting population. After 1815, competition between the two parties all but ceased as the Jeffersonian Republicans gained supremacy, moving the country into the so-called Era of Good Feelings.

The second party system is usually dated from 1828, the year of the first presidential election with substantial popular participation, which marked the resurgence of party competition for the presidency. Emerging ultimately from this renewed competition were the Democrats and the Whigs, parties that competed almost evenly for national power until the 1850s. Mass political participation increased, and party organizations were strengthened as both parties sought electoral support from the common people. Although the Democratic Party had come to prominence led by frontiersman Andrew Jackson, by the 1850s both Democrats and Whigs had adherents in all sections of the nation. Thus, when the issue of slavery broke full force on the nation, the existing parties could not easily cope with the sectional differences they found within their ranks. As the Whigs and Democrats compromised or failed to act because of internal disagreements, a flurry of minor parties appeared to push the cause of abolition. One of these, the Republican Party, eventually replaced the floundering Whigs as one of the two major parties that would dominate party systems thereafter.

The intense conflicts that preceded the Civil War led to the basic regional alignment of Democratic dominance in the South and Republican strength in the North that emerged from the war and that characterized the third-party system. But the extreme intensity and durability of the partisan loyalties were also significantly dependent on emotional attachments associated with the war. The strength of partisan attachments after the Civil War was not lessened by the sharp competitiveness of the two parties throughout the system. Electoral forces were so evenly balanced that the Republican Party could effectively control the presidency and Congress only by excluding the Southern Democrats from participation in elections. Once Reconstruction relaxed enough to permit the full expression of Democratic strength, the nation was narrowly divided, with the slightest deviation determining the outcome of elections.

The most dominant characteristic of the Civil War realignment was the regional division of party strongholds, but considerable Republican vote strength was found throughout much of the South and Democratic strength in most of the North. Especially in the North, states that regularly cast their electoral votes for Republican presidential candidates did so by slim margins. Within each region, persistent loyalty to the minority party was usually related to earlier opposition to the war. The intensity of feelings surrounding the war overwhelmed other issues, and the severity of the division over the war greatly inhibited the emergence of new issues along other lines. Thus, a significant feature of the Civil War realignment is its "freezing" of the party system.[22] Although later realignments have occurred and a fourth and fifth party system can be identified, after the Civil War the same two parties have remained dominant. New parties have found it impossible to compete effectively (although they may occasionally affect electoral outcomes). The subsequent realignments changed only the competitive position of these two parties relative to each other. Thus, although the choices were frozen following the Civil War, the relative strength of the parties was not. Political scientist Nathan Kalmoe has shown that the Civil War was a partisan war, where partisan voters were stable supporters of their party before and during the war, and created stable party cultures long after the war—as late as 1912![23]

Toward the end of the nineteenth century, Civil War loyalties weakened enough to allow new parties, particularly the Populists in the Midwest and South, to make inroads into the votes of both major parties. Following the economic recession of 1893, for which the Democrats suffered politically, the Republican Party began to improve its basic voting strength. In 1896, the formation of a coalition of Democrats and Populists and the unsuccessful presidential candidacy of their nominee, William Jennings Bryan, resulted in increased Republican strength in the East and a further strengthening of the secure position of the Democratic Party in the South. Republican domination was solidified in the Midwest by the popularity of Theodore Roosevelt in the election of 1904. By the early twentieth century, competitive areas were confined to the border states and a few mountain states.

The realignment of 1896 and the fourth party system that followed are appropriately viewed as an adjustment of the Civil War alignment. Few areas shifted far from the previous levels of voting; most individuals probably did not change their partisanship. The issue basis of the alignment was economic. The Republicans advocated development and modernization while opposing regulation of economic activity. The Democrats supported policies intended to provide remedies for particular economic hardships. At a minimum, these issues led the more prosperous, more modern areas in the North to shift toward the Republicans and the more backward, more depressed areas in the South to shift toward the Democrats. These tendencies are based on normal vote patterns and should not obscure the considerable variation in the vote for president during these years, particularly in the elections of 1912 and 1916.

Following the onset of the Great Depression in 1929 under a Republican president, Democrat Franklin D. Roosevelt rode the reaction to economic hardship to a landslide victory in 1932. In his first administration, Roosevelt launched a program of economic recovery and public assistance called the New Deal. The Democrats emerged as the majority party, signaling the start of the fifth party system. The New Deal realignment resulted in far greater shifts than the earlier realignment of 1896, because it moved many of the northern states from Republican to Democratic status. Because the policies of the Democratic administration during the New Deal appealed more to the working class than to the middle class, and more to poor farmers than to prosperous farmers, these groups responded differently to Democratic candidates. The New Deal and the electorate's response to Roosevelt's administration considerably sharpened the social class basis of party support. Especially for younger voters during these years, class politics was of greater salience than it had been before or has been since.

This realignment resulted in adjustments in previous loyalties, but it did not override them completely. The New Deal coalition was based on regional strength in the South, which was independent of social class, and further reinforced an already overwhelming dominance in the region. The most incompatible elements in the New Deal coalition were Southern middle-class whites, mainly conservative, and northern liberals, both white and Black, and this incompatibility led to the later unraveling of the New Deal alignment. The erosion of the New Deal coalition occurred first in presidential voting with the departure of Southern white voters from the Democratic Party. In 1964, the states of the Deep South were the only states carried by Republican candidate Barry Goldwater, a stark reversal of one hundred years of history. This pattern continued for the next four decades. Only when the Democratic candidate was a Southerner (Jimmy Carter in 1976 and Bill Clinton in 1992 and 1996) did the Democrats have a chance to carry some Southern states. In 2000, Al Gore, also a Southerner, was given a chance of winning only two Southern states—Florida and his home state of Tennessee. Ultimately, he won neither. (Of course, he was running against another Southerner, George W. Bush.) However, Obama's success in winning Florida, North Carolina, and Virginia in 2008 and Florida and Virginia again in 2012 needs to be viewed against this recent history.

The departure of the South from the Democratic fold is the major reason for the decline of the New Deal coalition. To a degree, working-class whites in the North also have been attracted to the Republican Party on occasion, and middle-class voters—particularly those in service professions—have shifted toward the Democrats.

Survey data on party identification over the past fifty years yield evidence of the New Deal alignment as well as its later deterioration (recall Table 5-1). In the early years of this period, the advantage that the Democrats enjoyed nationwide was largely a result of having an overwhelming Democratic majority in the South. The increased strength of the Republicans in the South after 1964 led to a number of years of fairly even balance nationwide between Democrats and Republicans. Since 2006, the Democrats have gained an advantage over the Republicans, as Democrats increased their strength in the North.

Another important element regarding shifts in the New Deal alignment, also reflected in these tables, was the increase beginning in 1966 in the proportion of independents. Supporters of George Wallace in the South represented part of this increase initially, but an even larger portion is composed of young voters who, since the early 1970s, have not chosen sides in politics as quickly as their elders did. The increase leveled off in the 1970s, and although the proportions have fluctuated, the number of independents remains near its highest point since the era of survey research began. The 42 percent of independents in 2000 is the largest proportion of independents in the history of the ANES.

The New Deal partisan realignment established in the 1930s remained intact longer in congressional voting. However, by the 1970s, additional shifts in the New Deal alignment became evident, as conservative Republicans began to show strength in races for other offices in many parts of the South. Long-standing

Southern Democratic incumbents in Congress were safe from competition. As they stepped down, though, their seats were won more often than not by Republicans. Conversely, in some areas of the North, moderate Republicans were replaced by liberal Democrats. In the 2008 congressional elections, not one Republican was elected to the House of Representatives from New England. Democratic strength in the South was crucial for the Democrats' control of the House of Representatives for much of this historical period.

We should be clear about what is changing and what is not. White Southerners have always been conservative, especially on matters concerning race. From the Civil War until the 1960s, the Democratic Party was at least as conservative as the Republican Party on the crucial issue of race. When the national Republican Party took the more conservative position on race in 1964, white Southerners began to vote for Republican presidential candidates; they continued to vote for Southern conservative Democratic candidates in state and local races. Meanwhile, for the same reasons in reverse, newly enfranchised Black Southern voters were moving into the Democratic Party. Over the years, the positions of the two parties have become more clearly distinguished—the Democratic Party as the more liberal party on racial as well as economic issues, the Republican Party as the more conservative party. Particularly in the South, voters have changed their partisanship and their votes accordingly. Figure 5-9,[24] showing the party identification of white voters, North and South, from 1952 to 2016, highlights the dramatic shift in the partisanship of white Southerners over this period. The congressional elections of 1994 were perhaps the moment when the shift became complete. Even so, white Southern Democratic Party identifiers have continued to drop in number while non-Southern white Democrats have continued to fluctuate around the 40–50 percent mark. When the Republicans took control of the House of Representatives and Senate, their leadership was predominantly Southern.

Are Conditions Right for a Realignment?

The decline of the New Deal coalition is best seen, we believe, as more of a process of conflict extension than of traditional dealignment.[25] Voter movement and electoral volatility have been in evidence since the 1960s. Furthermore, much of this movement has been a sorting-out process, whereby some voters are finding their natural home in a political party that shares their views on issues that concern them most. Over this same time period, however, a sizable number of voters have found neither political party a congenial place and have chosen instead to become independent—that is, not to adopt a party identification in the first place or support independent candidates such as Perot or, to a lesser extent, Nader. Through the 1990s, neither party was able to gather the political support to take firm control of government or complete initiatives that would appear to solve societal problems and win converts to their ranks. This sounds a lot like dealignment, so what gives?

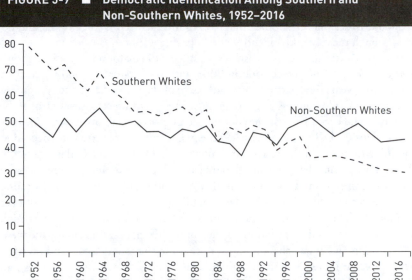

FIGURE 5-9 ■ Democratic Identification Among Southern and Non-Southern Whites, 1952–2016

Source: American National Election Studies, available at www.electionstudies.org.

Thomas Carsey and Geoffrey Layman have argued that what has occurred in American politics can best be described not as dealignment but as "conflict extension."[26] Along with other scholars, they show that the New Deal divide between Republicans and Democrats has remained on economic issues and that political conflict has been extended to include issues of race and social issues like abortion and gay rights. As Edward Carmines, Michael Ensley, and Michael Wagner have shown, some Americans have liberal attitudes across these issues and are strong Democrats, whereas others have conservative attitudes across these same issues and are strong Republicans.[27] However, plenty of people have views that are liberal on one set of issues and conservative on the other. (We discuss this in greater detail in Chapter 6.) Libertarians (conservative on economic issues, liberal on social issues) and populists (the opposite of libertarians) regularly identify as partisans but are more likely to switch their party identification due to short-term forces, are more likely to cast split-ticket ballots, and are less likely to participate. Thus, while elite conflict has extended to a left–right divide across the panoply of political issues currently contested in Washington, the public continues to organize its attitudes separately across economic and social issues. In other words, the New Deal divide has weakened, but it still remains at the same time the parties have adopted competing positions on a whole new set of issues that have pulled some people closer to the parties and pushed others further away. Those who have attitudes on social issues that match the positions offered by their political party have "extended" their conflict with the party on the other side of the aisle. Those who have attitudes on social issues that match one party and attitudes on economic issues that match the other have found themselves stuck in the middle, even though most (weakly) identify with a party.

Into this scenario rode a charismatic young candidate for president who promised change and won the election in 2008 with the largest margin of victory in twenty-four years. His party increased the size of the majorities it had recaptured in both houses of Congress in 2006, giving the new administration control of the legislative and executive branches of the federal government. Six months into the new Congress, the Democrats reached the magic number of sixty votes needed to shut off a filibuster in the Senate, after one switch of allegiance (Arlen Specter of Pennsylvania, who changed from Republican to Democrat) and one resolution to a long-running recount (Al Franken of Minnesota). Public opinion polls found fewer people who identified with the Republicans and more identifying with the Democrats. The new administration took office amid great euphoria, sky-high approval ratings, and an ambitious agenda of health care reform, energy independence, stopping climate change, and restoring international respect and prestige. Several of the ingredients for a realignment were there—a crisis (or crises); an electorate willing to throw the rascals out; a pool of voters without affiliation to either party, available for conversion; and unified control of government, giving the new administration the ability, in principle, to enact its policy agenda. Pundits argued that the opportunity was there for the new administration to capture the imagination of those available independents, turn them into Democrats, and change the partisan division in the country for the foreseeable future. The United States was poised for a true realignment and a new party system.

But . . .

As we contemplate this scenario, we need to keep in mind that many of the voters up for grabs in any given election have a series of issue preferences that do not match up perfectly with either party. In Chapter 6, we describe how Populist voters were more likely to be strong Trump supporters during the 2016 primaries—a departure from their relatively consistent association with Democrats over the previous few decades. If the 2008 election portended a true realignment, Hillary Clinton would have been elected president in 2016. On the one hand, she did win the popular vote, but on the other hand, Republicans made gains in Congress as well, something we would not expect in a realignment advantaging the Democratic Party.

Thus, long-term conversion of these voters is a difficult prospect. Carsey and Layman have also shown that people are willing to change their attitudes to align with their political party on issues that are not very important to them, but this has not occurred enough, nor has it been sufficiently durable, to result in a realignment.[28] Though the administration was moderately successful at enacting its policy agenda (with big victories, including health care reform, the auto bailout, and the economic stimulus plan), it also had some notable failures (failing to close the detention center at Guantánamo Bay, increase the minimum wage to $9.50 per hour, and usher in a new era of bipartisan cooperation in Washington, DC). The Democrats' dramatic loss of seats in Congress in 2010 reflected, in part, the frustration of citizens over the unified government of Democrats not getting more accomplished, which also helped to prevent a cementing of a new and durable Democratic majority.

PARTISAN CHANGE

Partisanship can be thought of as a basic attitude that establishes a normal or expected vote, an estimate about how individuals or populations will vote, other things being equal. However, partisanship itself is not unchangeable. Individuals may change not only their vote but also their long-term party identification from one party to another. More important, over extended periods of time, the partisan composition of the electorate may be altered as new voters of one political persuasion replace older voters of another. When the basic partisan division of the electorate changes, a partisan realignment occurs.

In the past, the absence of survey data limited analysis of realignments, but during the current period, the individual processes of partisan change that underlie aggregate shifts in the partisan division of the electorate can be studied. These processes have been a matter of some controversy. One perspective holds that individual partisans are *converted* from one party to the other during a realignment. Other analysts, noting the psychological difficulty in changing long-held and deeply felt attachments, argue that such change probably comes about through *mobilization*, not conversion. In other words, the independents or nonpolitical individuals, perhaps predominantly young voters just entering the electorate without strong partisan attachments, fuel a realignment by joining the electorate overwhelmingly on the side of one party.

Some evidence on these points comes from the New Deal era. Although survey research was then in its infancy, some scholars have creatively used data from early surveys to try to answer these questions. Research by Kristi Andersen, reported in *The Changing American Voter*, reveals high levels of nonvoting and nonpartisanship among young people and new citizens before the Great Depression.[29] Those uninvolved, uncommitted potential participants entered the electorate in the 1930s disproportionately as Democrats. Andersen's findings on the electorate of the 1920s and 1930s support the view that realignments are based on the mobilization of new, independent voters instead of on the conversion of partisans. In contrast, Robert S. Erikson and Kent L. Tedin argue on the basis of early Gallup poll data that much of the increase in the Democratic vote in the 1930s came from voters who had previously voted Republican.[30] In the next section, we examine the processes of partisan change in the contemporary period. Although we are in a better position to do so than we were for earlier eras, efforts are still hampered by a scarcity of panel data—that is, repeated interviews with the same individuals at different times. In most cases, it will be necessary to infer individual changes from the behavior of different individuals over time.

Changes in Individuals Over a Lifetime

Two types of change in partisan identification can be distinguished, both of which have significant implications for political behavior. First, an individual may change from one party to another or to independent or from independence to partisanship. Such change is important if a large proportion of the electorate shifts in the same direction at about the same time. Second, an individual's partisanship may strengthen or weaken in intensity. A long-standing hypothesis states that the longer individuals identify with a party, the stronger their partisanship will become.[31] In the electorate as a whole, the two types of change are not necessarily related to one another, so the occurrence of one form of change does not dictate or prevent the other. For example, recent decades saw an increase in the number of independents in the electorate, which can be accounted for by young people not choosing a party or by partisans moving to independence or both. At the same time, the remaining partisans have become more firmly committed and more party loyal, and polarization between the parties has increased.

Analysts have attempted to explain partisan change by referring to three types of causal effects: (1) *period effects*, or the impact of a particular historical period that briefly affects partisanship across all age groups; (2) a *generation effect*, which affects the partisanship of a particular age group for the remainder of their political lives; and (3) a *life-cycle effect*, which produces changes associated with an individual's age. In current political behavior, all three can be illustrated: a period effect that resulted in increased independence in all age groups, a generation effect that keeps Democratic partisan loyalty high in the generation that entered the electorate during the New Deal, and a life-cycle effect that yields greater independence among the young than among their elders.

The change in particular age cohorts is worth considering. For example, the youngest age cohort in 1972 was more than forty years old in 1992 and had a lower level of independence than it did when entering the electorate. By 2012, that same cohort was more than sixty years old and had stayed about the same in its level of independence. How do age cohorts identify as independents today? The difference between those thirty and under, those thirty-one to fifty-nine, and those over sixty in the proportion of independents in various age groups is shown in Figure 5-10. In 2020, the younger the cohort, the higher the percentage of people who identified themselves as independents. Of those under thirty, 37.2 percent did not prefer to affiliate with a party as compared to only 26.4 percent of those over sixty.

Contrary to political folklore, little evidence exists that people become Republicans as they grow older—that is, that a life-cycle effect favors Republicans. Older members of the electorate were, for some years, more likely to be Republicans than younger members. The generation of young people who came of age before the Great Depression contained large proportions of Republicans, an understandable situation given the advantage the Republicans enjoyed nationally at that time. Relatively few members of this generation changed partisanship

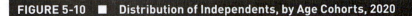

FIGURE 5-10   ■   Distribution of Independents, by Age Cohorts, 2020

Percent Independents

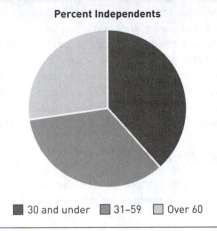

■ 30 and under   ■ 31–59   ☐ Over 60

Source: American National Election Studies, available at www.electionstudies.org.

over the years, and these individuals constituted the older, more heavily Republican segment of the electorate. By the same token, the generation that entered the electorate during the New Deal was disproportionately Democratic. Because they also remained stable in partisanship, older voters looked increasingly Democratic as this generation aged.

However, when party voting is frequently disrupted, this reinforcement of partisanship may not occur. Even if the strength of partisanship does not increase with age, older partisans are less likely to abandon their party and become independents. This explains in part why older partisans are less likely to vote for independent or third-party candidates than are younger partisans. In 1992, 19 percent of the Republican and Democratic partisans aged twenty-five and younger voted for Perot, but only 11 percent of partisans aged forty-five and older voted for him. In 2000, Nader's vote, although small, was greatest among the young.

Gradual changes in individual partisanship have not been assessed satisfactorily for the entire public because the few election studies based on repeated interviews of the same individuals have covered at most four years. Nevertheless, the possibility that individuals change their partisanship over longer time periods is of considerable interest. Speculation has focused on the possibility that the large number of young independents will become identified with one party or the other, thus creating a substantial shift in the overall partisan balance of the electorate. Obama's appeal to young people raised this as a possibility, but 5 percent fewer voters between eighteen and twenty-nine voted for Hillary Clinton in 2016 than Barack Obama in 2012.[32]

The best evidence of this type of change in the past comes from a major study of political socialization led by M. Kent Jennings. He surveyed a national sample of high school students and their parents in 1965, with follow-up interviews in 1973, 1982, and 1997.[33] This study provides a before-and-after picture of young people during the political traumas of the late 1960s and early 1970s, as well as later snapshots after a more quiescent period.

Table 5-5 shows the amount of change in partisanship between each wave of the study. Partisanship was least stable when the respondents were youngest, between 1965 and 1973. About two-thirds of the sample reported the same partisanship when interviewed in 1982 as in 1973 and, again, between 1982 and 1997. Most of the changes that did occur were between partisanship and independence; relatively few reported switching from Democrat to Republican or vice versa.

Changes Across Generations

A shift in the partisan composition of the electorate owing to generational change is ordinarily a gradual one, because political attitudes, including

TABLE 5-5 ■ Stability and Change of Partisanship, 1965–1997									
		1973					1982		
		Dem.	Ind.	Rep.			Dem.	Ind.	Rep.
	Dem.	24	14	3		Dem.	23	9	3
1965	Ind.	7	24	5	1973	Ind.	8	32	7
	Rep.	3	9	10		Rep.	2	4	13
	Total = 99%		N = 952			Total = 101%		N = 924	
		1997							
		Dem.	Ind.	Rep.					
	Dem.	23	7	2					
1982	Ind.	5	27	5					
	Rep.	4	10	17					
	Total = 100%		N = 896						

Source: Youth-Parent Socialization Panel Study, 1965–1997, Youth Wave. Data provided by Interuniversity Consortium for Political and Social Research, available at http://www.icpsr.umich.edu/.

Note: Dem. = Democrat; Ind. = Independent; Rep. = Republican. The highlighted cells (along the diagonal) represent those individuals who remained stable in their partisanship from one time period to the next. The off-diagonal cells represent individuals who changed their partisan identification.

partisanship, tend to be transmitted from parents to their children. Normally, more than two-thirds of the electorate identify with their parents' party if both parents had the same party identification. Adoption of parents' partisanship by their children is consistent with the notion of family socialization, but it is also consistent with the notion that political views are, in part, biological in nature. Children pick up the partisanship of their parents while young, but the parents' influence diminishes as the child comes into contact with other political and social influences during the teenage years. For most individuals, the political influence of their surroundings will be consistent with their family's political leanings, so the similarity between parents' and offspring's partisanship remains strong. In contrast, people who remember their parents as having conflicting loyalties are more likely to be independents than either Democrats or Republicans. This is even more true of the children of parents without any partisan attachments. Thus, in each political generation a sizable number of voters lack an inherited party loyalty.

The Jennings study permits the empirical examination of the process of generational change because it allows a comparison of party identification for parents and their children. Figure 5-11 shows that 58 percent of the seventeen-year-olds in 1965 had adopted the party identification of their parents. Of the high school seniors, 30 percent were Democratic and came from Democratic families. Another 10 percent of the seniors were Democratic but came from independent or Republican families. Although not explicitly shown in Figure 5-11, Democrats had a somewhat higher transmission rate than either Republicans or independents. Despite the higher transmission rate, there were so many more Democratic parents that their children also contributed substantial numbers to the independent ranks.

The latest wave of the Jennings study allows an examination of generational change in a more recent time, by comparing the partisanship of the 1965 high school seniors, now parents, with the partisanship of their high school–aged children (see Figure 5-12). (Not all the original 1965 students had children of that age in 1997, so the focus is on only a subset of those in the original sample reinterviewed in 1997. Therefore, the distribution of partisanship of these parents will not be the same as for the whole 1997 sample covered in Table 5-5. The group of parents is somewhat less Democratic and more Republican than the full group.) Figure 5-12 suggests that parents transmitted their partisanship to their children at a lower rate in the 1990s than they had a generation earlier. Hidden in these numbers, however, are traces of a modest recovery in partisanship. Unlike 1965, the younger generation is only slightly more independent than the parents, and the number of children leaving their parents' parties for independence is about equally offset by the children of independents adopting a partisanship. In 1965, twice as many children opted for independence as moved toward partisanship.

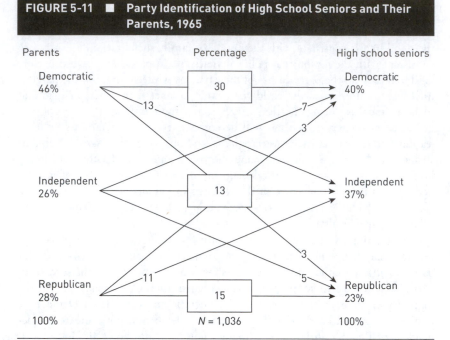

FIGURE 5-11 ■ Party Identification of High School Seniors and Their Parents, 1965

Source: Adapted from Paul A. Beck, Jere W. Bruner, and L. Douglas Dobson, *Political Socialization* (Washington, DC: American Political Science Association, 1974), 22.

Note: On the left of the figure is the distribution of the parents' party identification, and on the right is their children's. The numbers in the three boxes highlight the percentages of the children who had the same party identification as their parents. The numbers on the remaining arrows show various amounts of change from their parents' partisanship by the children. For example, 7 percent of the total number of children had independent parents but became Democrats.

THE FUTURE OF PARTIES AND PARTISANSHIP

Since the 1970s, some political observers have commented on the weakness of political parties, citing especially the overall increase in independents and the appeal of independent candidates, such as Anderson in 1980 or Perot in 1992 and 1996. These factors, combined with declines in trust and confidence in government, turnout, and attention to political news, have suggested to some that the American public has lost its capacity to identify with political parties in a meaningful way. A corollary would suggest there would likely never be another realignment because political parties would not be able to attract new partisans to their camps.

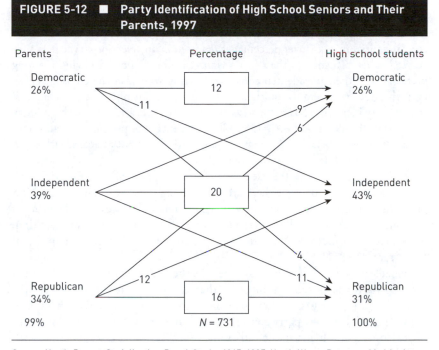

FIGURE 5-12 ■ **Party Identification of High School Seniors and Their Parents, 1997**

Parents	Percentage	High school students
Democratic 26%	12	Democratic 26%
Independent 39%	20	Independent 43%
Republican 34%	16	Republican 31%
99%	N = 731	100%

Source: Youth-Parent Socialization Panel Study, 1965–1997, Youth Wave. Data provided by Inter-university Consortium for Political and Social Research, available at http://www.icpsr.umich.edu/.

A contrary point of view argues that many of these trends slowed or stopped in the late 1970s, and that partisan stability and party-loyal behavior since then have been nearly as high as in the 1950s. Analysts cite increases in party-line voting in Congress, sharper ideological division between the parties, and an increase in uncivil political discourse in the mass media and in Congress as evidence of the increased commitment to, as well as the polarization of, political parties.

So is partisanship becoming stronger or weaker? It seems to us that both these phenomena are occurring—in different parts of the electorate. On the one hand, among political elites and party activists, the polarization and hostility are becoming greater. On the other hand, a large pool of individuals remain who do not strongly identify with either of the major parties and for whom the increased intensity of the partisan debate is off-putting. More generally, in the words of political scientist Julia Azari, the United States has weak parties and strong partisans. Party organizations have little power over office holders and candidates, Azari argues, but partisanship is strong in the electorate. This combination could be dangerous when it comes to the health of political institutions.[34]

The close competitiveness of recent presidential elections has raised the intensity of feelings about politics. As we showed in Chapter 3, almost half the public reported trying to influence other people's votes in 2004 and again in 2008. This is a substantial increase over percentages reported in any election in the past fifty years. Higher percentages than in previous elections reported having a strong preference for their presidential choice and caring who won the election. However, this does not seem to translate to stronger partisanship. The percentage of strong party identifiers has not increased in twenty years and is not as high today as it was in the 1950s and early 1960s. The percentage of people who call themselves "extremely liberal" or "extremely conservative" has not increased either and is generally a small fraction of the population.

A sizable segment of the electorate distrusts political parties, preferring divided government to keep either party from doing too much. The 2008 ANES found that a majority of the public (51 percent) preferred to see divided control of government, though a Gallup survey just four years later saw that number drop to 23 percent. In 2016, Gallup estimated preferences for divided government at 20 percent.[35]

For at least some of these nonparty people, the problem with the parties is the same partisan and ideological intensity that has been increasing. They see the party elites and activists as extreme in their views, whereas they see themselves as moderate. They view party conflict in Washington as divisive and contributing to, instead of solving, the country's problems. These are the people attracted to Trump's and Sanders's attacks on the party system. For such people, heightened partisan debate is unlikely to move them to embrace a political party. Becoming more engaged in political discussion, turning out to vote, and trying to influence the views of others are not unimportant aspects of the public's behavior, and they may signal changes in the partisan feelings of American citizens. However, the largest changes in partisan behavior are among leaders and political activists.

Study Questions

1. What is party identification, and how has Americans' attachment to their party changed over time?

2. What are some of the key characteristics of affective polarization?

3. How do different ways of categorizing independents influence how we understand the role they play in American elections?

4. What are some key characteristics of realignment?

Suggested Readings

Blum, Rachel M. *How the Tea Party Captured the GOP: Insurgent Factions in American Politics*. Chicago: University of Chicago Press, 2020. A book that chronicles how the Tea Party insurgents in the Republican Party increased their political influence in the two-party system.

Campbell, Angus, Philip E. Converse, Warren E. Miller, and Donald E. Stokes. *The American Voter*. New York: Wiley, 1960. The classic study of public opinion and voting behavior in the United States.

Green, Donald, Bradley Palmquist, and Eric Schickler. *Partisan Hearts and Minds: Political Parties and the Social Identities of Voters*. New Haven, CT: Yale University Press, 2004. A strong argument for party identification as a social-psychological orientation and a powerful determinant of vote choice and political attitudes.

Klar, Samara, and Yanna Krupnikov. *Independent Politics: How American Disdain for Parties Leads to Political Inaction*. New York: Cambridge University Press, 2016. Unique account of how some citizens have become embarrassed by their partisan attachments and started to identify as independents; Klar and Krupnikov then show the consequences of independent identification on political action in the United States.

Lavine, Howard G., Christopher D. Johnston, and Marco R. Steenbergen. *The Ambivalent Partisan: How Critical Loyalty Promotes Democracy*. New York: Oxford University Press, 2012. A fascinating analysis of partisans' willingness to view the world accurately and pay attention to issues and how this contributes to good democratic citizenship.

Lewis-Beck, Michael S., William G. Jacoby, Helmut Norpoth, and Herbert F. Weisberg. *The American Voter Revisited*. Ann Arbor: University of Michigan Press, 2008. A rich reanalysis of the themes from the classic work using mainly 2000 and 2004 data.

Mason, Lilliana. *Uncivil Agreement: How Politics Became Our Identity*. Chicago: University of Chicago Press, 2018. A careful and far-reaching study that highlights the rise of social polarization in American party politics.

Noel, Hans. *Political Ideologies and Political Parties in America*. New York: Cambridge University Press, 2013. A theoretically and empirically innovative study that shows how the growth of modern liberalism and conservatism developed independent of the Republican and Democratic Parties—and then restructured the parties in their image.

Wolbrecht, Christina. *The Politics of Women's Rights: Parties, Positions and Change*. Princeton, NJ: Princeton University Press, 2000. A detailed and persuasive analysis showing that the parties were transformed by the women's rights debate in American public life.

Notes

1. Lilliana Mason, *Uncivil Agreement: How Politics Became Our Identity* (Chicago: University of Chicago Press, 2018).

2. Chris Wells, Katherine J. Cramer, Michael W. Wagner, German Alvarez, Lewis A. Friedland, Dhavan V. Shah, Leticia Bode, Stephanie Edgerly, Itay Gabay, and Charles Franklin, "When We Stop Talking Politics: The Maintenance and Closing of Conversation in Contentious Times," *Journal of Communication* 67 (2017): 131–157.

3. E. E. Schattschneider, *Party Government* (New York: Farrar & Rinehart, 1942), 1.

4. The most important research cited on party identification is in Angus Campbell, Philip E. Converse, Warren E. Miller, and Donald E. Stokes, *The American Voter* (New York: Wiley, 1960), 120–167. For an updated treatment, see Michael S. Lewis-Beck, William G. Jacoby, Helmut Norpoth, and Herbert F. Weisberg, *The American Voter Revisited* (Ann Arbor: University of Michigan Press, 2008), Chapters 6 and 7.

5. Michael W. Wagner, "The Utility of Staying on Message: Competing Partisan Frames and Public Awareness of Elite Differences on Issues," *The Forum* 5 (2007): 1–18; Michael W. Wagner and Michael W. Gruszczynski, "When Framing Matters: How Partisan and Journalistic Frames Affect Public Opinion and Party Identification," *Journalism and Communication Monographs* 18, no. 1 (2016): 5–48. DOI: 10.1177/1522637915623965.

6. For the most important statement of these ideas, see Philip E. Converse, "The Concept of a Normal Vote," in *Elections and the Political Order*, eds. Angus Campbell, Philip E. Converse, Warren E. Miller, and Donald E. Stokes (New York: Wiley, 1966), 9–39.

7. This discussion and data presentation are based on earlier work by the authors of the first twelve editions of this book, William H. Flanigan and Nancy H. Zingale, "The Measurement of Electoral Change," *Political Methodology* 1 (Summer 1974): 49–82.

8. Alan I. Abramowitz, "Partisan Nation: The Rise of Affective Partisanship in the American Electorate," in *The State of the Parties: The Changing Role of Contemporary American Parties*, eds. John C. Green, Daniel J. Coffey, and David B. Cohen (Lanham, MD: Rowman and Littlefield, 2014).

9. Shanto Iyengar, Gaurav Sood, and Yphtach Lelkes, "Affect, Not Ideology: A Social Identity Perspective on Polarization," *Public Opinion Quarterly* 76, no. 3 (2012): 405–431.

10. "Presidential Election, 2020," Ballotpedia, accessed July 4, 2021, https://ballotpedia.org/Presidential_election,_2020.

11. Larry Bartels argues that partisan loyalty has been steadily increasing since its nadir in 1972, but this trend has been overlooked by analysts focusing on the weakness of the political parties. See Larry Bartels, "Partisanship and Voting Behavior, 1952–1996," *American Journal of Political Science* 44 (January 2000): 35–50.

12. Paul R. Abramson and John H. Aldrich, "The Decline of Electoral Participation in America," *American Political Science Review* 76 (September 1982): 502–521.

13. Kevin K. Banda, "Issue Ownership Cues and Candidate Support," *Party Politics* 27, no. 3 (2019): 552–564.

14. Had Bush adviser Karl Rove not implemented his strategy to turn out the vote among Christian conservatives in safe Republican states in the South, Bush would have again lost the popular vote nationwide, while winning in the Electoral College.

15. Arthur H. Miller and Martin P. Wattenberg, "Measuring Party Identification: Independent or No Partisan Preference?," *American Journal of Political Science* 27 (February 1983): 106–121.

16. John Petrocik, "An Analysis of Intransitivities in the Index of Party Identification," *Political Methodology* 1 (Summer 1974): 31–47.

17. Samara Klar and Yanna Krupnikov, *Independent Politics: How American Disdain for Parties Leads to Political Inaction* (New York: Cambridge University Press, 2016).

18. Nick Vivani, "Kanye West Won't Be on the Wisconsin Ballot, Elections Commission Rules," WSAW, August 20, 2020, https://www.wsaw.com/2020/08/20/kanye-west-wont-be-on-the-wisconsin-ballot-elections-commission-rules/.

19. This and most discussions of the classification of elections are based on the work of V. O. Key and Angus Campbell. See V. O. Key, "A Theory of Critical Elections," *Journal of Politics* 17 (1955): 3–18; and Angus Campbell, "A Classification of Presidential Elections," in *Elections and the Political Order*, eds. Angus Campbell, Philip E. Converse, Warren E. Miller, and Donald E. Stokes (New York: Wiley, 1966), 63–77.

20. This and the following discussion draw heavily on Jerome M. Clubb, William H. Flanigan, and Nancy H. Zingale, *Partisan Realignment: Voters, Parties, and Government in American History* (Boulder, CO: Westview Press, 1990). See especially Chapters 5 and 8.

21. See, for example, William N. Chambers and Walter Dean Burnham, eds., *The American Party Systems: Stages of Political Development* (New York: Oxford University Press, 1975).

22. This concept was developed by Seymour Martin Lipset and Stein Rokkan in their discussion of the development of the European party systems in *Party Systems and Voter Alignments* (New York: Free Press, 1967), 1–64.

23. Nathan P. Kalmoe, *With Ballots and Bullets: Partisanship and Violence in the American Civil War* (New York: Cambridge University Press, 2020).

24. At the time we submitted our book for publication, the ANES had not released data including which state the respondents lived in, so we could not update Figures 5-9 and 5-10 with 2020 data.

25. Some analysts have argued that the movement of white Southerners into the Republican Party and that of Blacks and some northern whites into the Democratic Party constitutes a realignment and should be regarded as the start of a new party system. Disagreement arises about when this realignment occurred. Some date it from the 1960s, with the start of Republican dominance in presidential voting; others view it as a Reagan realignment of the 1980s.

26. Thomas M. Carsey and Geoffrey C. Layman, "Changing Sides or Changing Minds? Party Identification and Policy Preferences in the American Electorate," *American Journal of Political Science* 50, no. 2 (2006): 464–477.

27. Edward G. Carmines, Michael J. Ensley, and Michael W. Wagner, "Political Ideology in American Politics: One, Two, or None?," *The Forum* 10, no. 4 (2012): 1–18.

28. Carsey and Layman, "Changing Sides or Changing Minds?"

29. Norman H. Nie, Sidney Verba, and John R. Petrocik, *The Changing American Voter* (Cambridge, MA: Harvard University Press, 1976), Chapter 5.

30. Robert S. Erikson and Kent L. Tedin, "The 1928–1936 Partisan Realignment: The Case for the Conversion Hypothesis," *American Political Science Review* 75 (December 1981): 951–962.

31. Philip E. Converse, *The Dynamics of Party Support: Cohort-Analyzing Party Identification* (Beverly Hills, CA: SAGE, 1976).

32. Jon Huang, Samuel Jacoby, Michael Strickland, and K. K. Rebecca Lai, producers, "Election 2016: Exit Polls," *New York Times*, November 8, 2016, https://www.nytimes.com/interactive/2016/11/08/us/politics/election-exit-polls.html?_r=0.

33. The parents were also reinterviewed in 1973. By 1997, many of the original high school seniors were parents of high school–aged students. The study also interviewed the children of the original sample, creating a second set of parent–child interviews to compare with the original data from 1965. See Figure 5-11.

34. Julia Azari, "Weak Parties and Strong Partisanship Are a Bad Combination," Vox, November 3, 2016, https://www.vox.com/mischiefs-of-faction/2016/11/3/13512362/weak-parties-strong-partisanship-bad-combination.

35. Art Swift, "In U.S., Preference for Divided Government Lowest in Fifteen Years," Gallup, September 28, 2016, http://www.gallup.com/poll/195857/preference-divided-government-lowest-years.aspx.

6

PUBLIC OPINION
AND IDEOLOGY

REPRESENTATIVE DEMOCRACY REQUIRES an understanding of *public opinion*—the collective attitudes of the public, or segments of the public, toward the issues of the day—and how well these preferences are reflected in what government does. Public opinion polls are an ever-present feature of American public life and contemporary journalism. You can scarcely flip on the TV or read a push notification from a media outlet on your phone without being inundated with the latest poll telling you what the American people think about issues ranging from whether people believe the 2020 election was stolen to whether Washington, DC, should become a state to how movements like Black Lives Matter (BLM) and policy proposals like the Green New Deal can be framed to maximize or minimize public support.[1] Understanding the nature, measurement, and content of public opinion is crucial to explaining American political behavior. In this chapter, our learning objectives are:

- Understanding how public opinion is measured and interpreted

- Learning about the array of views Americans have on economic, racial, social, defense, and international issues

- Considering the nature of political ideology and whether Americans have a political ideology representing a coherent set of fundamental beliefs or principles about politics that serves as a guide to current political issues, much as partisanship does

- Exploring state- and national-level relationships between leadership and public opinion

THE MEASUREMENT OF PUBLIC OPINION

The commercial opinion-polling organizations have spent more than eight decades asking Americans about their views on matters of public policy. Most of this investigation has taken one of two forms: (1) asking individuals whether they "approve or disapprove of" or "agree or disagree with" a statement of policy or (2) asking individuals to pick their preference among two or more alternative statements of policy. This form of questioning seriously exaggerates the number of people who hold views on political issues. People can easily say "agree" or "disapprove" in response to a question, even if they know nothing at all about the topic. If given the opportunity, many people will volunteer the information that they hold no views on specific items of public policy. For example, during the 2011 showdown between President Barack Obama and congressional Republicans over raising the debt ceiling, about 35 percent of those polled by Gallup said they did not know enough about the issue to have an opinion.[2] In contrast, in the past several decades, less than 5 percent of all adults had no opinion on issues such as abortion or the death penalty. Other issues, like the North American Free Trade Agreement, have gone from 16 percent of the public having no opinion in 1997 to 6 percent having no opinion in 2017—shortly after Donald Trump raised the salience of trade issues on the campaign trail.[3] More typically in recent years, approximately 10 percent of the electorate has had no opinion on major issues of public policy. Philip E. Converse has shown, in addition, that a number of those individuals who appear to have an opinion may be regarded as responding to policy questions at random.[4] One reason for this is that many people form opinions during a telephone survey off the top of their heads, usually based on the most recent or salient information about the issue they can immediately recall.[5] Indeed, people are more likely to be uninformed, rather than misinformed, about major issues in American politics.[6]

The lack of opinion and information on topics of public policy can be explained in several ways. In general, the factors that explain nonvoting also account for the absence of opinions. Individuals who are not very interested in or concerned about politics are the least likely to have opinions on matters of public policy. Beyond this basic relationship, those with lower socioeconomic status are associated with a lack of opinion on issues. Low income and little education create social circumstances in which individuals are less likely to be exposed to and learn the information they need to develop clear views on public policies.

Of course, not all issues are equal. Some issues of public policy, such as abortion or the death penalty, are relatively easy to understand; others may be much more difficult, requiring individuals to face complex considerations. Edward G. Carmines and James A. Stimson have argued that different segments of the public respond to "hard" issues that involve calculation of policy benefits and "easy" issues that call for symbolic, "gut responses." Relatively unsophisticated, uninterested members of the electorate respond to easy issues; the more sophisticated, most interested citizens are more likely to take positions on hard issues and are just as likely to take positions on easy ones.[7]

Partisan labels also affect people's opinions. Paul Sniderman and John Bullock found that adding words like "Democrats say" or "Republicans say" to an issue position increased individual ideological constraint.[8] That is, liberals were more likely to agree with a position when it carried a Democratic Party label, and conservatives were more likely to favor preferences with a Republican Party endorsement.

It is no simple matter to describe the distribution of opinions in the American electorate because no obvious, widely accepted method has been established to measure these opinions. Asking different questions in public opinion polls will elicit different answers. Even on the issue of abortion, on which most people have views, the distribution of opinions can be substantially altered by asking respondents whether they approve of "killing unborn children" as opposed to "letting women have control over their own bodies." Furthermore, unlike reports of voting behavior, no direct means exist to validate measures of opinions. As a consequence, descriptions of public opinion must be taken as more uncertain and more tentative than those drawn from the discussion of partisanship.

The mode of public opinion gathering can also affect the distribution of opinions. The results from surveys asking Americans for whom they planned to vote in the presidential election varied substantially, based on whether the survey was a phone survey using random-digit dialing of landlines, included cell phone numbers, was conducted on the internet, or was administered face-to-face. Now that more than half of American homes do not have landlines,[9] survey researchers who rely on phone calls mix an increasing percentage of cell phone numbers in the samples.[10] This is especially critical for capturing younger people in surveys. The American National Election Studies (ANES), which provides most of the data used in this book, used a mix of video, phone, and internet sampling in 2020.[11]

Beyond the mode of the survey, nonresponse to public opinion polling can skew results. The Elections Research Center (ERC) at the University of Wisconsin–Madison conducted a multiwave panel survey in 2020 in several swing states. In each wave, the ERC tried to reinterview the same people interviewed in the first wave, but of course, some people refused to participate again. This is called attrition. Working with the survey firm YouGov, the ERC replaced those who did not participate in multiple waves of the survey with new, carefully sampled respondents. Interestingly, the first survey the ERC conducted, back in February 2020,[12] was the most accurate prediction of the election results in the swing states. One reason for this could be that as the election got closer, and President Trump looked like he would lose, his supporters became less willing to participate in surveys, making it look like he was performing worse than he actually was. Another potential explanation is that survey firms were systematically undersampling a key group of Trump supporters so that their intent to vote for the president was not captured in surveys. The Pew Research Center has studied whether polls that significantly overestimated Joe Biden's vote in a state are a sign that polls about issues are similarly skewed, so far concluding that they are not.[13]

After public opinion is measured, it needs to be interpreted. When reading results from a public opinion survey, it is important to look for the nature of the sample (e.g., adults, registered voters, or likely voters) and the size of the sample. A good rule of thumb is that a national U.S. sample of one thousand adults will have a ±4 percent margin of error.[14] This means that if the survey firm conducted the poll one hundred times, the results would be within 4 percentage points of the survey result ninety-five out of one hundred times. So, if a survey reported that 53 percent of people favored a policy with a margin of error of 3 percent, we could be very confident that the true level of support for the whole population would be between 50 and 56 percent. With this knowledge in mind about how opinions are measured and how polls are interpreted, let us move on to describing some contours of American political opinion.

PUBLIC OPINION ON ISSUES

Domestic Economic Issues

The liberal–conservative ideological divide related to the government's role in managing the economy has dominated partisan politics since 1932. A little more than a month after he took office, major economic problems caused by the COVID-19 pandemic led President Biden to advocate for and sign a $1.9 trillion relief package that received no Republican votes, highlighting this ideological divide. The collapse of the financial sector in the fall of 2008 and the actions of both the Bush administration and the incoming Obama administration to stimulate the economy and to bail out and then reregulate banks and insurance companies brought cries of "socialism" from conservative politicians and commentators. Highly partisan debate over President Obama's health care plan reminded Democrats of the failure of the Clinton administration's health care plan in 1993. This failure helped usher in the loss of the House of Representatives to the Republicans in 1994 and promises of a "conservative revolution" that would reduce government involvement in the economy and cut support for various social programs. In similar fashion, Ronald Reagan's victory in 1980 and his administration's subsequent cutting of taxes and social programs was portrayed as a reversal of fifty years of economic liberalism. Elections have consequences, and in policy terms, there have certainly been consequences of Republican or Democratic victories. In terms of public opinion, however, broad and continuing public support remains for many governmental initiatives, regardless of election outcomes. As George W. Bush discovered when he proposed privatizing Social Security after winning reelection in 2004, long-standing programs that appear to benefit "deserving" segments of the population are difficult to reform because they enjoy widespread support.

The responses to public opinion questions, and public opinion itself, can be affected by political rhetoric and election slogans. For example, the General Social Survey asks a long series of questions on whether spending on various programs is "too much, not enough, or about right." Over the years, sizable proportions of the public have said that too much is being spent on "welfare." At the same time, even larger proportions have said not enough is being spent on "assistance to the poor."[15] Clearly, years of racist anecdotes about welfare queens and promises to end welfare as we know it have had their effect on the way particular programs are perceived, if not on the public's general willingness to use government as an instrument for social purposes.

Figure 6-1 shows the distribution of attitudes toward spending for different governmental purposes, using the 2020 ANES. It is clear that there are major partisan differences across spending preferences for almost every issue. Majorities of Democrats favor increasing spending on social security, public schools, welfare programs, highway maintenance, aiding the poor, and protecting the environment. Majorities of Republicans prefer more spending on border security, public schools, dealing with crime, and highway maintenance.

On some issues, the disagreements between the parties are about whether spending should be increased or decreased. For example, Democrats want more spending on welfare programs while Republicans want less. However, most differences are between a spending change and the status quo. Republicans prefer more spending on dealing with crime and on border security while a plurality of Democrats prefer spending to stay as it is on those issues. More than 60 percent of Democrats want more social security spending whereas Republicans were evenly divided between preferring more spending and preferring the same level of spending.

Overall, Figure 6-1 shows fairly widespread willingness to support government spending on domestic social programs, something that has been true for the past several decades. Importantly, many government benefits that come from spending are hidden from public view. Suzanne Mettler's *The Submerged State* shows that most Americans are unaware of the many government benefits they receive and are even less aware that the affluent are the most likely to benefit from these programs.[16]

Perhaps not surprisingly, examining how different social groups think about major political issues reveals some fairly dramatic differences in what people want from the government. Figure 6-2 is based on a question in the 2020 ANES that offers respondents a choice between "cutting spending and decreasing services" and "increasing services and increasing spending." We look at responses to this question for several social categories, using race and ethnicity, education, and religion as variables. The pattern in the figure is not difficult to discern. The least economically secure—Blacks, Hispanics, and whites with no religious preferences and some or no college—support government services most strongly. The groups most distinctively in favor of cutting spending and services are white Protestants and Catholics with no college or some college.

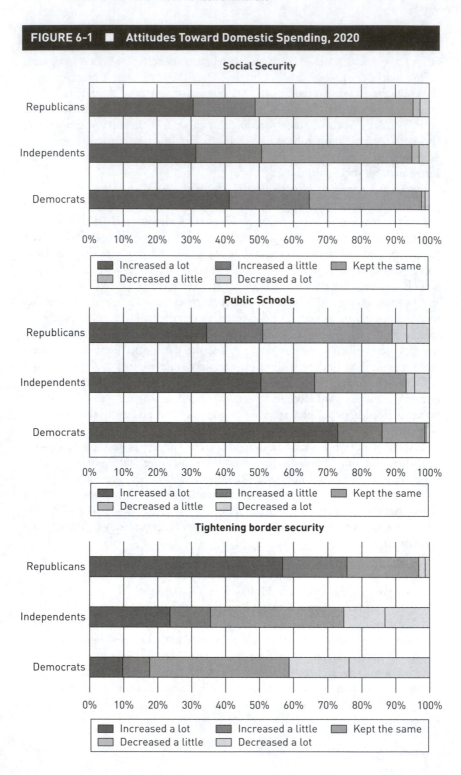

FIGURE 6-1 ■ Attitudes Toward Domestic Spending, 2020

Social Security

Public Schools

Tightening border security

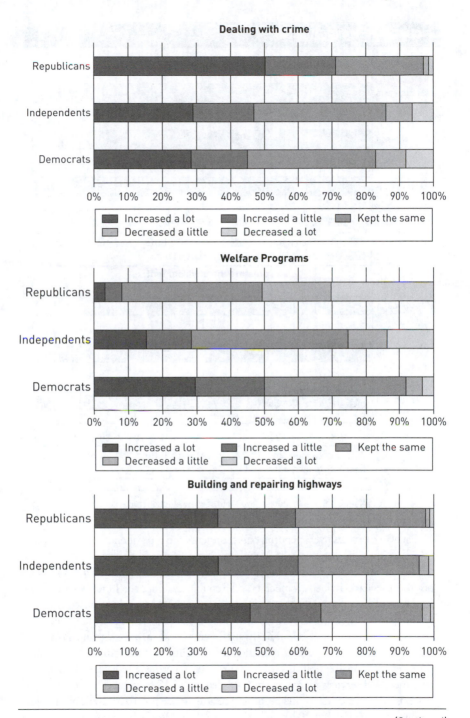

(Continued)

FIGURE 6-1 ■ (Continued)

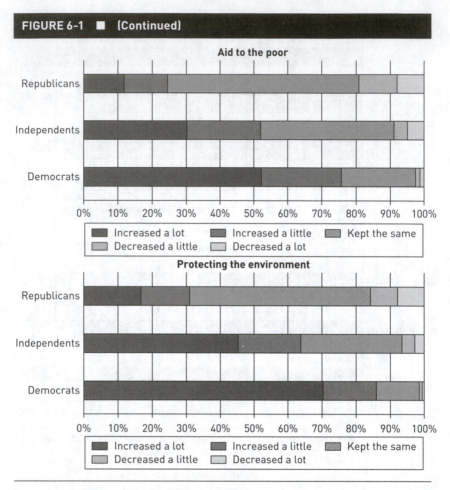

Source: American National Election Studies, available at www.electionstudies.org.

Favoring services over spending cuts represents the type of choice in governmental policy that characterized the New Deal. Thus, it would be reasonable to expect a dramatic difference between Democrats and Republicans on such an issue. Economic issues have divided Democrats and Republicans since the 1930s, whereas other issues have been of only temporary significance for the parties. As a consequence, the relationship in Table 6-1 showing that Democrats disproportionately favor increased government services and Republicans prefer cuts is no surprise. Strong Democrats favor increased services over a reduction in spending by a margin of 75 percent to 3 percent; strong Republicans are the opposite, favoring a reduction in spending over increased services by a margin of 48 percent to 15 percent. This basic pattern has existed for decades. While becoming steadily more polarized, Republican views became less polarized in 2020, perhaps due to the COVID-19 pandemic.

FIGURE 6-2 ■ Attitudes Toward Cutting Spending Versus Increasing Government Services, by Race, Ethnicity, Religion, and Education, 2020

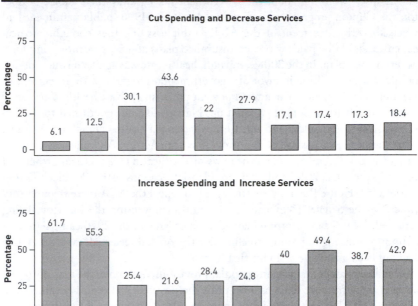

Source: 2020 American National Election Studies, available at www.electionstudies.org.

Rising health care costs have been a concern for years. Health care was the dominant issue in the first years of the Obama administration. Reforming the health care system was also attempted early in the Clinton administration, when President Bill Clinton appointed First Lady Hillary Rodham Clinton to head a group to develop a proposal for a national health care program. The managed competition program eventually proposed was not the national health care program favored by the most liberal advocates, but the ensuing debate was cast in terms of governmentally mandated and regulated programs versus private insurance companies with individual choice in health care providers. Ultimately, the Clinton administration lost the battle in Congress and in the arena of public opinion. Initially in 1992, the public favored a governmental insurance plan,

44 percent to 24 percent, over private insurance plans.[17] After health insurance and pharmaceutical companies and the American Medical Association launched an extensive advertising campaign featuring a middle American couple, "Harry and Louise," worrying about the government taking away their choice of doctor, the Clinton program went down in defeat. By 1996, public sentiment had reversed, with 40 percent of the ANES sample saying they thought medical expenses should be paid by private insurance plans and 34 percent opting for a governmental plan. In the 2008 campaign, health care was again an issue, and the public was again tilting in favor of a governmental program, with 48 percent in favor of a governmental plan and 34 percent preferring private health insurance.[18]

As the debate in Congress geared up, Harry and Louise returned to the airwaves, sixteen years older and this time *supporting* a health care reform package. After the successful passage of the Affordable Care Act (ACA), known as Obamacare by political opponents and the news media, health care was again front and center in the 2012, 2016, and 2020 presidential elections. After President Trump was elected, House Republicans attempted to repeal the ACA more than seventy times. In the Senate, Democrats closed ranks, preventing the bill from being repealed. Health care reform remained a major issue in the 2020 campaign with Trump continuing to promise to eliminate the ACA if reelected, even though he had not been able to do so in his first term.

While the law contains many popular provisions, opinion of the entirety of the act was more negative than positive until the possibility of repeal became more serious. In 2021, the ACA is slightly more popular than not.[19] Table 6-2 shows the durability of partisan divisions on health care issues as Democrats continued to favor government-sponsored health insurance and Republicans strongly favored private health insurance in 2020. Interestingly, after Trump's victory, when the possibility of the ACA being overturned was suddenly real, the legislation became much more popular. Strong Republican support of government health insurance doubled from 2016 to 2020.

TABLE 6-1 ■ Attitudes Toward Cutting Spending Versus Increasing Government Services, by Party Identification, 2020					
	Strong Democrats	Weak Democrats	Independents	Weak Republicans	Strong Republicans
Favor cutting spending	3%	6%	21%	35%	48%
Neutral	11	16	20	25	24
Favor increasing government services	75	62	43	20	15

Source: 2020 American National Election Studies, available at www.electionstudies.org.

TABLE 6-2 ■ Attitudes on Health Care, by Party Identification, 2020					
	Strong Democrats	Weak Democrats	Independents	Weak Republicans	Strong Republicans
Favor governmental health insurance	67%	57%	43%	23%	10%
Favor private health insurance	11	14	27	47	66

Source: 2020 American National Election Studies, available at www.electionstudies.org.

Racial Justice Issues

Race and attitudes associated with race hold a prominent place in American political history. For many years after Reconstruction, little overt public attention was paid to racial issues. The South was allowed to impose its system of segregation on its Black population by law, while informal, de facto methods created much the same system of separate neighborhoods and segregated schools in the North. After integration became a major national and international focal point of attention in the 1940s and 1950s, a number of significant developments in the political attitudes of the public occurred. First, Southern Blacks have become an organized, involved, politically motivated group. Removing the legal barriers to voting in the South enabled Black voters in Southern states to command the attention of politicians at the ballot box and in state legislatures and governors' mansions.

Second, large numbers of Southern whites have adjusted their opinions to accept the realities of the new legal and political position of Black Americans. The public, as a whole, has come to support the general principle of racial equality. The recent near unanimity on this point means that the vast majority of Americans no longer express support for policies and practices that explicitly discriminate against racial groups, and making political appeals based on blatant racism is no longer consistent with the dominant political culture.

At the same time, the public has not moved significantly closer to supporting governmental programs designed to improve the economic and social position of racial groups. Northern as well as Southern whites have consistently opposed busing for the purposes of integration. More than 80 percent of whites oppose affirmative action on behalf of racial minorities, and less than half support the federal government enforcing fair employment practices. The proportion of the public supporting various forms of governmental action to aid Blacks is shown in Table 6-3. In contrast to the near unanimity of support for "letting [B]lack and white children go to school together," less than half of the public supports positive actions on the part of government to improve the social and economic position of Blacks.

The lack of connection between broad principle and policy implementation has been the focus of both political debate and scholarly disagreement. One side argues that opposition to programs to aid Blacks is based, in general, on opposition to governmental activities and, in particular, on programs that benefit a subgroup of society.[20] This position, often referred to as "racial conservatism," is seen as stemming from a general philosophical commitment to limited government and a belief in individualism. The attitudes, it is argued, are based on principles, not racism.

The other view argues that opposition to policy proposals to use governmental programs to aid the social and economic circumstances of Blacks and other underrepresented groups stems from racial hostility, even though racial conservatives may have learned to cloak their racism in acceptable philosophical language. To complicate the matter further, scholars take different views of how racial hostility expresses itself in political attitudes. Scholars have used three dimensions of racial hostility to explain white support for or opposition to governmental policies regarding race:

1. Racial resentment (the feeling that Blacks are getting more than they deserve) or racial disapproval (the feeling that Blacks do not live up to certain value expectations, such as working hard).[21] These contentions are often referred to as *symbolic racism*.

2. Group conflict (zero-sum conflicts over scarce resources).[22]

3. Social dominance (protection of the status quo by a dominant group).[23]

These dimensions of racial hostility can be interrelated and may reinforce one another. It is difficult to separate them or to be confident in measuring them or evaluating which dimension contributes the most to racial attitudes. Measuring racial attitudes is especially tricky because social norms in twenty-first-century America dictate against making explicitly racist statements and people want to give answers to survey interviewers that are socially desirable. Interpreting racial attitudes can also be tricky. Although these dimensions are often labeled as if they were positive or negative in content, they have both pro-Black and anti-Black extremes. In other words, if a Black person believes strongly that Black people are not getting what they deserve, racial resentment may be involved just as much as when a white person believes that Blacks are getting more than they deserve.

To connect these dimensions with attitudes about policies designed to provide governmental aid to underrepresented groups, it seems reasonable to assume that people must view potential beneficiaries of governmental aid as deserving. The extent to which Blacks and other people of color are viewed as deserving by white Americans may depend on whether Blacks are seen as individually responsible for their position or whether they are seen as victims of social and economic forces beyond their control. Presumably, whites who believe that Blacks can improve their situation through their own efforts will not view them as deserving of special governmental programs on their behalf. This basis of opposition would fit the symbolic racism perspective. Whites who see social structures and conditions imposing special hardships on Blacks regardless of their individual efforts will view Blacks as deserving of special assistance.

Even if Blacks are viewed by whites as deserving of government assistance, special programs may be opposed if whites see these programs as coming at the expense of whites. Another similar basis for opposition to programs for Blacks is the expectation that the status quo, which favors whites, will be disrupted, which would be undesirable from the point of view of whites. These objections are examples of the group conflict and social dominance perspectives.

A racial conservative might make the argument that there was once a time when all the relevant democratic principles were on the side of helping Blacks but that more recently such principles work both ways. Blacks should have an equal chance to get an education, find a job, and so forth, but they should not be given advantages over other deserving people. Indeed, this was the argument that the majority of the Supreme Court used in its 2013 decision overturning key provisions of the Voting Rights Act that had required federal approval when states with a history of racial discrimination wanted to change voting procedures. However, great differences are found in the perceptions of Blacks and whites about whether or not Blacks have an equal chance in American society.

Racial attitudes have had a profound effect on the American political landscape. In their book *Issue Evolution*, Carmines and Stimson argue that an evolution of the racial issue since the early 1960s has led increasingly to the Democratic Party being perceived as the liberal party on civil rights issues and the Republican Party being perceived as the conservative party.[24] They see this distinction as the dominant perception of the parties in the eyes of the public, representing a fundamental redefinition of the issue alignment that has characterized the parties since the New Deal.

Before the 1960s, Republicans (the party of Abraham Lincoln) were seen as more progressive on civil rights than Democrats, particularly in light of the strongly segregationist cast to the Southern wing of the Democratic Party. Carmines and Stimson show that a change occurred during the 1960s and 1970s, when the elites of the two parties—members of Congress and presidential candidates—as well as party activists became distinctive in their racial views. The Democratic Party became dominated by northern liberals advocating stronger governmental action to ensure equal rights. At the same time, the leadership of the Republican Party became racially conservative—that is, opposed to government intervention to ensure equal rights for people of color. As the elites and activists sorted themselves into distinct groups on the basis of their attitudes toward racial issues, the perceptions that the mass public held of the parties followed suit. Increasingly through the late 1960s and 1970s, Carmines and Stimson argue, the partisan choices of individual citizens fell in line with their attitudes on racial questions.

The role of race and racial issues in American politics is not always easy to trace, however. Because certain issues that are not explicitly stated in terms of race are nevertheless symbols of race in the minds of some people, candidates can make appeals based on racist attitudes without using racial language. For example, "law and order" may mean "keeping Blacks in their place" to some, and "welfare" may carry racial overtones.[25] Furthermore, the lack of support among whites for policies that target assistance to Blacks gives both parties an incentive to avoid embracing such policies, according to Donald R. Kinder and Lynn M. Sanders.[26] Republican leaders can oppose these policies and win support from their overwhelmingly white constituency, particularly Southern whites. But Democratic leaders also have an incentive to avoid endorsing policies that would help Blacks, so as not to alienate white support.

If race is not an issue to be openly discussed in political campaigns, then uncovering the political significance of race in people's attitudes and perceptions of the political parties becomes difficult. On the whole, straightforward efforts to capture distinctive party images along racial lines do not succeed. Although more than half of Americans believe there are differences in what the parties stand for, typically only a small percentage characterize the differences in racial terms. Overwhelmingly, when people articulate differences between the parties, it is in terms of symbols and issues associated with the New Deal realignment. This in all likelihood reflects the lack of overt discussion of racial issues by the political leadership of either party. In fact, Paul Kellstedt's book *The Mass Media and the Dynamics of Racial Attitudes* has shown that shifts in mass opinion on racial attitudes have begun to mirror shifts in economic attitudes, suggesting that ideological opinions about race have "fused" onto economic preferences.[27]

In 2008, with the first Black presidential candidate nominated by a major party, race was an issue whether anyone talked about it or not. From Bill Clinton's remarks downplaying a Black candidate's win in the South Carolina primary, to the Reverend Jeremiah Wright's videotaped sermons, to Obama's March 18 speech on race, to the increased Black turnout and overwhelming support for Obama on Election Day in 2008 and 2012, race was an often unspoken but constant presence throughout the campaign. In retrospect, it needs to be remembered that Obama did not have the unanimous support of Black Democratic activists in the primaries. Former president Clinton was highly popular among Blacks during and after his presidency, and Hillary Clinton benefited from that association. And early on, Obama was seen in some circles as "not Black enough," given his mixed racial heritage and his upbringing by his white mother and grandparents. Once nominated, any Democratic presidential candidate can count on around 90 percent of the Black vote in the November election. After Obama's nomination, he received not only virtually unanimous support from Black voters but high enthusiasm and turnout as well in both 2008 and 2012. In their book *Steadfast Democrats: How Social Forces Shape Black Political Behavior*, Ismail White and Chryl Laird highlight how social pressure, built through strong social bonds of survival and resistance, is a critical element of Black Americans' electoral support for Democratic Party candidates.[28]

While explicit examples of race negatively affecting Obama's candidacy were few and far between, research examining people's implicit, or "automatic," responses to race showed that those with an implicit preference for whites over Blacks were more likely to support John McCain in 2008 and Mitt Romney in 2012, highlighting how complicated it is to untangle how racial attitudes affect public preferences and voting behavior. However, in the 2016 presidential elections, attitudes about race were a significant predictor of vote choice. An analysis of public opinion data led by Brian Schaffner showed that those individuals who thought racist incidents in the United States were few and far between were far more likely to vote for Trump than were those who thought racial incidents were a regular problem in the country.[29]

In 2020, the murder of George Floyd by a Minneapolis police officer sparked massive protests around the country, giving new energy to the BLM movement. As the protests grew, news coverage focused on what mass communication scholar Doug McLeod and colleagues have called the protest paradigm[30]—focusing on political elites as compared to ordinary citizens, framing coverage episodically instead of digging for the root causes of systemic racism, framing protesters as engaged in destructive action while police are framed as engaging in restoring order, and characterizing the movement based on the actions of a few.

Public opinion consequences of this kind of coverage can be inferred by looking at Table 6-3, which compares support for the BLM movement in June, shortly after Floyd was killed, and September, closer to Election Day. While support for the movement from Black people was steady, it dropped among every other group, though white Democrats continued to support the movement at a slightly higher level than Blacks.

TABLE 6-3 ■ Support for Black Lives Matter Movement in June and September 2020

Group	June	September
Adults	67%	55%
Whites	60	45
Blacks	86	87
Hispanics	77	66
Asians	75	69
White Republicans	37	16
White Democrats	92	88

Source: Deja Thomas and Juliana Menasce Horowitz, "Support for Black Lives Matter Has Decreased Since June but Remains Strong Among Black Americans," Pew Research Center, September 16, 2020, https://www.pewresearch.org/fact-tank/2020/09/16/support-for-black-lives-matter-has-decreased-since-june-but-remains-strong-among-black-americans/.

Social Issues

One of the more emotional aspects of the polarization of the two political parties over the past two decades has been conflict over so-called traditional values. Issues such as abortion, gay rights, transgender rights, pornography, and sex education and prayer in the public schools have risen in prominence over the past few decades. Common wisdom positions Democrats on the liberal side and Republicans on the conservative side of these "culture wars," as they are often called, but significant numbers of leaders and followers in both parties are not so easily placed. Like the process of sorting that occurred over racial issues in the 1960s and 1970s, a similar sorting over traditional values has been occurring more recently. The Republican Party, especially, has had a difficult time portraying itself as a "big tent" that welcomes a wide range of people with varying beliefs, but people who are pro-life or opposed to same-sex marriage have also come to feel uncomfortable in the Democratic Party.

Certainly, one of the most potent of these social issues is abortion. The 1973 Supreme Court decision in *Roe v. Wade* immediately generated a polarized response, turning election races in some areas into one-issue campaigns. Forty years later, intact dilation and extraction, far more commonly known as "partial birth" abortion, is a hot-button issue, and both sides in the abortion debate gird for battle over any anticipated retirement from the U.S. Supreme Court.

One of the difficulties in examining public opinion on abortion lies in the responses that different question wording elicits. Although responses to the same question are similar over time, different phrasing of questions produces differing proportions of "pro-choice" and "pro-life" answers. In the following analysis, we use data from the ANES, which has used the same question in each survey since 1980.

The public's views on abortion are associated with several personal characteristics, most notably age, education, and religion. No matter what combination of characteristics is examined in the general public, invariably more than half of the people in the ANES surveys support the right to abortion under at least some circumstances. The two response choices at the pro-life end of the continuum are that abortion should never be permitted and that abortion should be permitted only in cases of rape or incest or to save the life of the mother. The first is a more extreme position than many pro-life advocates would take; the second includes circumstances that have been explicitly rejected by pro-life advocates in and out of Congress. The most extreme pro-choice alternative offered is that by law a woman should always be able to obtain an abortion as a matter of personal choice. We have used the most extreme category at either end of the continuum to indicate pro-life and pro-choice positions.

In simple terms, older people are generally more likely to be pro-life than younger people, and the less educated are less supportive of legal abortion than are the better educated. Given the frequent labeling of abortion as a *women's* issue, it is worth noting that there is relatively little difference in the views of women and men, although women are more likely than men to take the extreme positions on both the pro-choice and pro-life sides.

Perhaps surprisingly, given the Roman Catholic Church's clear position in opposition to abortion, little difference is found between Catholics and Protestants in their positions on abortion. This is true even when the frequency of church attendance is taken into account. Figure 6-3 shows the percentages taking the most extreme pro-life position and the most extreme pro-choice position for Catholics and Protestants with different frequencies of church attendance. Among both Catholics and Protestants, opposition to abortion declines as church attendance declines, but the percentages expressing pro-choice and pro-life sentiments are quite similar for the Catholic and Protestant groups. Regular churchgoers among Catholics are about as pro-life as Protestant regular churchgoers. Catholic occasional attenders are more likely to be pro-choice than Protestants who attend church infrequently. Underlying this change is another trend—a smaller proportion of all Catholics claim to be regular churchgoers. Regardless of their religious denomination, the figure shows that those who are faithful churchgoers are more pro-life.

Beyond the policy preferences individuals have on abortion is the level of relative importance they place on the issue. If abortion was an issue where people had clear opinions, but the opinions were not very important to them, it would not be a very consequential issue in American politics. Table 6-4 shows that nearly 62 percent of Democrats say abortion is very or extremely important while more than 56 percent of Republicans feel the same way.

Perhaps not surprisingly, then, the public does a pretty good job of assessing candidate positions on the abortion issue. Table 6-5 shows that strong majorities of Democrats, independents, and Republicans placed Biden's position solidly on the pro-choice end of the spectrum. Table 6-6 reveals more of a partisan difference with the placement of Trump's position on abortion, with Democrats placing the president at the most extreme pro-life end of the spectrum, perhaps on the basis of the believed opinions about abortion that are held by Trump's picks for the Supreme Court. Republicans place Trump on the pro-life end of the spectrum, but less than a quarter of Republicans thought that Trump was a pro-life evangelist.

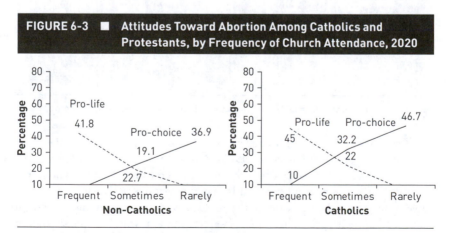

FIGURE 6-3 ■ Attitudes Toward Abortion Among Catholics and Protestants, by Frequency of Church Attendance, 2020

Source: 2020 American National Election Studies, available at www.electionstudies.org.

TABLE 6-4 ■ Importance of Abortion, by Party, 2020			
Importance of abortion issue	Democrats	Independents	Republicans
1. Not at all important	3.1%	5.8%	3.3%
2. Not too important	9.3	14.9	13.9
3. Somewhat important	25.8	31.5	26.5
4. Very important	30.7	23.9	27.5
5. Extremely important	31.1	23.9	28.8
Total	100%	100%	100%
N	1,855	1,895	1,644

Source: 2020 American National Election Studies, available at www.electionstudies.org.

TABLE 6-5 ■ Placement of Joe Biden's Position on Abortion, by Party, 2020			
	Democrats	Independents	Republicans
Never permit abortion	3.7%	5.9%	6.8%
Permit only in special cases	11	10.7	5.6
Permit for other reasons	20.6	19.3	8
Always permit as a woman's right	64.7	64.1	79.6
Total	100%	100%	100%
N	1,812	1,822	1,596

Source: 2020 American National Election Studies, available at www.electionstudies.org.

Their position on abortion has become a litmus test for presidential hopefuls in both parties ever since the 1970s. Not surprisingly, then, a fairly strong relationship exists between partisanship and views on abortion, as can be seen in Table 6-7. Perhaps more unexpected is that the relationship is not stronger. Sizable minorities of Republicans and some Democrats take positions contrary to the stand of their party. This is one of several ways in which the polarization of the political activists and elites of the parties is not reflected in the rank and file.

TABLE 6-6 ■ Placement of Donald Trump's Position on Abortion, by Party, 2020			
	Democrats	**Independents**	**Republicans**
Never permit abortion	59.6%	40.7%	22.8%
Permit only in special cases	25.6	35.2	54
Permit for other reasons	5.8	12.6	14.4
Always permit as a woman's right	9	11.5	8.8
Total	100%	100%	100%
N	1,811	1,815	1,598

Source: 2020 American National Election Studies, available at www.electionstudies.org.

TABLE 6-7 ■ Attitudes on Abortion, by Party Identification, 2020					
	Strong Democrats	**Weak Democrats**	**Independents**	**Weak Republicans**	**Strong Republicans**
Never permit abortion	3	6	8	13	24
Permit only in special cases	10	11	22	32	47
Permit for other reasons	10	13	15	20	13
Always permit as a woman's right	77	70	55	35	16
Total	100%	100%	100%	100%	100%
N	1,228	585	1,772	526	1,058

Source: 2020 American National Election Studies, available at www.electionstudies.org.

Note: The full text of choices is as follows:

1. By law, abortion should never be permitted.

2. The law should permit abortion only in case of rape, [in case of] incest, or when the woman's life is in danger.

3. The law should permit abortion for reasons other than rape, incest, or danger to the woman's life, but only after the need for the abortion has been clearly established.

4. By law, a woman should always be able to obtain an abortion as a matter of personal choice.

The issue of same-sex marriage was very contentious in the early 2000s, with some states banning same-sex marriage through legislative actions or referenda and others moving toward legalizing it. In 2004, the issue was suddenly injected into the presidential campaign when the Supreme Court of Massachusetts ruled that denying gay and lesbian people the right to marry was unconstitutional in that state, and when the mayor of San Francisco began issuing marriage licenses to same-sex couples. This was a no-win situation for the Democrats and their presidential candidate, given that the American public opposed same-sex marriage by a two-to-one margin at the time. Because proposed bans on same-sex marriage were on the ballot in several states that year, the issue also served to energize conservative voters in safe Republican states, thus raising President Bush's popular vote margin. President Obama famously "evolved" to a position of support for same-sex marriage, following growing public sentiment favoring such a position. In 2013, the Supreme Court ruled that the federal government could not define marriage as being between one man and one woman, striking down the Defense of Marriage Act signed by former president Clinton.

Over time, the American public has become more tolerant of the idea of same-sex marriage or, at least, civil unions for same-sex couples. This is another social issue that has a fairly strong relationship with partisanship, as can be seen in Table 6-8. Democratic partisans are more accepting of the idea than Republicans,

TABLE 6-8 ■ Attitudes Toward Same-Sex Marriage, by Party Identification, 2020					
	Strong Democrats	Weak Democrats	Independents	Weak Republicans	Strong Republicans
Allow same-sex marriage	85	84	74	63	40
Allow civil unions	8	10	16	22	33
Do not allow either	7	6	10	15	26
Total	100%	100%	100%	100%	99%
N	1,252	599	1,870	538	1,095

Source: 2020 American National Election Studies, available at www.electionstudies.org.

although a substantial minority of Democrats oppose it. Since 2008, strong Republicans' support for same-sex marriage has grown from 9 percent to 40 percent, and strong Democrats' support is up to 85 percent, from 46 percent in 2008. Weak Republicans' support was at 63 percent in 2020, and weak Democrats' support of same-sex marriage jumped to 84 percent, 17 points higher than in 2016.

Homeland Security, Terrorism, and International Affairs

After September 11, 2001, terrorism dominated the front page for years.[31] Not only have the events of that day been seared into people's memories, but the fear of future terrorist attacks remains pervasive also—although concern is ebbing a little as time passes without another attack. In the fall of 2011, a CBS News poll found that 83 percent of the public believed that the threat of terrorism will always exist, though more than half also believed that an attack was not likely in the next few months.[32]

A wide-ranging survey in 2004 on Americans' perceptions of the threat of terrorism showed that concerns about a terrorist attack focus on chemical and biological weapons as the most worrisome.[33] Terrorism is seen as multifaceted, taking many possible forms with a wide array of possible targets. Even without another attack, many years will pass before substantial numbers of the public have no personal memory of September 11, so the feelings and issues surrounding terrorism will be around for a long time.

Terrorism is a *valence* issue—that is, one in which virtually every citizen of the United States agrees that it is bad—as opposed to a *position* issue, which some support and others oppose. At one level, terrorism is also an *easy* issue, in the sense that Carmines and Stimson use the term. It is easy, on a gut level, to understand what happened on September 11 and to find it abhorrent. Beyond this, however, the terrorist threat becomes more complicated—a *hard* issue—as one tries to imagine who might be terrorists, what motivates them, and what array of possible weapons they might use. Even more difficult is assessing the steps proposed and taken to thwart terrorists. Do they work? Are they cost-effective? How would one know?

More than most other international issues, the threat of terrorism involves domestic policies aimed at preventing terrorist attacks, such as security searches at airports and on mass transit systems. Most initial survey research in this area has focused on the public's reaction to the USA PATRIOT Act. Among the roughly 80 percent of the public who had heard of the act, opinion was fairly evenly divided between those who saw it as a necessary tool for finding terrorists and those who thought it went too far and threatened civil liberties.[34] These responses were strongly influenced by partisanship. Only 15 percent of Republicans thought it went too far, while 53 percent of Democrats held that view when George W. Bush was president.

Up to some unknown point, Americans are willing to see their civil liberties compromised if they believe doing so will help prevent terrorism, even though three-fourths of the public has little confidence that the government will use personal information, gained through antiterror measures, appropriately.[35] Respondents are more willing to sacrifice the civil liberties of others than their own. For example, a CBS News poll in the spring of 2005 found that 56 percent of the public was willing to have governmental agencies monitor the telephone calls and emails of Americans the government finds suspicious; only 29 percent favored allowing this monitoring of "ordinary Americans."[36] These views are driven by partisanship as well. In 2013, with Democrat Barack Obama serving as commander in chief, 49 percent of Republicans supported the federal government's monitoring of Americans' phone calls, while 58 percent of Democrats did.

Typically, important valence issues, such as terrorism, have components that can be treated as position issues when segments of the public and their leaders hold differing views. So while everyone is opposed to terrorism, dissimilar views can be held about how well President Bush handled the war on terrorism or whether the Iraq war made the United States more or less safe from terrorism. As might be expected, the positions people take on these matters are related to partisanship.

Surprisingly, then, in 2020, worries that a terrorist attack might occur in the near future were surprisingly consistent across one's location on the party identification scale. Figure 6-4 shows that independents were the least worried group with almost 49 percent slightly or not at all worried. Strong Republicans were the most worried group, but their numbers were almost identical to those of strong Democrats.

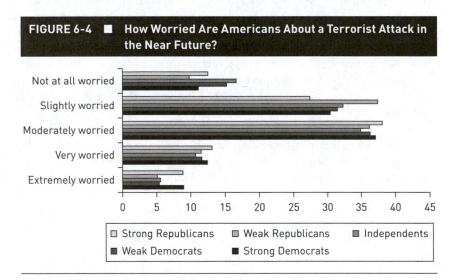

FIGURE 6-4 ■ How Worried Are Americans About a Terrorist Attack in the Near Future?

Source: 2020 American National Election Studies, available at www.electionstudies.org.

During the Cold War years (around 1947–1991), foreign policy—and the study of public opinion about foreign policy—focused on relations between the United States and the Soviet Union. Questions centered on the relative strength of the two countries, the likelihood of nuclear conflict between them, and the preference for negotiation or military strength as a strategy for keeping the peace. With the breakup of the Soviet Union, the focus of foreign policy has shifted away from superpower military relations toward involvement, or noninvolvement, in trouble spots around the world, such as the Persian Gulf in 1990 and 1991; Afghanistan and Iraq since 2001 and 2003, respectively; Libya in 2011; the ongoing violence in the Sudan; and the political disarray in Egypt and Syria.

Issues of foreign affairs vary greatly in salience, particularly in response to involvement of the nation in a military conflict. In analyzing the public's attitudes toward international events, a distinction needs to be made between brief conflicts and longer-lasting wars. A truism now in American politics says the American public will support—usually enthusiastically—brief military involvement in a foreign conflict that seems to be successful (and they will quickly forget if it is not successful). If, however, combat drags on, support typically diminishes, especially if there are significant U.S. casualties. In the case of Vietnam, opposition to the war developed at a sluggish pace over a considerable period of time, as did recognition of the seriousness of U.S. involvement. In the early years, opposition to the war (as measured by support for a prompt withdrawal) was low—less than 10 percent. By 1968, it had grown to 20 percent; by 1970, it was more than 30 percent; and by 1972, it had reached more than 40 percent. Clearly, as the war dragged on, support for military involvement declined dramatically. The Korean War more than seventy years ago offers similar evidence of the failure of public support for prolonged conflicts.

In contrast, military episodes that develop rapidly command great public attention and almost always garner public support. In the Persian Gulf War, deployment of American military forces to Saudi Arabia began in the late summer of 1990, in response to Iraq's invasion of Kuwait. In the late fall, as deployment of U.S. troops continued, the public was somewhat divided in its support of this policy. Fifty-nine percent of the public polled said they believed it was the correct policy to pursue, and 39 percent said they believed it was not. These views shifted fairly dramatically after the brief and well-televised war with Iraq in early 1991. When the same people were interviewed again in June 1991 following the war, 81 percent felt the war had been the right thing to do, and only 18 percent thought the United States should have stayed out.

In the beginning, support for the second war in Iraq was high among the American public. In March 2003, immediately after the invasion, 69 percent of the public thought the United States had done the right thing in taking military action against Iraq. Only a quarter of the public thought the United States should have stayed out.[37] A little over a year later, on the anniversary of the declared end of formal hostilities, the public was evenly divided on whether or not the United States had done the right thing—47 percent thought so; 46 percent did not.[38]

Small bursts of support appeared after the patriotic displays at both parties' national nominating conventions in the summer of 2004 and right before the presidential election in November 2004, but generally, the trend of support was downward. By the fall of 2008, 70 percent of the public disapproved of President Bush's handling of the war in Iraq.[39] Political analysts have long noted a rally-around-the-flag phenomenon that occurs at times of international crisis.[40] Presidents invariably get a boost in popularity ratings in the polls in the midst of an international incident, even when the actions of the administration are not particularly successful. John F. Kennedy got such a boost after the disastrous Bay of Pigs invasion of Cuba in 1961, as did Jimmy Carter—temporarily—after a militant student group seized the American embassy in Iran in 1979. And public approval of President George H. W. Bush's handling of the Persian Gulf War was extremely high during and immediately following the conflict, representing a substantial increase over his earlier ratings. Similarly, George W. Bush saw an immediate gain in presidential job approval after the attacks on the World Trade Center and Pentagon on September 11, 2001. ABC News and the *Washington Post* completed a national survey the weekend before the attacks in which Bush's job approval was at 55 percent, about average for modern presidents in the first year of their first term. Immediately after the disaster, his job approval climbed to 86 percent. The change in "strong" approval was from 26 to 63 percent.[41] This enthusiasm did not survive the passage of time as President Bush left office with approval ratings that rivaled the worst evaluations of presidential performance in modern polling history.

As with domestic issues, partisan differences are apparent, with partisans of the president in office more supportive of whatever actions are taken than are partisans of the party out of power. This was seen most clearly during the war in Vietnam. Republicans were more likely to think getting involved in Vietnam was a mistake before 1969, when Democratic president Lyndon B. Johnson was in charge; thereafter, with Republican Richard M. Nixon in the White House, Democrats were more likely to view the war as a mistake.

Similarly, in 2004, 61 percent of Republicans said that Iraq was an immediate threat that required military action, whereas only 14 percent of Democrats and 26 percent of independents held that view. The partisan differences extend to many attitudes toward the Iraq war. Republicans, for example, are much more likely than Democrats or independents to believe that the war in Iraq was a major part of the war on terrorism. Republican support for the war in Iraq remained strong, whereas the support of Democrats and independents fell faster. In March 2003, 87 percent of Republicans said that attacking Iraq was the right thing to do. A year later, their support was still at 80 percent. Democratic support, meanwhile, dropped from 50 percent to 24 percent over the same time period, and independent support declined a comparable amount, from 70 percent to 45 percent.[42] As can be seen in Table 6-9, what question was asked about Iraq did not matter much. Republicans, Democrats, and independents responded consistently. Republicans continued to support the Republican president, whereas Democrats did not. Independents were somewhere in between but became increasingly negative as time went on. Once Democrat Barack Obama took office, the percentage of Democrats who believed the war was going well jumped nearly 20 percentage points from 27 percent in September 2008 to 46 percent in June 2009, whereas Republican support fell from 88 percent to 76 percent during the same period.[43]

The public makes a distinction between the war in Iraq and the war in Afghanistan, although they share the characteristic of dragging on inconclusively. By the fall of 2008, 56 percent of the public thought sending military forces to Iraq had been a mistake, but only 28 percent thought it had been a mistake to send troops to Afghanistan.[44] Similarly, a little over 60 percent of the public thought the United States should keep troops in Afghanistan, while only 45 percent thought troops should be kept in Iraq. Republicans overwhelmingly thought troops should be kept in both countries, but Democrats were less sure. Fifty-three percent of all Democrats thought troops should be kept in Afghanistan, but only 25 percent felt that way about Iraq.[45] The fact that the war in Afghanistan has lasted longer shows that simple duration of a conflict does not determine the level of support. Most important, the connection between terrorism and the war in Afghanistan has not been questioned. Moreover, the cost in American lives and dollars has been less in Afghanistan than Iraq, and news coverage of successes and failures has been more extensive in Iraq. With the Obama administration's emphasis on Afghanistan as the right place to fight terrorism, partisan-shaped opinions were once again evident as a 2011 survey showed that while 72 percent of the public supported Obama's Afghanistan withdrawal plan, only 50 percent of Republicans liked the idea compared to 87 percent of Democrats and 74 percent of independents.[46]

TABLE 6-9 ■ **Attitudes Toward the War in Iraq According to Party Identification, 2004 and 2008 (in percentages)**

	Democrats	Independents	Republicans
Think the United States did the right thing in taking military action against Iraq (2004)	24	45	80
Think the war with Iraq has been worth the cost (2008)	8	19	56
Think Iraq was a threat to the United States that required immediate military action (2004)	14	26	61

(Continued)

TABLE 6-9 ■ (Continued)

	Democrats	Independents	Republicans
Think the Bush administration tried hard enough to reach a diplomatic solution in Iraq (2004)	12	31	64
Think the war with Iraq has decreased the threat of terrorism against the United States (2008)	12	23	49
Approve of the way President Bush is handling the war in Iraq (2008)	7	25	69
Oppose setting a deadline for the withdrawal of troops from Iraq (2008)	17	28	60

Sources: CBS News Poll, April 6–8, 2004, data provided by Inter-university Consortium for Political and Social Research, http://www.icpsr.umich.edu/icpsrweb/ICPSR/studies/4101; 2008 American National Election Studies, available at www.electionstudies.org.

Up until Vietnam, bipartisanship was touted as the hallmark of American foreign policy—that "politics stops at the water's edge." While strictly speaking this was never true, the division between internationalist and isolationist views on the United States' role in the world tended not to follow party lines. Today, the partisan polarization extends also to international issues, especially as they concern one or the other party's handling of them. As Table 6-10 demonstrates, although there is widespread bipartisan agreement on general principles, such as preventing the spread of nuclear weapons, there is disagreement on the role of the United Nations, on combating global hunger, and on assessing presidential performance on foreign policy issues.

As noted in previous sections, fairly strong and consistent relationships exist between partisanship and domestic issues and, increasingly, foreign policy issues. A leading assumption is that partisan identification provides guidance for the

TABLE 6-10 ■ Attitudes Toward Possible Foreign Policy Goals According to Party Identification, 2008–2020			
	Percentage Agreeing		
	Democrats	**Independents**	**Republicans**
Strengthening the United Nations should be a very important U.S. foreign policy goal (2008)	55	39	29
Combating world hunger should be a very important U.S. foreign policy goal (2008)	70	59	45
The war in Afghanistan has been worth the cost (2012)	24	26	37
Approve of Obama's handling of foreign relations (2012)	84	52	19
Approve of Obama's handling of foreign relations (2016)	76	42	19
Support sending U.S. ground troops to fight the Islamic State (2016)	32	39	55
Should allow Syrian refugees into the U.S. (2016)	46	17	10
Approve of Trump's handling of foreign relations (2020)	7	36	86
Favor free trade agreements with foreign countries (2020)	53	43	40

Source: American National Election Studies, available at www.electionstudies.org.

public on policy matters—that is, most Americans adopt opinions consistent with their partisanship. It also is likely that policy positions developed independently of one's partisanship, but consistent with it, will reinforce feelings of party loyalty or that attitudes on issues will lead to a preference for the party most in agreement with them. Furthermore, issue preferences inconsistent with party loyalty can erode or change it. For any particular individual, it would be extremely difficult to untangle the effects of partisanship and policy preferences over a long period of time.

Even though on many issues most partisans of one party will hold a position different from that held by the majority of the other party, considerable numbers of people with issue positions "inconsistent" with their party identification remain loyal to that party. To account for this, it is variously suggested that (1) issues are unimportant to many voters; (2) only the issues most important to individuals need to be congruent with their partisanship; (3) individuals regularly misperceive the positions of the parties to remain comfortable with both their party loyalty and their policy preferences; or (4) the positions of each party are ambiguous or dissimilar enough in different areas of the country that no clear distinction exists between the parties. Undoubtedly, all these explanations have some degree of truth, and no one should expect to find extremely strong relationships between partisanship and positions on particular issues. Nevertheless, as an indication of the recent increased polarization of the parties, racial issues and cultural issues have joined traditional domestic economic issues to clearly differentiate Democrats from Republicans. While this has led those with consistently liberal or consistently conservative positions to be increasingly polarized from each other, it has also led to a widening "middle" of ideological libertarians, populists, and moderates—people with dissimilar views to each other *and* the parties in government in Washington, DC. These individuals, who have a set of views that match Republicans on one issue dimension and Democrats on another, are less likely to participate in political activities, are less partisan, and are more likely to split their tickets when voting. As noted earlier, there are times when these voters (like populists in 2016) do meaningfully change their typical electoral behavior in ways that can affect the outcome of an election.

POLITICAL IDEOLOGY

A *political ideology* is a set of fundamental beliefs or principles about politics and government: what the scope of government should be, how decisions should be made, what values should be pursued, and so on. In the United States, the most prominent ideological patterns are those captured by the terms *liberalism* and *conservatism*. Although these words are used in a variety of ways, generally liberalism endorses the idea of social change and advocates the involvement of government in effecting such change, whereas conservatism seeks to defend the status quo and prescribes a more limited role for governmental activity. Another common conception of the terms portrays liberalism as advocating equality and individual freedom and conservatism as endorsing a more structured, ordered society. These two conceptions of liberalism and conservatism clash when considering differences in people's preferences about economic and social issues. That is, modern conservatives generally prefer that the government stay out of the deep management of economic issues while preferring that the government be more activist in regulating social issues. For example, conservatives generally want the government to relax business regulations and to outlaw abortion and define marriage traditionally. Contemporary liberals generally prefer more aggressive business regulations but want a government that stays out of abortion and does not define marriage.

"Ideological" views on social and economic issues are not always joined in the political thinking of Americans. That is, some Americans have views on economic issues, relating to the government's role in managing the economy, that are generally liberal or generally conservative, and some Americans have opinions on social issues, relating to the government's weighing in on what is morally right or wrong, that are broadly liberal or broadly conservative. However, there is no law or general psychological principle that requires Americans to have views that are consistently liberal or conservative across both dimensions. What's more, some people have attitudes that are moderate on these issues; still others just don't care. Thus, the ideological landscape of American public opinion certainly contains those who are either liberal or conservative across both economic and social issues, but it also contains those who are conservative economically and liberal socially (libertarians), those who are liberal economically and conservative socially (populists), and those who fall somewhere in between (moderates).[47] Usually, liberals and conservatives do the most participating in elections. In 2016, populists were uniquely important, both in the Republican primaries and in the general election itself.

While the experienced politicians running for the Republican presidential nomination in 2016 ran traditional campaigns that courted traditional primary voters, Donald Trump charted a different course. Aside from his behavior on Twitter and in the news media, Trump courted voters by espousing nationalist issue preferences that would "make America great again." Eric Oliver and Wendy Rahn showed that Trump supporters were especially strong with respect to their national identity.[48] Carmines and colleagues examined the support for nationalist policies among populists, libertarians, moderates, liberals, and conservatives, finding that populists held the strongest nationalist attitudes in 2008 (believing that immigrants take jobs, favoring torture, believing that Blacks have too much influence, and favoring less outsourcing).[49] In 2016, conservatives and populists tied for holding the highest percentage of nationalist views. Interestingly, populists typically are more likely to vote for Democrats in presidential elections, as the ratio of Democratic populists to Republican populists is 55 to 27 percent. However, in the 2016 primaries, populists participating in the Republican primaries were the group that was most supportive of Trump's candidacy for the Republican nomination.

Despite the ambiguities of ideological definitions, most commentators on the American political scene, as well as its active participants, describe much of what happens in terms of liberalism or conservatism—and with good reason. The news media routinely chronicle political debate as a contest between Republicans and Democrats in government. At the federal level, there is a clear "left–right" divide between Republicans, who are on the ideological right, and Democrats, who are on the ideological left. Indeed, Republicans and Democrats in the U.S. Congress are now more polarized in their roll call voting behavior than they were in the years immediately following the Civil War![50] Furthermore, most political history and commentary treats the Democratic Party as the liberal party and the Republican Party as the conservative one. Although considerable ideological variation remains in both parties, the trend in recent years is toward greater ideological distinctiveness between the two parties at both the elite and mass levels.[51] Candidates of both parties attempt to pin ideological labels on opposing candidates (usually candidates of the other party, but sometimes within their own). In recent years, *liberal* has been portrayed more negatively than *conservative*, and some candidates for office portray themselves as *progressive* or use other such terms to avoid the *liberal* label.

Analysts of American political history pay special attention to those rare periods when a single-issue dimension dominates the public's views of governmental policy. Periods such as the Civil War or the New Deal revealed deep divisions in the public, paralleled by a distinctiveness in the issue stands of the political parties. Electoral realignments of voters are forged by unusually strong issue alignments, and during such times a close correspondence can be expected between attitudes on the relevant issues and partisanship.

At other times, highly salient issues may capture the attention of the public, but they often cut across, rather than reinforce, other issue positions and party loyalties. If the parties do not take clearly differentiated stands on such issues and if party supporters are divided in their feelings toward the issues, party loyalty and the existing partisan alignment are undermined. On the other hand, if parties do take clear but competing positions on such issues, they run the risk of alienating some of their supporters. In a complex political system, such as that of the United States, new, dissimilar issue divisions accumulate until a crisis causes one dimension to dominate and obscure other issues. An example of these kinds of issues—and their electoral consequences—that we will explore in this chapter is issues related to nationalism.

The most consistent and the most distinctive ideological difference between the parties emerged during the New Deal realignment (see also Chapter 5). It focused on domestic economic issues, specifically on the question of what role the government should take in regulating the economy and providing social welfare benefits. These issues still underlie the division between the parties. Since the 1930s, the Democratic Party has advocated more governmental activity, and the Republican Party has preferred less. Historically, American political parties have not been viewed as particularly ideological, in part because other issues—such as racial or social issues—have cut across the economic dimension and blurred distinctions between the parties.

For example, in the 1940s and 1950s, the Republican Party was at least as liberal on race (i.e., supportive of civil rights legislation) as was the Democratic Party, with its strong Southern base. Similarly, in the 1970s, the two parties were both divided internally on the issue of abortion. Currently, immigration has the potential to be a crosscutting issue, though it seems to divide Republicans more than it does Democrats. What makes the two parties especially interesting today is that they are in the rare historical position of being quite consistent and ideologically distinctive. The two parties have become more ideologically polarized over a broader range of issues, and their supporters seem to have sorted themselves out, as increasing numbers of Democrats have liberal positions on social and economic issues, while more and more Republicans have conservative positions on them.[52]

So, a political ideology is a set of interrelated attitudes that fit together into some coherent and consistent view of or orientation toward the political world. Americans have opinions on a wide range of issues, and political analysts and commentators characterize these positions as "liberal" or "conservative." Does this mean, then, that the typical American voter has an ideology that serves as a guide to political thought and action, much the same way partisanship does?

When Americans are asked to identify themselves as liberal or conservative, most are able to do so. The categories have some meaning for most Americans, although the identifications are not of overriding importance. Table 6-11 presents the ideological identification of Americans over the past five decades. A consistently larger proportion of respondents call themselves conservative as opposed to liberal. At the same time, about a quarter of the population regards itself as middle-of-the-road ideologically. The question wording provides respondents with the opportunity to say they "haven't thought much about this," and fully a quarter to a third typically respond this way, though that number dropped to 15 percent in 2020. The series of liberal and conservative responses has been remarkably stable over the years. Ideological identification, in the aggregate, is even more stable than party identification. The slight drop in the percentages saying they "haven't thought about" themselves in these terms, and the corresponding increase in the proportion of those calling themselves conservatives in 1994 and beyond, may be a response to the heightened ideological rhetoric of the 1994 campaign and the increased polarization of the political parties. The overall stability of these numbers, however, should make one cautious of commentary that finds big shifts in liberalism or conservatism in the American electorate.

Table 6-12 shows the relationship between ideological self-identification and party identification. Democrats are more liberal than conservative, Republicans are disproportionately conservative, and independents are fairly evenly balanced. But conservatives are three times as likely to be Republicans as Democrats, and liberals are far more likely to be Democrats. The relationship between ideology and partisanship is shown in the low coincidence of liberal Republicans and

TABLE 6-11 ■ Distribution of Ideological Identification, 1972–2020

	1972	1976	1980	1984	1988	1992	1996	2000	2004	2008	2012	2016	2020
Extremely liberal	1%	1%	2%	2%	2%	2%	1%	2%	2%	3%	2%	3%	4%
Liberal	7	7	6	7	6	8	7	9	9	10	10	11	15
Slightly liberal	10	8	9	9	9	10	10	9	8	9	9	9	11
Middle-of-the-road	27	25	20	23	22	23	24	23	25	22	24	20	23
Slightly conservative	15	12	13	14	15	15	15	12	12	12	13	14	10
Conservative	10	11	13	13	14	13	15	15	16	17	15	16	7
Extremely conservative	1	2	2	2	3	3	3	3	3	3	4	4	5
Haven't thought about it	28	33	36	30	30	27	25	27	25	25	23	25	15
Total	99%	99%	101%	100%	101%	101%	100%	100%	100%	101%	100%	102%	100%
(N)	2,155	2,839	1,565	2,229	2,035	2,483	1,712	849	1,211	2,319	2,048	1,174	5,419

Source: American National Election Studies, available at www.electionstudies.org.

TABLE 6-12 ■ Relationship Between Ideological Self-Identification and Party Identification, 2020				
	Democrats	**Independents**	**Republicans**	**Total**
Liberal	71	31	3	36%
Middle-of-the-road	23	41	15	26%
Conservative	6	28	82	38%
Total	100%	100%	100%	100%
N	1,561	1,567	1,464	

Source: 2020 American National Election Studies, available at www.electionstudies.org.

"No opinion" and "haven't thought about it" responses omitted.

conservative Democrats. Also, the electorate tends to perceive the Democratic Party as liberal and the Republican Party as conservative. Those who see an ideological difference between the parties believe Republicans are more conservative than Democrats by a ratio of more than four to one.

There is also a relationship between social characteristics and ideological self-identification. Self-identified liberals are most frequent among better-educated whites who claim no religious affiliation or a non-Christian affiliation. Figure 6-5 also shows that a plurality of Hispanics (35 percent) self-identify as liberal, a significant change from 2016, while 29 percent identify as conservative. Self-identified conservatives are most common among white "other" Christians who went to college, but they are also found in substantial numbers among white "Other" Christians with no college and among Catholics. The major impact of education is to reduce the proportion of respondents who opt for the middle category. The better educated are more likely to call themselves either liberal or conservative than the high school educated. This tendency would be even greater if those who offered no self-identification were included.

Approximately three-quarters of the public identifies itself as liberal or conservative. Do these individuals use ideological orientation to organize political information and attitudes? Does political ideology play a role for Americans similar to the role of partisanship as a basic determinant of specific political views? Analysis has usually centered on two kinds of evidence to assess the extent of ideological thinking in the American electorate—the use of ideological concepts in discussing politics and the consistency of attitudes on related issues—suggesting an underlying perspective in the individual's approach to politics.

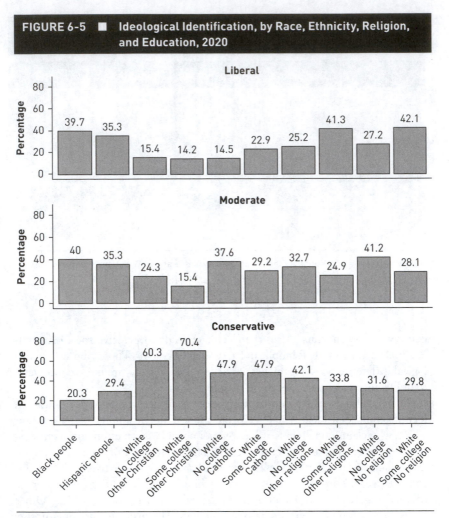

FIGURE 6-5 ■ Ideological Identification, by Race, Ethnicity, Religion, and Education, 2020

Source: 2020 American National Election Studies, available at www.electionstudies.org.

Data reported in *The American Voter*, by Angus Campbell, Philip E. Converse, Warren E. Miller, and Donald E. Stokes, showed that few members of the electorate discussed their evaluations of the parties and the candidates in ideological language; only 12 percent did so in 1956.[53] Other scholars have contributed similar analysis of subsequent years.[54]

It is possible that individuals may simply be unsophisticated in the verbal descriptions of their feelings about politics and political parties. Their ideology may guide their political decisions, but they may be unable to articulate it. In that case, the individuals' attitudes toward public issues might be expected to show a degree of coherence and consistency; they would arrive at those positions by applying a common underlying set of political ideals. If individuals are liberal on one issue, one would expect them to be liberal on other related issues; if they are conservative on one issue, they likely are conservative on others. The most sophisticated analysis of ideological perspectives and consistency in issue positions, usually called *issue constraint*, was carried out by Philip E. Converse using data from 1956, 1958, and 1960.[55] He found that the strength of the relationship *among* domestic issues and *among* foreign policy issues was about twice as strong as that *between* domestic and foreign issues. By normal standards, even the strongest relationship among domestic issues did not suggest particularly impressive issue consistency, but consistency does increase when survey questions reference which party holds a particular position on an issue. Additionally, the degree of issue constraint on various policy matters increased in 1964 and remains at this higher level to the present.

As might be expected, the degree of consistency among attitudes on different issues varies with the level of education of the individual; the more educated are substantially more consistent in their views than the less educated. However, increasing levels of education do not appear to account for the increase in issue constraint. The work of Norman Nie, Sidney Verba, and John Petrocik (see *The Changing American Voter*) shows convincingly that interest in politics is more critical. In other words, as members of the public become more concerned with issues and more attentive to political leaders, they perceive, and reflect, a higher degree of issue coherence. Almost certainly, the electorate has the capacity for greater issue constraint than it has shown. However, the exercise of the capacity depends much more on political leaders and events than on the characteristics of the electorate. When political leaders use ideological terms to describe themselves and the clusters of issues that they support, the electorate is capable of following suit.

The degree of issue constraint also depends on the range of issues considered. *The American Voter* documented a coherent set of attitudes on welfare policies and governmental activity, even in the 1950s. When the analysis moves to more disparate issues, such as support for welfare policies and civil liberties, the relationship weakens substantially. It can be argued that little relationship should be expected between positions in these different issue areas because they tap different ideological dimensions with no logical or necessary connections among them. For example, there is nothing logically inconsistent in a person's opposing government regulation of business and believing in racial equality. In the first half of the twentieth century, internationalist views in foreign policy were considered the liberal position and isolationist attitudes conservative. However, the Cold War and Vietnam did much to rearrange these notions as liberals argued against American involvement and conservatives became more aggressive internationalists. In considering the question of issue constraint, two points should be kept in mind: (1) The meaning of the terms *liberal* and *conservative* changes with time, as do the connections between these ideologies and specific historical events, and (2) analysts, in studying issue constraint, invariably impose on the analysis their own version of ideological consistency, which, in light of the ambiguities surrounding the terms, is likely to be somewhat artificial.

A less strenuous criterion than issue constraint for assessing the impact of ideology on political attitudes is simply to look at the relationship between individuals' ideological identification and their positions on various issues taken one at a time. Here, substantial relationships are found. The relationship between ideological identification and liberal views on various policy matters over the past thirty-six years is shown in Table 6-13. Between one-fourth and one-third of the people sampled did not have an ideological position or did not profess attitudes on these issues and are, therefore, missing in the analysis. Nevertheless, the data in Table 6-13 document strong, consistent relationships between ideological identification and many issue positions. The data do not, however, demonstrate that ideology determines issue positions.

If everyone had a strong ideology, attitudes would be determined by that ideology. To a considerable extent, this appears to happen to the most politically alert and concerned in the society, but this group is a small minority of the total adult population. To the extent that the major American political parties are ideologically oriented—by following the parties or political leaders in these parties—Americans have their opinions determined indirectly by ideology. American political parties are often characterized as nonideological, and the country has passed through substantial historical periods when the parties have seemed bent on obscuring the differences between them. At other times, such as 1964 and since the early 1990s, political leaders were more intent on drawing distinctions between themselves and the opposing party in ideological terms. At these times, the public responds by appearing more ideological as well.

Whether tightly constrained or seemingly built at random, ideology and issue preferences have to come from somewhere. For years, the dominant explanation was that preferences, ideology, and partisanship came from a process of socialization from one's parents, schools, religion, and socioeconomic status. In recent years, scholars have started to demonstrate that while socialization certainly affects our opinions, ideology, and partisanship, biological factors do as well. In one study, from John Alford, Carolyn Funk, and John Hibbing, researchers compared issue preferences of identical twins to those of fraternal twins, finding that identical twins (ones from the same zygote, sharing 100 percent of their DNA) had views that were more alike than fraternal twins (from two zygotes, sharing roughly 50 percent of their DNA).[56] Jeffrey J. Mondak has shown how people's personality characteristics inform their ideology and preferences,[57] and other scholars such as Peter Hatemi, Kevin Smith, James Fowler, Rose McDermott, and Hibbing have provided evidence on matters as diverse as the role that genes play in one's likelihood of identifying as a partisan (but not with which party), how physiological responses to threatening and disgusting images correlate with liberalism and conservatism, and how genes are related to voter turnout.[58] These studies have elicited plenty of controversy, with some scholars arguing that such studies are dangerous, whereas other scholars question the precision of measurements connecting deep-seated biological orientations with expressed political attitudes and behaviors.

TABLE 6-13 ■ Relationship Between Ideological Identification and Liberal Positions on Issues, 1972–2020				
	Liberal	Somewhat Liberal	Middle-of-the-Road	Somewhat Conservative	Conservative
Favor increased regulation on greenhouse gas emissions (2020)	92	87	69	53	26
Federal government should make it harder to buy a gun (2020)	86	75	56	38	17
Increase government services (2008)	81	55	54	29	28
Favor government health insurance (2008)	72	62	50	45	19
Pro-choice on abortion (2008)	79	50	43	34	16
Should allow same-sex marriage (2008)	72	53	43	28	12
Iraq war increased terrorist threat (2008)	46	45	30	22	12
Government help for Blacks (2004)	48	26	20	14	11

(Continued)

TABLE 6-13 ■ (Continued)					
	Liberal	Somewhat Liberal	Middle-of-the-Road	Somewhat Conservative	Conservative
Protect the environment (2004)	63	55	40	37	27
Oppose school vouchers (2000)	44	48	52	46	28
Protect gay men and lesbians from job discrimination (1996)	87	79	68	63	39
Not worth it to fight in Persian Gulf (1992)	66	45	41	30	24
Support for the Equal Rights Amendment (1980)	91	78	64	48	38
Legalize marijuana (1976)	60	49	24	24	10
Oppose the Vietnam War (1972)	76	61	39	33	27

Source: American National Election Studies, available at www.electionstudies.org.

Note: The numbers in the table are the percentages (in each group) taking the liberal position on each issue.

PUBLIC OPINION AND POLITICAL LEADERSHIP

The study of public opinion is of obvious relevance to public officials and political journalists who wish to assess the mood of the people on various topics, but the extent to which decision makers are influenced by public opinion on any particular policy is almost impossible to determine. Although policy makers must have some sense of the public mood, no one supposes that they measure precisely the attitudes of the public or are influenced by public opinion alone.

Political analysts and public officials both have difficulty assessing the likely impact of public opinion as measured by public opinion polls because the intensity of feelings will influence the willingness of the public to act on their views. Public officials who value their careers must be conscious of the issues that raise feelings strong enough to cause people to contribute money, to campaign, and to cast their ballots solely on the basis of that issue. As a result, public officials may be more responsive to the desires of small, intense groups than to larger, but basically indifferent, segments of the public.

In American society, public attitudes toward policies usually can be described in one of two ways: (1) as permissive opinion, whereby a wide range of possible governmental activities are acceptable to the public, or (2) as directive opinion, either supportive or negative, whereby specific alternatives are definitely demanded or opposed. Ordinarily, policy alternatives advocated by both political parties are within the range of permissive opinion, a situation that does not create highly salient issues or sharp cleavages in the public, even though political leaders may present their positions dramatically. Only when many people hold directive opinions will the level of issue salience rise or issue clashes appear among the public. For example, widespread directive support exists for public education in the United States. Most individuals demand a system of public education or would demand one were it threatened. At the same time, permissive support is evident for a wide range of policies and programs in public education. Governments at several levels may engage in a variety of programs without arousing the public to opposition or support. Within this permissive range the public is indifferent.

Occasionally, the public may out-and-out oppose some programs and form directive opinions that impose limits on how far government can go. For example, the widespread opposition to busing children out of their neighborhoods for purposes of integration has perhaps become a directive, negative opinion. Political analysts or politicians cannot easily discover the boundaries between permissive and directive opinions. Political leaders are likely to argue that there are supportive, directive opinions for their own positions and negative, directive opinions for their opponents' views. One should be skeptical of these claims because it is much more likely that there are permissive opinions and casual indifference toward the alternative views. Indifference is widespread and, of course, does not create political pressure. It frees political leaders of restrictions on issue positions but, on balance, is probably more frustrating than welcome. When comparing the general ideological orientation of states to the general public policies produced by state legislatures, Robert Erikson, Gerald Wright, and John McIver have found that states with more liberal publics have state legislatures that produce more liberal public policies and vice versa.[59] At the national level, James Stimson provides evidence of federal representation, showing that as the overall public mood becomes more liberal, liberals are more likely to get elected and produce left-leaning policies, and that as public mood swings to the conservative side, conservatives are more likely to enter office and produce more conservative policies.[60]

Study Questions

- What are some of the ways that people organize their attitudes about politics?

- What are some challenges involved with the measuring and interpretation of public opinion?

- How do Americans' attitudes array across various economic, social, racial, and international issues, and how have these changed over time?

Suggested Readings

Althaus, Scott. *Collective Preferences in Democratic Politics: Opinion Surveys and the Will of the People*. New York: Cambridge University Press, 2003. A compelling demonstration that measures of public opinion do not represent the public equally.

Carmines, Edward G., and James A. Stimson. *Issue Evolution: Race and the Transformation of American Politics*. Princeton, NJ: Princeton University Press, 1989. A fascinating account of the role of racial issues and policies in American politics in recent decades.

Converse, Philip E. "The Nature of Belief Systems in Mass Publics." In *Ideology and Discontent*, edited by David Apter, 206–261. New York: Free Press, 1964. A classic analysis of the levels of sophistication in the American public.

Erikson, Robert S., Michael B. MacKuen, and James A. Stimson. *The Macro Polity*. Cambridge, England: Cambridge University Press, 2002. A methodologically sophisticated study of representation in the United States.

Hibbing, John R., Kevin B. Smith, and John R. Alford. *Predisposed: Liberals, Conservatives, and the Biology of Political Differences*. New York: Routledge, 2013. An in-depth look at the evidence supporting the biological roots of the notion that political opponents experience and respond to the world differently.

Hochschild, Jennifer L. *What's Fair*. Cambridge, MA: Harvard University Press, 1981. An intensive, in-depth study of the beliefs and attitudes of a few people that deals with traditional topics from a different perspective.

Kellstedt, Paul. *The Mass Media and the Dynamics of Racial Attitudes*. New York: Cambridge University Press, 2003.

Kinder, Donald R., and Nathan P. Kalmoe. *Neither Liberal nor Conservative: Ideological Innocence in the American Public*. Chicago: University of Chicago Press, 2017. A provocative analysis of public opinion arguing that Americans are not ideological but group-centric in their political decision making.

Lewis-Beck, Michael S., William G. Jacoby, Helmut Norpoth, and Herbert F. Weisberg. *The American Voter Revisited*. Ann Arbor: University of Michigan Press, 2008. A rich reanalysis of the themes from the classic work, using mainly 2000 and 2004 data.

Stimson, James A. *The Tides of Consent: How Public Opinion Shapes American Politics*. Cambridge, England: Cambridge University Press, 2004. A complex analysis of changing policy views and their impact.

White, Ismail K., and Chryl N. Laird. *Steadfast Democrats: How Social Forces Shape Black Political Behavior*. Princeton, NJ: Princeton University Press, 2020. Rich, innovative analyses of why Black Americans' social expectations of other Black Americans encourage Democratic Party support.

Internet Resources

The website of the American National Election Studies, www.electionstudies.org, has extensive data on the topics covered in this chapter. Go to the Resources menu and click on "Guide to Public Opinion and Electoral Behavior," then scroll down to "Ideological Self-Identifications" for ideological items in a number of election years. Scroll to "Public Opinion on Public Policy Issues" for a wide range of attitudes from 1952 to the present. Each political item is broken down by an extensive set of social characteristics.

The Roper Center for Public Opinion Research, www.ropercenter.uconn.edu, at the University of Connecticut has an enormous collection of survey data on American public opinion from the 1930s to the present.

The General Social Survey, https://gss.norc.org/, has been collecting public opinion data since 1972 on a wide range of topics. Some of these data can be analyzed online at http://sda.berkeley.edu.

Notes

1. Jianing Li, Michael W. Wagner, Lewis A. Friedland, and Dhavan V. Shah, "When Do Voters Support Black Lives Matter or the Green New Deal?,"

Washington Post, December 8, 2020, https://www.washingtonpost.com/politics/2020/12/08/when-do-voters-support-black-lives-matter-or-green-new-deal/.

2. Lydia Saad, "U.S. Debt Ceiling Increase Remains Unpopular With Americans," Gallup Politics, July 12, 2011, http://www.gallup.com/poll/148454/debt-ceiling-increase-remains-unpopular-americans.aspx.

3. Art Swift, "Americans Split on Whether NAFTA Is Good or Bad for U.S.," Gallup Politics, February 24, 2017, http://www.gallup.com/poll/204269/americans-split-whether-nafta-good-bad.aspx?g_source=&g_medium=&g_campaign=tiles.

4. Philip E. Converse, "The Nature of Belief Systems in Mass Publics," in *Ideology and Discontent*, ed. David Apter (New York: Free Press, 1964), 206–261.

5. John R. Zaller, *The Nature and Origin of Mass Opinion* (New York: Cambridge University Press, 1980).

6. Jianing Li and Michael W. Wagner, "The Value of Not Knowing: Partisan Cue-Taking and Belief Updating of the Informed, Uniformed and Ambiguous," *Journal of Communication* 70, no. 5 (2020): 646–669.

7. Edward G. Carmines and James A. Stimson, "The Two Faces of Issue Voting," *American Political Science Review* 74 (1980): 78–91.

8. Paul M. Sniderman and John G. Bullock, "A Consistency Theory of Public Opinion and Political Choice: The Hypothesis of Menu Dependence," in *Studies in Public Opinion: Gauging Attitudes, Nonattitudes, Measurement Error, and Change*, ed. Willem E. Saris and Paul M. Sniderman (Princeton, NJ: Princeton University Press, 2004), 337–357.

9. Brett Creech, "Are Most Americans Cutting the Cord on Landlines?," *Beyond the Numbers* 8, no. 7 (May 2019), U.S. Bureau of Labor Statistics, accessed July 6, 2021, https://www.bls.gov/opub/btn/volume-8/are-most-americans-cutting-the-cord-on-landlines.htm.

10. "In U.S., Decline of Christianity Continues at Rapid Pace," Pew Research Center, October 17, 2019, https://www.pewforum.org/2019/10/17/methodology-28/.

11. "2020 Time Series Study," American National Election Studies, accessed July 6, 2021, https://electionstudies.org/data-center/2020-time-series-study/.

12. "2020 Election Surveys," Elections Research Center at the University of Wisconsin–Madison, accessed July 6, 2021, https://elections.wisc.edu/2020-election-survey/.

13. Drew DeSilver, "Q&A: After Misses in 2016 and 2020, Does Polling Need to Be Fixed Again? What Our Survey Experts Say," Pew Research Center,

April 8, 2021, https://www.pewresearch.org/fact-tank/2021/04/08/qa-after-misses-in-2016-and-2020-does-polling-need-to-be-fixed-again-what-our-survey-experts-say/.

14. "How Does Gallup Polling Work?," Gallup, accessed July 6, 2021, https://news.gallup.com/poll/101872/how-does-gallup-polling-work.aspx.

15. In the 2006 General Social Survey, for example, 38 percent said "too much" was being spent on "welfare"; however, 70 percent said "too little" was being spent on "assistance to the poor." See https://gss.norc.org/.

16. Suzanne Mettler, *The Submerged State: How Invisible Government Policies Undermine American Democracy* (Chicago: University of Chicago Press, 2011).

17. "1992 Time Series Study," American National Election Studies, accessed July 6, 2021, https://electionstudies.org/data-center/1992-time-series-study.

18. "2008 Time Series Study," American National Election Studies, accessed July 6, 2021, https://electionstudies.org/data-center/2008-time-series-study/.

19. "KFF Health Tracking Poll: The Public's Views on the ACA," Kaiser Family Foundation, June 3, 2021, https://www.kff.org/interactive/kff-health-tracking-poll-the-publics-views-on-the-aca/.

20. This view is most prominently associated with Paul M. Sniderman and Edward G. Carmines, *Reaching Beyond Race* (Cambridge, MA: Harvard University Press, 1997). See also Paul M. Sniderman, Philip E. Tetlock, and Edward G. Carmines, *Prejudice, Politics, and the American Dilemma* (Stanford, CA: Stanford University Press, 1993).

21. A strong statement of the symbolic racism position is in Donald R. Kinder and Lynn M. Sanders, *Divided by Color* (Chicago: University of Chicago Press, 1996).

22. This position is most commonly associated with Lawrence Bobo. See his "Race and Beliefs About Affirmative Action" in *Racialized Politics*, eds. David Sears, Jim Sidanius, and Lawrence Bobo (Chicago: University of Chicago Press, 2000), Chapter 5.

23. This position is represented by Jim Sidanius and Felicia Pratto in *Social Dominance: An Intergroup Theory of Social Dominance and Oppression* (Cambridge, England: Cambridge University Press, 1999).

24. Edward G. Carmines and James A. Stimson, *Issue Evolution: Race and the Transformation of American Politics* (Princeton, NJ: Princeton University Press, 1989).

25. Martin Gilens, *Why Americans Hate Welfare* (Chicago: University of Chicago Press, 1999).

26. Kinder and Sanders, *Divided by Color*.

27. Paul M. Kellstedt, *The Mass Media and the Dynamics of American Racial Attitudes* (New York: Cambridge University Press, 2003).

28. Ismail K. White and Chryl N. Laird, *Steadfast Democrats: How Social Forces Shape Black Political Behavior* (Princeton, NJ: Princeton University Press, 2020).

29. Brian F. Schaffner, Matthew MacWilliams, and Tatishe Nteta, "Explaining White Polarization in the 2016 Vote for President: The Sobering Role of Racism and Sexism," paper prepared for presentation at the Conference on The U.S. Elections of 2016: Domestic and International Aspects, January 8–9, 2017, IDC Herzliya Campus, accessed July 6, 2021, https://www.idc.ac.il/en/schools/government/uselections/documents/schaffner-brian%20.pdf.

30. Doug McLeod, "Five Problems With How the Media Cover Protests," Poynter, June 25, 2020, https://www.poynter.org/ethics-trust/2020/five-problems-with-how-the-media-covers-protests/.

31. Amber Boydstun, *Making the News: Politics, the Media, and Agenda Setting* (Chicago: University of Chicago Press, 2013).

32. Brian Montopoli, "Most Say U.S. Will Always Face Terrorism Threat," CBS News, September 9, 2011, http://www.cbsnews.com/8301-503544_162-20103461-503544/most-say-u-s-will-always-face-terrorism-threat/.

33. "America Speaks Out About Homeland Security Survey," conducted by Hart and Teeter Research Companies for the Council for Excellence in Government, February 5–8, 2004, Roper Center for Public Opinion Research, www.ropercenter.uconn.edu/.

34. Pew News Interest Index Poll, January 4–8, 2006, Roper Center for Public Opinion Research.

35. "America Speaks Out About Homeland Security Survey," Roper Center for Public Opinion Research.

36. CBS News Poll, April 2005, Roper Center for Public Opinion Research.

37. "CBS News Monthly Poll #5, March 2003" (ICPSR 3787), Inter-university Consortium for Political and Social Research, April 29, 2009, version, http://www.icpsr.umich.edu/icpsrweb/ICPSR/studies/3787.

38. CBS News/*New York Times* Poll, April 23–27, 2004, http://www.icpsr.umich.edu/.

39. "2008 Time Series Study," American National Election Studies.

40. John E. Mueller, *War, Presidents, and Public Opinion* (New York: Wiley, 1973), 208–213.

41. These data are available at www.pollingreport.com. See "President Bush: Job Ratings," PollingReport.com, accessed July 6, 2021, http://www.polling report.com/BushJob1.htm.

42. "CBS News Monthly Poll #5"; and CBS News/*New York Times* Poll, April 23–27, 2004. Data provided by the Inter-university Consortium for Political and Social Research, http://www.icpsr.umich.edu/.

43. Jeffrey M. Jones, "Americans Divided on How Well Iraq War Is Going for U.S.," Gallup Politics, August 5, 2010, http://www.gallup.com/poll/141773/Americans-Divided-Iraq-War-Going.aspx.

44. Gallup/*USA Today* Poll, July 2008, Roper Center for Public Opinion Research, www.ropercenter.uconn.edu/.

45. Pew Research Center for the People and the Press, September 2008, http://www.people-press.org/.

46. Lydia Saad, "Americans Broadly Favor Obama's Afghanistan Pullout Plan," Gallup Politics, June 29, 2011, http://www.gallup.com/poll/148313/Americans-Broadly-Favor-Obama-Afghanistan-Pullout-Plan.aspx.

47. Edward G. Carmines, Michael J. Ensley, and Michael W. Wagner, "Political Ideology in American Politics: One, Two, or None?" *The Forum* 10, no. 4 (2012): 1–18.

48. J. Eric Oliver and Wendy M. Rahn, "Rise of the *Trumpenvolk*: Populism in the 2016 Election," *The ANNALS* 667, no. 1 (2016): 189–206.

49. Edward G. Carmines, Michael J. Ensley, and Michael W. Wagner, "Ideological Heterogeneity and the Rise of Donald Trump," *The Forum* 14, no. 4 (2016): 385–397.

50. Nolan McCarty, Keith T. Poole, and Howard Rosenthal, *Polarized America: The Dance of Ideology and Unequal Riches* (Cambridge, MA: MIT Press, 2006). Updated data can be found at https://voteview.com/parties/all.

51. Marc J. Hetherington, "Resurgent Mass Partisanship: The Role of Elite Polarization," *American Political Science Review* 95, no. 3 (2001): 619–656.

52. Matthew Levendusky, *The Partisan Sort: How Liberals Became Democrats and Conservatives Became Republicans* (Chicago: University of Chicago Press, 2009).

53. Angus Campbell, Philip E. Converse, Warren E. Miller, and Donald E. Stokes, *The American Voter* (New York: Wiley, 1960), 249.

54. John C. Pierce, "Ideology, Attitudes, and Voting Behavior of the American Electorate: 1956, 1960, 1964" (PhD dissertation, University of Minnesota, 1969), 63, Table 3.1; Paul R. Hagner and John C. Pierce, "Conceptualization and Consistency in Political Beliefs: 1956–1976" (paper presented at the annual meeting of the Midwest Political Science Association, Chicago, 1981); and Michael Lewis-Beck, William G. Jacoby, Helmut Norpoth, and Herbert F. Weisberg, *The American Voter Revisited* (Ann Arbor: University of Michigan Press, 2008), Chapter 10. See also Norman H. Nie, Sidney Verba, and John R. Petrocik, *The Changing American Voter* (Cambridge, MA: Harvard University Press, 1976), Chapter 7.

55. Converse, "Nature of Belief Systems in Mass Publics."

56. John R. Alford, Carolyn L. Funk, and John R. Hibbing, "Are Political Orientations Genetically Transmitted?," *American Political Science Review* 99 (May 2005): 153–167.

57. Jeffery J. Mondak, *Personality and the Foundations of Political Behavior* (New York: Cambridge University Press, 2010).

58. P. K. Hatemi and R. McDermott, "The Genetics of Politics: Discovery, Challenges and Progress," *Trends in Genetics* 28, no. 10 (2012): 525–533; John R. Hibbing, Kevin B. Smith, and John R. Alford, *Predisposed: Liberals, Conservatives, and the Biology of Political Differences* (New York: Routledge, 2013); James H. Fowler and Christopher T. Dawes, "In Defense of Genopolitics," *American Political Science Review* 107, no. 2 (2013): 362–374.

59. Robert S. Erikson, Gerald C. Wright, and John P. McIver, *Statehouse Democracy: Public Opinion, and Policy in the American States* (Cambridge, England: Cambridge University Press, 1993).

60. James A. Stimson, *Public Opinion in America: Moods, Cycles, and Swings*, 2nd ed. (Boulder, CO: Westview Press, 1999).

7

POLITICAL COMMUNICATION AND THE MASS MEDIA

AS THE 2020 ELECTION DREW NEAR, a group of nearly seventy political communication scholars wrote what they called an emergency set of recommendations for how the news media should approach covering the end of the election season, what to do if the results were contested or one of the candidates would not concede, and what to do if there was civil unrest after the election.[1] They were worried that there would be attempts to undermine the integrity of the election and even efforts to subvert the will of the people on Election Day. Their recommendations—such as denying platforms to those making baseless claims about the election, striving for equity in news coverage, and publicizing plans regarding the decision process on who won a state—were made with the knowledge that the news media had considerable power with respect to shaping public confidence in American electoral administration.

Americans are almost wholly dependent on the news media to learn about politics. At the same time, Americans are notoriously critical of the news media. Less than 20 percent of the public have "a lot" of trust in the information they get from national or local news sources.[2] Three-quarters of citizens believe the news tends to favor one side in coverage of politics.[3] Of course, newspapers, television news, magazines, and online outlets are not the only places people learn about politics. People also talk with their friends, coworkers, and family members about contemporary issues. Moreover, they increasingly use social media to share, engage, learn, and express their own ideas about politics.

The American people are not the only ones engaged in a need–hate relationship with the news media. Politicians are chronic critics of journalists as well. President Donald Trump regularly derided coverage with which he disagreed as "fake," "unfair," and "nasty." Fact-checkers were particularly busy during the

Trump era; as the *Washington Post*'s Glenn Kessler and colleagues noted, the president made 30,573 false or misleading claims while in office.[4] In this chapter, our learning objectives for understanding the state and consequences of political communication include:

- Applying the major functions of the news media to our own assessments of media performance

- Learning how individuals select and assess their news and bias in the media

- Exploring the media's role in polarization, persuasion, and participation

- Examining how social media is changing politics

- Identifying how political communication can change individual attitudes

THE NEWS MEDIA: FUNCTIONS, TYPES, AND USERS

Despite being a crucial intermediary that connects a diverse array of people in myriad ways, the news media are a frequent punching bag for politicians, scholars, and the public alike. Much of the ire aimed at the media stems from critiques of the ways in which the media perform their basic functions. Doris Graber has argued that there are four functions of the mass media: surveillance, interpretation, socialization, and manipulation.[5]

Surveillance is the process by which the news media inform people of important events. Since most people do not wake up asking themselves, "How do I hold my government accountable today?," journalists convey to readers, listeners, and viewers which events are important and which are not. This begins with judgments about what is newsworthy. In general, newsworthy stories are those that are timely, proximal, and familiar and contain some kind of conflict, violence, or scandal. The surveillance function of the media is closely connected to the concept of *gatekeeping*—which is the power the media have to convey to the audience what is important and what isn't. Which of the fifteen items on the city council agenda merit public attention? Does a public protest merit media coverage, or is it small potatoes? Which elements of the COVID-19 recovery legislation deserve emphasis in the story, and which can be ignored? Surveillance is public in the sense that it brings attention to public officials, organized interests, and the like, and it is private in that it helps provide people an avenue to stay informed. Some critics argue that the media's choices about what to cover rely too much on the discourse of political elites and ignore the challenges and issues facing everyday citizens. Others accept that the news media will spend most of their attention on public figures, but blanch at the amount of coverage some politicians receive as compared to others, especially since more ideologically extreme politicians get more media attention.[6]

In the 2020 campaign, Trump got the most attention—by far. Political scientist Stuart Soroka's chronicling of 2020 coverage found that out of every ten stories about the campaign, Trump received seven to eight, and Joe Biden received two to three.[7] While incumbents tend to get more attention than challengers, the disparity in 2020 was the largest in the forty years of data Soroka analyzed.

Interpretation is the function of the media that puts an issue into context. Interpretation goes beyond surveillance to explain to the audience what an event *means*. For example, when Biden selected Kamala Harris to be his running mate, NPR's website ran an article arguing that Biden's choice was a "statement on what it means to be an American" and that Biden is willing to listen to people who disagree with him.[8] These kinds of articles praising Biden's choice were common in 2020, with more conservative critics complaining that the news media favored the Biden–Harris ticket.[9] While the surveillance function of the media certainly contains some biases regarding who gets covered the most, the interpretation function is often home to charges of ideological bias in news coverage, something we consider later in the chapter.

Despite the positive interpretation of Harris's selection as the vice-presidential nominee, news coverage of politics tends to be negative. Campaign coverage, however, tends to be more positive for one candidate and more negative for the other. Though Trump received far more coverage than Biden, Biden received more positive coverage. Table 7-1 shows analyses from the Shorenstein Center on Media, Politics and Public Policy that compared coverage from Fox News and CBS News. A cursory look at this result might suggest a bias that the news media had in favor of Biden. However, a closer look at the topics that generated positive and negative coverage for each candidate reveals that the news media's interpretation of events on the campaign trail is highly predictable and largely governed by

TABLE 7-1 ■ Percentage of Positive and Negative News Coverage for Donald Trump and Joe Biden From Fox News and CBS News, 2020 General Election				
	CBS News Positive	CBS News Negative	Fox News Positive	Fox News Negative
Biden Horserace	98	2	80	20
Trump Horserace	8	92	44	56
Biden Non-horserace	61	39	15	85
Trump Non-horserace	5	95	42	58

Source: Thomas E. Patterson, "A Tale of Two Elections: CBS and Fox News' Portrayal of the 2020 Presidential Campaign," Shorenstein Center on Media, Politics and Public Policy, December 17, 2020, https://shorensteincenter.org/patterson-2020-election-coverage/.

professional norms that reporters apply to all candidates. While Biden enjoyed more positive coverage than Trump, Table 7-1 shows that the main reasons were related to the tone of horserace stories—coverage that examined campaign strategy and who was winning and losing in the polls—and stories about COVID-19, which were overwhelmingly negative for Trump. In other words, since nearly every poll showed Biden winning the race and the public being dissatisfied with the Trump administration's handling of the pandemic, the news media's coverage of the polls was more positive for Biden.

The third media function, according to Graber, is *socialization*. This is the function in which the mass media help citizens learn basic values that prepare them to live in their society. For instance, the news media tend to cover the two major political parties but largely ignore third parties. When third parties are covered, it is usually to speculate about which of the major parties might lose votes to the third party. Thus, news coverage helps socialize Americans to accept the two-party system of government and see important differences between the parties.[10] Broader, cultural socialization can come from the mass media as well; notable examples include changing attitudes about premarital sexual behavior, sexual orientation, and racial attitudes. An example of socialization on display in 2016 occurred when Trump apologized after the *Access Hollywood* video, mentioned in Chapter 2, leaked. The early news coverage of the video focused on both the objectionable nature of the comments Trump made in the video and speculation about when Trump would apologize, which media commentators reasoned he would surely have to do to survive politically. The news media socialize the public to expect an apology from a lawmaker when one has said something incredibly offensive about a large group of people.

Finally, the news media engage in what some scholars call *manipulation*. Manipulation can mean many different things, including journalists engaging in "muckraking," the digging up of dirt on government behavior designed to force lawmakers to "clean up their act." However, Graber notes that manipulation also can mean the sensationalizing of facts to try to increase an audience's interest in a story to boost ratings and profits, and it can even mean the media surreptitiously advocating for the positions of some politicians or trying to alter the preferences of other politicians. One example of manipulation in the 2020 campaign was the news media's focus on Joe Biden's son Hunter and his dealings with a Ukrainian energy company called Burisma. Though a Republican-led Senate report about the younger Biden's dealings with the company found no evidence of wrongdoing or influence on foreign policy, they concluded the former vice president's behavior was problematic.[11] For most of the general election season, conservative news outlets aired hundreds of stories about Hunter Biden, calling the situation a scandal.

Other scholars think about the functions of the news media with respect to whether news coverage enhances the prospects and performance of democratic citizenship. A number of scholars have pointed out that it may be rational for voters to ignore much of the political information around them. Rational choice theorists, following the lead of economist Anthony Downs, argue that the benefits derived from reaching a "correct" decision on a candidate or policy may not be worth the costs the voter incurs in finding out the information.[12] It is rational, therefore, for the voter to take a number of information shortcuts, such as relying on someone else's judgment or voting according to one's established party identification. Samuel L. Popkin uses the analogy of "fire alarms" versus "police patrols" to explain how most people view political information.[13] Instead of patrolling the political "neighborhood" constantly to make sure nothing there requires their attention, most citizens rely on others to raise the alarm when something truly important happens. Television news and newspaper headlines may be enough to tell average citizens whether they need to delve deeper into a story.

Michael Schudson, a sociologist of news, argues that good citizens need not be fully informed on all issues of the day but that they ought to be "monitorial."[14] That is, a good citizen scans the headlines for issues that might be important enough about which to form an opinion or on which to take some action. Political scientist John Zaller argues for a "burglar alarm" standard of media coverage in which reporters regularly cover nonemergency but important issues in focused, dramatic ways that simultaneously entertain and allow traditional news makers like political parties and interest groups to express their views about the issue.[15]

For the media to have an impact on an individual's political attitudes and behavior, the individual must give some degree of attention to the media when political information is being reported. Even in an age of difficult economic times for newspapers and local television news stations, there is the ever-expanding number of media outlets and platforms. People can read newspapers; watch local television news, national network news, mainstream cable news, or ideologically oriented cable news; listen to the radio over the air or via paid satellite services or listen to podcasts; read magazines; read web-only news sites; share information via social media; and do all of the above on a computer, tablet, or phone.

Almost all Americans have access to television and watch political news at least some of the time. In 2021, 86 percent of Americans claimed to get at least some news from their smartphones.[16] On the one hand, use of smartphones expands access to political information, but as Johanna Dunaway and colleagues discovered, excessive smartphone use for political information could be a problem for the acquisition of political knowledge as people pay less attention for less time to news on their smartphones.[17] While a majority of Americans reported reading a daily newspaper regularly, often online, only about 5 percent of people said they prefer using a hard copy of a newspaper.[18] Somewhat fewer reported reading a newspaper for political news. This represents a decline in daily newspaper readership from more than 70 percent early in the 1990s. Occasional newspaper reading is higher. Television remains the main source of news for most Americans, but the internet has passed newspapers and radio as the second most commonly used source.[19]

Network television news viewership is down over the past several decades, but increased by five million between 2016 and 2020 to about twenty-nine million

QU: Please add text callout.

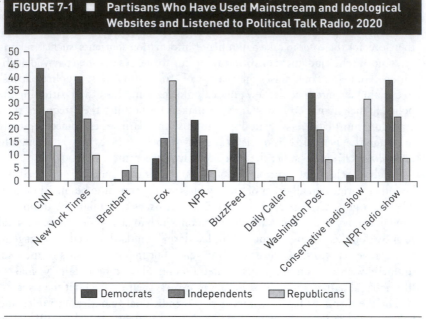

FIGURE 7-1 ■ Partisans Who Have Used Mainstream and Ideological Websites and Listened to Political Talk Radio, 2020

Source: 2020 American National Election Studies, available at https://electionstudies.org/.

Americans who watch the NBC, ABC, or CBS evening news programs on an average weeknight.[20] Prime-time viewers of CNN, Fox News, and MSNBC combined averaged just under six million people each weeknight.[21] While over 90 percent of Americans listen to the radio at some point during the week, only about one-third told the Pew Research Center that they listened "yesterday." The percentage of people listening to the radio online has increased to over 50 percent.[22] In 2020, the public continued reporting that television was a main source for campaign news. The use of mobile technologies—from reading newspapers online to listening to podcasts—all continued to grow in 2020. More than a fifth of Americans now say they get some of their news from podcasts.[23]

The American National Election Studies (ANES) asked respondents whether they had used various news websites and listened to political talk radio. Republicans were far more likely to choose Fox News's website while Democrats preferred CNN and the *New York Times*. Republicans listened to conservative talk radio while Democrats and independents were more likely to use NPR. Only 6 percent of Republicans used the far-right, and frequent misinformation purveyor, Breitbart.

One major consequence of the growth of technologies that can deliver the news is the increased choice media consumers have about what they will watch on television, read in a paper or magazine, listen to on the radio or in a podcast, or surf on the web. Markus Prior has called the era in which we live a period of "post-broadcast democracy," meaning that the rise of cable news and the internet has fundamentally altered who gets the news, which, in turn, has affected citizen political knowledge, voter turnout, polarization, and congressional and presidential elections.[24] During the early age of television, there was a limited number of networks (and no cable), thus constraining the choice of what people could watch. Moreover, they all tended to air the news at the same time, so if you wanted the television to be on in your home at 5:30 on a Wednesday night in Madison, Wisconsin, you had to be watching the news. This meant that some people who were not so interested in politics, but interested in watching television, would learn a bit about what was going on in spite of their own interests. Prior calls this "by-product learning." During the 1950s and 1960s, by-product learning helped produce a more informed, moderate, and participatory electorate. The television news media tended to air broad, nonideological journalism because that was the best way to appeal to the highest number of potential viewers in an era of constrained viewer choice. The moderate coverage helped produce more moderate public preferences, and the increased (if unintended) attention to politics spurred enough interest in enough people to increase voter turnout.

The development and growth of cable news, with cable networks like CNN, Fox News, ESPN, and HBO, changed all of that. Now, you can have the tube on at 5:30 p.m. and watch a movie on HBO instead of the news. You can even watch a show you digitally recorded a year ago. Or you can play a game on your phone, or Snapchat with a friend. Thus, those with a higher preference for entertainment compared to news are now opting out of watching the news and choosing instead to watch ESPN's *SportsCenter* or binge *Bridgerton* or *Cobra Kai* on Netflix. As the opportunities for by-product learning dropped for those who preferred entertainment to hard news coverage, so did their political knowledge and civic engagement. Moreover, those who like politics do not have to watch the broad, nonideological network news anymore. They can watch Fox News or MSNBC, stations whose prime-time lineup is full of ideological opinion programs hosted by strong personalities like Rachel Maddow and Sean Hannity. One consequence of the availability of these kinds of choices was that those who prefer ideological news are able to watch programs that spend more time providing justification for their points of view and attacking opposing points of view, leading to a greater polarization of the politically engaged.

What's more, Shanto Iyengar and Kyu Hahn have shown that when given the choice of stories to select from a variety of different news outlets, conservatives are more likely to choose Fox News, and liberals are more likely to reject Fox News for almost anything else. A Pew Research Center study similarly revealed that liberals had a wide variety of "main sources" for news, including CNN, MSNBC, NPR, and the *New York Times* (all ranging from 10 to 15 percent of liberals choosing a particular source). Conservatives, on the other hand, overwhelmingly chose Fox. Moreover, liberals had more trust than distrust for a variety of sources, from the major television networks and public broadcasting outlets to the *Daily Show* and the *New Yorker*. Conservatives had more trust than distrust for specific, conservative-oriented talk shows like Hannity's show on Fox, Glenn Beck's show on TheBlaze, and Rush Limbaugh's radio show.[25] This emergence of "red media" and "blue media" could exacerbate polarization and further turn off those who find themselves in the middle.[26]

Though partisans engage in some selective exposure to news sources, people have different media repertoires—the overall constellation of sources from which people prefer to get the news. A study of the media repertoires of Trump supporters in the swing state of Wisconsin found that while some Trump supporters lived in a Fox News bubble, others were news "omnivores," using a variety of sources and platforms for news. Nearly one-fifth of Trump supporters exposed themselves to ideologically heterogeneous sources (in their case, sources advocating more liberal positions). The *largest* group of Trump supporters, however, were media avoiders, people who consumed less news, on average, than other adults.[27]

MEDIA BIAS AND AUDIENCE BIAS

One reason those highly interested in politics choose more ideological outlets to serve their information-consuming desires is that they believe that the mainstream media are biased. Most scholarly researchers investigating questions of media bias find that the biases exhibited by the media are more structural than ideological. That is, they favor the two-party system, give more attention to the president, provide more positive coverage to parties on issues for which the parties have a strong public reputation, and cover partisan lawmakers who disagree with their party more than they cover members of the loyal rank and file. These slants in coverage, though, are a far cry from ideological bias that favors one political point of view over another.

Political scientist and economist Tim Groseclose, sometimes along with economist Jeffrey Milyo, has argued that the mainstream media are stunningly left wing in their coverage of national and international affairs. The main measure used to demonstrate this claim is a comparison of how often partisan members of Congress cite particular think tanks when they are speaking on the floor of the House or Senate to how often the news media use those same think tanks in their reporting. Groseclose and Milyo found a news media far more likely in their reporting to use think tanks favored by liberals compared to those favored by conservatives.[28] Even the *Wall Street Journal*, a paper with a conservative editorial page, produced news coverage using think tanks favored by Democrats more often than those cited by Republicans. Political scientist Brendan Nyhan has argued that Groseclose's evidence is not persuasive, as liberal members of Congress tend to favor quoting nonpartisan think tanks, which feeds into the media norm of providing balanced coverage, while conservative lawmakers speaking on the floor of the House or Senate prefer think tanks with a professed conservative point of view. Nyhan concludes that this is evidence not of media bias but of a difference in lawmakers' preference for the use of particular kinds of evidence.[29]

Despite the fact that most bias research finds little to no evidence of ideological bias from the mainstream media[30]—finding instead biases toward entertainment, scandal, and conflict—research has not stopped the public from believing that ideological bias is pervasive in the mainstream news media. Nearly three times more Republican voters than Democratic voters thought that the press influenced the outcome of the 2012 presidential election.[31] A Gallup poll from September 2012 showed distrust in the news media hitting a new high of 60 percent of the American people. Of course, there are partisan differences in media trust. Attitudes about the media are also strongly driven by political context. In 2016, when the election was closely contested, a nearly equal number of Republicans and Democrats agreed that media criticism keeps leaders from doing things they should not do. After Trump took office, the percentage of Democrats holding that belief leapt from 74 percent to 89 percent while the percentage of Republicans holding that attitude plunged from 77 percent to 42 percent![32] Thus, despite fairly paltry empirical evidence that the media are providing ideologically biased coverage, individuals are not convinced. In fact, people tend to view the news media as hostile to their own point of view, regardless of what that point of view is.

Research investigating this "hostile media" perception has repeatedly shown that people of different ideological orientations can read the same story and think that it is biased in completely different directions. Joel Turner has shown that people also judge how fair a story is based on the source reporting the news rather than the content of the story. He found that liberals who thought they were watching a CNN story thought it was fair, while liberals who saw the exact same story, but thought they were watching Fox News, thought that the story was conservatively biased. He found the exact same relationship for conservatives: they more favorably evaluated the Fox version of the story compared to the exact same story under the CNN banner.[33] In a study of how people interpreted election polls in 2016, research led by Mallory Perryman discovered that partisans were more likely to believe that bad news (their candidate was losing in a poll) was biased.[34] Social and political psychologists argue that one reason these attitudes persist is because of a concept called *motivated reasoning*. Motivated reasoning refers to a kind of information processing that fits conclusions about an issue to an individual's preexisting goals or views. Ironically, those with the most education are often the guiltiest of motivated reasoning because they have had more schooling and more training in the evaluation of evidence and the art of debate. Thus, they are more able to produce counterarguments to evidence that challenges their point of view. Indeed, conservatives who had a college education were more likely to falsely believe that Barack Obama was born in Kenya and not the United States. It is not hard to imagine an astute arguer countering evidence of the president's birthplace with questions about whether the birth certificate the president produced was a forgery or asking why it took as long as it did for the president to produce it, even though the fact remains that the president was born in the United States.

After President George W. Bush declared the end of "formal hostilities" in Iraq in May 2003, many surveys documented a pattern of beliefs among partisans about the factual evidence for the existence of weapons of mass destruction (WMDs) in Iraq, Iraqi nuclear arms development, and Iraqi dictator Saddam Hussein's involvement in the attacks on September 11. A year later, Bush supporters disproportionately believed that Iraq had WMDs and, to a lesser degree, that they had actually been found in Iraq. People not sympathetic to the president believed the opposite. *Newsweek* magazine polls in 2003 and 2004 showed that nearly one-half of the American people believed that Hussein was involved in the September 11 attacks on the United States. Figure 7-2 shows that views on the existence of WMDs were strongly associated with vote intention in 2004.

The motivated reasoning argument turns the traditional view—that misinformation or ignorance is the result of apathy or inattention—on its head. Rather than expecting the better educated and more interested to be accurately informed about WMDs in Iraq, the motivated reasoning argument suggests the opposite. But is the traditional view wrong? No. In fact, both the traditional view and the motivated reasoning argument are right. Among Bush supporters, those who were highly attentive and those who were least attentive to the election campaign were equally likely to believe there were WMDs in Iraq. That is, they held an inaccurate opinion. The supporters of challenger John Kerry, represented by the sloping line in Figure 7-2, had different views depending on their level of interest in the campaign. The least attentive Kerry supporters had about the same views as the Bush supporters.

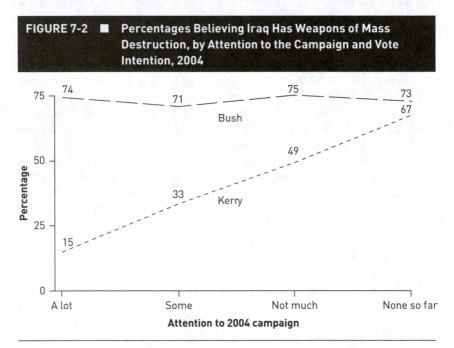

FIGURE 7-2 ■ Percentages Believing Iraq Has Weapons of Mass Destruction, by Attention to the Campaign and Vote Intention, 2004

Source: CBS News/*New York Times* Monthly Poll, April 2004.

Scholars like Brendan Nyhan and Jason Reifler have shown how persistent misperceptions are and how difficult they can be to overcome for conservatives and liberals alike. One thing that helps people change their attitudes in the face of facts that dispute their own point of view is the presence of visual data. Nyhan and Reifler showed that when liberals saw visual evidence of fewer American soldier deaths after President Bush's "surge" plan in Iraq, they were more likely to believe the surge had worked, and conservatives who saw visual evidence of an economy adding more jobs under the Obama administration were more likely to believe that the economy was getting better.[35]

Media sources are not the only context in which motivated reasoning and the holding onto misperceptions occurs. Another kind of thinking, supporting conspiracy theories, is largely driven by individuals with low levels of trust toward institutions such as government and the media and high levels of interest in politics. Political scientists Joanne Miller, Kyle Saunders, and Christina Farhat have found that the party that controls the presidency also affects who is more likely to endorse conspiracy theories. For example, a set of surveys conducted by the scholars found Republicans more likely to endorse conspiratorial thinking when Obama was in the White House, but the propensity to endorse conspiracy theory thinking shifted from Republicans to Democrats shortly after Trump took the oath of office.[36] Media use, or lack thereof, can also help account for conspiracism. Those who believe "news finds me"—that is, those who think they do not need to follow the news because they will eventually hear about the important stuff on social media or somewhere else—are more likely to engage in conspiratorial thinking.[37]

The rise of ideological media is not the only major change to the information environment in recent years. One major area of growth in journalism is in the area of fact-checking. Journalists have always engaged in a rigorous checking of basic facts in their stories—how to spell the names of the people quoted and so forth—but the fact-checking movement is something different. Fact-checking outlets like PolitiFact and fact-checkers like the *Washington Post*'s Glenn Kessler conduct fact-checks about the veracity of politicians' statements. In the 2016 primary campaign, Trump accused Grand Old Party (GOP) opponent Ted Cruz's father of being involved in the assassination of John F. Kennedy, falsely claiming that the elder Cruz had been photographed with Kennedy assassin Lee Harvey Oswald. Later, Trump claimed that Cruz had never denied that his father was in the photograph. PolitiFact checked Trump's claim, noting that it was so false that it deserved the rating "pants on fire." Cruz had denied his father was in the photograph, his campaign denied it, and Cruz's father denied it.

Fact-checkers hope that their work makes it less likely that politicians will lie and more likely that people will believe the corrected record that fact-checkers provide. The early evidence on the effects of fact-checking suggests that people often approach their interpretation of fact-checkers' conclusions with the same partisan-colored glasses that they use to approach other kinds of news coverage. Those who are willing to admit what they do not know are the most likely to benefit from a fact-check. But, fact-checks can come at a cost—even when fact-checks help people learn what is true, they also lead to people believing the news source conducting the fact-check is biased.[38]

THE NEWS, THE PUBLIC AGENDA, AND PARTISAN POLARIZATION

As noted in the section about the surveillance function of the media, much discussion has ensued in the scholarly literature on mass media about the capacity to bring matters to the attention of the public or to conceal them.[39] This is usually referred to as *agenda setting*. The literature suggests that the media have great influence over what the public is aware of and concerned with, issue wise. Television news and front-page stories in newspapers focus the public's attention on a few major stories each day. With just under eight billion people living in 196 countries on the planet, the front page of the *New York Times* averages about eight stories a day. Indeed, there are so few words spoken during a typical half-hour network television newscast that they could all fit on the front page of a newspaper. Thus, the stories that the news media choose to cover are of great consequence because the media's agenda sends a strong signal to the public about what is important, and what is worth their time. While the media's agenda is generally fairly stable, major political events, such as the killing of Osama bin Laden; the September 11, 2001, terrorist attacks; or scandals such as President Bill Clinton's sexual liaison with White House intern Monica Lewinsky, along with celebrity milestones, such as the death of Kobe Bryant, push other stories off the agenda.[40] The media make it almost impossible for an ordinary American to be unaware of these events. These are examples of agenda setting, but the concept also refers to the consequences of people finding an issue to be more important than they did before as a direct result of increased media coverage about that issue.

Candidates for office want to set the public's agenda for a variety of reasons. First, if you are thinking about issues a candidate wants you to be thinking about, you are not thinking about other things that could be damaging to the candidate. For example, in 2008, John McCain's campaign staff knew that McCain was being tied to the Bush economy, which had fallen off a cliff just a month before the election. McCain tried to burnish his foreign policy credentials, hoping some voters would focus on Obama's comparative lack of foreign policy experience. Second, the issue ownership hypothesis developed by John Petrocik (see Chapter 5) shows evidence that the public thinks that each party is better at dealing with certain issues.[41] For example, people think Democrats are strong on health care and Republicans are better on handling crime. Thus, candidates for office want to set our agendas on issues on which we favorably evaluate their political party. Recent evidence shows that candidates even pivot away from tough questions in debate settings to circle back and highlight issues they want the public to be thinking about when they enter the voting booth.[42] Moreover, studies reveal that the coverage candidates receive on issues that their party owns is more positive than their media attention about other issues.[43]

Television often plays a critical role in bringing events and issues to the public's attention, presenting certain types of information in an exceptionally dramatic or impressive way. The Persian Gulf War and the start of the Iraq war were televised to an unprecedented extent. The American public watched a real-life video arcade of modern warfare. In January 1991, 67 percent of a national sample reported following the Persian Gulf War "very closely."[44] Attention was not as high in 2003, but over half the public followed the invasion of Iraq very closely.[45] In the short run, the coverage created the impression of an overwhelming military victory and great satisfaction with the performance of each president. In each instance, the president's job approval ratings soared, and support for the war increased dramatically.[46] Evaluations became more mixed with the passage of time.

Perhaps nothing in television history compares with the coverage of the attacks on the World Trade Center and the Pentagon on September 11, 2001. The major news channels abandoned regular programming and focused on the attacks and their aftermath for days. Virtually everyone in the country was attentive to this coverage, and most people had strong emotional reactions to the graphic, disturbing, and frightening images they saw.

In the information age, scholars are starting to find consistent evidence that there is more to agenda setting than the news media signaling to the public what the important issues are so that the public comes to think the issues are important too. In an era in which the news media carefully track the number of clicks their web stories get, there is evidence that the people can set the media's agenda as well. Individuals' own information search behavior on tools like Google signals to the media that there is enough interest in some issues to ensure that news coverage about those issues is likely to "earn clicks." In other words, when many people search the web for information at about the same time, the mainstream media respond by being more likely to produce stories about that topic.[47] Later in this chapter, we will review evidence of how social media platforms like Twitter are also influencing both the public's and the media's agenda.

Because the most interested voters are also the most partisan, a relationship exists between attention to the media and partisanship. The fact that strong partisans and politically interested people are most attentive to the media accounts for the somewhat paradoxical finding that those with the most exposure to the media are among the least affected by it. Philip E. Converse, in his study of the impact of mass media exposure on voting behavior in elections in the 1950s, drew several conclusions.[48] The voters most stable in their preferences (whether stability is measured during a campaign or between elections) are those who are highly attentive to mass media but firmly committed to their party or candidate. Those who pay no attention to media communication remain stable in their vote choices because no new information is introduced to change their votes. The shifting, unstable voters are more likely to be those with moderate exposure to mass media. However, efforts at replicating Converse's findings for other election years have failed to uncover similar patterns. One difficulty may be that in recent years, there have been hardly any voters with no exposure to the mass media. Nevertheless, the reasoning behind this expected relationship is compelling: the impact of the media is likely to be greatest when the recipients of the message have little information and few existing attitudes or attitudes that are not strongly held.

Kevin Arceneaux and Martin Johnson tested this idea experimentally by first randomly assigning some participants to watch Fox News and others to watch MSNBC. Next, with other participants, they gave people the choice of what to watch. When people were randomly assigned to watch particular media, they found outlets broadcasting counterattitudinal ideas to be biased. When people chose what to watch themselves, as most people usually do outside of an experimental lab, the effects diminished significantly.[49] Thus, some of the worries about partisan media exacerbating polarization might be overstated because it is the people who are already polarized who are choosing the ideological news organizations in the first place. On the other hand, Natalie Jomini Stroud, in her book *Niche News*, found that using media that reinforces one's political beliefs can increase partisan divisions between people while also spurring greater participation.[50]

In general, there is clear evidence that liberals and conservatives prefer different news media sources. The differences in information preferences do not stop there.[51] One analysis of web use showed that liberals and conservatives also prefer to use different political blogs to learn about politics. While liberals are slightly more likely than conservatives to check out the other side's websites online, neither group is very likely to spend much time on websites that offer views supportive of a different political perspective. These choices have consequences for the issues people learn about from their news sources, the perspectives they are exposed to, and their political knowledge.

Liberals and conservatives also showed differences in their assessments of how well the news media do at keeping people informed. As with other media attitudes, the people's views are largely driven by which political party is in power. In 2016, the Pew Research Center reported little difference between Republicans and Democrats with respect to their beliefs about the job the news media did at informing the public. After President Trump took office, liberals became 5 percent more likely to positively evaluate the media's performance while conservatives became 6 percent more likely to negatively evaluate the news media.[52]

The news media can also exacerbate polarization by the lawmakers they choose to cover. From 1993 to 2013, an analysis of which members of Congress got covered by the *New York Times* and by network television news programs revealed that ideologically extreme members of the House of Representatives earned three times the media attention as moderates. The same trend did not hold up in the Senate because the institutional practice of using the filibuster focuses media attention on more moderate lawmakers, whose votes are required to either keep filibusters going or invoke closure to stop them. Interestingly, extreme Republicans were more likely to get news media attention than extreme Democrats. This could be a sign of ideological bias from reporters, casting

Republican lawmakers as extremists. However, recent analyses also show that the average incoming Republican in Congress is more conservative than the average returning (reelected) Republican in Congress and the average newly elected Democrat is more moderate than the average returning Democrat. That is, extreme Republicans may get more media attention not because journalists are trying to paint Republicans as ideologically extreme, but because more ideologically extremist Republicans are getting elected to office.[53]

When the COVID-19 pandemic hit, an analysis from Ceren Budak, Ashley Muddiman, and Talia Stroud showed that cable sources like MSNBC and Fox News were more likely to interview partisans than health officials about the health crisis.[54] Fox was 46.7 times more likely than CNN to discuss China, using the words "Chinese communist" to describe the origins of the virus. Fox also was more likely than CNN and MSNBC to positively characterize unproven treatments of the coronavirus touted by President Trump. When he famously speculated about the potential of injecting bleach or using ultraviolet light inside human bodies to fight COVID-19, fact-checkers leapt to report the danger of these methods while Fox News was less likely to cover the president's words. Moreover, the Pew Research Center presented evidence that Americans' news choices influenced how they perceived COVID-19.[55]

An underappreciated aspect of political communication is the simple, everyday political talk people engage in with friends, family, and coworkers. While many people avoid talking about politics, Kathy Cramer has found that a wide variety of Americans include political talk in their regular conversations with others. In her focus group conversations with individuals in rural areas in Wisconsin, Cramer found that political talk in these parts of the country focuses on people's sense of "rural consciousness"—the feeling that those in rural areas are hardworking, deserving of benefits yet ignored, and even mocked for their way of life by urbanites, including political and university elites. This leads to resentment of urbanites, including political and university elites, and contributed to Trump's success in 2016. Trump visited rural areas, reified rural Americans' deservingness of government benefits, and promised to take their concerns seriously.[56] Other analyses have found that when politics gets particularly contentious and polarized, it infiltrates parts of lives that were previously apolitical. A group of scholars led by Chris Wells found that fully one-third of Wisconsinites stopped talking to someone in their social network in the wake of the contentious recall election of Republican Scott Walker, who survived his recall election that was called after a Walker-led effort to end collective bargaining rights for public employees in Wisconsin.[57]

SOCIAL MEDIA AND CONTEMPORARY POLITICS

Perhaps the most consequential change to the media landscape over the past two decades has been the rise of social media. Nearly 90 percent of Americans say that they use the internet. Nearly all of them use some form of social media.

About 81 percent of adults use YouTube, and 70 percent of adults use Facebook, making them the most used, by far, social media platforms. Forty percent of people use Instagram, 25 percent use Snapchat, and 21 percent use TikTok.[58] While Twitter is heavily used by politicians, journalists, and activists, only 23 percent of Americans report using the platform. This makes the finding that the attention people give to issues on Twitter affects the news media's agenda all the more impressive—and potentially troubling, since such a modest percentage of the public can drive what the news media cover for the entire public. Of course, young people are more likely than those over the age of sixty-five to use social media, but 50 percent of senior citizens reported using Facebook in 2021. Interestingly, urban and rural Americans are just as likely to use Facebook while suburban Americans are slightly less likely to use the social networking site.[59]

About seven in ten Americans get news from social media, with 53 percent using social media sometimes or often for political information.[60] Some platforms are more likely to be used by political information seekers than others. Users of Reddit, Facebook, and Twitter are especially likely to get news from those platforms while users of Tumblr, YouTube, Instagram, LinkedIn, and Snapchat do not get much political information from those sites. In general, there are more Democrats using social media sites than Republicans, but this is largely a reflection of there being more Democrats than Republicans in the electorate. People of color make up a higher percentage of Twitter, YouTube, and Instagram users than their national demographics would suggest.[61]

One way social media use has affected contemporary politics is through the practice of "second screening"—using an internet platform to comment on one's use of a more traditional media platform. For example, citizens used to be passive viewers of presidential debates. Now, people can comment on Twitter or Facebook during the debates, potentially shaping the interpretation others, including the media, have of who won the debates. Evidence gathered by Dhavan Shah and his colleagues show that people become more likely to tweet about a moment in a debate when candidates use particular kinds of body language. In fact, body language appears to drive more of the commenting behavior on Twitter than the actual content of what candidates are saying. What is more, many politically interested individuals and media outlets alike use social media to engage in "real-time" fact-checking of candidates during debates and other major speeches.

Social media provide people increased opportunities to learn about the views of a wide array of people, but they also make it easier for folks to cloister themselves in ideological echo chambers that serve to reinforce their own views. As noted in Chapter 4, when people build friendship networks on Facebook or follower networks on Twitter that are primarily filled with like-minded people, it becomes easier for individuals to become more confident and extreme in their views, serving to further exacerbate polarization in the electorate.

Since social media are constant, they are a platform through which rumors and misinformation can be spread very quickly. During and after the 2016 campaign, Trump and some of his staffers claimed that negative stories about Trump were examples of "fake news." While satirical news sites like The Onion prided themselves on being fake news sources, reporters working in the mainstream news media did not appreciate the characterization that what they were doing was fake. Disputes over what constitutes fake news have sprung up in political and scholarly communities. From our point of view, fake news is not bad news that politicians do not like; it is stories that are demonstrably false. These kinds of stories can have real-world consequences. For example, a fake story widely circulated on the internet falsely and recklessly claimed that Hillary Clinton was involved in running a secret child-sex ring that was being operated out of a Washington, DC, pizzeria. One person took the story so seriously he showed up at the pizzeria with a gun, demanding to know where the kids were so he could save them. Thankfully, the situation was defused before anyone got hurt.

Social media are not all fake news and ideologically cloistered networks of followers. Some people enjoy rich and varied networks of people who espouse a wide range of views. These users tend to express higher degrees of political tolerance than those with more homogeneous social networks. Among young people in advanced democracies like the United States, Facebook use is positively correlated with increased political participation (see Chapters 3 and 4).[62]

Members of Congress have also gotten deeply involved in social media. Congressional lawmakers use Twitter to spread news about their voting behavior and availability to meet with constituents as well as to support their party and criticize the other major party. Female candidates for office are a little more likely to use Twitter than male candidates. In terms of the styles of Twitter use, Heather Evans and her colleagues found that challengers engage in more attacking behavior, while most candidates spend about 30 percent of their Twitter time sharing personal information, 10 to 15 percent of their tweets on issues, and 15 to 25 percent of their tweets on the campaign.[63]

Social media is also critically important to social movements. In a comprehensive report about social media and the Black Lives Matter movement, Deen Freelon and colleagues found that activists on Twitter were critical to the spreading of BLM messages. Moreover, users of the #BLM hashtag were successful at building new narratives about police relationships with Black communities and in sharing media criticism of how the movement was covered.[64] They also found that supportive online communities attracted more attention than unaligned people and opposed communities. The authors concluded that the unconventional participation (see Chapter 4) in the BLM movement might be a model for future civics education.

POLITICAL COMMUNICATION AND ATTITUDE CHANGE IN POLITICAL CAMPAIGNS

It is clear that individuals receive ideas and information intended to alter their political opinions from a variety of sources. Some sources are political leaders and commentators whose views arrive impersonally through the mass media; others are friends, coworkers, and family members who influence opinions through personal contact. Much remains to be learned about political persuasion and communication, but at least occasionally, many Americans engage in attempts to influence others, and almost everyone is regularly the recipient of large quantities of political communication.

A useful but oversimplified perspective on the transmission of political information would have the media presenting a uniform message to a mass audience made up of isolated individuals. The audience would receive all or most of its information from the media. Thus, public opinion would be a direct product of the information and perspective provided through the media. A more complex view suggests that information is transmitted in a "two-step flow of communication."[65] Information is transmitted from *opinion elites* (leaders in society, such as politicians, organizational heads, and news commentators) to a minority of the public—the *opinion leaders*—and from them to the remainder of the public.

The information from opinion elites usually is sent through the mass media, but this view implies that only a portion of the audience—the opinion leaders— is attentive to any particular type of information such as political news. The opinion leaders, as intermediaries, then interpret, modify, and explain facts and events to those friends and neighbors who are less interested in or concerned with these happenings. In the process, the original message conveyed through the media becomes many somewhat different messages as it reaches the public. Of course, this same process can skip over the traditional media in contemporary society as politicians and activists use social media to communicate with people, and people increasingly expose themselves selectively to the news outlets that tend to share their ideological perspective.

The two-step flow model may not be strictly true in most cases, and public opinion research has generally failed to turn up many people who recognize themselves as opinion leaders. Even so, most members of the public probably receive information from the mass media in the context of their social groups. Thus, they filter the information and interpretations of the media through not only their own perceptions, experiences, and existing attitudes but also those of people around them. Only when the media have the attention of most members of the audience, and a virtual monopoly over the kinds of information received by a public that has few existing attitudes about the subject, can the media produce anything like a uniform change in public attitudes. As noted earlier, the twenty-first century's media ecology is one in which the two-step flow is further complicated by individuals' ability to interact directly with the news media, elites, and each other on social media platforms like Twitter and Facebook. While the primary direction of influence may still flow through the media from political elites to the public, it is certainly the case that individuals expressing their own views in the contemporary media landscape can influence how journalists do their jobs and how politicians read public opinion.

Another factor that affects how political elites' messages are accepted by individuals is how they are framed in media coverage. An analysis of issue frames (e.g., "women should have the right to choose what happens to their body") used by Democratic politicians showed they were more effective at affecting attitudes when they focused on specific policy ideals while Republican politicians' frames were more persuasive when they dealt with more symbolic frames that were not policy specific. Simple consistency matters as well. The more consistent the messages that Democrats and Republicans espoused in the media, the more likely their frames were to influence public opinion, thanks, in part, to the clear signal they sent about what the party's position was on a particular issue.[66]

A different argument, also based on the role of social influences on the development of public opinion, has been made by Elisabeth Noelle-Neumann in *The Spiral of Silence*.[67] She argues that members of society sense that some views are increasing in popularity, even if these ascending viewpoints are held only by a minority. Under such circumstances, people become reluctant to express opinions contrary to the presumed ascending view, whereas individuals holding that view are emboldened and express themselves more freely. This effect can often occur in social situations from conversations in a church group to jury deliberations. This furthers the illusion that one viewpoint is widely shared. People then become more likely to adopt the viewpoint because of this (perhaps) imaginary public pressure.

The internet as a news source is a more recent development, with intriguing characteristics. Providing almost unlimited access to information, it requires the consumer to seek out that information actively. As noted earlier, it also offers opportunities to "talk back" or comment on the news, share information within social networks, and be in touch with other like-minded people. Few gatekeepers operate on the internet, and the issues of the reliability and credibility of information are largely left to the user to determine. Opportunities abound for whispering campaigns of rumor and misinformation.

One factor we have not yet considered is the impact of editorial endorsements by newspapers (television and radio stations rarely make endorsements). These should be assessed independently of news coverage, although editorial preferences may bias news stories. Newspaper endorsements seemingly have a minimal impact in presidential elections, given that many other sources of influence exist.[68] In less visible, local races, a newspaper editorial may influence many voters.[69] Some concern exists that major newspaper chains could wield significant power nationally by lining up their papers behind one candidate. In recent years, however, the large chains have generally left their papers free to make decisions locally. Still, additional concerns come from evidence showing that candidates who receive editorial endorsements receive more favorable coverage on the news side of the paper as well.[70]

We also need to make the distinction between the impact of news coverage by the media and political advertising carried by the media (see Chapter 2). This is not an easy task, especially because the news media often cover political advertising as if it were news and consciously or unconsciously pick up themes from political ads and weave them into their own coverage.[71] Placing political advertising in news programs makes it harder to separate news from ads. Even the "ad watches" that news organizations use to critique candidates' advertising may contribute to the confusion over what is news and what is paid advertising. Moreover, the growth of advertising on social media sites like Facebook is complicating political campaign strategies and scholars' ability to isolate advertising effects.[72] One study showed that, in 2016, the groups that did not file with the Federal Election Commission (FEC) ran the most divisive issue ads. Perhaps worse, many of those ads appear to have been sponsored by Russian groups.[73]

The Impact of Political Campaigns

Political campaigns are efforts to present candidates or issues to voters with information, rationales, characterizations, and images to convince them that one candidate or position is better than the alternatives and to get them to act on that preference. Massive amounts of money are spent in modern campaigns to saturate the airwaves in an effort to influence voters. A perennial question for politicians, political commentators, and scholars is "How much difference does a campaign make?"

Although most professional politicians take for granted the efficacy of political campaigns, scholarly analysis has often questioned their impact. In most elections, the majority of voters decide how they will vote, based on partisanship or ideological leanings, before the general election campaign begins. Beyond this, the generally low level of political information among the less politically interested throws doubt on the ability of undecided voters to absorb ideas during a campaign. Indeed, Andrew Gelman and Gary King have offered an especially interesting form of this argument.[74] They contend that a voter's eventual choice can be predicted satisfactorily at the start of a campaign, well before the candidates are even known. Furthermore, because a voter may move away from this ultimate choice during the course of a campaign, intermediate predictions—so popular in media coverage and campaign organizations—are misleading.

Recall from Chapter 2 that some political scientists, using economic forecasting models, argue that the outcome of the election—and the margin of victory—can be predicted long before the election campaign from such variables as the rates of economic growth, inflation, and unemployment.[75] It may be difficult to believe that an individual voter's choice is made before the start of a campaign or is determined by economic forces; yet evidence indicates that in most years, the vote choices of most voters are not affected by the general election campaigns. The ANES regularly asks voters when, during the presidential campaign, they made their voting decisions.[76] In most years, about two-thirds of the electorate reports deciding before or during the conventions, with the final one-third deciding during the campaign. Over the years, fewer people report deciding during the conventions—presumably because, in recent decades, the candidates have essentially been chosen by the end of the presidential primaries in the late spring.

The decision times of partisans and independents are different because the loyal party voters line up early behind the party's candidate. In all recent presidential elections, the strong partisans made their decisions by the end of the conventions, whereas many of the less committed partisans and independents were typically still undecided at the start of the general election campaign. In close elections (2012, 2016, and 2020, for example), this relatively uncommitted group can swing the election either way, with 10 to 15 percent of the voters claiming to decide in the last days of the election campaign.

Campaigning influences a small but crucial proportion of the electorate, and many elections are close enough that the winning margin could well be a result of campaigning. Professional politicians drive themselves and their organizations toward influencing undecided voters in the expectation that they are the key to providing, or maintaining, the winning margin. One can easily think of examples of elections in which the only explanation for the outcome was the aggressive campaign of one of the candidates. In 2016, the Republican Party elite did not want Trump to be their nominee, but they could not stop him as the attention he received in the primary campaign eclipsed that of his several opponents many times over.

The Impact of Debates

New information has the greatest impact in situations in which little is known about the candidate or issue and in which the voters have few existing attitudes. The application of this generalization can be seen in many areas. For example, the candidate who is less well known has the most to gain (or lose) from joint appearances, such as debates. The 1960 debates between Kennedy and Richard M. Nixon, the first-ever series of televised presidential debates, appear to have had a substantial impact on the election outcome, in large part because at the time Kennedy was not well known to the public. According to several different public opinion polls in 1960, about half of the voters reported that they were influenced by the debates, with Kennedy holding an advantage of three to one over Nixon.[77] Although Nixon's poor showing is often blamed on his five o'clock shadow, it is unlikely that his appearance caused many to turn against him, because he had been in the public eye as vice president for eight years. Instead, Kennedy's advantage came from undecided Democrats who had little information about Kennedy (but were favorably disposed toward him because he was the Democratic candidate) and who were influenced by his appearance and good performance. The immediate effect of the 1960 experience was the abandonment of presidential debates until 1976. Incumbent presidents or campaign front-runners were unwilling to offer such opportunities to their lesser-known challengers.

The 2008 debates presented a similar situation for Barack Obama. As the younger, less experienced, and less familiar candidate, he had the chance and the challenge to shape the impressions that voters had about him to a greater extent than the more familiar candidate, John McCain. Although public opinion polls generally showed that Obama "won" all the debates,[78] his greater victory was probably in reassuring those already leaning in his direction that he had the right characteristics to be president, as Kennedy had done in 1960.

In 2012, the general consensus was that Mitt Romney won the first debate. Much ink was spilled and airtime was spent analyzing President Obama's performance, looking for slight changes in the day-to-day tracking polls (which gave Romney a small, short-lived boost) and speculating about whether the first contest was a "game changer." It wasn't. The remaining debates, including Vice President Biden's lone contest with Congressman Paul Ryan, failed to meaningfully influence the polls.

Postelection polls and social media sentiment on Twitter and Facebook revealed that most people thought Hillary Clinton won all three debates against Donald Trump in 2016. Even so, there is not much evidence that these debate wins helped Clinton, who was very well known to the public. Trump's attacking style; willingness to violate traditional norms, such as not interrupting his opponent; and making claims that were easily demonstrable as false did not give his supporters pause. On the contrary, Trump's behavior fit with his campaign's narrative that he was not a phony politician but a strong leader who would make America great again by the sheer will of his winning personality.

Controlling the Message

Campaigns and the information they provide are also effective in influencing attitudes when counterinformation is not available. The obvious example is when one candidate has substantial resources for campaigning and the opponents do not. Such well-financed candidates can present a favorable image of themselves—or an unflattering image of their opponents—without having those images contradicted. This situation is more likely to occur in primaries, when candidates must rely on their own funds and whatever they can raise from others, than in general elections, when both candidates can tap party resources. However, strategic decisions may also lead to a failure to counter information. In 2004, Kerry delayed responding to the Swift Boat Veterans for Truth ads attacking his war record. The Swift Boat Veterans had been following him with similar accusations for years. He may have underestimated their potential harm to him when these allegations were played on a national stage, with higher stakes and an audience less knowledgeable about him than were his constituents in Massachusetts. Most major campaigns now have a "rapid response team" as part of their campaign staff to fire back when hit with unexpected and potentially damaging attacks. Obama reportedly beefed up his team after his campaign was slow to respond when allegations about his connections to 1960s radical William Ayers and indicted Chicago developer Tony Rezko surfaced in the spring of 2008. Even with the capability to respond quickly, candidates and their advisers still must make the strategic decision whether a response will be effective or will only serve to keep the story alive.

In presidential elections, the national nominating conventions offer each party the opportunity, at least temporarily, to get its message to the public without the annoyance of sharing the stage with the other party. The televised acceptance speech of the nominee and the ability to showcase rising stars and celebrate past heroes— all before a prime-time audience—offer unique opportunities for the political parties to present themselves and their campaign themes as they wish the public to see them. Although the news media interject commentary and analysis, the media's view of what is interesting generally leads them to emphasize strategy and motives instead of outright contradiction of a party's claims. The result of this nationwide opportunity for favorable publicity is the convention "bounce" that presidential nominees typically receive in their approval ratings and trial heat results immediately after their party's convention.[79] Obama had a 2008 convention bounce of about 5 percent at the end of August, and McCain's bounce was of the same amount after the Republican convention a week later. In 2012, Gallup reported a small, 3-point bounce for Obama after the Democratic National Convention (DNC) and no bounce for Romney after the Republican National Convention (RNC).

The 2012 election showed that political parties have not always been able to use the nominating convention to their advantage. Many previous nominating conventions corroborate this point. The battle-marred DNC in 1968 and George McGovern's acceptance speech long after midnight in 1972 represent dramatic failures to use this opportunity to benefit the party's nominee. Opponents within one's party may present the case against a nominee as effectively as the opposing party could. In recent years, when the nomination has been a foregone conclusion well before the nominating convention, both parties have tried to control their conventions as tightly as possible, keeping controversial issues and personalities under wraps. However, as the conventions have become more staged in an effort to promote the most favorable image of the candidate, the audience and the news coverage for them have shrunk, making it less likely that those images will be conveyed to the public. In 2008, the Obama campaign sought to increase the audience appeal of the DNC by showcasing the nominee's acceptance speech in a stadium filled with over eighty thousand enthusiastic supporters. Although the speech was well received, the effect was short lived, as McCain countered by announcing his running mate the following morning.

In 2016, the two parties' nominating conventions diverged widely in their execution. The RNC earned low marks from the news media for being poorly organized. Senator Cruz made headlines (and earned boos from the convention crowd) when he spoke about, but did not endorse, Trump at the convention. Trump's wife Melania got unwanted attention for taking passages of Michelle Obama's 2008 DNC speech and repeating them as her own. Trump's own speech was ridiculed for statements that suggested he did not understand how democratic governance worked. At one point in his speech, Trump said, "Nobody knows the system better than me, which is why I alone can fix it."[80] While pundits panned Trump's speech, the often appealing message (see Chapter 1) played well with his supporters, many of whom preferred a more authoritarian leadership style.[81]

The Democratic Party's convention was dramatic for reasons the party would have preferred to avoid as well. The head of the DNC, Congresswoman Debbie Wasserman Schultz, was not able to continue serving in her party position, a consequence of the anger Bernie Sanders supporters felt after leaked DNC emails suggested that the party apparatus was favoring the Clinton candidacy over the Vermont senator's presidential bid. On the other hand, Clinton's speech, and the speeches of many of her surrogates, was generally praised. The DNC, on the whole, received favorable appraisals from the news media and the voters when compared to the Republican effort. In 2020, the campaign was conducted in very different ways—with President Trump continuing to hold in-person events while Biden mostly campaigned virtually.

The fact that voters respond differently to information depending on its presentation offers campaign managers opportunities to use sophisticated techniques to create favorable images of their candidates. Highly paid political consultants use an arsenal of social science knowledge and techniques in an attempt to do just that. Although some of these attempts have been notably successful, serious limitations also exist.

To successfully "sell" a candidate with advertising techniques, image makers must be able to control the information available about their candidates, thereby controlling the perceptions the voters hold about them. Ronald Reagan was more successfully handled in this way than most other presidential candidates. Perhaps his training as an actor made him more amenable to management by his advisers. However, to a considerable degree, maintaining his public image depended more on protecting him from the press and public exposure than on manipulating the content of publicity about him. This approach was especially effective in the 1980 campaign, when the focus of attention and public dissatisfaction rested on President Jimmy Carter and not the challenger, Reagan.

For most candidates, however, manipulating a public image by controlling information is either impossible or self-defeating. For a relatively unknown challenger, such as Bill Clinton in 1992 or Barack Obama in 2008, this type of strategy would appear self-defeating because few candidates have had the resources to become well known nationwide through advertising and staged appearances alone. Billionaire Ross Perot was an exception in 1992, purchasing blocks of airtime to speak to the American voters. Billionaire Donald Trump was another exception in 2016, earning six times the free media attention of his nearest competitor in the primaries.

Typically, unknowns scramble for exposure in any forum they can find, and this prevents the careful manipulation of an image. Conversely, well-known candidates or incumbents, who can afford to sit back and let the public relations people campaign for them, probably already have images that are impossible to improve in any significant way over the relatively short period of time available in an election campaign. The most famous alleged attempt to repackage a candidate was the effort of the Nixon campaign staff in the 1968 presidential election.[82] However, the evidence suggests that more voters decided to vote for other candidates during the course of the campaign than decided to vote for Nixon. After about twenty years of nationwide public exposure, a "new Nixon" reinforced existing images, both negative and positive. He simply could not create a new, more attractive image. Romney faced criticism in 2012 for what critics called repeated attempts to change his image. Fearing his moderate record as governor of Massachusetts could hurt him in the GOP primary, Romney used one of the primary debates to refer to himself as a "severe" conservative. However, once Romney secured the nomination, a staffer of his went on television to claim that it was time to "shake" the Etch A Sketch and remake Romney's image for the general election. Al Gore received criticism in the 2000 election for a switch to "earth tones" in the way he dressed on the campaign trail.[83]

Campaign organizations also attempt to affect the public image of their candidates by supplying the news media with favorable information. If successful, this strategy can be particularly effective, because the information arrives through the more credible medium of news coverage instead of paid advertising. Media events can be staged that provide the media—particularly television—with an attention-grabbing headline, sound bite, or photo opportunity. The campaigns of Nixon in 1968 and George H. W. Bush in 1988 were particularly successful in manipulating news coverage favorable to their candidates by staging media events and otherwise limiting access to the candidates. In 2004, the campaign of George W. Bush went to great lengths to handpick the audiences at appearances of the president or vice president, thereby ensuring an enthusiastically supportive crowd. President Trump followed suit in 2020, but was sometimes thwarted by the new information environment. For one rally in Tulsa, Oklahoma, TikTok users who opposed the president requested upwards of one million tickets for the event, though they had no intention of showing up. The result was fewer than 6,200 people having their tickets scanned for the event in the nineteen-thousand-seat arena.[84]

Limiting exposure of the candidate to staged media events works better for well-known incumbents than for challengers. Attempts by the McCain campaign to keep national politics newcomer Sarah Palin under wraps in 2008 were ultimately unsuccessful because the press and public demanded to know more about a person who might be a heartbeat away from the presidency. Furthermore, recent advances in technology make carefully controlling the image of a candidate even more daunting. A casual remark at a reception of supporters, captured by cell phone video and uploaded to YouTube, can become an overnight sensation on the internet with catastrophic consequences for the candidate. In 2016, Trump's *Access Hollywood* video was an example of how a secretly taped conversation can affect a campaign. Hillary Clinton's campaign suffered with respect to the media attention it received when a video of Clinton at a fundraiser showed her referring to some Trump supporters as a "basket of deplorables." In 2020, the Trump campaign regularly argued that Biden was being managed and controlled, arguing he was campaigning from his basement.

In recent years, campaign organizations have had difficulty getting news stories aired or printed about their issue positions and policy stands, but they have had more success with negative stories and attacks on other candidates. A key tactic is to seduce the media into covering paid political advertising, usually negative, as if it were news. In her book *Dirty Politics*, Kathleen Hall Jamieson details how, in 1988, the news media continually reinforced the premise behind the infamous Willie Horton ads that attacked Democratic candidate Michael Dukakis's position on crime.[85] For some years afterward, television and newspapers regularly featured ad watches that attempted to dissect the claims made in candidates' paid advertising; ironically, in the course of doing so they provided the ads with a wider audience. Clinton's 2016 campaign was atypical in that her advertising was largely devoid of policy information, as compared to the general election candidates of the past twenty years.

Negative campaigning and advertising offer an effective way to hurt an opponent's image. In recent years, candidates' campaigns and independent organizations have attacked the images of candidates in personal and political terms. The volume of this particular form of negative advertising, sometimes called attack ads, has increased greatly. Many of these ads are paid for by committees, interest groups, and organizations not connected directly to a candidate or a campaign. The Supreme Court has ruled that such attack ads are issue advocacy and therefore cannot be limited because of the First Amendment.[86] As a result, a candidate can be hit with a massive campaign for which the opposing candidate need take no responsibility and that is basically outside the regulations and agreements governing the candidates and their campaign organizations. Three generalizations about negative campaigning can be made: (1) The public disapproves of negative campaigning; (2) even so, it sometimes works; and (3) negative advertising typically contains more useful policy information than positive ads. Because the public disapproves of negative advertising, some candidates have managed to be positive in their own ads while allowing independent organizations to trash their opponents for them, though presidential candidates in recent years have aired a high percentage of negative ads on their own.

If negative campaigning illustrates the capacity to use the mass media to accomplish political purposes, the difficulty candidates have in using the media to respond to these attacks reveals its limitations. Victims of negative campaigning have tried to ignore the attacks, attempted to answer the charges, or counterattacked with their own negative campaign. None of these responses appears to be notably successful—a fact that encourages the continued use of negative campaigning. Attacks in the form of ridicule or humor may be particularly difficult to answer. Some strategists have urged the victims of negative campaigning to respond immediately and defend themselves aggressively. This may be good advice, but following it requires much from the victim. To respond promptly with advertising requires a great deal of money (perhaps near the end of a campaign, when resources are limited) and a skilled staff. Moreover, victims of negative campaigning need to have a strong, effective answer to such attacks.

In their study of the 1992 presidential campaign, Marion R. Just, Ann N. Crigler, Dean E. Alger, Timothy E. Cook, Montague Kern, and Darrell M. West offer a useful way to look at the "construction" of a candidate's persona over the course of an election campaign.[87] Instead of the candidate's image being the creation of a campaign staff or the product of straight news coverage, it will evolve through the three-way interaction of the candidate's campaign, the news media, and the public. The candidates' initial attempts at establishing themselves face a range of reactions from the press and public—encouragement, incredulity, boredom—and the candidates adjust accordingly. Likewise, the news reporters assess and react to the response of colleagues and the public to their coverage of candidates. Finally, the public's judgments in public opinion polls, radio call-in programs, live interviews, and email indicate displeasure or support of the behavior of both candidates and news media. The final picture may not be a faithful reflection of the candidate's inner being, but neither is it an artificial creation of campaign technicians, nor is it the distortion of an overbearing press.

The Special Case of Primary Elections

Because the impact of new information is greatest when there are few existing attitudes, the impact of campaigns should be greatest in primary elections, especially with little-known candidates. In primaries, when all the candidates are of the same party, the voter does not have partisanship to help in the evaluation of candidates. In such situations, whenever new information is provided, it can have a substantial impact.

After 1968, reforms in the presidential nominating process led to an increased use of presidential primaries as a means of selecting delegates to the Democratic and Republican nominating conventions. The purpose of the reforms was to make the choice of the presidential candidates more reflective of the preferences of the party's supporters in the electorate. In fact, the increased use of presidential primaries opened the door, at least initially, to the nomination of candidates little known to the general public. Political newcomers, such as Carter in 1976, Gary Hart in 1984, Steve Forbes in 1996, and Howard Dean in 2004, had an opportunity to focus their energy and campaign resources on a few early primaries or caucuses, gain national media attention by winning or doing surprisingly well in those early contests, and generate momentum to allow them to challenge more established and well-known potential nominees. Such candidates often do not have long-term viability. Their early appeal, based on little information, dissipates as more, often less flattering, information becomes available. Nevertheless, by the time this happens, the candidate may already have secured the nomination (Carter in 1976) or severely damaged the front-runner, as Hart damaged Walter F. Mondale in 1984. Primaries can do considerable harm to candidates' images under some circumstances. Well-known front-runners such as George H. W. Bush in 1992 and Bob Dole in 1996 suffered a loss of popularity that they never recovered under the campaign attacks of fellow Republicans. Intraparty fighting is typically destructive for established candidates.

Before the 1988 election season, Southern Democratic leaders decided that concentrating their states' primaries early in the election year would focus media and candidates' attention on the Southern states as well as give a head start to more conservative candidates who could pick up a large bloc of delegate votes from these states. Although this strategy did not work in the short run—the Democrats nominated the liberal northeastern governor Dukakis in 1988—the creation of Super Tuesday considerably shortened the primary season by allowing candidates to amass enough delegates to secure the nomination months before the summer convention.

Every four years since 1988, additional states have moved their primaries forward, hoping to capture some media attention or, at least, to have a say before the nominations are decided. By 2008 and 2012, this process had gone so far that half the states had their primaries or caucuses by early February, far supplanting the old Super Tuesday in early March. This "front-loading" of primaries originally had the effect of favoring the front-runner and decreasing the opportunity for lesser-known candidates. Because the primaries are so close together in time, candidates cannot concentrate their resources in a few states and use victories there to generate favorable coverage in other states. Instead, after the early states of Iowa and New Hampshire, which now have their caucuses and primary in early January, candidates must campaign all across the country in many states. Unknown candidates have almost no time to capitalize on early success in Iowa or New Hampshire by raising money and creating state campaign organizations. The established, well-known candidates again seem to have the advantage.

Although the Obama phenomenon in 2008 seems to contradict the conventional wisdom about the front-loading of primaries advantaging the front-runner, we should be careful about jumping to conclusions, especially given how the primary calendar benefited Hillary Clinton in 2016. Obama was unusual among lesser-known candidates because he was able to raise an enormous amount of money and create a substantial grassroots organization across many states before the primary season began in January 2008. None of the other non-front-runners (except Dean in 2004 and Sanders in 2016) were able to come close to that. Whether other lesser-known candidates of the future will have those fundraising and organizational skills—and the staying power that Obama and, to a slightly lesser extent, Sanders had and Dean did not—is unclear. In any event, if the Democrats had held a national primary on February 5 (a national primary being the logical outcome of the current process of moving more and more primaries to the beginning of the season), it is quite likely that Clinton, the established front-runner, would have won, according to the nationwide trial heat results of the time in 2008.

The role of the news media in influencing presidential primaries with their coverage has changed as the format of the primaries has changed. In the 1970s and 1980s, the media had considerable potential to enhance one candidate's campaign momentum and to consign others to obscurity. Thomas E. Patterson's study of the role of the media in 1976 shows that, during the primaries, Carter benefited from the tendency of the press to cover only the winner of a primary, regardless of the narrowness of the victory or the number of convention delegates won.[88] Even the accident of winning primaries in the eastern time zone gave Carter disproportion-ately large, prime-time coverage on evenings when other candidates enjoyed bigger victories farther west.[89] This was possible because few voters were well informed about or committed to any of the many Democratic candidates. During the same period, the media exaggerated the significance of President Gerald R. Ford's early primary victories without noticeably influencing the public's feelings about him or his challenger, then governor of California Reagan.[90] It is much more difficult to influence voters who have well-informed preferences.

Attention focuses on who does better or worse than expected, regardless of the number of votes they receive. This was the case with Clinton's third-place finish in Iowa in 2008 (which led to the media writing her candidacy off), as well as her "surprise" win in New Hampshire, where she won more votes—but ultimately fewer delegates—than Obama. The same thing happened to Rick Santorum, who won the Iowa caucus after all the votes were counted; the media named Romney the winner on the night of the caucus even though the results were not all in and too close to call. The irony of this type of commentary is that it essen-tially converts the errors in the media's preelection coverage into newsworthy political change. With the front-loading of the primaries, however, media cover-age becomes less relevant after the first few primaries.

Inequality in the resources available to candidates in presidential primary campaigns is likely to have a greater effect than in the presidential general elec-tion, in which public financing is available to both major-party candidates. In the 2000 election campaign, George W. Bush raised more than $100 million, more money by far than any of the other candidates and more than twice as much as any previous candidates for president. He also raised his money early. Six months before the first primary, he had raised more than half his eventual total. This enormous war chest served both to discourage other potential candidates and to defeat his most serious rival for the nomination, John McCain. In 2008, Hillary Clinton followed a similar strategy of raising and spending so much money that it would create an aura of invincibility and scare off would-be rivals for the nomi-nation. Unfortunately for the strategy, her fundraising was more than matched by Obama's, and Clinton's campaign was chronically short of funds later in the season. Indeed, Obama's fundraising prowess was so formidable that it enabled him to forgo public financing in the general election, giving him a consider-able financial advantage over Republican candidate McCain, who had accepted public financing. Both Romney and Obama eschewed public financing in 2012. Those choices, along with the *Citizens United* decision from the Supreme Court, led to record spending from the candidates and from outside groups.

In 2016, the largest inequalities were related not to fundraising, but to earned media coverage. Figure 7-3 shows that Trump received more than $1.8 billion in free media attention, outpacing his closest competitors, Cruz, Jeb Bush, and Marco Rubio, by well over a billion dollars' worth of news coverage. Clinton enjoyed more attention than Sanders, though her advantage was more typical, getting twice the free media Sanders received.

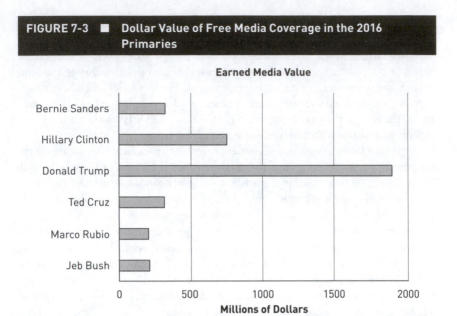

FIGURE 7-3 ■ Dollar Value of Free Media Coverage in the 2016 Primaries

Earned Media Value

Millions of Dollars

Source: Nicholas Confessore and Karen Yourish, "$2 Billion Worth of Free Media for Donald Trump," *Upshot, New York Times,* March 15, 2016, https://www.nytimes.com/2016/03/16/upshot/measuring-donald-trumps-mammoth-advantage-in-free-media.html?mcubz=0.

In 2020, presidential campaign financing skyrocketed. Biden raised over $1 billion, significantly outraising Trump, who came in just under $775 million. Even though Biden spent a record amount on advertising, he ended the campaign with money left in his campaign coffers and no debt. Trump's campaign, in contrast, ended up in debt.[91] Near the end of the campaign, Biden had more money on hand, and handily outspent Trump on television advertising three to one. Trump, as noted in Chapter 2, spent a lot on internet advertising.[92] In the end, it is unclear what impact all of this spending had on the election outcome, given that most people had decided to vote for or against Trump long before Election Day.

CONCLUSION

The current media environment is a vast, immediate, and polarized one. Politically interested individuals can, and often do, select news sources that reinforce their own views, while people who are not living and breathing politics find it easier than ever to avoid politics given the wide array of alternative forms of entertainment. Politicians devote considerable effort in trying to influence us to change our attitudes and participate in politics. Our own partisan blinders can affect what we believe to be true and who we are willing to trust—especially when the information we come in contact with suggests that our views might be incorrect. Still, those who regularly read newspapers, watch television news, or share news stories on social media are more likely to be interested in politics, knowledgeable about politics, and engaged civically.

Study Questions

1. What are the different sources and platforms that make up the news media?

2. What is selective exposure, and what are some of the consequences it has on American elections?

3. How does evidence related to media bias compare to evidence related to biases in the audience?

Suggested Readings

Graber, Doris. *Processing the News.* New York: Longman, 1988. An in-depth study of a few respondents on the handling of political information from the media.

Jamieson, Kathleen Hall. *Dirty Politics: Deception, Distraction, and Democracy.* New York: Oxford University Press, 1992. A blistering commentary on political advertising strategies and the interaction between advertising and news coverage.

Just, Marion R., Ann N. Crigler, Dean E. Alger, Timothy E. Cook, Montague Kern, and Darrell M. West. *Crosstalk: Citizens, Candidates, and the Media in a Presidential Campaign.* Chicago: University of Chicago Press, 1996. A multimethod study of the 1992 presidential election campaign.

Peeck, Reece. *Fox Populism: Branding Conservatism as Working Class.* New York: Cambridge University Press. Fascinating treatment of how Fox News blended tabloid journalism and populism to define its audience as the "real" Americans.

Popkin, Samuel L. *The Reasoning Voter.* Chicago: University of Chicago Press, 1991. A wide-ranging discussion of campaigning and presidential vote choice.

Sides, John, and Lynn Vavreck. *The Gamble: Choice and Chance in the 2012 Presidential Election.* Princeton, NJ: Princeton University Press, 2013. A political science-oriented election book produced as the 2012 campaign was occurring.

Stroud, Natalie Jomini. *Niche News: The Politics of News Choice.* New York: Oxford University Press, 2011. A groundbreaking examination of how expanding news choice divides us.

Vavreck, Lynn. *The Message Matters: The Economy and Presidential Campaigns.* Princeton, NJ: Princeton University Press, 2009. A creative and original account of when and how candidates' campaign messages ought to include economic messages as compared to messages on other issues.

West, Darrell M. *Air Wars: Television Advertising in Election Campaigns, 1952–2008.* Washington, DC: CQ Press, 2009. The fifth edition of a study of many aspects of television advertising in presidential elections.

Internet Resources

The Pew Research Center conducts numerous political surveys throughout the year as well as the best study of American media behavior done in the spring of even-numbered years. Not only does the center make the data available freely, at www.pewresearch.org/topic/politics-policy, but the website offers extensive analysis of many political and media topics as well. During election years, most major news organizations have websites with survey data on many political items, but poll aggregating websites, such as elections.huffingtonpost.com/pollster, provide stronger estimates of candidate support and changes thereof in real time.

Notes

1. "Recommendations for Media Covering the 2020 U.S. Presidential Election," Election Coverage and Democracy Network, accessed July 9, 2021, https://mediafordemocracy.org/recommendations-for-media-covering-the-2020-u-s-presidential-election/.

2. Amy Mitchell, Jeffrey Gottfried, Michael Barthel, and Elisa Shearer, "Trust and Accuracy," Pew Research Center, July 7, 2016, http://www.journalism.org/2016/07/07/trust-and-accuracy/.

3. "2017 Pew Research Center's American Trends Panel," Pew Research Center, March 17–27, 2017, http://assets.pewresearch.org/wp-content/uploads/sites/13/2017/05/09125944/PJ_2017.05.10_Media-Attitudes_TOPLINE.pdf.

4. Glenn Kessler, Salvador Rizzo, and Meg Kelly, "Trump's False or Misleading Claims Total 30,573 Over 4 Years," *Washington Post*, January 24, 2021, https://www.washingtonpost.com/politics/2021/01/24/trumps-false-or-misleading-claims-total-30573-over-four-years/.

5. Doris A. Graber, *Mass Media and American Politics*, 8th ed. (Washington, DC: CQ Press, 2010).

6. Michael W. Wagner and Mike Gruszczynski, "Who Gets Covered? Ideological Extremity and News Coverage of Members of the U.S. Congress," *Journalism and Mass Communication Quarterly* 95, no. 3 (2018): 670–690; Jeremy Padgett, Johanna L. Dunaway, and Joshua P. Darr, "As Seen on TV? How Gatekeeping Makes the U.S. House Seem More Extreme," *Journal of Communication* 69, no. 6 (2019): 696–719.

7. "News Coverage of the 2020 Presidential Election," Institute for Social Research, Center for Political Studies, University of Michigan, October 16, 2020, https://cpsblog.isr.umich.edu/?p=2871.

8. Domenico Montanaro, "5 Takeaways on the New Biden-Harris Presidential Ticket," NPR, August 12, 2020, https://www.npr.org/2020/08/12/901537144/5-takeaways-on-the-new-biden-harris-presidential-ticket.

9. Tim Murtaugh, "More Evidence Emerges That the Media Is on Team Biden," Heritage Foundation, March 17, 2021, https://www.heritage.org/civil-society/commentary/more-evidence-emerges-the-media-team-biden.

10. Michael W. Wagner, "The Utility of Staying on Message: Competing Partisan Frames and Public Awareness of Elite Differences on Issues," *The Forum* 5 (2007): 1–18.

11. "Hunter Biden: Republicans Release Report on Joe Biden's Son," BBC News, September 23, 2020, https://www.bbc.com/news/election-us-2020-54268887.

12. Anthony Downs, *An Economic Theory of Democracy* (New York: Harper and Brothers, 1957).

13. Samuel L. Popkin, *The Reasoning Voter* (Chicago: University of Chicago Press, 1991), 47–49.

14. Michael Schudson, *The Good Citizen: A History of American Public Life* (New York: Free Press, 1998).

15. John Zaller, "A New Standard for News Quality: Burglar Alarms for the Monitorial Citizen," *Political Communication* 20, no. 2 (2003): 109–130.

16. Elisa Shearer, "More Than Eight-in-Ten Americans Get News From Digital Devices," Pew Research Center, January 12, 2021, https://www.pewresearch.org/fact-tank/2021/01/12/more-than-eight-in-ten-americans-get-news-from-digital-devices/.

17. Johanna Dunaway, Kathleen Searles, Mingxiao Sui, and Newly Paul, "News Attention in a Mobile Era," *Journal of Computer-Mediated Communication* 23, no. 2 (2018): 107–124.

18. Shearer, "More Than Eight-in-Ten Americans Get News From Digital Devices."

19. "Internet Overtakes Newspapers as News Outlet," Pew Research Center, News Interest Index, December 23, 2008, http://www.pewresearch.org/politics/2008/12/23/internet-overtakes-newspapers-as-news-outlet/.

20. Brad Adgate, "TV News Ratings Remain Strong, but Pandemic Fatigue Seems to Be Setting In," *Forbes*, May 13, 2020, https://www.forbes.com/sites/bradadgate/2020/05/13/tv-news-ratings-remain-strong-but-pandemic-fatigue-seems-to-be-setting-in/?sh=721773fa6f12; Katerina Eva Matsa, "Network News: Fact Sheet," last updated June 2016, p. 37, in *State of the News Media 2016*, Pew Research Center, June 15, 2016, https://assets.pewresearch.org/wp-content/uploads/sites/13/2016/06/30143308/state-of-the-news-media-report-2016-final.pdf.

21. A. J. Katz, "Thursday, May 27 Scoreboard: Tucker Carlson, Hannity Lead Fox News to No. 1," TVNewser, May 28, 2021, https://www.adweek.com/tvnewser/thursday-may-27-scoreboard-tucker-carlson-hannity-lead-fox-news-to-no-1/479694/.

22. Nancy Vogt, "Audio: Fact Sheet," last updated June 2016, p. 68, in *State of the News Media 2016*, Pew Research Center, June 15, 2016, https://assets.pewresearch.org/wp-content/uploads/sites/13/2016/06/30143308/state-of-the-news-media-report-2016-final.pdf.

23. Shearer, "More Than Eight-in-Ten Americans Get News From Digital Devices."

24. Markus Prior, *Post-broadcast Democracy: How Media Choice Increases Inequality in Political Involvement and Polarizes Elections* (New York: Cambridge University Press, 2007).

25. Amy Mitchell, Jeffrey Gottfried, Jocelyn Kiley, and Katerina Eva Mitsu, "Political Polarization & Media Habits," Pew Research Center, October 21, 2014, http://www.journalism.org/2014/10/21/political-polarization-media-habits/.

26. Shanto Iyengar and Kyu S. Hahn, "Red Media, Blue Media: Evidence of Ideological Selectivity in Media Use," *Journal of Communication* 59, no. 1 (2009): 19–39.

27. Sadie Dempsey, Jiyoun Suk, Katherine J. Cramer, Lewis A. Friedland, Michael W. Wagner, and Dhavan V. Shah, "Understanding Trump Supporters' News Use: Beyond the Fox News Bubble," *The Forum* 18, no. 3 (2020): 319–346.

28. Tim Groseclose and Jeffrey Milyo, "A Measure of Media Bias," *Quarterly Journal of Economics* 120, no. 4 (2005): 1191–1237.

29. Brendan Nyhan, "Does the U.S. Media Have a Liberal Bias? A Discussion of Tim Groseclose's Left Turn: How Liberal Media Bias Distorts the American Mind," *Perspectives on Politics* 10, no. 3 (2012): 767–771; and "The Problems With the Groseclose/Milyo Study of Media Bias," Brendan-Nyhan.com, December 22, 2005, http://www.brendan-nyhan.com/blog/2005/12/the_problems_wi.html.

30. Hans J. G. Hassell, John B. Holbein, and Matthew R. Miles, "There Is No Liberal Media Bias in Which News Stories Political Journalists Choose to Cover," *Science Advances* 6, no. 14 (2020), doi: 10.1126/sciadv.aay9344.

31. "Low Marks for 2012 Election," Pew Research Center, November 15, 2012, http://www.pewresearch.org/politics/2012/11/15/section-4-news-sources-election-night-and-views-of-press-coverage/.

32. Michael Barthel and Amy Mitchell, "Americans' Attitudes About the News Media Deeply Divided Along Partisan Lines," Pew Research Center, May 10, 2017, http://www.journalism.org/2017/05/10/americans-attitudes-about-the-news-media-deeply-divided-along-partisan-lines/.

33. Joel Turner, "The Messenger Overwhelming the Message: Ideological Cues and Perceptions of Bias in Television News," *Political Behavior* 29 (April 2007): 441–464.

34. Mallory Perryman, Jordan Foley, and Michael W. Wagner, "Is Bad News Biased? How Poll Reporting Affects Perceptions of Media Bias and Voter Behavior," *International Journal of Communication* 14 (2020): 1–21.

35. Brendan Nyhan and Jason Reifler, "When Corrections Fail: The Persistence of Political Misperceptions," *Political Behavior* 32, no. 2 (2010): 303–330.

36. Christina E. Farhat, Kyle L. Saunders, and Joanne M. Miller, "The Relationship Between Perceptions of Loser Status and Conspiracy Theory Endorsement" (paper presented at the Annual Meeting of the Midwest Political Science Association, 2017). Other descriptions of this evidence came from Professor Miller during a panel of the 2017 conference, "Truth, Trust, and the Future of Journalism," sponsored by the Center for Journalism Ethics and the University of Wisconsin–Madison.

37. Jordan Foley and Michael W. Wagner, "How Media Consumption Patterns Fuel Conspiratorial Thinking," *TechStream*, Brookings Institution, May 26, 2020, https://www.brookings.edu/techstream/how-media-consumption-patterns-fuel-conspiratorial-thinking/.

38. Jianing Li and Michael W. Wagner, "The Value of Not Knowing: Partisan Cue-Taking and Belief Updating of the Informed, Uniformed and Ambiguous," *Journal of Communication* 70, no. 5 (2020): 646–669; Jianing Li, Jordan Foley, Omar Dumdum, and Michael W. Wagner, "The Power of a Genre: Political News Presented as Fact-Checking Increases Accurate Belief Updating *and* Hostile Media Perceptions," *Mass Communication and Society*, published online June 1, 2021, https://doi.org/10.1080/15205436.2021.1924382.

39. For an early statement of this point, see Bernard C. Cohen, *The Press and Foreign Policy* (Princeton, NJ: Princeton University Press, 1963).

40. Amber E. Boydstun, *Making the News: Politics, the Media, and Agenda-Setting* (Chicago: University of Chicago Press, 2013).

41. John R. Petrocik, "Issue Ownership in Presidential Elections, With a 1980 Case Study," *American Journal of Political Science* 40 (August 1996): 825–850.

42. Amber E. Boydstun, Rebecca A. Glazier, and Claire Phillips, "Agenda Control in the 2008 Presidential Debates," *American Politics Research* 41, no. 5 (2013): 863–889.

43. Danny Hayes, "Party Reputations, Journalistic Expectations: How Issue Ownership Influences Election News," *Political Communication* 25, no. 4 (2008): 377–400.

44. "The People, the Press and the War in the Gulf," Pew Research Center, January 31, 1991, http://www.people-press.org/1991/01/31/the-people-the-press-and-the-war-in-the-gulf/.

45. "March 20–April 7, 2003 Iraq War Tracking Poll," Pew Research Center, accessed July 9, 2021, http://www.pewresearch.org/politics/dataset/march-20-april-7-2003-iraq-war-tracking-poll/.

46. CBS News/*New York Times* Poll, press release, January 17, 1991, and CNN/*USA Today*/Gallup Poll, March–April 2003, available at www.pollingreport.com.

47. Mike Gruszczynski and Michael W. Wagner, "Information Flow in the 21st Century: The Dynamics of Agenda-Uptake," *Mass Communication and Society* 20, no. 3 (2017): 378–402.

48. Philip E. Converse, "Information Flow and the Stability of Partisan Attitudes," *Public Opinion Quarterly* 26 (Winter 1962): 578–599.

49. Kevin Arceneaux and Martin Johnson, *Changing Minds or Changing Channels? Partisan News in an Age of Choice* (Chicago: University of Chicago Press, 2013).

50. Natalie Jomini Stroud, *Niche News: The Politics of News Choice* (New York: Oxford University Press, 2011).

51. Eric Lawrence, John Sides, and Henry Farrell, "Self-Segregation or Deliberation? Blog Readership, Participation, and Polarization in American Politics," *Perspectives on Politics* 8, no. 1 (March 2010): 141–157.

52. "Americans' Attitudes About the News, Media Deeply Divided Along Partisan Lines," Pew Research Center, May 10, 2017, http://www.journalism.org/2017/05/10/americans-attitudes-about-the-news-media-deeply-divided-along-partisan-lines/.

53. Wagner and Gruszczynski, "Who Gets Covered?"

54. Ceren Budak, Ashley Muddiman, and Natalie (Talia) Stroud, "How Did U.S. Television News Networks Cover the Pandemic? Here's a Scorecard," *Monkey Cage* (newsletter), *Washington Post*, February 3, 2021, https://www.washingtonpost.com/politics/2021/02/03/how-did-different-us-television-news-networks-cover-pandemic-heres-scorecard/.

55. Mark Jurkowitz and Amy Mitchell, "Cable TV and COVID-19: How Americans Perceive the Outbreak and View Media Coverage Differ by Main News Source," Pew Research Center, April 1, 2020, https://www.journalism.org/2020/04/01/cable-tv-and-covid-19-how-americans-perceive-the-outbreak-and-view-media-coverage-differ-by-main-news-source/.

56. Claudia Wallis, "Trump's Victory and the Politics of Resentment," *Scientific American*, November 12, 2006, https://www.scientificamerican.com/article/trump-s-victory-and-the-politics-of-resentment/.

57. Chris Wells, Katherine J. Cramer, Michael W. Wagner, German Alvarez, Lewis A. Friedland, Dhavan V. Shah, Leticia Bode, Stephanie Edgerly, Itay Gabay, and Charles Franklin, "When We Stop Talking Politics: The Maintenance and Closing of Conversation in Contentious Times," *Journal of Communication* 67, no. 1 (2017): 131–157.

58. Brooke Auxier and Monica Anderson, "Social Media Use in 2021," Pew Research Center, April 7, 2021, https://www.pewresearch.org/internet/2021/04/07/social-media-use-in-2021/.

59. Shannon Greenwood, Andrew Perrin, and Maeve Duggan, "Social Media Update 2016," Pew Research Center, November 11, 2016, http://www.pewresearch.org/internet/2016/11/11/social-media-update-2016/.

60. Elisa Shearer and Amy Mitchell, "News Use Across Social Media Platforms in 2020," Pew Research Center, January 12, 2021, https://www.journalism.org/2021/01/12/news-use-across-social-media-platforms-in-2020/.

61. Jeffrey Gottfried and Elisa Shearer, "News Use Across Social Media Platforms 2016," Pew Research Center, May 26, 2016, http://www.journalism.org/2016/05/26/news-use-across-social-media-platforms-2016/.

62. Michael Xenos, Ariadne Vromen, and Brian D. Loader, "The Great Equalizer? Patterns of Social Media Use and Youth Political Engagement in Three Advanced Democracies," *Information, Communication, & Society* 17, no. 2 (2014): 151–167.

63. Heather K. Evans, Victoria Cordova, and Savannah Sipole, "Twitter Style: An Analysis of How House Candidates Used Twitter in Their 2012 Campaigns," *PS: Political Science and Politics* (April 2014): 454–462.

64. Deen Freelon, Charlton D. McIlwain, and Meredith D. Clark, *Beyond the Hashtags: #Ferguson, #BlackLivesMatter, and the Online Struggle for Offline Justice* (Washington, DC: Center for Media and Social Impact, February 2016), https://cmsimpact.org/wp-content/uploads/2016/03/beyond_the_hashtags_2016.pdf.

65. Elihu Katz and Paul F. Lazarsfeld, *Personal Influence: The Part Played by People in the Flow of Mass Communications* (New York: Free Press, 1964).

66. Michael W. Wagner and Mike Gruszcsynski, "When Framing Matters: How Partisan and Journalistic Frames Affect Individual Opinions and Party Identification," *Journalism & Communication Monographs* 18, no. 1 (2016): 5–48.

67. Elisabeth Noelle-Neumann, *The Spiral of Silence* (Chicago: University of Chicago Press, 1984).

68. Everette E. Dennis, *The Media Society* (Dubuque, IA: Wm. C. Brown, 1978), 37–41.

69. Michael B. MacKuen and Steven L. Coombs, *More Than News* (Beverly Hills, CA: SAGE, 1981).

70. Kim Fridkin Kahn and Patrick J. Kenney, "The Slant of the News: How Editorial Endorsements Influence Campaign Coverage and Citizens' Views of Candidates," *American Political Science Review* 96 (2002): 381–394.

71. Kathleen Hall Jamieson, *Dirty Politics: Deception, Distraction, and Democracy* (New York: Oxford University Press, 1992).

72. Adina Gitomer, Ravel V. Oleinikov, Laura M. Baum, Erika Franklin Fowler, and Saray Shai, "Geographic Impressions in Facebook Political Ads," *Applied Network Science* 6, no. 18 (2021), https://link.springer.com/article/10.1007/s41109-020-00350-7.

73. Young Mie Kim, Jordan Hsu, David Neiman, Colin Kou, Levi Bankston, Soo Yun Kim, Richard Heinrich, Robyn Baragwanath, and Garvesh Raskutt, "The Stealth Media? Groups and Targets Behind Divisive Issue Campaigns on Facebook," *Political Communication* 35, no. 4 (2018): 515–541, https://www.tandfonline.com/doi/abs/10.1080/10584609.2018.1476425?journalCode=upcp20.

74. Andrew Gelman and Gary King, *Why Do Presidential Election Campaign Polls Vary So Much When the Vote Is So Predictable?* (Cambridge, MA: Littauer Center, 1992).

75. Michael S. Lewis-Beck and Tom W. Rice, *Forecasting Elections* (Washington, DC: CQ Press, 1992). These economic forecasts limit themselves to two-party races and cannot accommodate third-party candidates, such as Ross Perot.

76. American National Election Studies, 1948–2004, www.electionstudies.org.

77. Recomputed from Elihu Katz and Jacob J. Feldman, "The Debates in the Light of Research: A Survey of Surveys," in *The Great Debates: Background,*

Perspective, Effects, ed. Sidney Kraus (Bloomington: Indiana University Press, 1962), 212.

78. Post-debate polls by *USA Today*/Gallup and CNN/Opinion Research Corporation, "Campaign 2008," October–December 2008, available at www.pollingreport .com.

79. James E. Campbell, Lynna L. Cherry, and Kenneth A. Wink, "The Convention Bump," *American Politics Quarterly* 20 (July 1992): 287–307.

80. Politico Staff, "Full Text: Donald Trump 2016 RNC Draft Speech Transcript," Politico, July 21, 2016, http://www.politico.com/story/2016/07/full-transcript-donald-trump-nomination-acceptance-speech-at-rnc-225974.

81. Wendy Rahn and Eric Oliver, "Trump's Voters Aren't Authoritarians, New Research Says. So What Are They?," *Monkey Cage* (newsletter), *Washington Post*, March 9, 2016, https://www.washingtonpost.com/news/monkey-cage/wp/2016/03/09/trumps-voters-arent-authoritarians-new-research-says-so-what-are-they/?utm_term=.a1d5fa972912.

82. Joe McGinniss, *The Selling of the President* (New York: Trident Press, 1969).

83. Dana Millbank, "For Al Gore, It Was Too, Too Tuesday," *Washington Post*, March 8, 2020, https://www.washingtonpost.com/archive/lifestyle/2000/03/08/for-al-gore-it-was-too-too-tuesday/52103f71-85f5-481f-8347-50d48a2d7ba1/.

84. Taylor Lorenz, Kellen Browning, and Sheera Frenkel, "TikTok Teens and K-Pop Stans Say They Sank Trump Rally," *New York Times*, first published June 21, 2020, last updated November 6, 2020, https://www.nytimes.com/2020/06/21/style/tiktok-trump-rally-tulsa.html.

85. Jamieson, *Dirty Politics*, Chapter 1.

86. Federal legislative attempts to curb negative ads, such as the McCain–Feingold Act, have generally been thwarted by the courts. In 2007, the Supreme Court ruled in *FEC v. Wisconsin Right to Life, Inc.* (551 U.S. 449) that issue ads may not be banned.

87. Marion R. Just, Ann N. Crigler, Dean E. Alger, Timothy E. Cook, Montague Kern, and Darrell M. West, *Crosstalk: Citizens, Candidates, and the Media in a Presidential Campaign* (Chicago: University of Chicago Press, 1996).

88. Thomas E. Patterson, "Press Coverage and Candidate Success in Presidential Primaries: The 1976 Democratic Race" (paper presented at the annual meeting of the American Political Science Association, Washington, DC, 1977).

89. James D. Barber, ed., *Race for the Presidency* (Englewood Cliffs, NJ: Prentice Hall, 1978), Chapter 2.

90. Thomas E. Patterson, *The Mass Media Election* (New York: Praeger, 1980), 130–132.

91. "2020 Presidential Race," OpenSecrets.org, accessed July 10, 2021, https://www.opensecrets.org/2020-presidential-race.

92. Elena Schneider, "Biden Takes Huge Cash Lead Over Trump While Outspending Him 2 to 1," Politico, September 21, 2020, https://www.politico.com/news/2020/09/21/joe-biden-fundraising-surge-419308.

VOTE CHOICE AND ELECTORAL DECISIONS

A CENTRAL FOCUS of research on American political behavior is vote choice, especially presidential vote choice. Most Americans follow presidential campaigns with greater attention than they give other elections, and eventually over 50 percent of the electorate expresses a preference by voting. The results of presidential balloting are reported and analyzed far more extensively than any others. This chapter explores the main determinants of vote choice and the interpretation of election outcomes in light of these determinants. The 2020 election was different from past elections in many ways. It took place during the COVID-19 pandemic when health and the economy were front and center. The United States was (and is) more polarized than it has been in a very long time. The racial reckoning following the killing of George Floyd led to widespread protests. The sitting president, Donald Trump, had lost the popular vote but won the Electoral College vote in 2016 and never saw his approval ratings hit 50 percent.[1] As we will show in this chapter, what is striking about the 2020 election is not only how different it was but also how normal it was in terms of the factors that explain vote choice.

In their pioneering work *The American Voter*, Angus Campbell, Philip E. Converse, Warren E. Miller, and Donald E. Stokes introduced the metaphor of the "funnel of causality" to depict the way multiple factors have an impact on an individual's vote choice.[2] As they envisioned it, at the narrow end of the funnel is the dependent variable, vote choice. At the wide end of the funnel are social characteristics, such as race, gender, social class, and level of education—factors that shape many facets of an individual's life and that are related to political attitudes and, ultimately, vote choice. These relationships, however, are not especially strong. Next in the funnel are long-term predispositions, including partisanship (Chapter 5) and ideology (Chapter 6), that orient and predispose an individual to view the world and act in particular ways. These predispositions are related to social characteristics, but not wholly determined by them. They are also more strongly related to vote choice than are the social characteristics, but by no means do they determine it. Moving further toward the narrow end of the funnel, we find attitudes toward issues that are important to the individual as well as evaluations of the current parties' candidates. Again, these attitudes are related to the long-term predispositions of party and ideology and, to a lesser extent, to the individual's social characteristics. They are also more closely linked to, and more predictive of, how the individual will vote. The preceding chapters have looked in depth at the various factors. In this chapter, we bring them all together to answer the question "Why do people vote the way they do?" starting with the factors that are furthest from vote choice.

Learning objectives for Chapter 8 include:

- Exploring how the long-term factors that people bring into any given election affect their presidential vote choice

- Learning what short-term factors add to predicting election outcomes

- Engaging with ideas for changing the Electoral College as the way Americans elect their president

- Examining voters' choices in lower-level elections

- Interpreting the meaning of the 2020 election

LONG-TERM DETERMINANTS OF PRESIDENTIAL VOTE CHOICE

Social Characteristics

Social characteristics such as an individual's race, religion, social class, and gender are unlikely to change over the course of a campaign. They are, rather, a set of long-term factors that both analysts and politicians link to vote choice. Social analysis of the 2020 presidential election reveals striking patterns, shown in Figure 8-1. A key feature of the 2020 election was the demographic makeup of the American people and how this played out in support for the two major-party candidates. According to the 2019 U.S. Census Bureau American Community Survey data, Hispanics and Latin@s make up 18 percent of the American population. Among non-Hispanics, the American population consists of 60 percent whites, 12 percent Black and African Americans, 6 percent Asians and Pacific Islanders, 1 percent Native North Americans, and 2.5 percent more than one race.[3] The United States has become increasingly diverse in its population over time. If the various racial and ethnic groups all had the same vote choice distribution, the changing demographics would be politically uninteresting. Instead, they are highly interesting. Figure 8-1 shows that whites were more likely to support Republican Donald Trump than Democrat Joe Biden, whereas every other racial and ethnic group was much more likely to support Biden over Trump.

In 2020, Black voters heavily favored Democratic candidate Joe Biden, but their support for him was lower than was their support for Barack Obama in 2008 and 2012. Drawing on data from the American National Election Studies (ANES), Blacks were nearly unanimous in voting for Obama in 2008 (99.5 percent) and in 2012 (98 percent). Their vote dropped to 90 percent for Democratic candidate Hillary Clinton in 2016 and to 88 percent for Biden in 2020. Recall that Black voters have overwhelmingly supported the Democratic candidate—usually by 90 percent or more—for decades (see also Chapter 6). The impact that a Black candidate had on Black voting behavior was seen both in heightened turnout and in enthusiasm for his candidacy. Clinton and Biden did not generate an equal level of enthusiasm or votes.

Biden also did quite well among other people of color (see Figure 8-1). In recent years, Republicans have had hopes of making inroads among Hispanic and Latin@ voters, but since 2004 the numbers overall seem to be moving in the wrong direction for the Grand Old Party (GOP). Hispanics and Latin@s gave Democrat John Kerry 60 percent of their vote in 2004, Obama 73 percent in 2008 and 76.5 percent in 2012, and Clinton 69 percent in 2016. Biden comparatively did very well among Hispanics and Latin@s, with 74 percent voting for him compared to only 21 percent for Trump. Asian Americans have turned to the Democratic Party over the past couple of decades. The Democratic share of the Asian American vote was 31 percent in 1992, 62 percent in 2008, 73 percent in 2012, and 63 percent in 2016. In 2020, Biden garnered 69 percent of the Asian American vote.[4] The number of Native Americans and people who identify as more than one race included in the 2020 ANES survey was very small, so the percentages provided in Figure 8-1 are not as reliable, in terms of the results being generalizable to the Native American

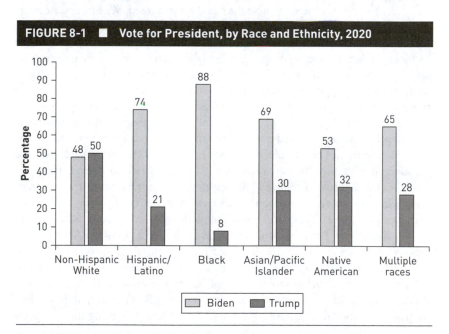

FIGURE 8-1 ■ Vote for President, by Race and Ethnicity, 2020

Source: 2020 American National Election Studies, available at www.electionstudies.org.

and mixed-race populations, as the other numbers. The results, however, fit the pattern of other people of color: support for Democrat Joe Biden was much stronger among these groups than was support for Republican Donald Trump.

White Americans were more supportive of Trump than were the other major racial and ethnic groups, with 50 percent supporting Trump and 48 percent supporting Biden. Trump did worse among whites in 2020 than he had in 2016, when he received 53 percent of the white vote (and Clinton won only 42 percent). We further break down the white vote by education, a social characteristic that increasingly differentiates white Republican and Democratic voters. Whites with a bachelor's or graduate degree strongly backed Biden, giving him 62 percent of their vote. In contrast, whites who had not graduated from college were supporters of Trump, with 61 percent voting for the sitting president.

With a woman on the ticket as the Democrats' vice-presidential candidate, pundits wondered if this would draw more women to vote for Biden. Overall, women voted for Biden over Trump, 58 percent to 39 percent. Unlike in 2016, when men were evenly divided in their votes for Trump and Clinton, men in 2020 were strong supporters of Biden, giving him 55 percent of their vote to Trump's 42 percent. These data hide the large differences between whites and people of color. White women were slightly more likely to vote for Trump (49 percent) than Biden (48.5 percent). Women of color overwhelmingly voted for Biden (79 percent) over Trump (16 percent). Among men, 51 percent of white men voted for Trump and 47 percent for Biden, whereas 22.5 percent of men of color voted for Trump and 73 percent for Biden.

We can also look at the ways various social groups contributed to the vote totals of the two candidates. Figure 8-2 shows the analysis of the "composition" of Trump's and Biden's votes, in contrast to how the social groups voted. We further categorize white voters by gender and education level to determine from whom each candidate drew his white support. The composition of Biden's vote total reflects his and the Democratic Party's appeal to diverse groups in American society: Black people made up 17 percent of Biden's vote, Hispanics 14 percent, other people of color 11 percent, and white people 58 percent. Among these white supporters, Biden received most of his support from those with a college education. White, college-educated women made up 17 percent of his voters, and white, college-educated men made up another 16 percent. Less-educated whites made up a smaller portion of his voter base (11 percent men and 14 percent women). Trump voters were much less diverse racially and ethnically. Trump voters were 2 percent Black, 6 percent Hispanic, 7 percent other people of color, and 85 percent white. Among white Trump voters, those without a college degree were much more numerous (59 percent) than those with a college degree (26 percent), fairly evenly divided between men and women.

The Republican Party, in assessing its loss in the 2012 election, pointed to the problem of diversity within the party as a possible culprit. Republican National Committee chairman Reince Priebus argued that Americans viewed the party as a "'narrow-minded, out-of-touch' party of 'stuffy old men'" and that the GOP needed to do something about this party image. Young Republicans, in the College Republican National Committee, were especially blunt in arguing that the party

FIGURE 8-2   ■   Social Composition of the Vote for President, by Race, Ethnicity, Gender, and Education, 2020

BIDEN VOTERS

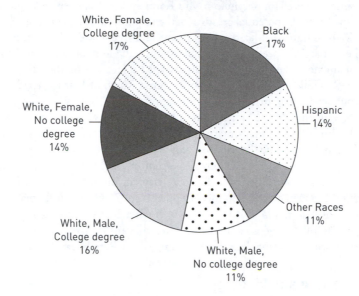

White, Female, College degree 17%

Black 17%

Hispanic 14%

White, Female, No college degree 14%

Other Races 11%

White, Male, College degree 16%

White, Male, No college degree 11%

TRUMP VOTERS

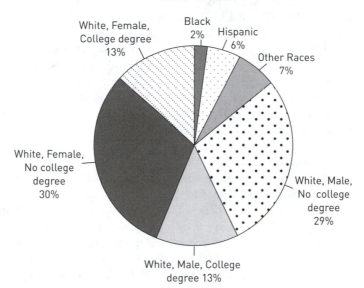

White, Female, College degree 13%

Black 2%

Hispanic 6%

Other Races 7%

White, Female, No college degree 30%

White, Male, No college degree 29%

White, Male, College degree 13%

Source: 2020 American National Election Studies, available at www.electionstudies.org.

needed to take steps to broaden its appeal, including reaching out to women, gay voters, younger people, and other underrepresented groups. Of particular concern to Republicans was the trend toward the Democratic Party of Latinos and Latinas. Three-quarters of Latin@s voted for Democrat Barack Obama, compared to only 22 percent who voted for Republican Mitt Romney. Political scientist Sergio Wals's research points to the potential positives of the Republican Party courting Hispanic voters. Wals found that Mexican immigrants aren't guaranteed Democrats. They span the ideological spectrum, and as a bonus to the Republican Party, those on the right are more likely to be politically engaged than those on the left.[5]

Some Republicans, including Senator Marco Rubio of Florida, tried to push the Republican Party to support immigration reform that was more sensitive to Latin@s in the United States.[6] Not all Republicans were on board with the idea. The 2016 Republican primaries pitted pro-immigration Rubio against anti-immigration Trump, and Trump won handily. Even so, Hispanic support for the Republican nominee increased from 22 percent in 2012 (Romney) to 32 percent in 2016 (Trump), but dropped again to 21 percent in 2020 (Trump). Hispanic support for the Democratic nominee dropped from 76 percent (Obama in 2012) to 69 percent (Clinton in 2016) but rose to 74 percent in the most recent election (Biden in 2020). The desire among some Republicans to diversify their base has not been a priority during Trump's leadership of the Republican Party.

Partisanship and Ideology

As seen in earlier chapters, party loyalty is a basic characteristic that influences many aspects of an individual's political behavior and is itself influenced by an individual's social characteristics. In Table 8-1, we see the relationship between partisanship and vote choice in 2020. As strength of partisanship increases, so does the likelihood of voting for one's party so that strong Democrats and strong Republicans are overwhelmingly supportive of their respective party's nominee. As shown in Chapter 5's discussion of defection rates, what makes 2020 different from previous years is the much larger percentage of Republican-leaning independents and weak Republicans who chose Joe Biden over Donald Trump. In 2016, less than 10 percent of both groups voted for Democrat Hillary Clinton. Democrats, in contrast, were much more successful at keeping weak and leaning Democrats in their fold. Over 90 percent voted for Biden in 2020, compared to only about 80 percent who voted for Clinton in 2016. Trump was a highly polarizing figure, and more Republicans than is normal jumped ship.

Ideology works in much the same way as partisanship as a long-term predisposition that shapes attitudes and behavior (see Chapter 6). When voters have a clear ideological viewpoint, it is highly related to vote choice, as can be seen in Table 8-2. Among those who call themselves "moderate" or who disclaim any ideology, voters can try to discern which candidate is more moderate or, as is often the case, rely on other factors to help them decide how to vote.

Also included in Tables 8-1 and 8-2 is the "other" category. In many elections, third-party or minor candidate votes are so minimal they hardly deserve mention.

TABLE 8-1 ■ Presidential Vote, by Party Identification, 2020

	Strong Democrat	Weak Democrat	Independent Democrat	Independent	Independent Republican	Weak Republican	Strong Republican
Joe Biden	97%	91%	92%	56%	19%	22%	4%
Donald Trump	2	8	3	31	74	77	95
Other	1	2	5	13	7	2	0
Total	100%	101%	100%	100%	100%	101%	99%
(N)	(960)	(429)	(502)	(315)	(396)	(412)	(807)

Source: 2020 American National Election Studies, available at www.electionstudies.org.

TABLE 8-2 ■ Presidential Vote, by Ideological Identification, 2020

	Extremely Liberal	Liberal	Slightly Liberal	Moderate	Slightly Conservative	Conservative	Extremely Conservative
Joe Biden	95%	94%	94%	65%	34%	6%	4%
Donald Trump	2	4	5	31	61	93	95
Other	3	2	2	5	5	1	1
Total	**100%**	**100%**	**101%**	**101%**	**100%**	**100%**	**100%**
[N]	[170]	[561]	[445]	[858]	[417]	[678]	[190]

Source: 2020 American National Election Studies, available at www.electionstudies.org.

In some years, however, third-party candidates do fairly well among some segments of the population. For 2016, when many voters did not like either of the major party candidates, ANES data show that 5 percent of respondents said they voted for Libertarian candidate Gary Johnson, 1 percent said they voted for Green Party candidate Jill Stein, and another 2 percent said they voted for a different alternative. Third-party candidate support was much more muted in 2020, although 13 percent of pure independents said they voted for someone other than Biden or Trump.[7] Not surprisingly, people who claim to be independents are more likely to vote for a third-party candidate.

As we have seen in Chapter 6, partisanship and ideology are related to each other—increasingly so, given the partisan sort—and it would be very difficult to untangle the causal connections between the two. No doubt some individuals adopt a party because it fits their ideological worldview or because their admired party leaders are so labeled. For most people, though, partisanship takes a more central role in explaining voting behavior in part because more Americans think of themselves as partisans or independents than as ideologues. Candidates are also more explicitly connected to their party than to their ideology because they have chosen a party label under which to run (while possibly avoiding or obfuscating an ideological label for another one like "reformer," "maverick," or "outsider"). Trump is a good example of a politician who does not fit the label "conservative" well, but he ran for office as a Republican. Nonetheless, as we think about the factors that influence a person's vote, we can think of ideology as holding a similar place in the chain of factors—or funnel of causality—that leads to the final voting decision, especially now that the parties have more clearly become ideologically sorted.

SHORT-TERM DETERMINANTS OF PRESIDENTIAL VOTE CHOICE

Candidate Image

In seeking to understand vote choice, an individual's partisanship can be construed as a long-term predisposition to vote for one party or another, other things being equal. In other words, in the absence of any information about candidates and issues or other short-term forces in an election, individuals can be expected to vote according to their partisanship. However, to the extent that such short-term forces have an impact on them, voters may be deflected away from their usual party loyalty toward an out-party candidate. The more short-term forces there are in an election—or the more a voter is aware of them—the less impact partisanship might have on a person's vote choice. This idea is crucial for understanding the relative impact of partisanship in different types of elections. In highly visible presidential elections, when information about candidates and issues is widely available, partisanship will typically be less overriding in the voter's decision than in less visible races down the ticket. Furthermore, more potent short-term forces would be required to cause a very strong partisan to vote for another party than would be necessary to prompt a weak partisan to defect. An individual's vote in an election can be viewed as the product of the strength of partisanship and the impact of short-term forces on the individual.

In most elections, both candidates and political commentators give their attention to short-term forces, such as the candidates' personalities and the issues, because they want to pull in the votes of weaker partisans and independents. This section considers the impact of the short-term forces of candidate image and issues within a setting of stable party loyalties.

During the past seventy years, national samples have been extensively questioned about their views of the presidential candidates. During this period, several very popular candidates such as Republican Dwight Eisenhower and Democrat Lyndon Johnson had extremely favorable images, and several others such as Republican Barry Goldwater and Democrat George McGovern were rejected by the electorate in part on the basis of their personal attributes.

Figure 8-3 displays the mean ratings of presidential candidates since 1968 on the ANES feeling thermometer, which asks respondents to rate how "warmly," or favorably, they feel toward a candidate on a scale of 0 to 100, with 100 being *very warm* and 0 being *very cold*. Perhaps the most prominent feature of this series is the unfavorable view Americans had of both candidates in the 2016 election. Neither Trump nor Clinton broke the 50-degree mark, thereby coming in on the cold side of the thermometer. This is the first time in recent history that at least one of the two major-party candidates did not generate at least some overall warm feelings among the public. Trump stayed well below the 50-degree mark, and Biden almost topped the midpoint but didn't make it above 49 degrees in 2020. A second feature of the feeling thermometer data is the downward trend for the Republican candidates. Democratic candidates experienced something of a downward trend as well until Obama became their candidate in 2008 and again in 2012. Other indicators of candidate image show that the downward trend would be even steeper if elections in the 1950s and early 1960s were included. The disenchantment with government and politics, catalogued in Chapter 1, clearly extends to the personal images of the presidential candidates.

Incumbent presidents face a different situation than challengers do in that voters have the previous four years to judge whether the president has been doing a good job or not. If the president is doing a bad job, it does not make a lot of sense to put the same person back in office for another four years. Part of voters' calculus when deciding for whom to vote when an incumbent is running includes an assessment of the president's performance in office (see Chapter 2 on presidential approval). Even if an incumbent is not running, as was the case in 2016, people judge the incumbent party, and therefore the incumbent party's candidate, based on the success of the outgoing president. One question asked by many polling organizations and included in the ANES survey is the presidential

FIGURE 8-3 ■ **Democratic and Republican Presidential Candidate Feeling Thermometers, 1968–2020**

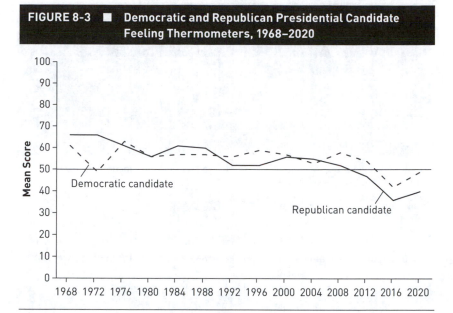

Source: American National Election Studies, available at www.electionstudies.org.

Note: The values in the figure represent "thermometer scores," in which respondents are asked to rate the candidates on a scale of 0 to 100, where 0 is *very cold*, or negative, and 100 is *very warm*, or positive.

approval question, which asks if people approve or disapprove of the way the president is handling the job. While presidential approval is not a direct measure of candidate image, it acts as a gauge of the perceived leadership ability of the incumbent president and party. Table 8-3 shows the presidential approval level in the preelection survey and whether the incumbent or the incumbent's party won reelection. Since 1972, there have been nine elections in which an incumbent ran for reelection (or election, in Gerald Ford's case). Of those nine, the incumbent has won reelection five times and lost four times. The average approval rating of those who won their bid for reelection is 59 percent. For those who lost, the average is 44 percent.

When the incumbent president's approval level dips below 50 percent, the likelihood of winning reelection is slim. Jimmy Carter was originally elected in 1976. When he came up for reelection in 1980, his presidency was associated with both a bad economy and the Iran hostage crisis. With only 39 percent approval, he lost his reelection bid to Ronald Reagan. George H. W. Bush, who had been Reagan's vice president and won his bid for the presidency in 1988, similarly had to try to get past a struggling economy to be reelected. His approval rating was only 42 percent as the 1992 election approached, and he was defeated by Bill Clinton. Chapter 2's discussion of structural factors and presidential voting reminds us that Donald Trump faced the COVID-19 crisis and a struggling

TABLE 8-3 ■ Presidential Approval and Reelection, 1972–2020			
Year	Incumbent President	Approval Level	Won/Lost Reelection
1972	Richard Nixon	65	Won
1976	Gerald Ford	56	Lost
1980	Jimmy Carter	39	Lost
1984	Ronald Reagan	59	Won
1988	Open seat (after Republican president)	57	Incumbent party won
1992	George H. W. Bush	42	Lost
1996	Bill Clinton	68	Won
2000	Open seat (after Democratic president)	66	Incumbent party lost
2004	George W. Bush	51	Won
2008	Open seat (after Republican president)	22	Incumbent party lost
2012	Barack Obama	54	Won
2016	Open seat (after Democratic president)	54	Incumbent party lost
2020	Donald Trump	40	Lost

Source: American National Election Studies, available at www.electionstudies.org.

Note: The shaded rows are elections in which the incumbent ran for reelection or Ford ran for election. Ford became president after Richard Nixon resigned in the aftermath of the Watergate scandal. He ran for election to the presidency for the first time in 1976 but was defeated.

economy when he ran against Joe Biden in 2020, and he lost his reelection bid with an approval rating of only 40 percent.

Open-seat races are difficult for the incumbent party to win. Negative images of a president can wrap themselves around the neck of the party's next presidential candidate. Though John McCain had run against George W. Bush in the 2000 Republican primaries and had been an occasional antagonist of President Bush, Democratic candidate Barack Obama tied McCain to Bush every chance he got, helping to link voters' unusually negative perceptions of Bush to the McCain candidacy. Even positive evaluations of the exiting president do not lead to a sure win for the incumbent party. Republicans won the open seat in 1988 when Ronald Reagan was highly popular. Bill Clinton's 66 percent approval rating led to a popular vote win for Al Gore but not an Electoral College victory. The Democrats experienced a similar loss in 2016 when a popular president's party won the popular vote but not the Electoral College vote.

Analysts have tried to get at how the electorate evaluates candidates on a more personal level. In most presidential election years, political reporters gauge which candidate people think is more likable. In 2016, a Rasmussen poll asked voters with which candidate they would rather have a beer and which candidate they would like to have home for dinner with them or their family. Respondents were more likely to choose Trump to have a beer with (45 percent Trump, 37 percent Clinton) and leaned toward Trump as a dinner guest (42 percent Trump, 41 percent Clinton).[8] These questions were not asked in 2020, which might strike some people as a good thing. Asking people with whom they would rather have a beer or dinner might seem frivolous—the best dinner date is not necessarily a good president—but candidate image can help people assess what kind of a job the candidates would do in office and if they would understand the needs and concerns of everyday Americans.

On average, presidential candidates score higher on traits associated with their political party. That is, people assume a party's candidate is characterized by the traits they associate with the party. People generally assume Republican candidates are stronger leaders and more moral, whereas Democratic candidates are assumed to be more compassionate and empathetic.[9] In 2020, voters knew both candidates well (one having served as president for four years and the other as vice president for eight years) and saw the two as highly different people. The ANES survey asked respondents the extent to which a variety of traits—leadership, caring, knowledgeability, and honesty—described the two candidates. The response options ranged from *not well at all* to *extremely well*. Figure 8-4 shows the means for Trump and Biden for each of the traits. Biden received higher ratings than Trump on all four traits, although the difference was small on leadership. It is interesting to note that Biden's knowledge score was higher than Trump's even

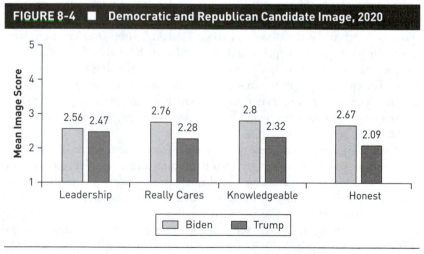

FIGURE 8-4 ■ Democratic and Republican Candidate Image, 2020

Source: 2020 American National Election Studies, available at www.electionstudies.org.

though the latter had spent four years in office as president. Overall, respondents had a negative view of both candidates in the sense that none of their ratings was above the midpoint. For all of the traits and both of the candidates, people rated them more negatively than positively.

Political scientists have increasingly taken seriously the important role emotions play in politics.[10] Contrary to the view that people are rational and policy oriented, constantly weighing the costs and benefits of candidates' policy proposals, research shows that people's reactions to much of what goes on in politics is emotional. Candidates can make people feel angry or afraid, proud or hopeful. Obama framed his run for the presidency in 2008 on the idea that many people wanted to see change but had given up hope. He told Americans that if he were elected, he would bring the change they wanted. Trump framed his message in 2016 very differently. His campaign message was "Make America Great Again," but his vision of America was dystopian. Even in his inaugural address, Trump painted a picture of the United States as one of "American carnage" in which crime was rampant in American cities, jobs were gone overseas, and America's wealth and standing in the world had "dissipated."[11] The president couldn't run on a dystopian message in 2020 since doing so would raise questions about what he had accomplished over the previous four years. Trump instead raised fears about what would happen if the Democrats won, played up the gains made in the stock market, and claimed that the only way he could lose the election was if there was rampant voter fraud. Biden's primary message was that he wanted to bring the country back together after the tumultuous Trump presidency. He emphasized that he was not Trump, that he would handle the pandemic very differently from Trump, and that he would restore America's international image. The messages candidates focus on and their actions during the campaign, in addition to the media stories about the candidates, can affect how people emotionally react to them.

A George Washington University Politics Poll fielded in October 2020 asked respondents, "How often would you say you've felt the following emotions because of the kind of person Joe Biden is or because of something he has done?" They were asked the same question about Donald Trump. The emotions were angry, afraid, disgusted, hopeful, and proud.[12] Figure 8-5 shows the percentage of people who answered *most of the time* or *always* to experiencing each of the emotions. Trump made people feel much more angry, afraid, and disgusted than did Biden. Biden was able to generate slightly more hope and pride than Trump, but the main story is that many people had a strong and negative emotional reaction to Trump.

A major question, given these differences, is whether candidates can manipulate their image to their advantage. That is, do campaign managers come up with an ideal image for their candidate and then create that image in the mind of the American public? It is highly unlikely that campaign managers have this kind of power, especially for well-established candidates about whom voters are reasonably well informed. Overall, the public's impressions of candidates for major office seem to be realistic, gained primarily through ordinary news coverage.

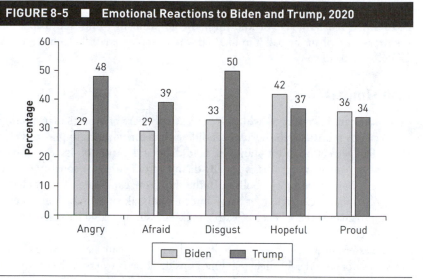

FIGURE 8-5 ■ Emotional Reactions to Biden and Trump, 2020

Source: George Washington University Politics Poll, October 16–26, 2020.

Note: Percentage of people responding *most of the time* or *always* to each of the emotions questions.

This is not to say that these images are accurate, fair, or sophisticated, but they are not fictitious pictures created by public relations personnel. In 2020, both Trump and Biden were well-known political figures who had already established who they were in the minds of the public. Trump was seen as a highly divisive figure whose followers praised him for telling it like it is and being strong and action oriented while his opponents viewed him as corrupt and antidemocratic. Biden was less divisive, with his supporters appreciating his calm, reasoned solutions to problems and his opponents seeing him as weak and against freedom. There was little either candidate could do during the campaign to change these images.

Few candidates for other offices are as well known or as well publicized as candidates for the presidency. Typically, voters will be aware of candidates' party affiliation and whether they are incumbents, but not much more. In fact, these pieces of information may come to the voter's attention only if they are indicated on the ballot. Because of low information, unimportant things like the order of candidate names on the ballot can affect the vote. Candidates whose names come first on the ballot tend to get more votes than candidates whose names appear further down on the list.[13]

Lynn Vavreck has shown that the messages candidates promote and the images they try to cultivate are the most effective when they coincide with broader, structural forces that shape electoral outcomes (as discussed in Chapter 2).[14] For example, having empathy and focusing on economic issues served Bill Clinton well in the 1992 campaign season, which occurred during an economic recession. Donald Trump's image of being willing to speak his mind and not fit the politics-as-usual model helped him in 2016 when Americans were fed up with politics. Joe Biden's image of knowing how government works and using it to solve major problems helped him in 2020 when people were still reeling from the COVID-19 pandemic.

Issue Impact

Unlike candidate image, which is contextually part of a particular election, issues can be specific to the current candidates or a carryover from previous elections. The perception of the stands of candidates and parties on issues is a basis for making vote choices, a basis usually distinct from either personality characteristics or long-standing symbolism. In the short run, candidates cannot change their job experience, religion, or party, but they can take new stands on issues or attempt to change the salience of issues, making issue appeals a basis for people's vote choice.

The extent to which voters are concerned with issues in making vote choices is a subject of considerable debate.[15] One consideration is whether the candidates themselves offer distinct issue choices. There was a rise in issue voting associated with the election of 1964, when the correlation between attitudes on issues and vote choice peaked in the ideological Johnson/Goldwater campaign, but issue voting remained through 1972 at a considerably higher level than in the "issueless" 1950s.[16] What makes these elections stand out is the clear contrast the candidates offered in their issue positions. If candidates take highly divergent stands on important issues of the day, people will be able to vote on the basis of issues. If, however, candidates' issue stands are quite similar, people will have a difficult time being issue voters. This was the case in the elections of 1988 and 1992.[17] Even if people don't vote on the basis of candidates' issue stands, they could vote using the heuristic, or shortcut, of party issue image. Candidates and their issue stands come and go and are more or less transparent, but the reputations parties develop within certain issue areas can easily be used by voters when determining which party's candidate is likely to pursue which policy areas. When people have low information about the candidates' issue stands, they can be issue voters indirectly by voting for the candidate whose party's issue positions come closest to their own.[18] Benjamin Highton has found that candidate issue contrast has a much bigger impact on vote choice from election to election than party issue contrast, but both play a role in elections.[19]

A second consideration focuses on the voters themselves. In most elections, many voters are unaware of the stands candidates take on issues. Voters commonly believe that the candidates they support agree with them. This suggests that voters may project their issue positions onto their favorite candidates more often than they decide to vote for candidates on the basis of their position on issues. Furthermore, when voters agree with a candidate's issue stand, they may have adopted this position merely to agree with their favored candidate. Candidates and other political leaders frequently provide issue leadership for their followers.

Within the enormous range of possible issues at any given time, complete indifference to many is common. Most issues important to political leaders remain in this indifferent category for the general public.

Over the years, considerable commentary has focused on the rise of single-issue voting. Collections of voters, caring intensely about a particular issue, vote for whichever candidate is closest to their views on that issue, regardless of the candidate's party, personal characteristics, or positions on other issues. There is nothing new about this phenomenon. The classic example of single-issue voting in American politics was abolition, an issue so intense that it destroyed the Whig Party, launched several new parties including the Republican Party, and was a major contributing factor to the Civil War. Abortion is a current issue that determines the way some people will vote. Intense concentration on a single issue, however, is potentially divisive and damaging to parties that must appeal to a broad range of voters or to those in office who must cast votes on a wide range of issues.

In some ways, 2020 was an odd year for issues. Normally, the two major parties put together a platform at their national conventions that reflect the issue stands of the party and of the party's nominee for the presidency. The Democratic Party did this, highlighting issues related to the economy, racial justice, health care, climate change, and so on.[20] The Republican Party, in contrast, chose not to release a platform, stating instead, "Resolved, That the Republican Party has and will continue to enthusiastically support the President's America-first agenda" and "Resolved, That the Republican National Convention will adjourn without adopting a new platform until the 2024 Republican National Convention."[21] Rather than spell out the issue differences between the parties, the Republican Party simply backed its presidential candidate, Donald Trump. We nonetheless quickly examine a handful of issues that were relevant to the presidential election. (See Chapter 6 for a fuller discussion of party differences on major issues.) We begin with a major issue that has divided the two major parties for many decades, the extent to which government spending and services should be increased or decreased. As Figure 8-6 shows, those who favored increasing government services and spending were much more likely to vote overwhelmingly for Biden over Trump, although a plurality of Trump voters were at the midpoint of the scale rather than calling for fewer services.

On another domestic issue—whether the government should provide assistance to Black people versus letting them help themselves, shown in Figure 8-7—Biden voters were much more likely to endorse the "government should help" side of the scale, with a third placing themselves at a 1 on the scale. Trump voters, on the other hand, were much more likely to place themselves on the "help themselves" side of the scale, with almost a third of Trump voters placing themselves at 7 on the scale.

Because both these issues deal with themes that have long divided the parties, it is not surprising that substantial relationships exist between holding a certain view and supporting a particular candidate. The issue of abortion is a more recent

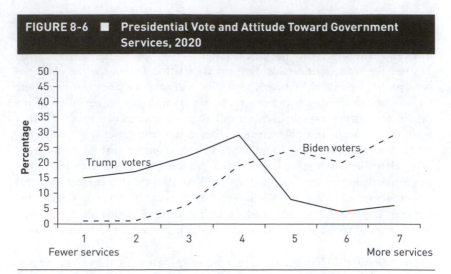

FIGURE 8-6 ■ Presidential Vote and Attitude Toward Government Services, 2020

Source: 2020 American National Election Studies, available at www.electionstudies.org.

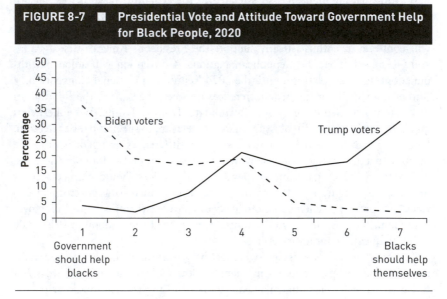

FIGURE 8-7 ■ Presidential Vote and Attitude Toward Government Help for Black People, 2020

Source: 2020 American National Election Studies, available at www.electionstudies.org.

divisive issue. The strong relationship found in 2020 and shown in Figure 8-8, also true from 2000 through 2016, suggests increasing polarization especially among Democrats. Trump's supporters were more likely to be on the pro-life side of the issue, with 20 percent choosing the option that abortion should never be allowed and 43 percent allowing abortion only in cases of rape or incest or when the woman's life is in danger. Over one-third of his supporters, however, were more open to laws allowing abortion (responses 3 and 4). Biden voters were overwhelmingly on the pro-choice side, with 73 percent choosing the option that women should be able to choose whether to have an abortion. Nonetheless, over a quarter of Biden voters supported some restrictions on abortion. (See Chapter 6 for a more extensive discussion of how abortion preferences are arrayed in the American public.)

A major issue in recent years, especially among liberals, has been climate change. The scientific evidence supporting the idea that human actions have caused the unprecedented increase in global temperatures over the past fifty years is "unequivocal."[22] Unfortunately, climate change has become a partisan issue. Respondents were asked how much climate change is affecting severe weather and temperatures in the United States. Response options ranged from 1 (*not at all*) to 5 (*a great deal*). Trump voters had an average score of 2.5 on this scale whereas Biden voters had an average score of 4.4. Respondents were also asked if they thought the government should be doing more or less about rising temperatures. Figure 8-9 shows the partisan split between Trump and Biden voters on this issue. Almost all of the Biden voters (87 percent) said the government should be doing more about this issue. Most Trump voters (60 percent) were happy with

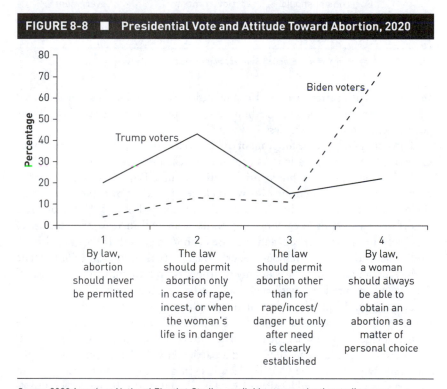

FIGURE 8-8 ■ Presidential Vote and Attitude Toward Abortion, 2020

Source: 2020 American National Election Studies, available at www.electionstudies.org.

FIGURE 8-9 ■ Presidential Vote and Attitude Toward Government Efforts on Global Warming, 2020

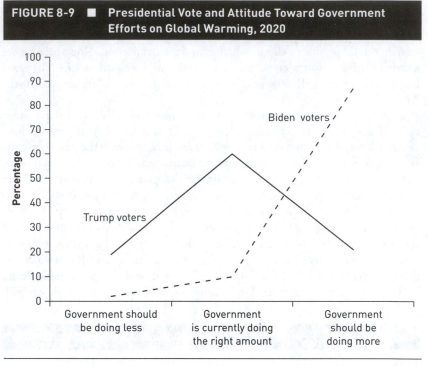

Source: 2020 American National Election Studies, available at www.electionstudies.org.

the government's current actions. Keep in mind that the survey was administered while Trump was still president. Almost 20 percent of Trump voters thought the government should be doing less.

Three issues were at the forefront of the 2020 election: the state of the economy, COVID-19, and immigration. As explained in Chapter 2, economic conditions are highly correlated with presidential election results. People naturally want the economy to be strong and for whoever is elected president to make sound decisions that will lead to or shore up a healthy economy. Both of the major-party candidates must work to convince voters that they will increase the number of jobs, keep inflation in check, and increase economic growth if they are elected. Presidents tend to be held responsible, or at least partially responsible, for the state of the economy, so when the economy is strong, people are more likely to reward the incumbent president with reelection. When the economy is weak, on the other hand, punishing the president at the polls is an obvious option people can take.[23] If the seat is open, as it was in 2016, people base their predictions on the parties' images and on what the candidates project concerning economic policy.

The sitting president in 2020 faced a particularly difficult economic hurdle, the havoc wreaked by the COVID-19 crisis. In an effort to stop the spread of the virus, many states and localities issued mask and stay-at-home orders. People stopped traveling, eating at restaurants, shopping at local stores, and participating

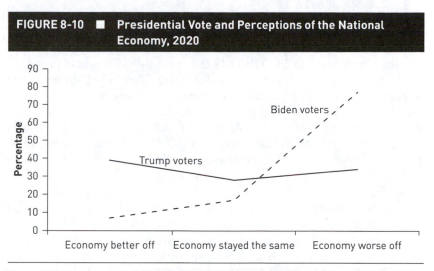

FIGURE 8-10 ■ **Presidential Vote and Perceptions of the National Economy, 2020**

Source: 2020 American National Election Studies, available at www.electionstudies.org.

in many other activities that keep the economy strong. Because of the lack of business, many people were furloughed or laid off. The economy tanked. Figure 8-10 shows how perceptions of the state of the economy were related to people's vote choice. Trump voters were fairly evenly divided, with 39 percent thinking the economy was better off than one year earlier, 28 percent thinking it had stayed about the same, and 34 percent thinking it was worse off. Biden voters were not nearly so positive. Over three-quarters thought the economy was worse off than a year earlier, and only 7 percent thought it was better off. People who supported Trump clearly wanted to put a more positive spin on the economy, just as Biden supporters wanted to put a more negative spin on the same situation. The bottom line, though, is that Trump faced a difficult economic situation when he ran for reelection, and even his voters could not put a highly positive spin on it.

The second and related issue of the 2020 campaign, of course, was the pandemic. Donald Trump used the bully pulpit of the presidency to downplay the COVID-19 virus and to play up the idea that people needed to get back to life as normal. Trump's main concern was getting the economy back on track, and if people would only keep doing what they normally did, businesses and the economy would bounce back quickly. The president therefore claimed that the virus would simply disappear, refused to wear a mask, and frequently ridiculed his experts in the Centers for Disease Control and Prevention for their calls for restrictions to limit the spread of the virus. He promised more of the same if he were reelected. Joe Biden, in contrast, supported a stricter COVID-19 response, including mask wearing, limiting crowd sizes, and closing businesses to in-person traffic. He severely limited his campaigning to online meetings or extremely small, socially distanced gatherings, and emphasized that everyone should take these steps in the hope that getting the virus under control would be better for the economy in the long run. Biden said that if elected, he would follow the advice of scientists, who strongly supported the need for greater restrictions to get the virus under control.

Not surprisingly, Trump and Biden voters differed in their views on the role of science in decisions about COVID-19 and in what they thought of the restrictions put in place to combat the spread of the virus. When asked how important it was to base COVID-19 decisions on science, most Americans readily agreed that doing so was very or extremely important, but there were large differences between Biden and Trump voters. Almost all Biden voters (94 percent) thought it important to have scientifically based COVID-19 decisions, compared to 58 percent of Trump voters. Biden and Trump voters differed as well in their reactions to the restrictions put in place to try to prevent the spread of the virus. Figure 8-11 shows the extent to which Americans thought the COVID-19 restrictions were too lenient or too strict. Similar percentages of Trump and Biden voters thought the restrictions put in place were about right. However, almost half of Biden voters thought the restrictions were not strict enough whereas almost half of Trump voters thought they were too strict. Not surprisingly, Biden voters disapproved (97 percent) whereas Trump voters approved (85 percent) of the president's handling of COVID-19.

The third major issue was immigration, a continuation from 2016. Donald Trump promised throughout his first campaign to crack down on illegal immigration, deport people who were in the United States illegally, build a wall along the southern border of the United States, and not support amnesty for people already in the United States. Hillary Clinton promised comprehensive

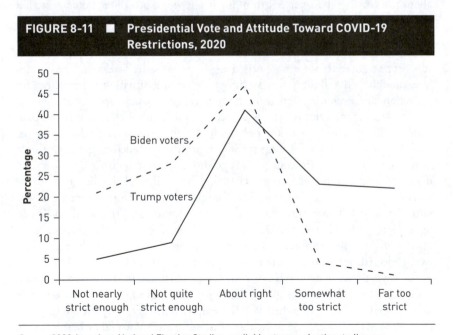

FIGURE 8-11 ■ Presidential Vote and Attitude Toward COVID-19 Restrictions, 2020

Source: 2020 American National Election Studies, available at www.electionstudies.org.

immigration reform and highlighted a path to citizenship for undocumented immigrants in the United States.[24] During the four years of the Trump presidency, immigration remained a hot issue. President Trump decreased the number of refugees and immigrants given permanent residency visas and increased the number of people given temporary work visas; continued the rate of deportations established in the last two years of the Obama administration, although there was a significant increase in the number of detentions at the border in 2019; and dedicated resources to build 450 miles of wall on the southern border of the United States.[25] Joe Biden, like Clinton four years earlier, promised immigration reform. He also promised to overturn Trump's immigration policies if elected, including ending Trump's policy of separating parents and children at the border and reinstating the Deferred Action for Childhood Arrivals (DACA) program.[26] The building of the wall on the border with Mexico starkly divided voters in 2016 and continued to do so in 2020, as seen in Figure 8-12. About 60 percent of Biden voters opposed building the wall a great deal, and the same percentage of Trump voters favored building the wall a great deal.

Attitudes toward immigration are more nuanced than the wall findings suggest. When people were asked to choose their preferred policy among four options, Biden and Trump voters differed, but a majority in both camps preferred the option of allowing undocumented immigrants to remain in the United States and eventually qualify for citizenship if they met certain requirements such as paying back taxes, learning English, and passing background checks. Figure 8-13 shows that 62 percent of Biden voters and 51 percent of Trump voters chose this option. The agreement on the preferred policy concerning how to treat immigrants currently in the United States suggests a pathway for immigration reform.

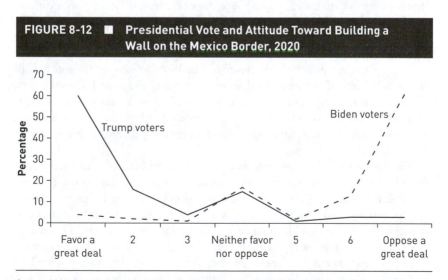

FIGURE 8-12 ■ Presidential Vote and Attitude Toward Building a Wall on the Mexico Border, 2020

Source: 2020 American National Election Studies, available at www.electionstudies.org.

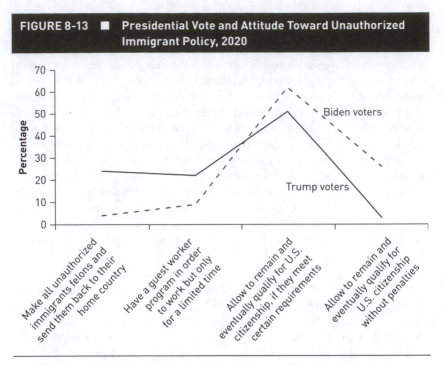

FIGURE 8-13 ■ Presidential Vote and Attitude Toward Unauthorized Immigrant Policy, 2020

Source: 2020 American National Election Studies, available at www.electionstudies.org.

Figure 8-14 looks at vote choice in a somewhat different manner by illustrating the differences in the ideological positions of Biden and Trump voters (similar to what we did with issue stands) as well as the electorate's perceptions of the ideological positions of Biden and Trump. In the 2020 ANES survey, voters were asked about their own ideological position using a 7-point scale ranging from *extremely liberal* to *extremely conservative.* The distributions in the top half of Figure 8-14 indicate the ideological self-placements of Biden and Trump voters. They show that a large plurality (46 percent) of Trump voters classified themselves as conservatives, with others seeing themselves as anywhere from moderate to extremely conservative. Biden voters were more evenly spread out across liberal, slightly liberal, and moderate.

The ANES also asked respondents to indicate how liberal or conservative they thought the two candidates were using the same 7-point ideology scale. The bottom half of Figure 8-14 shows that people generally thought Biden was liberal, but not extremely so, and that Trump was conservative. The two frequency distributions in the top and bottom of the figure look very similar. This makes sense. Americans tend not to be extremely ideological, and partisans have sorted themselves over recent years such that liberals tend to identify with and vote for Democrats and conservatives tend to identify with and vote for Republicans.

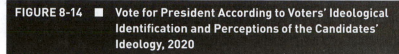

FIGURE 8-14 ■ Vote for President According to Voters' Ideological Identification and Perceptions of the Candidates' Ideology, 2020

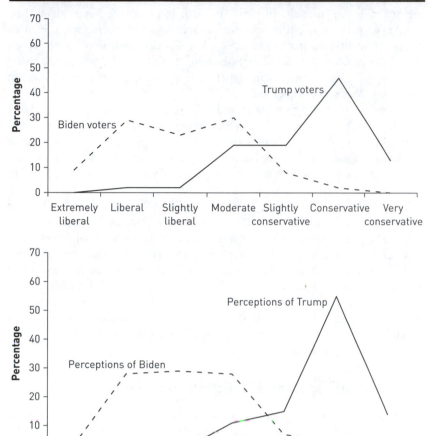

Source: 2020 American National Election Studies, available at www.electionstudies.org.

The pattern in the bottom half of the figure, however, hides large differences in perceptions among partisans (data not shown). Trump voters overwhelmingly thought Biden was extremely liberal (42 percent) or liberal (38 percent), and Biden voters overwhelmingly thought Trump was extremely conservative (45 percent) or conservative (26 percent). People were much more likely to view their own candidate as more ideologically tame.

A number of factors must be present for issues to have an impact on vote choice. First, voters must be informed and concerned about an issue; second, candidates must take distinguishable stands on an issue; and third, voters must perceive the candidates' stands in relation to their own. These conditions often are not achieved, especially the first. In 2020, 16 percent of Americans had no opinion on the issue of cutting government services and spending versus increasing government spending and services, a key aspect of Biden's platform. Voters may also misperceive the candidates' positions. For example, quite a few voters misperceived Biden as an extreme conservative or Trump as an extreme liberal on the government services question.

A weak relationship between an individual's issue positions and vote choice may result from the fact that the analyst chooses the issues for analysis, and these might be issues that are not important to the individual. People who vote on the basis of agricultural policy but are never asked about this issue in a survey will appear not to be issue voters when they actually are. If voters are allowed to define what they see as the most important issue, a somewhat stronger relationship between their position on issues and voting decisions is found.[27] Another problem with the generic approach to issue voting is that candidates are strategic actors who play up (or try to ignore) certain issues if doing so will win votes. Lynn Vavreck found that incumbent party candidates talk a lot about the economy when it is strong, whereas challengers talk a lot about the economy when it is weak. It is strategically advantageous for both sides to do so.[28] Candidates even pivot toward or away from these kinds of positions during presidential debates.[29] The bottom line is that although many voters lack opinions on issues or on the candidates' positions, those who do have opinions show considerable consistency between issue positions and vote choice.

Putting It All Together: Predicting Vote Choice

The preceding sections considered candidate image and issues as short-term forces that either reinforce or deflect voters from their long-term party loyalty. An interesting, but far more difficult, question is the relative impact of these factors on vote choice. Because all these factors are strongly interrelated and almost certainly influence each other, disentangling their effects using the kinds of data available in nationwide surveys is difficult, but we give it a try using binary logistic regression. We include the long-term factors of gender, race, age, and education along with party identification, as well as short-term factors, including both policy stands and candidate image. The numbers in Table 8-4 are the odds ratios, which basically indicate the impact of the variable on the probability of voting for Biden rather than Trump while holding everything else equal. Odds ratios of 1 indicate a 1-to-1 probability of voting for Biden or Trump, which means the variable doesn't help us predict for whom people would vote. Odds ratios over 1 show a net gain for Biden, and odds ratios under 1 show a net gain for Trump. The further away from 1 the odds ratio is, either higher or lower, the stronger an impact the variable has in predicting a vote for Biden or Trump. The numbers in bold are significant, meaning we can be fairly certain they have an impact on predicting vote choice. We include three different models: the first column of numbers includes just the long-term factors; the second column of numbers includes both the long-term factors and people's policy stands; the third column of numbers has all of the variables, including candidate image.

Starting with Model 1, Table 8-4 shows that all of the long-term factors except the respondent's gender are significant predictors of vote choice when they alone are in the model. White people were significantly less likely to vote for Biden (the odds ratio is below 1) and Black people were significantly more likely to vote for Biden (the odds ratio is above 1) compared to other people of color (the excluded category). Older people were significantly less likely to vote for Biden, all else equal. The odds ratio is 0.99 but is significant. It's important to keep in mind that the odds ratio is the impact of a one-unit change in the independent variable (age in this case) on a vote for Biden, so each year older a person is increases the likelihood of voting for Trump. More education increased votes for Biden. The best predictor of these long-term factors, though, was party identification. As we saw earlier in Table 8-1, partisans tended to vote for their party's candidate. When holding all of the other variables in Model 1 equal, moving each unit toward strong Republican (say from independent-leaning Republican to not-so-strong Republican) decreased the odds of voting for Biden by 0.30 to 1. Essentially, there was very little risk that a strong Republican would vote for Biden.

In Model 2 of Table 8-4, we introduce issues that are either issues that play a role in just about every election (the state of the economy and government spending to help Black Americans) or issues more specific to the Trump presidency and the 2020 election (the border wall, climate change, and COVID-19 restrictions). All of these issues were significant predictors of vote choice. The more people thought the economy was doing well, and the more they wanted the United States to build a wall at the Mexican border, the more likely they were to vote for Trump. People who wanted more assistance for Blacks, more government action on climate change, and stricter COVID-19 restrictions were more likely to vote for Biden. Note that the long-term factors become less predictive of vote choice when policy stands are taken into account. For example, if the differences between white and Black people are largely based on their different stands on policies, then the stands on policies explain their vote choice, not the color of their skin.

In the last model, Model 3, we add candidate image as an explanatory variable. We created a candidate image scale for Biden and for Trump by adding up responses for each candidate on the four traits of leadership, caring, knowledgeability, and honesty. The scales range from 4 (*extremely negative*) to 20 (*extremely positive*). Trump's and Biden's image had a very large impact on the probability of voting for the candidate. A one-unit move in the candidate image score (say from 11 to 12) increased the odds of voting for the candidate by 30 percent. This was true for both Biden and Trump. Party identification, age, and some of the policy stands remain significant predictors of vote choice, even with Biden and Trump image included.

TABLE 8-4 ■ Determinants of Presidential Vote Choice, Donald Trump Versus Joe Biden, 2020

	Probability of a Vote for Joe Biden Odds Ratios		
	Model 1 Long-Term Factors	Model 2 With Policy Positions	Model 3 With Candidate Image
Long-Term Factors			
Sex (Male = 1)	1.05	1.00	0.98
Whites, non-Hispanic (White = 1)	**0.57**	0.80	0.83
Blacks (Black = 1)	**1.42**	1.41	0.71
Age (80 = 80 and older)	**0.99**	1.00	**0.98**
Education (5 = Graduate degree)	**1.34**	**1.16**	1.07
Party identification (7 = Strong Republican)	**0.30**	**0.49**	**0.70**
Policy Positions			
Perception of the state of the economy (5 = Gotten much better over past year)	—	**0.69**	**0.79**
Government should provide assistance for Blacks (7 = Government should assist)	—	**1.37**	**1.25**
Support building a wall at border with Mexico (7 = Favor a great deal)	—	**0.63**	**0.88**
Support government action on climate change (7 = A great deal more government action is needed)	—	**1.39**	1.10
Support COVID-19 restrictions (5 = Not nearly enough restrictions)	—	**1.24**	0.90
Candidate Image			
Biden's candidate image	—	—	**1.31**
Trump's candidate image	—	—	**0.70**

	Probability of a Vote for Joe Biden Odds Ratios		
	Model 1 Long-Term Factors	Model 2 With Policy Positions	Model 3 With Candidate Image
Model Fit			
Model chi-square	**2542.0**	**3130.0**	**3480.8**
Nagelkerke R^2	0.748	0.851	0.903
Percent correct prediction	90.4	93.7	96.0

Source: 2020 American National Election Studies, available at www.electionstudies.org.

Note: The odds ratios are used to represent the strength and direction of the relationship between each variable and presidential vote choice controlling for the other variables. The odds ratios show the odds of voting for Biden and not Trump.

THE POPULAR VOTE AND THE ELECTORAL COLLEGE

One aspect of the American electoral system that often raises questions is the Electoral College. If one requirement of a democracy is a reasonably faithful translation of popular votes into governmental control, then the Electoral College is a potential impediment to democracy. (See Chapter 2 for further discussion of the Electoral College as an electoral structure.) When voters cast a ballot for president in the November election, they are actually casting a ballot for that party's slate of electors, which was certified months before by the party's formal submission of the slate to a state official.

The framers wrote the Electoral College into the Constitution as a compromise between those who wanted the president to be popularly elected and those who wanted Congress to choose the president. Under the constitutional system adopted in 1787 and amended in 1804, the president is selected by the Electoral College, with each state having electoral votes equal to the combined seats that it has in the U.S. House of Representatives and Senate. The Electoral College is currently made up of 538 electors who, on the first Monday after the second Wednesday in December, meet in their respective states and cast their votes for president and vice president. Political parties in each state are the organizations in charge of selecting a slate of electors for their candidate. These electors are most often dedicated, loyal party activists who are motivated to do what the party wants.

In forty-eight states and the District of Columbia, the electors for the winner of the popular vote in the state are appointed as the state's electors. That is, the winner-take-all feature means that the state's electors are all from the winning party, even if the popular vote margin was small. Only two states, Nebraska and Maine, have a proportional system. The party of the statewide winner gets to appoint two electors.

The rest of the state's delegation is determined by which presidential candidate wins each of the congressional districts. In 2020, Maine's overall vote was for Joe Biden, but one of its congressional districts voted for Biden and the other for Donald Trump. Maine's Electoral College delegation therefore consisted of three electors chosen by the state's Democratic Party and one elector chosen by the state's Republican Party. Nebraska similarly split its Electoral College vote in 2020: the state overall voted for Trump, as did two of its three congressional districts. One congressional district, covering the city of Omaha and the surrounding area, voted for Biden. Of Nebraska's five Electoral College electors, four were chosen by the state's Republican Party, and one was chosen by the state's Democratic Party.

While no federal law requires electors to vote for the state's popular vote winner, some states have laws on the books that require electors to cast their votes for the winner, or they allow the political parties to require a pledge from electors to vote for the winner. So-called faithless electors, those who vote for someone other than the winner, can be fined according to some of these laws, but no state has made an elector pay a fine. Since electors are chosen by the party and are considered loyal to the party, the number of faithless electors is small. In 2020, all of the electors voted for the candidate who won their state (or congressional district in Maine and Nebraska). Most presidential elections have no faithless electors, although elections occasionally have one elector vote for someone other than the winner.[30]

After the electors have met in each state and cast their votes, the "Certificate of Vote" from each state is sent to Congress, which, in a joint session on January 6, tallies the votes. The president of the Senate, who is the sitting vice president, declares who has been elected president and vice president.[31] A majority of the electoral votes is required to elect a president—270 electoral votes at this time. Normally this process is a quiet affair that simply continues the process of formalizing the public votes cast in November and the electoral votes cast in December. This process was anything but quiet on January 6, 2021, and the United States has never before experienced in its history an insurrection such as occurred on that day.

The Electoral College is certainly an oddity in American politics, but it most often does not lead to results that differ from the popular vote. There have, however, been five elections in which the popular vote winner did not win the Electoral College vote and therefore did not become president: 1824—Andrew Jackson beat John Quincy Adams in both the Electoral College and the popular vote, but because no candidate received a majority of the Electoral College vote, the House of Representatives made the decision to make Adams president; 1876—Republican Rutherford B. Hayes won the Electoral College by 1 vote, and Democrat Samuel Tilden won the popular vote by more than 250,000 votes; 1888—Republican Benjamin Harrison won the Electoral College by 65 votes, while Democrat Grover Cleveland won the popular vote by more than 90,000 votes; 2000—Republican George W. Bush won the Electoral College by 5 votes, and Democrat Al Gore won the popular vote by more than 540,000 votes; 2016—Republican Donald Trump won the Electoral College by 77 votes, while Democrat Hillary Clinton won the popular vote by over 2.8 million votes.

To understand how the Electoral College could produce a winner who is not the popular vote winner, it is important to remember that all states (except Maine and Nebraska) use a winner-take-all procedure for deciding who wins the states' electoral votes. In other words, it does not matter whether a candidate wins the state narrowly or by a wide margin—all of the electoral votes go to the winner. If one candidate wins many states narrowly and the other candidate wins states by a wide margin, the first candidate can win in the Electoral College vote while the second candidate can have more popular votes. This occurred in 2016, when Hillary Clinton won by large margins big states such as California (Clinton 61.5 percent, Trump 31.5 percent) and New York (Clinton 59 percent, Trump 36.5 percent), accumulating a huge number of popular votes, while Trump won some big states, such as Florida, narrowly (Trump 48.6 percent, Clinton 47.4 percent), along with many small states. Since every state is assigned two electoral votes to represent its seats in the U.S. Senate, each electoral vote in a small state represents fewer voters than in a large state. In 2016, each electoral vote in Wyoming represented 149,305 potential voters, and in California, each electoral vote represented 559,696 potential voters.[32] Overall, Clinton won 65,853,625 votes (48.0 percent) to Trump's 62,985,106 votes (45.9 percent), but Trump won 306 electoral votes to Clinton's 232.

The presidential election of 2020 led to the popular vote and the Electoral College vote choosing the same winner. Joe Biden won 51.3 percent (81,283,361 votes) and Donald Trump won 46.8 percent (74,222,960 votes) of the popular vote, with the remaining votes going to third-party candidates. The Electoral College similarly went to Biden, 306 votes to 232 votes.[33]

Although only rarely does the Electoral College produce a winner who has not won the popular vote, the consequences of a winner-take-all system are well known to campaign strategists in presidential elections. The Electoral College arrangement strongly influences presidential campaign strategy. The closer the expected margin in a state and the larger the number of electoral votes available, the more resources the campaigns will put in the state, and the more aggressively the candidates will attempt to respond to the political interests in the state. These are the battleground states, where both candidates have a chance to win and much is at stake. In contrast, safe states are relatively unimportant to both candidates in a general election campaign—taken for granted by one and written off by the other—although they may be visited by one or both candidates to raise funds to spend in competitive states. This strategy clearly played out in both 2016 and 2020, as can be seen in Figure 8-15, which shows the quantity of ads aired in each state.[34] In 2016, television ads supporting Trump or Clinton were almost exclusively aired in the swing states. States that were safe for one candidate or the other were virtually, if not completely, ignored. In 2020, the main thing that stands out is the higher rate of advertising across the country (see also Chapter 2). According to the Wesleyan Media Project, 2020 was a "record shattering" year for ad volume.[35] Even given the overall higher ad volume, though, a pattern still emerges: the areas getting the most election ads were in competitive states: Arizona, Georgia, Michigan, and so on.

FIGURE 8-15 ■ The Strategic Placing of Ads in Swing States, 2016 and 2020

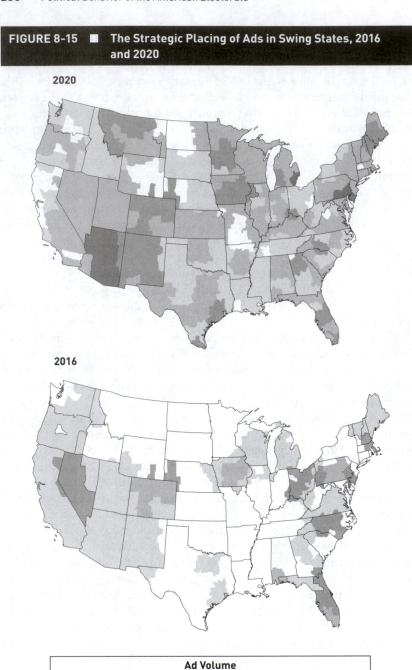

2020

2016

Ad Volume

☐ 0–500   ☐ 501–5,000   ☐ 5,001–25,000
☐ 25,001–40,000   ☐ 40,000+

Source: Wesleyan Media Project, https://mediaproject.wesleyan.edu/releases-102920/#fig1.

The fact that the Electoral College is not very democratic was not a concern for the founders; most of them were wary of too much democracy and approved the idea of state legislatures selecting the electors. Whenever there is a clash between the popular and Electoral College vote, calls for change become louder. Over the years, proposals have been put forth to change or abandon the Electoral College.[36] Some proposals are modest, such as getting rid of the slate of electors (who occasionally do not vote the way they are pledged) and having each secretary of state simply certify the state's electoral votes.

The most sweeping proposal, and the one most commonly discussed by political commentators, is electing the president in a nationwide popular election and getting rid of the Electoral College. This is an obvious alternative method of selecting the president, answering the main criticism of the Electoral College— the potential that the popular vote winner is not the Electoral College winner. A nationwide popular election, however, has problems of its own. It is generally believed that a national popular election would attract more and more candidates—third-party candidates, independent candidates, and major-party candidates who failed to get their party's nomination. Candidates with a small but crucial constituency could threaten to take votes away from the major-party nominees as a way to win concessions. But presumably more candidates would stay in the race to demonstrate their strength, so gradually the percentage of the vote needed to win would shrink. The popular vote winner could have 35 percent or 25 percent of the total vote, and arguably this would undermine the legitimacy of the winner. As a consequence, most proposals for a national popular election have included provisions for a run-off election if the winner's percentage was below, say, 40 percent. The prospect of two presidential elections and the political maneuvering associated with run-off elections has reduced enthusiasm for making such a change.

The current interest in adopting an *instant run-off*, also known as ranked-choice voting, in some local and state elections offers a possible solution. Under instant run-off arrangements, if there are more than two candidates in a race, voters rank their preferences among them. When the votes are counted, the candidate with the fewest number of votes is eliminated, and the second choices of the voters who voted for the eliminated candidate are then counted and added to those candidates' totals. This process is continued until one candidate has a majority (50 percent plus one) of all votes cast. Such a system would produce a majority winner without a run-off. There are a number of objections that have been raised against instant run-off, but several large cities, including San Francisco and Minneapolis, and the state of Maine have adopted ranked-choice voting for some elected positions.[37] If these experiments prove the approach is workable, it might answer some of the perennial concerns about a direct popular vote for president.

Two other proposals have been advanced that would not require a constitutional amendment, although a constitutional amendment would be required to adopt them uniformly across the country. The district method, now used in Maine and Nebraska, could be adoped more broadly. The proposal does not eliminate the winner-take-all characteristic, but it does allow for a distribution of electoral votes that is more reflective of the popular vote. Maine started using the district method in 1972 and has divided its Electoral College vote twice (in 2016 and 2020). Nebraska started using the district method in 1991 and has also divided its vote twice (in 2008 and 2020). Some Republicans in the Nebraska state legislature, unhappy with this outcome, have introduced legislation several times to go back to the winner-take-all system but have been unsuccessful thus far in getting this legislation passed.

An alternative, the proportional method, would allocate all of the electoral votes on a statewide basis but proportionally instead of to the plurality winner. Given the typical margin of victory in the popular vote in a state, a winning candidate would be unlikely to gain more than a one-vote electoral margin from a state using the proportional method. No individual state is likely to adopt this method because the state would become much less strategically attractive to presidential candidates.

For years, political scientists and some political commentators predicted that the Electoral College would be immediately abandoned if, in the modern age, it produced a non–popular vote winner. Why, then, has so little happened to jettison the Electoral College since the 2000 election? A major part of the answer is that any major changes to the Electoral College system would require a constitutional amendment, and small states have no interest in getting rid of a system from which they benefit. Another reason is that politicians and campaign managers at least understand how the current system affects their candidates, even if they think it is flawed. Many alternatives have been aired, but some question the sense of trying to game the Electoral College system for electoral advantage. Former Republican Speaker of the Florida House Will Weatherford said, "To me, that's like saying in a football game, 'We should have only three quarters, because we were winning after three quarters and they beat us in the fourth.' I don't think we need to change the rules of the game, I think we need to get better."[38] State legislatures are reluctant to change Electoral College rules because a rule change that benefits the majority party one year could end up hurting the party in a following year. Most people agree that the Electoral College system has major problems, including electing the less popular candidate, but there is no agreement on a clean fix, and the two major parties do not want to alter the system in a way that will hurt their party in the future.

VOTE CHOICE IN OTHER TYPES OF ELECTIONS

In voting for members of Congress, most of the electorate has relatively little information about the candidates, especially candidates challenging incumbents. A major determinant of votes, then, is party identification. People are likely to know the party of the candidates or to see the party designation on the ballot, making party-line voting much stronger in less visible races, including Congress. Another significant factor in congressional elections is incumbency. Studies have shown that voters are about twice as likely to be able to identify the incumbent as the challenger in congressional races, and almost all the defections from partisanship are in favor of the more familiar incumbent.[39] Both Republicans and Democrats have historically been susceptible to voting for incumbents, especially in the early 1980s when party-line voting dropped to 70 percent in House races and voting for the incumbent of the out-party increased, but the pull of partisanship has grown stronger with the increase in polarization over the recent past.[40] Party-line voting for House races in 2020, according to ANES data, was about 80 percent for weak partisans and 90 percent for strong partisans.

The advantage that incumbents have does not mean that congressional districts are invariably safe for one party, though most are. Instead, it suggests that even if districts were virtual toss-ups in open-seat races, the representatives who manage to survive a term or two find reelection almost ensured. This tendency becomes accentuated as the opposition party finds it increasingly difficult to field an attractive candidate to challenge a secure incumbent. Thus, many incumbent representatives are elected again and again by safe margins. This tendency is exacerbated by the partisan drawing of district lines after the census is completed every ten years.

A Senate election has relatively high visibility and is more likely to gain heavy media attention, unlike most House races. The more information about the election that gets through to the voters, the less they rely on either partisanship or the familiarity of the incumbent's name. The visibility of a Senate race makes an incumbent senator more vulnerable to a well-financed campaign by an attractive opponent.

Despite the advantages of incumbency, national electoral tides can make enough of a difference in enough districts to change the balance of power in one or both houses of Congress. Which party controls the houses of Congress matters. The majority party not only has more people in the chamber who are predisposed to vote for its legislation, but it also controls leadership positions, rules, and procedures that have a major impact on the day-to-day operations of Congress and, ultimately, the passage of legislation. Elections that shift the party control of the House or Senate are therefore key to understanding politics in the United States.

After years of stability in the party control of the two houses of Congress, especially the House, recent elections have introduced a great deal of volatility. In 2014, Republicans maintained their control of the House and also won the Senate. In 2016, the status quo held with the Republicans retaining control of both chambers. The 2018 midterms shifted control of the House back to the Democrats, but the Republicans held the Senate. The 2020 elections did nothing to dispel the notion that we are living through volatile times. The Democrats retained control of the House but lost seats, making their majority the tightest House majority since 2001. In the same election, Democrats won three seats in the Senate, making it a 50 (Democrats and independents) to 50 (Republicans) split. Because the sitting vice president has the power to cast tie-breaking votes in the Senate, the fact that Democrat Kamala Harris was elected vice president in 2020 meant that the Democrats officially controlled the Senate.

Even with all of this volatility in control of the House and Senate, the bottom line is that incumbents get reelected at extremely high rates. In 2020, 95 percent of House incumbents and 84 percent of Senate incumbents were reelected.[41] These high reelection rates are not unusual, but they might be surprising given people's feelings about Congress. When people were asked by Gallup if they approved or disapproved of the job Congress was doing prior to the election, only 19 percent said they approved. Over three-quarters of Americans said they disapproved. Americans clearly do not like what Congress is doing, and it would make perfect sense to "throw the rascals out." Why, then, are so many members of Congress reelected when people are so dissatisfied with Congress? Richard Fenno Jr. has pointed out the interesting paradox that people hate Congress but love their own member of Congress. Members of Congress take great pains to make sure their constituents are happy, including cultivating trust and being seen as "one of us."[42] John Hibbing and Elizabeth Theiss-Morse questioned what it is about Congress that people hate. They found that most Americans approve of Congress as an institution (88 percent) but are highly disapproving of the members of Congress, the 435 House members and the 100 Senators. Only 24 percent approved of the members of Congress.[43] People might like their own representative and senators, although even this has declined in recent years, but they heartily dislike the other members of Congress. They are limited, though, in being able to vote only for or against their own representatives. This helps explain why reelection rates remain so high even though people are so thoroughly disgusted with Congress.

THE MEANING OF AN ELECTION

Politicians and news commentators spend much time and energy interpreting and explaining the outcome of an election. The most important element is usually clear—the winner—although in 2020 the claims made by some top Republicans, including Trump, that the election was stolen raised doubts in many Republicans' minds. Accepting election results when there is no evidence of fraud is an essential aspect of living in a democracy. Nevertheless, analysts and the public in general often try to discover the policy implications of patterns of voting and to read meaning into the outcome of elections. This effort raises two problems for analysis: first, the issue content of the voters' decisions and, second, the policy implications of the winning and losing candidates' issue stands.

It is very difficult to establish that the voters' preferences have certain policy meanings or that the votes for a particular candidate provide a policy mandate. After all, people do not mark on their ballot "Trump, anti-immigration, and opposed to government spending on services." The only information they provide is the vote they cast for a particular candidate and not why they voted that way. Several obstacles lie in the way of stating simply what policies are implied by the behavior of the voters. In many elections, the voters are unaware of the candidates' stands on issues, and sometimes the voters are mistaken in their perceptions.

Furthermore, many voters are not concerned with issues as such in a campaign but vote according to their party loyalty or a candidate's image. As John Sides points out, voters "choose a candidate based on party or whatever, and then line up their views on issues to match the candidates."[44] Voters who supported Reagan in 1980 had an unfavorable view of Carter's performance as president, especially his handling of the Iran hostage crisis. The dissatisfaction with Carter was clear enough. However, the expectations about Reagan were vague and perhaps limited to the hope that he would strengthen national defense and balance the budget. Reagan's supporters came around to support his issues, but not liking Carter and liking Reagan were the bigger drivers behind people's votes in 1980. In 2020, people who voted for Trump were very pro-Trump, but people who voted for Biden were primarily anti-Trump. That is, people either loved Trump or hated him, and their votes reflected these reactions.[45] What this doesn't tell us is what issue mandate was given to Biden when he won the election. He could easily not be Trump, because he is not, but what did voters want him to do over the next four years?

The extent to which mandates occur depends more heavily on politicians than on voters.[46] Newly elected presidents, especially those who win decisively, play up the idea that the voters gave them a mandate to pursue their policy interests. They quickly push their policy agenda in Congress, usually trying to get as much done as possible in the first one hundred days, because it is during this period that members of Congress are still trying to figure out what message the voters were sending. When members of Congress perceive election returns to be significant, they are more willing to change their voting behavior to go along with the new president's agenda. This does not happen often—clear cases are Johnson's election in 1964 and his Great Society policy agenda, Reagan's election in 1980 and the subsequent Reagan Revolution, and the 1994 congressional elections putting in place the Contract with America—but when it does, policy changes are dramatic. The window of opportunity is narrow, and most elections are not perceived to be significant, but at times mandates do happen. Did a mandate happen in 2020? Americans gave Biden a decisive win in the election, both in popular and Electoral College votes, but they were and continue to be deeply divided in their issue stands and in their visions of what kind of country they want the United States to be. Many people voted for Trump because he was not the usual politician, but seven million more voted for Biden, a long-serving politician and Washington insider. In his first hundred days in office, Biden moved ahead as if he had a mandate, whether he actually did or not. This is what new presidents have to do if they want to get their policies in place.

One factor that can help new presidents is their popularity with the general public. Presidents can use their popularity to let members of Congress know what a mistake it would be to vote against their policy agendas. Presidents tend to have higher approval ratings right after an election, although Trump's election in 2016 did not spark the usual "give him a chance" attitude among many people. As Figure 8-16 shows, Obama left office with almost 60 percent approval, after climbing from a low point in mid-2014. Trump started his term with an approval rating of 45 percent, the lowest approval rating of any newly inaugurated president

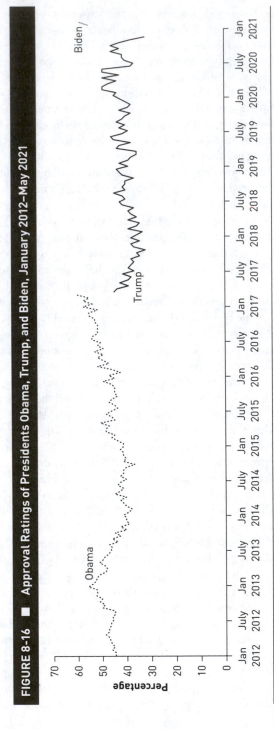

FIGURE 8-16 ■ Approval Ratings of Presidents Obama, Trump, and Biden, January 2012–May 2021

Sources: "President Obama: Gallup Daily Tracking," PollingReport.com, http://pollingreport.com/obama_job1.htm; "President Trump: Gallup Daily Tracking," PollingReport.com, http://pollingreport.com/djt_job1.htm; "Presidential Job Approval Center," Gallup, https://news.gallup.com/interactives/185273/presidential-job-approval-center.aspx.

since the time Gallup started asking its approval question. Because of his low approval, Trump had less leverage to use when trying to get his policy initiatives passed in Congress even though he had a Republican Congress with which to work. Biden began his presidency with an approval rating of 57 percent—much higher than Trump's but lower than most new presidents'.[47] In these highly polarized times, Biden will need to be a skilled politician to get his agenda passed. He would need to be a miracle worker to unite Americans.

American elections are hardly a classic model of democracy with rational, well-informed voters making dispassionate decisions. Yet American elections provide an acceptable opportunity for parties and candidates to attempt to win or hold public office. Despite the polarization in the United States today, a sizable portion of the electorate is moderate or unconcerned about ideology and lacking in firm partisan attachments. For the present at least, this segment of the electorate holds the key to electoral victory. The political parties, their officeholders, and their candidates ignore this situation at their peril.

Study Questions

1. What explains why people vote the way they do? What has a bigger impact on vote choice: long-term or short-term factors?

2. Should Americans keep the Electoral College? What impact would the alternatives have on presidential election outcomes?

3. What explains votes in lower-level elections?

4. How should we interpret the meaning of the 2020 election? Did Americans give Joe Biden a clear mandate to lead?

Suggested Readings

Albertson, Bethany, and Shana Kushner Gadarian. *Anxious Politics: Democratic Citizenship in a Threatening World*. New York: Cambridge University Press, 2015. Excellent analysis of the impact of emotions on people's consumption of news, reactions to issues, and overall support of the government.

Bartels, Larry M. *Presidential Primaries and the Dynamics of Public Choice*. Princeton, NJ: Princeton University Press, 1988. The best available analysis of public opinion and vote choice during presidential primaries.

Cramer, Katherine J. *The Politics of Resentment: Rural Consciousness in Wisconsin and the Rise of Scott Walker*. Chicago: University of Chicago Press, 2016. A deep and perceptive examination of rural identity and resentment of political elites.

Fiorina, Morris P. *Retrospective Voting in American National Elections*. New Haven, CT: Yale University Press, 1981. An important conceptual argument for viewing vote choice as judgments about the past.

Jacobson, Gary C. *The Politics of Congressional Elections*, 6th ed. New York: Longman, 2006. An authoritative survey of a broad topic and the literature surrounding it.

Lau, Richard R., and David P. Redlawsk. *How Voters Decide: Information Processing in Election Campaigns*. New York: Cambridge University Press, 2006. An innovative use of experiments shows how successful voters are at selecting the candidate closest to their own preferences.

Lewis-Beck, Michael S., William G. Jacoby, Helmut Norpoth, and Herbert F. Weisberg. *The American Voter Revisited*. Ann Arbor: University of Michigan Press, 2008. A rich reanalysis of the themes from the classic work, using mainly 2000 and 2004 data.

Mayer, William G., ed. *The Swing Voter in American Politics*. Washington, DC: Brookings Institution Press, 2008. A collection using several definitions of "swing voters" to analyze them currently and over time.

Niemi, Richard G., and Herbert F. Weisberg, eds. *Classics in Voting Behavior.* Washington, DC: CQ Press, 1993; Niemi, Richard G., and Herbert F. Weisberg, eds. *Controversies in Voting Behavior*, 4th ed. Washington, DC: CQ Press, 2001. These two collections offer the best readings from decades of research on public opinion and voting behavior.

Shanks, J. Merrill, and Warren E. Miller. *The New American Voter.* Cambridge, MA: Harvard University Press, 1996. A sophisticated analysis using an elaborate model of vote choice.

Internet Resources

The website of the American National Election Studies, www.electionstudies.org, has extensive data on topics covered in this chapter. Under the Resources menu, click "Guide to Public Opinion and Electoral Behavior." Scroll down to "Evaluation of the Presidential Candidates," "Evaluation of Congressional Candidates," and "Vote Choice" for a variety of political items from 1952 to the present. In addition, all of these items can be broken down by social characteristics.

PollingReport.com and Gallup (https://news.gallup.com/topic/politics.aspx) have current political information on elections as well as public opinion data. Major news organizations like CNN and the *New York Times* post results of exit polls on their websites. Candidates for office, like the political parties, have websites that can be located with search engines.

Notes

1. Presidential Job Approval Center, Gallup, accessed July 13, 2021, https://news.gallup.com/interactives/185273/presidential-job-approval-center.aspx.

2. Angus Campbell, Philip E. Converse, Warren E. Miller, and Donald E. Stokes, *The American Voter* (New York: Wiley, 1960), Chapter 2.

3. "ACS Demographic and Housing Estimates: 2019 American Community Survey 1-Year Estimates," U.S. Census Bureau, accessed July 13, 2021, https://data.census.gov/cedsci/table?q=race&tid=ACSDP1Y2019.DP05&hidePreview=true.

4. Taeku Lee and Karthick Ramakrishnan, "Asian Americans Turn Democratic," *Los Angeles Times*, November 23, 2012, http://articles.latimes.com/2012/nov/23/opinion/la-oe-lee-asian-american-voters-20121123. The vote percentages for Clinton in 2016 and Biden in 2020 were taken from the 2016 and 2020 American National Election Studies.

5. Sergio C. Wals, "Made in the USA? Immigrants' Imported Ideology and Political Engagement," *Electoral Studies* 32 (December 2013): 756–767.

6. Susan Heavey, "Republicans Aim to Rebrand Party, Attract Voters," Reuters, March 18, 2013, http://www.reuters.com/article/2013/03/18/us-usa-republicans-idUSBRE92H0HL20130318; Katie Glueck, "Reince Priebus Hails College GOP Report," Politico, June 3, 2013, http://www.politico.com/story/2013/06/reince-priebus-college-gop-report-92146.html; Ron Elving, "RNC Post-election Report a Line in the Sand for Divided GOP," *It's All Politics*, NPR, March 19, 2013, http://www.npr.org/blogs/itsallpolitics/2013/03/18/174689113/rnc-chairs-postmortem-report-a-line-in-the-sand-for-divided-gop.

7. To the astute reader, the numbers in Table 8-1 might look a bit different from the 2020 numbers in Table 5-3. The reason for this is that all independents, leaners and "pure," are combined in Table 5-3, whereas they are separated out in Table 8-1.

8. "Would You Rather Have a Beer With Clinton or Trump?," Rasmussen Reports, June 15, 2016, http://www.rasmussenreports.com/public_content/politics/elections/election_2016/would_you_rather_have_a_beer_with_clinton_or_trump.

9. Danny Hayes, "Candidate Qualities Through a Partisan Lens: A Theory of Trait Ownership," *American Journal of Political Science* 49 (October 2005): 908–923.

10. Bethany Albertson and Shana Kushner Gadarian, *Anxious Politics: Democratic Citizenship in a Threatening World* (New York: Cambridge University Press, 2015); Ted Brader, *Campaigning for Hearts and Minds* (Chicago: University of Chicago Press, 2006); W. Russell Neuman, George E. Marcus, Ann N. Crigler, and Michael MacKuen, eds., *The Affect Effect* (Chicago: University of Chicago Press, 2007).

11. David A. Fahrenthold, Robert Costa, and John Wagner, "Donald Trump Is Sworn In as President, Vows to End 'American Carnage,'" *Washington Post*, January 20, 2017, https://www.washingtonpost.com/politics/trump-to-be-sworn-in-marking-a-transformative-shift-in-the-countrys-leadership/2017/01/20/954b9cac-de7d-11e6-ad42-f3375f271c9c_story.html?utm_term=.adc527c1bb54.

12. Danny Hayes and Kimberly Gross, "Trump Makes More Voters Feel Bad Than Biden Does. That's a Problem for the President," *Monkey Cage* (newsletter), *Washington Post* (November 2, 2020), https://www.washington post.com/politics/2020/11/02/trump-makes-more-voters-feel-bad-than-biden-does-thats-problem-president/. A heartfelt thanks to Danny Hayes for sharing the data on all of the emotions asked in the poll.

13. Joanne M. Miller and Jon A. Krosnick, "The Impact of Candidate Name Order on Election Outcomes," *Public Opinion Quarterly* 62 (Autumn 1998): 291–330; Jonathan G. S. Koppell and Jennifer A. Steen, "The Effects of Ballot Position on Election Outcomes," *Journal of Politics* 66 (February 2004): 267–281.

14. Lynn Vavreck, *The Message Matters: The Economy and Presidential Campaigns* (Princeton, NJ: Princeton University Press, 2009).

15. A good discussion of this topic in a single source is the collection of articles and commentary by Gerald Pomper, Richard Boyd, Richard Brody, Benjamin Page, and John Kessel in *American Political Science Review* 66 (June 1972): 415–470. See also Benjamin I. Page, *Choices and Echoes in Presidential Elections* (Chicago: University of Chicago Press, 1978).

16. Norman H. Nie, Sidney Verba, and John R. Petrocik, *The Changing American Voter* (Cambridge, MA: Harvard University Press, 1976), Chapter 10; see also Benjamin I. Page and Richard A. Brody, "Policy Voting and the Electoral Process: The Vietnam War Issue," *American Political Science Review* 66 (September 1972): 979–995.

17. J. Merrill Shanks and Warren E. Miller, *The New American Voter* (Cambridge, MA: Harvard University Press, 1996).

18. James M. Snyder Jr. and Michael M. Ting, "An Informational Rationale for Political Parties," *American Journal of Political Science* 46 (January 2002): 90–110; Jonathan Woon and Jeremy C. Pope, "Made in Congress? Testing the Electoral Implications of Party Ideological Brand Names," *Journal of Politics* 70 (July 2008): 823–836.

19. Benjamin Highton, "The Contextual Causes of Issue and Party Voting in American Presidential Elections," *Political Behavior* 32 (December 2010): 453–471.

20. "Party Platform: The 2020 Democratic Platform," Democratic National Committee, accessed July 13, 2021, https://democrats.org/where-we-stand/party-platform/.

21. "Resolution Regarding the Republican Party Platform," Republican National Committee, accessed July 13, 2021, https://prod-cdn-static.gop.com/docs/Resolution_Platform_2020.pdf; Tom Wheeler, "The 2020 Republican Party Platform: 'L'etat, c'est moi,'" Brookings, August 25, 2020, https://www.brookings.edu/blog/up-front/2020/08/25/the-2020-republican-party-platform-letat-cest-moi/.

22. Global Climate Change, NASA, accessed May 12, 2021, https://climate.nasa.gov/evidence/.

23. Gerald H. Kramer, "Short-Term Fluctuations in U.S. Voting Behavior, 1896–1964," *American Political Science Review* 65 (March 1971): 131–143; Thomas J. Rudolph, "Who's Responsible for the Economy? The Formation and Consequences of Responsibility Attributions," *American Journal of Political Science* 47 (October 2003): 698–713.

24. Benjy Sarlin and Alex Seitz-Wald, "Donald Trump and Hillary Clinton Are Universes Apart on Immigration," NBC News, September 2, 2016, http://www.nbcnews.com/politics/2016-election/donald-trump-hillary-clinton-are-universes-apart-immigration-n641686.

25. Ed Lowther, "US Election 2020: Trump's Impact on Immigration—in Seven Charts," BBC News, October 22, 2020, https://www.bbc.com/news/election-us-2020-54638643.

26. Marianna Sotomayor and Mike Memoli, "Joe Biden Releases Two Immigration-Focused Plans," NBC News, updated May 11, 2021, https://www.nbcnews.com/politics/meet-the-press/blog/meet-press-blog-latest-news-analysis-data-driving-political-discussion-n988541/ncrd1099821#blogHeader.

27. David RePass, "Issue Salience and Party Choice," *American Political Science Review* 65 (June 1971): 368–400.

28. Vavreck, *Message Matters*.

29. Amber E. Boydstun, Rebecca A. Glazier, and Claire Phillips, "Agenda Control in the 2008 Presidential Debate," *American Politics Research* 41 (September 2013): 863–899.

30. "Faithless Electors," FairVote, last updated July 6, 2020, http://www.fairvote.org/faithless_electors.

31. "What Is the Electoral College?," Electoral College, U.S. National Archives and Records Administration, last reviewed December 23, 2019, https://www.archives.gov/federal-register/electoral-college/about.html; "About the Electors," Electoral College, U.S. National Archives and Records Administration, last reviewed May 11, 2021, https://www.archives.gov/federal-register/electoral-college/electors.html#selection.

32. Alex Daugherty, "Your Vote in Texas Isn't Worth as Much as Some Other States," McClatchy DC Bureau, November 14, 2016, http://www.mcclatchydc.com/news/politics-government/election/article114635878.html.

33. "Presidential Election Results: Biden Wins," *New York Times*, accessed May 14, 2021, https://www.nytimes.com/interactive/2020/11/03/us/elections/results-president.html.

34. "Presidential General Election Ad Spending Tops $1.5 Billion," Wesleyan Media Project, October 29, 2020, https://mediaproject.wesleyan.edu/releases-102920/#fig1.

35. "Record Shattering 2020 Ad Volumes," Wesleyan Media Project, October 21, 2020, https://mediaproject.wesleyan.edu/releases-102120/.

36. See Lawrence D. Longley and Alan G. Braun, *The Politics of Electoral College Reform* (New Haven, CT: Yale University Press, 1972), for a survey of the proposals for Electoral College reform; see A. C. Thomas, Andrew Gelman, Gary King, and Jonathan N. Katz, "Estimating Partisan Bias of the Electoral College Under Proposed Changes in Elector Apportionment," *Statistics, Politics, and Policy* 4, no. 1 (2013): 1–13, for an empirical test of the effects of various reform proposals.

37. Katharine Q. Seelye, "Maine Adopts Ranked-Choice Voting. What Is It, and How Will It Work?," *New York Times*, December 3, 2016, https://www.nytimes.com/2016/12/03/us/maine-ranked-choice-voting.html?_r=0.

38. Alan Greenblatt, "Some in GOP Want New Electoral College Rules," *It's All Politics*, NPR, January 28, 2013, http://www.npr.org/blogs/itsallpolitics/2013/01/25/170276794/some-in-gop-want-new-electoral-college-rules; see "Gaming the Electoral College," http://www.270towin.com/alternative-electoral-college-allocation-methods/, to see how changing the Electoral College rules would affect who wins the presidential elections.

39. Donald E. Stokes and Warren E. Miller, "Party Government and the Saliency of Congress," *Public Opinion Quarterly* 26 (Winter 1962): 531–546.

40. "Vital Statistics on Congress," Brookings, February 8, 2021, https://www.brookings.edu/multi-chapter-report/vital-statistics-on-congress/.

41. Tom Murse, "Do Members of Congress Ever Lose Re-election?," ThoughtCo, December 10, 2020, https://www.thoughtco.com/do-congressmen-ever-lose-re-election-3367511.

42. Richard F. Fenno Jr., "If, as Ralph Nader Says, Congress Is 'The Broken Branch,' How Come We Love Our Congressmen So Much?," in *Congress in Change: Evolution and Reform*, ed. Norman J. Ornstein (New York: Praeger, 1975), 277–287; Richard F. Fenno Jr., *Home Style: House Members in Their Districts* (New York: Pearson, 2002).

43. John R. Hibbing and Elizabeth Theiss-Morse, *Congress as Public Enemy* (New York: Cambridge University Press, 1995), 45.

44. John Sides, "The 2012 Election Was Not a Mandate," *Monkey Cage* (blog), November 7, 2012, http://themonkeycage.org/2012/11/07/the-2012-election-was-not-a-mandate/.

45. "The Trump-Biden Presidential Contest," Pew Research Center, October 9, 2020, https://www.pewresearch.org/politics/2020/10/09/the-trump-biden-presidential-contest/.

46. David A. M. Peterson, Lawrence J. Grossback, James A. Stimson, and Amy Gangl, "Congressional Response to Mandate Elections," *American Journal of Political Science* 47 (July 2003): 411–426; Lawrence J. Grossback, David A. M. Peterson, and James A. Stimson, *Mandate Politics* (New York: Cambridge University Press, 2007).

47. "Presidential Job Approval Center," Gallup, accessed July 13, 2021, https://news.gallup.com/interactives/185273/presidential-job-approval-center.aspx.

APPENDIX

Survey Research Methods

M ANY OF THE DATA in this book have come from survey research, and most of the analyses cited have been based on findings from survey research. For more than seventy years, the data from the American National Election Studies (ANES), as well as from other major survey projects in political science, have been available through the Inter-university Consortium for Political and Social Research and have formed the basis for countless research projects in many fields by scholars, graduate students, and undergraduates. Given this widespread use of survey data, it is appropriate to give some description of the data-collection methods that underlie them.

During the past eighty years, social scientists have developed an impressive array of techniques for discovering and measuring individual attitudes and behavior. Basically, survey research relies on giving a standard questionnaire to the individuals to be studied. In most major studies of the national electorate over the years, trained interviewers ask the questions and record the responses in a face-to-face interview with each respondent. A few studies depend on the respondents themselves filling out the questionnaires. Recently, the rising costs of survey research, the pressure for quick results, and the availability of random-digit telephone dialing have led both commercial and academic pollsters to rely increasingly on telephone interviewing. The ANES used both face-to-face and telephone interviewing in 2000 but returned to using face-to-face interviews exclusively in 2004 and 2008. Beginning in 2012 and continuing in 2016, the ANES used face-to-face interviews but also had a sample of respondents answer the survey on the web. Due to COVID-19 in 2020, the ANES used a combination of web, phone, and video to administer the surveys. Web-based surveys are increasingly common, with organizations having respondents fill out questionnaires on a survey organization's website. Also, for several decades, news organizations have conducted exit polls on Election Day to give an early estimate of the outcome and gather additional information about voters that election statistics do not provide.

SURVEY DATA COLLECTION

We describe four data-collection phases in the survey research process, noting the ways these steps vary depending on whether the surveys are face-to-face, telephone, internet, or an exit poll. The four phases are sampling, questionnaire constructing, interviewing, and coding.

Sampling

The key to survey research is probability sampling. It may seem inappropriate to analyze the entire American electorate using studies composed of fewer than two thousand individuals, which is about the average number of respondents in the studies used in this book. But it would be prohibitively expensive to interview the entire electorate, and the only way to study public opinion nationally is by interviewing relatively few individuals who accurately represent the entire electorate. Probability sampling is the method used to ensure that the individuals selected for interviewing will be representative of the total population. Probability sampling attempts to select respondents in such a way that every individual in the population has an equal chance of being selected for interviewing. If the respondents are selected in this way, the analyst can be confident that the characteristics of the sample are approximately the same as those of the whole population.

It would be impossible to make a list of every adult in the United States and then draw names from the list randomly. All survey organizations depart from such strict random procedures in some way. The ANES surveys, the General Social Survey (GSS), and other high-quality surveys using face-to-face interviews employ stratified cluster samples, based on households.

Stratification means that random selection occurs within subpopulations. In the United States, the sample is customarily selected within regions to guarantee that all sections are represented and within communities of different sizes as well. *Clustering* means that relatively small geographical areas, called primary sampling units, are randomly selected within the stratified categories so that many interviews are concentrated within a small area to reduce the costs and inconvenience for interviewers. Finally, the ANES samples *households* instead of individuals (although within households individuals are randomly selected and interviewed), which means that within sampling areas households are enumerated and selected at random. (This sampling procedure means that no respondents are selected in military bases, hospitals, hotels, prisons, or other places where people do not live in households. However, after the enfranchisement of eighteen-year-olds, the ANES and GSS began to include college dormitories as residences to be sampled.)

Increasingly, the commercial polling organizations have turned to telephone interviewing as a faster and cheaper alternative to field interviewing. Random-digit dialing is typically used by these polling operations to select both listed and unlisted numbers and to give each residential number the same chance of being called. Telephone sampling has an advantage over field surveys because it does not require clustering.

Telephone sampling added cell phone–only households only recently and still ignores individuals without telephones. Otherwise, no major obstacles prevent drawing an excellent sample of telephone numbers. The problems begin at that point. Success in reaching a person and completing a telephone interview is uneven, and failures may run as high as 50 percent, or even higher. Some polling organizations make repeated callbacks, as the chances of getting an answer increase with the number of callbacks. Repeated callbacks, however, slow the data collection and increase the costs. Because an important reason for using the telephone is speed and low costs, most polling organizations do not call back.

Once the telephone is answered or the household is contacted for a face-to-face interview, a respondent from the household must be selected. Some randomizing procedure is typically used to select the respondent. There are two methods for selecting respondents, and they have different consequences. The best sampling procedure, but a costly and time-consuming one, is to identify all the eligible members of the household and select one at random. If the respondent selected is not at home, an appointment is arranged for a callback. In a high-quality survey such as the ANES, many attempts are made to interview the individual randomly selected, but no substitutions are made. Telephone surveys typically allow a huge proportion of their respondents to be substitutes for the respondents who should have been interviewed. The alternative, and more common, method of selection identifies the respondent among those eligible who is available, and the interview is conducted immediately. This further compromises the sample, making it a selection among those people who happen to be at home or answer their phone when the interviewer calls.

The more often the randomly selected respondents cannot be contacted or refuse to be interviewed, the more the sample departs from its original design. Probability samples, with either face-to-face or telephone interviews, can result in unrepresentative samples if the *nonresponse rate* is high. The nonresponse rate refers to the number of respondents originally selected who, for whatever reason, are not interviewed and thus do not appear in the sample.[1] Should these nonrespondents share some characteristic disproportionately, the resulting sample will underrepresent that type of person. For example, residents of high-crime neighborhoods and the elderly may be reluctant to answer the door for a face-to-face interview; busy people with multiple jobs may not be at home enough to be reached by landline telephone. When this happens, the sample will have fewer of these people than occur in the population, and thus the sample will be biased. All the polling organizations take steps to counter these tendencies by weighting the results to compensate for various demographic biases.[2] This is a difficult problem to solve, however. The likelihood is high that the people who consent to be interviewed are different from, and therefore not representative of, those who refuse. If this is the case, counting those who are interviewed more heavily (which is essentially what weighting the sample does) does not eliminate the bias.

Internet polls and exit polls have their own sampling problems. Self-administered internet polls are increasingly common. Random-digit dialing is used to draw a sample of residential telephones, similar to a telephone poll, and create a "panel"—a large group of individuals who agree to answer a questionnaire and participate in future studies. These individuals are provided with internet access and a computer, if necessary, so the panel is not limited to those who already have such access. Each study draws a sample from the larger panel, and these respondents are informed of the opportunity to go online to answer a questionnaire at a secure website. Although the sampling design initially produces a representative set of potential respondents, people who are willing to join the panel and participate in particular studies may be different from the rest of the public. The ANES has started to use internet surveys in addition to the traditional face-to-face method. The ANES selects households in a manner similar to the face-to-face interviews and sends an invitation to participate in the study via the mail. A screening instrument is used to sample one person living at the address to complete the survey. Given the potential differences of these two methods with respect to comparability over time, we report only the face-to-face ANES results from 1952 to 2016 in this book. In 2020, due to COVID-19, ANES did telephone or web, not face-to-face, surveys. We utilize these phone and web data that were fresh samples (not the panel samples).

Internet polls have nothing in common with the self-selected "vote on the internet" polls favored by some television programs and social media. When people take the initiative to respond, instead of being chosen to respond through a random selection procedure, there can be no claim that they are a representative sample of the public.

Exit polls involve random selection of polling places. Interviewers go to each of the randomly selected polling places and are instructed to select, say, every tenth voter emerging from the polling place for an interview. At midday, the interviewers call in the results of the first set of completed interviews, and at this time the central office may adjust the interval of voters to speed up or slow down the pace of interviewing. A number of biases can be introduced in the sampling process, as busy voters refuse to be interviewed and other voters avoid interviewers on the basis of age or race. With so many people not voting in person on Election Day in 2020, exit polls in that year became even less representative.

Questionnaire Constructing

In survey questionnaires, several types of questions will ordinarily be used. Public opinion surveys began years ago with forced-choice questions that a respondent was asked to answer by choosing among a set of offered alternatives, none of which included "don't know" or "no opinion." For example, forced-choice questions frequently take the form of stating a position on public policy and asking the respondent to "agree" or "disagree" with the statement. The analysis in Chapter 6 was based in part on the answers to forced-choice questions on public policy that were used in ANES questionnaires in which respondents were asked to "agree strongly," "agree," "disagree," or "disagree strongly." Some respondents gave qualified answers that did not fit into these prearranged categories or volunteered that they had no opinions.

A major innovation associated with the Survey Research Center at the University of Michigan is the use of open-ended questioning. Open-ended questions give respondents the opportunity to express their opinions in their own way without being forced to select among categories provided by the questionnaire. Questions such as "Is there anything in particular you like about the Democratic Party?" or "What are the most important problems facing the country today?" permit the respondents to answer in their own terms. Interviewers encourage respondents to answer such questions as fully as they can with neutral "probes" such as "Could you tell me more about that?" or "Anything else?" or similar queries that draw forth more discussion. Open-ended questions are a superior method of eliciting accurate expressions of opinion, but they have two major disadvantages: (1) They place more of a burden on interviewers to record the responses, and (2) the burden of reducing the many responses to a dimension that can be analyzed is left for the coders. For example, if Americans are asked, "Do you think of yourself as a Democrat, a Republican, an independent, or something else?," almost all the responses will fit usefully into the designated categories:

Democrat

Independent

Republican

Something else

Don't know

If a relatively unstructured, open-ended question is used, however—such as "How do you think of yourself politically?"—some people will answer with "Democrat," "Republican," and so forth, but many others will give answers that are substantially different, such as "liberal," "conservative," "radical," "moderate," "pragmatic," or "I hate politics"—and these cannot easily be compared with the partisan categories. Analysts often intend to force responses into a single dimension, such as partisanship, whether the respondents would have volunteered an answer along that dimension or not. This is essential if researchers are to develop single dimensions for analytic purposes. Modern survey research includes questions and techniques considerably more complex than these examples for establishing dimensions.

Questionnaires differ a great deal in their complexity and sophistication. Face-to-face interviews with well-trained interviewers may have many open-ended questions or questions with *branching*, conditional on the responses to previous questions. Telephone interviews using computer-assisted telephone interview (CATI) technology and online internet polls can also be complex, relying on computer branching to guide the respondent through the questionnaire. At the other extreme, exit polls are entirely forced-choice questions that can be completed quickly by the voter without instruction.

Writing good survey questions is an art. The questions should be clear, direct, and able to be understood in the same way by all respondents, regardless of age, education, or regional or subcultural differences. They need to avoid various technical mistakes, like asking two things in one question (a so-called double-barreled question). A professionally done poll that seeks accurate results—whether an academic survey, a journalistic poll, or a political poll that wants both the good news and the bad news for its client—will try very hard to ask unbiased questions that reflect the actual opinions of the respondents rather than leading them to answer in any particular way. Not all survey operations have this as a goal, however. The following examples come from a Republican Party survey, the "Mainstream Media Accountability Survey," conducted in February 2017. Respondents were asked, "Do you believe the mainstream media does not do their due diligence fact-checking before publishing stories on the Trump administration?" and "Do you believe the media uses slurs rather than facts to attack conservative stances on issues like border control, religious liberties, and ObamaCare?"[3] The purpose of the questions was not to elicit an accurate picture of public opinion on media coverage of the Trump administration but to reinforce the view among some Republicans that the media are out to get Donald Trump and other Republicans.

Interviewing

The selection of the sample can depend in part on the interviewer, but even more important is the role of the interviewer in asking questions of the respondent and in recording the answers. Motivated, well-trained interviewers are crucial to the success of face-to-face and telephone survey research. The interviewer has several major responsibilities. First, the interviewer must select the respondents according to sampling instructions. Second, the interviewer must develop rapport with the respondents so that they will be willing to go through with the interview, which may last an hour or more. Third, the interviewer must ask the questions in a friendly way and encourage the respondents to answer fully without leading them to distort their views. Fourth, the interviewer must record the answers of the respondents fully and accurately. The best survey organizations keep a permanent staff of highly trained interviewers for this purpose.

A technological innovation used in telephone interviewing is the CATI system. The interviewer sits at the telephone, with the questionnaire appearing on a computer screen. As the interviewer moves through the questionnaire, responses are entered directly into the computer and automatically coded. Complicated branching to different questions, conditional on the responses given to preceding questions, is possible.

Telephone interviewing has some real advantages. The travel costs of a field staff are eliminated. Having interviewing conducted from a call room allows for direct supervision of the interviewing staff, enhancing the uniformity of the administration of the questionnaires. Within-interview "experiments" are possible with the CATI system. Also, changing the content of the questionnaire during the course of the study is easy and inexpensive. The great disadvantage is that face-to-face interviews yield higher-quality data.

In internet polling, on the one hand, there are no interviewers, which is a great saving in cost. On the other hand, there is no interviewer to help the respondents navigate the questionnaire or to keep the respondents motivated—or to make judgments about the plausibility of the responses.

Exit polls generally use a combination of self-administered questionnaires with interviewers available to read the questionnaires and record responses for those voters who need assistance. Given that exit polls might provide one day of work every couple of years, exit poll interviewers are not seasoned professionals. They also work in scattered locations with no direct supervision. Errors in implementing the sampling technique or in administering the questionnaires would rarely be caught and unlikely to be corrected in the short time span of Election Day.

Coding

Once the interviewers administer the questionnaires to respondents, the verbal information is reduced to a numerical form, according to a code. Numeric information, unlike verbal information, can be processed and manipulated by high-speed data-processing equipment. The coder's task may be simple or complex. For example, to code the respondent's voter registration status can be as simple as requiring a simple code: 1 = registered to vote, 2 = not registered to vote. A data field that contains information on the respondent will have a location designated for indicating the respondent's registration status. A value of 1 will indicate registered, and a value of 2 will indicate not registered. Printed questionnaires for face-to-face interviews are precoded for many of the more straightforward questions, and the CATI system allows precoded categories to be assigned automatically as the interviewer records the respondent's answers.

Some coding is complicated, with elaborate arrays of categories. For example, coding the responses to a question such as "Is there anything in particular you like about the Democratic Party?" might include hundreds of categories covering such details as "I like the party's farm policies," "I like the party's tax program," and "I've just always been a Democrat." Some codes require coders to make judgments about the respondents' answers. In political surveys, these codes have included judgments on the level of sophistication of the respondents' answers and about the main reason for respondents' vote choices.

After the verbal information has been converted into numbers according to the coding instructions, the data are ready for analysis by computer. At this point, the survey research process ends, and the political analysts take over to make what use of the data they can.

VALIDITY OF SURVEY QUESTIONS

A frequent set of criticisms directed at public opinion research questions the validity of the responses to survey items. *Validity* simply means the extent to which there is correspondence between the response given to a question and the attitude or behavior of the respondent that the question is designed to measure. There is no one answer to doubts about validity because each item has a validity applicable to it alone. Some items are notoriously invalid; others have nearly perfect validity. Many survey items have not been independently tested for their validity, and for practical purposes, researchers are forced to say that they are interested in analyzing the responses, whatever they mean to the respondent. In other instances, the sample result can be compared with the known population value.

The items with the most questionable validity in political studies come from those situations in which respondents have some incentive to misrepresent the facts or when their memories may not be accurate. Questions about voter turnout or level of income are noteworthy in this regard. Validity checks reveal that respondents are about as likely to underestimate their income as overestimate it, and a noticeable percentage of respondents claim to have voted when they did not.[4]

ADVANTAGES AND DISADVANTAGES OF DIFFERENT TYPES OF SURVEYS

Face-to-face interviews with respondents drawn from a sample of households

Advantages
    High-quality data
    Allows for longer, more in-depth interviews

Disadvantages
    High cost
    Slow data collection and processing

Telephone interviews of respondents drawn from a sample of residential and cell phone numbers

Advantages
    Lower cost
    Fast turnaround, especially using a CATI system
    Allows direct supervision of interviewing process

Disadvantages
    No-phone households are excluded
    Call screening and resistance to stranger calls further degrade the sample

Self-administered internet polls

Advantages
    Less expensive once the panel is set up
    Subsamples with particular characteristics can be drawn from the panel

(Continued)

(Continued)

Disadvantages
   Those who agree to participate may be unrepresentative of the population

Exit polls

Advantages
   Provides a large number of journalists with material for reporting and commentary immediately after an election

Disadvantages
   Lack of training and supervision of interviewers
   With increase in absentee and mail-in voting, poll needs to be supplemented with telephone survey of voters who do not go to a polling place

Recall of past voting behavior falls victim to failing memories and intervening events. Changes in party identification, past votes cast, the party identification of one's parents—all may contain substantial error. For example, during November and December immediately after the 1960 election, respondents were asked how they had voted for president. Most remembered voting for either John F. Kennedy or Richard M. Nixon, and as shown in Table A-1, they were divided about evenly between the two. (The slight deviation of 1 percent from the actual results is within sampling error by any reasonable standards.) The 1962 and 1964 sample estimates of the 1960 vote reveal increasing departures from the actual outcome. Granting that some change in the population over four years may affect vote-choice percentages, a substantial proportion of the 1964 sample gave responses to the question of 1960 presidential vote choice that misrepresented their vote. The validity of this item always declines over a four-year period, but President Kennedy's assassination in the intervening years created an unusually large distortion in recalled vote.

TABLE A-1 ■ Recalled Vote for President in 1960, 1962, and 1964				
Recalled Vote	**1960**	**1962**	**1964**	**Actual Vote in 1960[a]**
John F. Kennedy	49%	56%	64%	49.7%
Richard M. Nixon	51	43	36	49.5
Other	[b]	[b]	[b]	0.7
Total	**100%**	**99%**	**100%**	**99.9%**
(*N*)	(1,428)	(940)	(1,124)	

Sources: American National Election Studies, available at www.electionstudies.org, and U.S. House of Representatives, Office of the Clerk, clerk.house.gov.

[a]The 1960 popular vote can be tallied in a number of ways, including those that show Nixon with a slight popular vote majority. No matter how the votes are counted, the election was very close.

[b]Less than 0.5 percent.

VALIDITY VERSUS CONTINUITY

One of the important features of the ANES is its continuity over a seventy-year time span. Samples of the American population have been asked the same questions during every national election campaign throughout this period, offering an extraordinary opportunity for studying trends in the attitudes of the American electorate. The development of this valuable, continuous series does have one unfortunate aspect, however. Because the value of the series depends on the comparability of the questions, researchers are reluctant to alter questions, even when doubts about their validity arise. Improving the questions undermines comparability. Therefore, a choice between continuity and validity must be made.

The ANES questions concerning religious preference provide a recent example in which validity was chosen over continuity. For years, respondents were simply asked, "What is your religious preference?" Although a small percentage in each survey answered "none," it was clear that a significant number of those answering "Protestant," and fewer numbers citing other religions, had no meaningful religious affiliation. In the 1992 survey, the ANES began asking the question differently. Respondents were first asked, "Do you ever attend religious services, apart from occasional weddings, baptisms, and funerals?" Those who answered "no" were asked an additional question about their religious preference: "Regardless of whether you now attend any religious services, do you ever think of yourself as part of a particular church or denomination?" Those who did not answer "yes" to one of these two screening questions were not asked the traditional question about religious affiliation that then followed. As a result, the percentage of the population categorized as having no religious affiliation increased dramatically. This new question more validly reflects the religious sentiments of the American public, but it is now impossible to compare these later results with those of previous years. We cannot infer a large drop in religious affiliation on the basis of the responses to these new and different questions. In this instance, continuity has been sacrificed in favor of validity.

Despite inevitable concerns about validity, survey research provides the best means of investigating the attitudes and behavior of large populations of individuals such as the American electorate.

Suggested Readings

Fowler, Floyd J., Jr. *Survey Research Methods*, 5th ed. Thousand Oaks, CA: SAGE, 2014. Comprehensive overview of survey research.

Groves, Robert M., Floyd J. Fowler Jr., Mick P. Couper, James M. Lepkowski, Eleanor Singer, and Roger Tourangeau. *Survey Methodology*, 2nd ed. Hoboken, NJ: Wiley, 2009. Excellent coverage of the many topics of survey methods.

Kish, Leslie. *Survey Sampling.* New York: Wiley, 1965. By far the most authoritative work on survey sampling.

Mann, Thomas E., and Gary R. Orren, eds. *Media Polls in American Politics.* Washington, DC: Brookings Institution Press, 1992. An excellent collection of essays on the use of polls in contemporary media analysis.

Marsden, Peter V., and James D. Wright, eds. *Handbook of Survey Research.* Bingley, England: Emerald, 2010. Excellent source from top survey researchers.

Weisberg, Herbert F. *The Total Survey Error Approach.* Chicago: University of Chicago Press, 2005. A comprehensive treatment of survey research methods.

Weisberg, Herbert F., Jon Krosnick, and Bruce D. Bowen. *An Introduction to Survey Research and Data Analysis.* San Francisco: W. H. Freeman, 1989. A good, methodological textbook on survey research and the interpretation of statistical analysis.

Internet Resources

The website of the American National Election Studies, www.electionstudies.org, has extensive information on survey methodology.

Some other websites with methodological information are the Gallup poll, www.gallup.com, and the General Social Survey, http://gss.norc.org/.

The Pew Research Center, www.pewresearch.org/topic/methodological-research/, has done interesting methodological analyses and offers important information on survey sampling and methods.

Notes

1. See John Brehm, *The Phantom Respondents* (Ann Arbor: University of Michigan Press, 1993).

2. Jelke G. Bethlehem, "Weighting Nonresponse Adjustments Based on Auxiliary Information," in *Survey Nonresponse*, eds. Robert M. Groves, Don A. Dillman, John L. Eltinge, and Roderick J. A. Little (New York: Wiley, 2002), Chapter 18, 275–288.

3. Danielle Kurtzleben, "The Trump Media Survey Is Phenomenally Biased. It's Also Useful," NPR, February 17, 2017, http://www.npr.org/2017/02/17/515791540/the-trump-media-survey-is-phenomenally-biased-it-also-does-its-job-well.

4. Paul Abramson and William Claggett, "Race-Related Differences in Self-Reported and Validated Turnout," *Journal of Politics* 46 (August 1984): 719–738.

INDEX

boycott, 99–101, 109
Bush supporters, 224
businesses, 11, 97, 101, 109, 118,
    203, 275

California, 75, 105–6, 285
campaign activities, 14, 80, 83–84, 86–87
campaign activities scale, 85, 87
campaign managers, 268, 288
campaign organizations, 83, 234, 239–40
campaign participation, 85, 87
campaigns, 46–48, 50, 52–53, 55–56,
    58–59, 64, 70, 81–85, 87, 94, 96–98,
    104–5, 178, 217–18, 224–25, 230–31,
    234, 236, 238–42, 244–45
candidate image, 149, 240, 263–65, 267,
    270, 280–82
candidates, 45–48, 52–55, 63–64, 72–73,
    82–84, 127–28, 130, 136–38, 141,
    198, 217–19, 226–27, 230–31,
    233–43, 263–65, 267–71, 278–85,
    287–88, 290–91, 293–94
  congressional, 53, 294
  independent, 126, 138, 145, 154,
    162, 287
  lesser-known, 242
  particular, 271, 290
candidates and issues, 138, 145, 263
candidates for office, 108, 128, 226, 294
candidate support, 167, 246
Capitol, 13, 18, 35, 107, 114–15,
    123, 125
Carmines, Edward G., 168, 170,
    210–11, 213
Carter, 141, 241–43, 291
Catholics, 133–34, 173, 177, 185, 201
Catholics and Protestants, 185
caucuses, 47, 241–42
CBS News, 120, 135, 212–13, 217,
    224, 250
change, partisan, 125–26, 157–58
Changing American Voter, 157, 168, 203,
    214, 296
children, 80, 110, 161–62, 168, 277
cities, 97, 103, 106, 284
citizenship, 80, 277–78

Citizens United, 50, 243
civil liberties, 26, 37–38, 190, 203
Civil War, 72, 128, 149, 151–52, 154,
    198, 271
climate change, 156, 271, 273, 281–82
Clinton, Hillary 45, 47–48, 53–55, 58, 236,
    239–40, 242–43, 257–58, 260, 264,
    267, 285, 295
college degree, 69, 72, 102-3, 117, 131,
    133, 173, 177, 201-2, 258-59
color, 77, 79, 86–87, 96, 111, 117, 131,
    180–81, 211–12, 257–58, 281
composition, partisan, 157, 160
compromise, 24, 27–29, 32, 283
Congress, 21–23, 45, 48–49, 51, 75–76,
    149, 151, 156–57, 163, 177–78, 222,
    228–29, 283–84, 288–91, 298–99
congressional elections, 45–46, 50, 66,
    68, 138, 154, 288, 291, 294
congressional races, 48, 50, 138,
    140, 289
congressional Republicans, 13, 170
congressional voting, 138–40, 153
conservatives, 103–4, 117, 197–203,
    205–6, 208–9, 213–14, 221–23, 225,
    228, 262–63, 278–79
consistency, 201–3
conventions, 234–35, 237
costs, 23–24, 75, 77, 79, 83, 104, 107, 111,
    193, 195, 219, 226
coverage, 22, 183, 215–18, 222, 227, 233,
    241–42
COVID-19 Restrictions, 276, 281
crisis, 30, 56, 149–50, 156, 198

deadline, 75, 148, 194
debates, 24–25, 27, 46, 52, 58, 76, 177–78,
    223, 230, 235–36, 252
defection rates, 136–38, 260
degree of issue constraint, 203
degrees, 107, 134–35, 148, 153, 196,
    202–3, 219, 259, 264
delegates, 46–47, 242–43
democracy, 11, 13–14, 18, 24–25, 27,
    30–33, 35–38, 63, 65, 116, 118–20,
    123, 245, 247, 283